Ernest Renan, Joseph Henry Allen

Antichrist, Including the Period from the Arrival of Paul in Rome

To the End of the Jewish revolution

Ernest Renan, Joseph Henry Allen

Antichrist, Including the Period from the Arrival of Paul in Rome
To the End of the Jewish revolution

ISBN/EAN: 9783744764506

Printed in Europe, USA, Canada, Australia, Japan

Cover: Foto ©Lupo / pixelio.de

More available books at **www.hansebooks.com**

ANTICHRIST

INCLUDING

THE PERIOD FROM THE ARRIVAL OF PAUL IN ROME
TO THE END OF THE JEWISH REVOLUTION

BY

ERNEST RENAN

AUTHOR OF "THE HISTORY OF THE PEOPLE OF ISRAEL"
"LIFE OF JESUS," "FUTURE OF SCIENCE," ETC.

TRANSLATED AND EDITED

BY

JOSEPH HENRY ALLEN

LATE LECTURER ON ECCLESIASTICAL HISTORY IN HARVARD UNIVERSITY

BOSTON
ROBERTS BROTHERS
1897

EDITOR'S NOTE.

THIS volume is the fourth in a series entitled "Beginnings of Christian History" (*Histoire des Origines du Christianisme*), published at intervals from 1863 to 1882. The titles and dates of the several volumes are the following: — Life of Jesus, 1863; The Apostles, 1866; Saint Paul, 1869; Antichrist, 1873; The Gospels, 1877; The Church, 1879; Marcus Aurelius, 1882. The selection of this for separate publication is in accordance with a judgment thus expressed by Sir Mountstuart E. Grant Duff, a personal friend of the author: "If any one who did not wish to read through the seven volumes of the *Origines*, but only desired to form an opinion of Renan as an historian, were to ask me what part of them he should read, I should certainly reply, the fourth volume, that to which the author gave the name of *L'Antéchrist.*" (Ernest Renan, *In Memoriam*, p. 132.)

Imperfect translations of the first three volumes, and perhaps of others, have already appeared in English; and the first, the "Life of Jesus," was given to the public a year ago under the present editorship. The critical reader will notice a certain freedom in dealing with the grammatical structure of some of M. Renan's periods; an occasional transference of matter from the notes to the text, or the reverse; the rendering into English of many sentences or phrases given by the author in the original tongues; an Index of contents; and the insertion of the text of numerous citations, and explanations where they seemed to be required, especially of oriental words and phrases and of later views regarding the structure of the Apocalypse, in which the Editor acknowledges the kind aid of his friend Professor Toy.[1] In all other respects his aim has been to give an absolutely faithful transcription of the substance, style, spirit, and literary colouring of the original.

J. H. A.

CAMBRIDGE, MASS.,
October, 1897.

[1] I have not hesitated to translate βασιλεύς (1 Pet. ii. 13) "emperor," and διάβολος (id. v. 8) "false accuser," where Renan follows the traditional rendering.

CONTENTS.

		PAGE
INTRODUCTION: ON CERTAIN ORIGINAL AUTHORITIES CONSULTED IN THE PREPARATION OF THIS VOLUME		1

CHAPTER
I. PAUL IN PRISON 31
II. PETER AT ROME 48
III. THE CHURCHES IN JUDÆA 62
IV. LATEST ACTS OF PAUL 81
V. NEARING THE CRISIS 106
VI. CONFLAGRATION OF ROME 116
VII. THE CHRISTIAN MARTYRS 138
VIII. DEATH OF PETER AND PAUL 159
IX. AFTER THE CRISIS 172
X. THE REVOLT IN JUDÆA 189
XI. MASSACRES IN SYRIA AND EGYPT 206
XII. VESPASIAN IN GALILEE; TERROR AT JERUSALEM . . 217
XIII. THE DEATH OF NERO 244
XIV. DISASTERS AND SIGNS 259
XV. THE APOSTLES IN ASIA 272
XVI. THE APOCALYPSE 299
XVII. LATER FORTUNES OF THE BOOK 351
XVIII. ACCESSION OF THE FLAVII 371
XIX. THE FALL OF JERUSALEM 385
XX. RESULTS OF THE FALL OF JERUSALEM 403

APPENDIX: OF PETER'S COMING TO ROME, AND OF JOHN'S STAY AT EPHESUS 423
INDEX 439

INTRODUCTION.

ON CERTAIN ORIGINAL AUTHORITIES CONSULTED IN THE PREPARATION OF THIS VOLUME.

THE period covered by the present volume is, after the three or four years of the public life of Jesus, the most extraordinary in the entire development of Christianity. Here, by a singular touch of the great unconscious Artist who appears to rule in the seeming caprice of historic evolution, we shall see Jesus and Nero — Christ and Antichrist — set, as it were, in contrast, face to face, like heaven and hell. The Christian consciousness is now full-grown. Hitherto it has known little else than the law of love: Jewish intolerance, though harsh, could not fret away the bond of grateful attachment cherished in the heart of the infant Church for her mother the Synagogue, from whom she is still hardly sundered. Now at length the Christian has before him an object of hate and terror. Over against the memory of Jesus rises a monstrous form, the ideal of evil, as He had been the ideal of holiness. Held in reserve, like Enoch or Elias, to play his part in the last great tragedy of the world, Nero completes the cycle of Christian mythology: he inspires the first sacred book of the new canon; by a frightful massacre he lays the corner-stone of Romish primacy, and opens the way to that revolution which is to make of Rome a second Jerusalem, a holy city. At the same time, by a mysterious coincidence not infrequent in great crises of human destiny, Jerusalem is overthrown; the Temple disappears; Christianity, disburdened of a restraint already painful and advancing to a broadening freedom, follows out its own destinies apart from conquered Judaism.

The later epistles of Paul, the epistle to the Hebrews, and those ascribed to Peter and James, with the Apocalypse, are chief among the canonical documents of this period. Valuable testimony comes to us, besides, from the first epistle of the Roman Clement, and from the historians Tacitus and Josephus. At many a point, notably the death of the Apostles and the relations of John with the churches in Asia, our picture must lie in shadow; upon others we may gather rays of real light. Almost all the material facts of the earliest Christian history are obscure; what we can see clearly is the eager enthusiasm, the superhuman boldness, the scorn of circumstance, which make this the most powerful effort towards the ideal still treasured in human memory.

In the Introduction to "Saint Paul" I have treated of the genuineness of the Letters ascribed to that chief of the Apostles. The four referred to in this volume — "Philippians," "Colossians," "Philemon," and "Ephesians" — offer some ground of doubt. The objections brought against "Philippians" are of so small account that I have scarcely urged them. As we shall see hereafter, "Colossians" gives more ground for scruple, while "Ephesians" stands quite by itself among the Pauline writings. In spite of its grave difficulties, however, I still hold "Colossians" to be genuine. The interpolations recently alleged by able critics are not apparent.[1] On this point Holtzmann's treatment is worthy of its learned author; but the way, too common in Germany, of assuming an *a priori* type to serve as the absolute criterion of a writer's genuineness is very hazardous. We cannot, indeed, deny that interpolation and fabrication were common enough, in the so-called apostolic writings, during the first two Christian centuries; but, in a matter like this, it is impossible to draw a sharp line between true and false, genuine and spurious. We say confidently that the epistles to the Romans, Corinthians, and Galatians are genuine; we say just as confidently that those to Timothy and Titus are apocryphal. In the border ground between, we but grope our way. The chief fault of the so-called

[1] H. J. Holtzmann, *Kritik der Epheser- und Kolosserbriefe*, Leipzig, 1872.

Tübingen school, dating from F. C. Baur, has been to conceive the Jews of the first century in the mass as fed on logic and rigid in their deductions. Peter, Paul, even Jesus, in the writings of this school, argue like Protestant professors in a German university; each has his own doctrine; each has but one, which he keeps always just the same. The truth is, those noble men, the true heroes of this story, often change their view and contradict themselves; in the course of their life they assume three or four varying theories; at one time they borrow views from their opponents, which at another time they sharply contradict. Seen from our point of view, these men are open to quick impressions, personal, irritable, changeful; what makes fixity in opinion, science or pure reason, is wholly unknown to them. Like Jews of every time, they have angry disputes among themselves, yet make together a very compact body. To understand them, we must clear ourselves of the pedantry inseparable from all academic methods; we must rather study the petty groups and cliques of the religious world, the Congregations of England and America, and in particular what goes on in the founding of all religious Orders. In this regard the theological faculties in German universities — the best in the world to supply the enormous toil needed to bring into shape the chaos of documents bearing on these obscure beginnings — are the worst in the world to undertake the task of a real history. For history is the interpretation of an unfolding life, an expanding germ, while theology (so to speak) reads life backward. Attending merely to what confirms or invalidates his doctrine, even the most liberal of theologians is unconsciously an advocate: his aim is to defend or else refute. The aim of the historian is simply to tell the fact. He finds a value in what may be in substance false, in documents even spurious; for they paint the soul, and are often truer than barren fact. In his view it were the greatest of errors to regard as defenders of abstract opinions those good and simple-minded dreamers, whose dreams through all these ages have been a consolation and a joy.

What I have said of "Colossians," and especially of "Ephesians," must be said emphatically of the first epistle ascribed to Peter, and of those of James and Jude.[1] The second of Peter (so called) is certainly apocryphal. We see at a glance that it is an artificial compound, an imitation made up of scraps of apostolic writings, especially the epistle of Jude.[2] I do not urge this point, as I do not suppose "Second Peter" has a single defender among true critics. But its very falsity — having as its main object to inspire patience in the faithful, weary with long waiting for the reappearing of Christ — in a sense confirms the genuineness of "First Peter." Though apocryphal it is still a very ancient writing, whose author fully believes in the other as really the work of Peter, making his own a "second" to it (see ch. iii. 1).[3] "First Peter," on the other hand, is one of the earliest and most frequently cited, as genuine, among all the New Testament writings.[4] Only one serious objection has been made, — namely, to passages taken (it is thought) from certain letters of Paul, particularly the so-called "Ephesians."[5] But the copyist whom Peter must have employed (if the letter is really his) may well have allowed himself to borrow thus. In all times, preachers and journalists have laid hands without scruple on phrases that have come to be part of the common stock and are, as we say, "in the air." So Paul's amanuensis, who wrote "Ephesians," copied freely from "Colossians." Epistolary writing is very apt

---

[1] Of the latter, see "Saint Paul," chap. x., near the end.

[2] Compare especially 2 Pet. ii. with Jude. Such passages as i. 14, 16, 18; and iii. 1, 2, 5–7, 15, 16, also clearly prove it spurious. Its style, further, — as Jerome has remarked in *Epist. ad Hedib.* 11 ; cf. *De viris illustr.* 1, — is no way like that of 1 Peter. Finally, it is not cited before the third century. Irenæus (*Adv. Hær.* iv. 9, 2) and Origen (in Euseb. *Hist. Eccl.* vi. 25; cf. iii. 25) ignore or exclude it.

[3] Supposed imitations of 1 Peter, found in "Timothy" and "Titus," touching the duties of women and of elders, are not so clear. But compare 1 Tim. ii. 9–15, iii. 11, with 1 Pet. iii. 1–4, v. 1–4; Tit. i. 5–9.

[4] Papias in Euseb. *H. E.* iii. 39; Polycarp, *Epist.* 1 (cf. 1 Pet. i. 8; Euseb. iv. 14); Irenæus, *Adv. Hær.* iv. 9, 2; 16, 5 (cf. Euseb. v. 8); Clem. Alex. *Strom.* iii. 18, iv. 7; Tertull. *Scorp.* 12; Origen in Euseb. vi. 25; Euseb. iii. 25.

[5] See below, pp. 108, 109.

to show a good deal that has been so taken from earlier like compositions.[1]

Suspicion has been raised by the passage 1 Pet. v. 1–4, which recalls the pious but somewhat feeble admonitions, wholly priestly in tone, of the spurious epistles to Timothy and Titus. Besides, the insistence with which the writer depicts himself [in v. 1] as "a witness of the sufferings of Christ" stirs doubts like those raised by the persistent assertions of an eye-witness in the writings falsely ascribed to John. Still, we should not stick at this. There are many tokens of genuineness as well. For example, the advance towards a hierarchy is hardly noticeable. Not only there is no hint of a bishopric (for the phrase "bishop of your souls" in ii. 25 proves that the word has as yet no official meaning), but each church has not even a Presbyter: it has "presbyters," or "elders," with nothing to imply that they make a distinct official body.[2] A point worth noting is that the writer,[3] even when laying stress on the self-surrender of Jesus on the cross, omits the striking feature given by Luke ["Father, forgive them," etc.], leading us to think that when he wrote the legendary narrative was not yet full-grown.

The eclectic and reconciling tendencies observed in the epistle of Peter bear against its genuineness only in the view of those who, like Baur and his school, regard the difference of Peter and Paul as flat hostility. If party hate in the primitive church was as deep as this school thinks, reconciliation would never have come about. Peter was not, like James, a stiff-necked Jew. In composing this history we must not think merely of "Galatians" and the pseudo-Clementine homilies; we must remember, too, the "Acts of the Apostles." An historian's skill should exhibit the event so as no way to belittle party strifes, which were doubtless profounder than we could

---

[1] Besides the canonical epistles, see those of Clem. Rom., Ignatius, and Polycarp.

[2] Πρεσβυτέρους ἐν ὑμῖν (Vat. and Sin. MSS.); the common reading is τοὺς ἐν ὑμῖν.

[3] 1 Peter ii. 23; cf. Luke xxiii. 34.

even think; yet so as to let us see how such strifes were soothed and fused into a noble harmony.

The epistle of James comes to the bar of criticism under like conditions with that of Peter. The difficulties of detail alleged against it are of little account. A more serious matter is the broad charge that writings of fictitious authorship were easily produced at a time when there was no sound test of genuineness, and no scruple at pious frauds. For writers like Paul, who by common consent have left us genuine writings, and whose biography is fairly well known, there are two sure tests, — comparison of doubtful works with those universally acknowledged genuine, and inquiry whether the document in dispute answers to the biographical data in our possession. But if the case is that of an author from whom we have only a few doubtful pages, and whose life is little known, we must decide mostly on grounds of feeling, which are not imperative. If we are of easy judgment, we may take much that is false for true; if too rigid, we may reject much that is true as false. For such questions the theologian, who thinks to walk by certainties, is (I say again) a bad judge. The critical historian has a quiet conscience when he has done his best to mark the various steps of certain, probable, plausible, possible. If at all capable, he may succeed in being true in the general colour, while as to special statements he makes free with his question-marks and his may-be's.

One thing I have found in favour of writings too strictly thrown out by critics of a certain school, — such as the first epistle of Peter, with those of James and Jude, — is the way they fit in with a narrative organically knit together. While the second ascribed to Peter, with those alleged to be from Paul to Timothy and Titus, have no place in the pattern of a connected story, the three I have mentioned fit themselves to it (as I may say) of their own accord. The features of detail in them anticipate facts known through outside testimony, and are embraced easily among them. "Peter" well corresponds with what we know, chiefly from Tacitus, of the situation of Christians at Rome about A.D. 63 or 64. "James," again, is a perfect picture of the *Ebionim* at Jerusalem in the years just before the great revolt, quite like the information given us by Josephus.[1] There is nothing to be gained by a theory that it was written by another James, not "the Lord's brother." True, this epistle was not admitted, in the early centuries, so unanimously as that of Peter;[2] but the hesitation would seem to have been rather on dogmatic grounds than on critical. The Greek Fathers had little liking for the Jewish-Christian writings: that is the real reason.

It may be remarked, as to the evidence regarding these minor apostolic writings, that they were composed before the fall of Jerusalem. This event so altered the situation as between Jew and Christian that we can easily distinguish between a document later than the catastrophe of A. D. 70 and one belonging to the period while Herod's temple was yet standing. Descriptions which clearly refer to class-jealousies in Jerusalem society, such as we find in "James" (v. 1–6), would be unmeaning if made later than the revolt of A. D. 66, which ended the rule of the Sadducees.

From the fact that there were pseudo-apostolic writings — such as the letters to Timothy and Titus, "Second Peter," and the epistle of Barnabas, whose practice is to imitate or dilute older compositions — it follows that there were writings genuinely apostolic held in reverence, which it was sought to multiply.[3] As every Arabic poet of the classic period had his *Kasida*, a complete expression of his personality, so every apostle had his "epistle," more or less genuine, which was supposed to preserve the fine flower of his thought.

I have elsewhere spoken of the epistle to the Hebrews.[4] I

---

[1] See below, pp. 52–53.

[2] Clem. Rom. 1 Cor. x., xi. (cf. Jas. ii. 21, 23, 25); "Hermas," *Mand.* xii. 5 (cf. Jas. iv. 7); Iren. *Adv. Hær.* iv. 16, 2 (cf. Jas. ii. 23); these writers seem to have known the epistle. Origen (*In Joh.* xix. 6), Eusebius (*H. E.* ii. 23), and Jerome (*De viris illustr.* 2) express doubts.

[3] See 2 Pet. iii. 15, 16, where the Pauline epistles are expressly named as sacred writings.

[4] Saint Paul, Introd., pp. 52–61.

have shown that this work is not by Paul, as has been held in some lines of Christian tradition; and that its probable date may be fixed at about A. D. 66. I have now to consider whether we may be sure of its real author, where it was written, and who were the "Hebrews" to whom by title it is addressed.

Circumstantial points are these: The writer speaks to the church addressed in the tone of a well-known master, — indeed, almost in a tone of reproach. The church has long since accepted the faith, but has fallen away in doctrine; so that it needs elementary instruction, and cannot comprehend the higher theology.[1] Further, this church has shown and still shows proofs of courage and devotion, especially in service to the saints. ["Ye have ministered to the saints and do minister."] It had endured cruel persecutions in the day when it received the full light of faith, when it was "made a gazing stock."[2] That was but a little while ago; for those now members of the church had part in the merits of that persecution — sympathising with the confessors, visiting those in prison, and, above all, bearing bravely the loss of their goods. In that trial, however, there were some deserters, and there was question whether such apostates could rejoin the church. It would seem that some were even now in prison (xiii. 3). There have been noble leaders ($\dot{\eta}\gamma o \dot{\upsilon}\mu \epsilon \nu o \iota$), preachers of the Word, whose end was glorious and inspiring (xiii. 7). But still there are chiefs well known to the writer (ver. 17, 24), who has himself had knowledge of the church, and seems to have held a high post of service in it; he means to return to it, and wishes his return to be as soon as possible (ver. 19). He and those to whom he writes are acquainted with Timothy, who has been a prisoner in some other place, but is now at liberty; he hopes that Timothy may come and join him, that they may visit this church of the "Hebrews" together (ver. 23). The epistle ends with the words, "Those away from

---

[1] See v. 11-14; vi. 11, 12; x. 24, 25; xiii., throughout.
[2] $\theta \epsilon \alpha \tau \rho \iota \zeta \acute{o} \mu \epsilon \nu o \iota$ ("exhibited on the stage"), x. 33-34; xii. 4-8, 23.

(ἀπό) Italy salute you," which must mean those who are just now absent from Italy.[1]

What chiefly distinguishes this writer is his incessant use of the [Jewish] scriptures, with a subtile and allegorical mode of exposition, and a Greek style more ample, more classic, less dry, but also less natural than that in most apostolic writings. He has slight acquaintance with the ritual of the temple at Jerusalem (ix. 1–5), which, however, strongly impresses him. He uses only the Alexandrian version, and reasons from errors in the Greek copyists (x. 5, 37, 38). He is not a Jew of Jerusalem, but a Hellenist, related to the school of Paul (iii. 23); and represents himself as having been a hearer, not of Jesus, but of those who had heard him, and as a witness of the "signs and wonders" manifested by the apostles by "the gift of the Holy Spirit" (ii. 3, 4). Still, he has high rank in the church: he speaks with authority (v. 11, 12; vi. 11, 12; x. 24, 25; xiii. *pass.*); is held in great respect by those to whom he writes (xiii. 19–24); and Timothy seems to be his inferior. The mere fact of addressing an epistle to an important church shows him to be a man of consequence, one of name and high standing among the apostles.

Still, all this is not enough to determine the authorship. It has been variously ascribed to Barnabas, Luke, Silas, Apollos, and Clement of Rome. The likeliest of all is Barnabas. This has the authority of Tertullian, who speaks of it as a well-known fact;[2] and it is contradicted by not a single feature offered by the epistle. Barnabas was a Hellenist of Cyprus, at once linked with Paul and independent

---

[1] Compare οἱ ἐν τῇ 'Ασίᾳ, 2 Tim. i. 15; ἡ ἐν Βαβυλῶνι συνεκλεκτή, i. Pet. v. 13. (But see Acts xvii. 13.)

[2] *De Pudic.* 20: *Exstat enim et Barnabæ titulus ad Hebræos.* These words show that the manuscript in the hands of Tertullian was inscribed with the name of Barnabas. (Cf. Jerome, *De viris illustr.* 5.) Tertullian's assertion has been wrongly regarded as a mere conjecture, put forth to give authority to a writing that favoured his Montanist notions. On the argument from the stichometry of the *Codex claromontanus*, see Introd. to "Saint Paul," note on pp. 53–4. The "epistle of Barnabas," commonly so called, is apocryphal, written about A. D. 110.

of him, known and esteemed by all. This view, further, suggests a reason for ascribing the composition to Paul: it was the destiny of Barnabas to be in a manner lost in the halo of the great apostle; and, if he did leave any writing, as seems not unlikely, we should naturally seek it among those of Paul.

The church to which this letter is addressed may be fixed on with some likelihood. From what has been already said, our choice lies, with little doubt, between Rome and Jerusalem. Alexandria has been suggested, but on slight grounds. First, there is no proof that Alexandria had a church as early as A. D. 66. Even if it had, it could have no relation with the school of Paul, or any knowledge of Timothy; while such passages as v. 12, x. 32-34, and others would be wholly inappropriate. The title, "to the Hebrews," makes us think at once of Jerusalem.[1] But this is not enough. Passages like v. 11-14, vi. 11, 12, and even vi. 10 ("minister to the saints")[2] are nonsense if we suppose them addressed by a follower of the apostles to the mother church of all, the source of all instruction. What is said of Timothy in xiii. 23 is no more intelligible; persons so committed as were the writer and Timothy to the party of Paul could not have sent to that church a missive implying special intimacy with their affairs. How, for instance, could the writer — with his exegesis founded wholly on the Septuagint, his imperfect Jewish knowledge, his slight acquaintance with the temple service — have dared to lecture so loftily those past masters of the field, men who talked Hebrew (very nearly), who lived every day close to the Temple, and who knew much better than he all he could say to them? How, indeed, could he address them as catechumens, barely initiated, and incapable of deep theology? On the other hand, if we suppose those addressed to be the faithful in Rome, all fits to a marvel. Such pas-

---

[1] Compare Acts vi. 1; Iren. *Adv. Hær.* III. i. 1; Euseb. *H. E.* iii. 24, 25.

[2] Compare Rom. xv. 25. This signifies the service due from all other churches to that at Jerusalem, but would hardly befit this latter.

sages as vi. 10, x. 32–34, xiii. 3, 7, allude to Nero's persecution; xiii. 7 refers to the death of Peter and Paul; the expression, "those away from Italy," is fully justified, since it is natural that the writer should send to those in Rome the salutations of the Italian colony about him. Add that the first epistle of the Roman Clement (certainly a Roman composition) borrows consecutively from "Hebrews," and evidently models its exposition upon that.[1]

One difficulty remains: Why does the title say "to the Hebrews"? Such titles, we know, are not always apostolic: they were sometimes late additions, and even erroneous, as we see in the case of "Ephesians." "Hebrews" was written, under the stress of persecution, to the church that suffered most. In several places (as in xiii. 23) the writer evidently expresses himself guardedly. Perhaps the inscription "to the Hebrews" was a password, to save the letter from being put to an evil use. Possibly the title came from the letter's being regarded in the second century as a confutation of the Ebionites, who were called "Judaisers." It is noteworthy that the church of Rome always had special light on this epistle; here it first appeared, and here it was first brought into use. While Alexandria is ready to call it Paul's, the church at Rome always maintains that it is not his, and that it is wrongly joined to his genuine writings.[2]

From what place was "Hebrews" written? This is harder to answer. The expression "those away from Italy" shows that the writer was not in that country. It is certain, too, that he wrote from an important town where there was a colony of Italian Christians closely allied with those of Rome, who had probably escaped the persecution of A. D. 64. We shall see that the stream of those who so escaped flowed towards Ephesus, where the church had had as its first nucleus two Jews from Rome, Aquila and Priscilla, and had always continued in direct relations with Rome. Thus we are led to think

---

[1] Compare chap. 17 with xi. 37; chap. 36 with i. 3, 5, 7, 13; chap. 9 with xi. 5, 7; chap. 12 with xi. 31.

[2] See "Saint Paul," p. lvii.

that it was here the epistle was written. The words in xiii. 23, it is true, are perplexing in that case: in what city, neither Rome nor Ephesus, yet closely connected with both, had Timothy been imprisoned? Whatever we may conjecture, this is a riddle hard to answer.

The most important document of this period is the Apocalypse. An attentive reading of chaps. xv.-xvii. will show, I think, that its date is fixed more positively than that of any other writing in the canon.[1] It may even be determined within a few days. The place where it was written may also be plausibly assigned. Who was its author is far more uncertain. As to this, I think, we cannot speak with confidence. The writer gives his name at the very beginning: "I, John, your brother and companion in tribulation and in the kingdom and patience of Christ."[2] But here two questions occur: 1. Is the claim genuine, or is it one of the pious frauds common to all apocalyptic writers? In other words, is it not an anonymous writing ascribed to John the apostle, as a man of highest authority in the churches, whose views are here communicated in visions? 2. Granting the claim to be sincere, is not the writer another John than the apostle?

To begin with the second question, as the easier to decide. The John who speaks or is thought to speak in the Apocalypse expresses himself with such emphasis; he is so sure of being known and of not being confounded with any other; he knows so well the secret things of the churches, and meets them with so firm a bearing, — that we can hardly fail to see in him an

---

[1] The theory of Vischer, accepted by Harnack and others (see "Life of Jesus," note on page 477), is that the body of the Apocalypse — iv. 1-xxii. 5 — is a Jewish composition, adopted and probably translated from a Hebrew original by some Christian writer near the end of the first century, who prefixed the first three chapters and interpolated numerous brief passages to adapt it to Christian uses. A valuable criticism of this view, defending the general unity of the composition, but excepting from this unity a series of visions beginning with chapter xi. was contributed by M. Louis Auguste Sabatier to the *Revue de Théologie et de Philosophie:* Paris, *Librairie Fischbacher*, 1888, pp. 37. — ED.

[2] Rev. i. 9; see also 1, 2, 4; xxii. 8.

apostle, or else a dignitary of very high rank in the Church. But in the second half of the first century there was no other of that name who approached such dignity. John Mark is here quite out of the question, whatever Hitzig may say. Mark never had consecutive relations with the churches in Asia, such as to embolden him to address them in this tone. There is, indeed, one "John the Elder," a dubious personage, a sort of double of the apostle, who haunts like a spectre the record of the church at Ephesus, and gives much trouble to the critics.[1] Though his very existence has been denied, and though we cannot positively refute the theory of those who make him a personified shadow of the apostle, I incline to think that he had an identity apart;[2] but I absolutely deny that he wrote the Apocalypse in A. D. 68 or 69, as maintained by Ewald. Such a man would not have been known to us merely through an obscure passage of Papias or an apologetic writing of Dionysius. We should find his name in the Gospels, or Acts, or an Epistle. He would be a man from Jerusalem. The writer of the Apocalypse is the best versed in Scripture, most attached to the Temple, most Hebraic, of all the New Testament writers. Such a man cannot have had his training out of Palestine; he must have been a native of Judæa; at the bottom of his heart he clings to the Church of Israel. If there was any such person as John the Elder, he was a disciple of John in his extreme old age. Admitting that the passage in the "Apostolical Constitutions" (vii. 46) refers to him, and that

---

[1] See "Life of Jesus," p. 58, note.

[2] See Papias (Euseb. iii. 39) and Dionysius of Alexandria (id. vii. 25). These two passages are not proof. The latter, in fact, deduces his opinion *a priori* from the difference [in style] between the Apocalypse and the Fourth Gospel, finding confirmation in two tombs which "are said to have existed at Ephesus, each bearing the name of John." The passage of Papias is vague; at all events it needs correction. That in the Apostolical Constitutions is of weak authority. Eusebius (iii. 39) simply brings together the statements of Papias and Dionysius, not confirming the existence of the two tombs. Jerome (*De viris illustr.* 9, 18) says there were two there, but that many regarded them as being two memorials of the apostle.

it has any value, he would be the apostle's successor in the episcopate of Ephesus. Papias seems to have been close beside him, at least his contemporary.[1] We may even admit that he sometimes held the pen for his master, and that he may have been the composer of the Fourth Gospel and the First Epistle of John. The second and third (so called), in which the writer calls himself "the Elder," would seem to be his own work, acknowledged as such.[2] But surely, if we admit that John the Elder counts for anything in the second class of Johannine writings (the Gospel and Epistles), he has no part in the composition of the Apocalypse. If anything is plain, it is that the two cannot have come from the same hand. This was evident to Dionysius of Alexandria, in the latter half of the third century, whose essay on the point is a model of learned and critical dissertation.[3] Of all the New Testament writings, the Apocalypse is the most Jewish, and the Fourth Gospel the least so. Thus the word "Jew," which in that Gospel always means "enemy of Jesus," is in the Apocalypse the highest title of honour (ii. 9, iii. 9). Admitting that the Apostle John is the author of any of the writings traditionally ascribed to him, it is certainly the Apocalypse, not the Gospel. The former corresponds perfectly to the settled opinion which he seems to have held in the dispute between Paul and the Jewish Christians, while the latter does not. The efforts made in the third century by some of the Greek Fathers to assign the Apocalypse to "John the Elder"[4] result from the aversion then felt for that book among the orthodox teachers.[5] They could not endure that an apostle should be thought the writer of a book

---

[1] Euseb. iii. 39. We should, as it appears, read in this passage "the disciples of the Lord's *disciples* say;" since Aristion and John the Elder are represented as living in the time of Papias, and do not stand in the same class with the apostles ("disciples of the Lord"). In any case, Eusebius goes beyond the mark in inferring that Papias himself was a listener to Aristion and "John the Elder."

[2] All these points will be further considered in the succeeding volume.

[3] Eusebius, vii. 25.

[4] Dion-Alex. in Euseb. vii. 25 (cf. iii. 39); Jerome, *De viris illustr.* 9.

[5] See "Life of Jesus," p. 290, note 3; also below, p. 355.

whose style they found barbarous and its spirit stamped with Jewish bitterness. Their opinion was an induction *a priori*, worthless in itself, expressing neither tradition nor critical judgment.

If, then, the expression "I, John," in the first chapter, is genuine, the Apocalypse is certainly from the hand of the Apostle John. But it is of the essence of an apocalypse to be pseudonymous. The writers of "Daniel," "Enoch," "Baruch," and "Esdras," all assume those names as their own. The Church of the second century accepted an apocalypse of Peter, certainly apocryphal, just as they did that of John.[1] If the writer gives his true name in the Apocalypse of our canon, it is a surprising exception to the rule. Let us grant the exception: in fact, this book differs essentially from other similar writings that have come down to us. Most of these are ascribed to writers who flourished (or were supposed to flourish) five or six centuries, or even [as Enoch, "the seventh from Adam"] some thousands of years before. Those of the second century were ascribed to men of the apostolic age. The "Shepherd" and the pseudo-Clementines are some fifty or sixty years after their assumed writers. So it was, probably, with the apocalypse of Peter; at least nothing shows that it makes any exception as to topic or author. On the other hand, the Apocalypse of the canon, if it is pseudonymous, seems to have been ascribed to John in his lifetime, or very soon after his death. Were it not for the first three chapters, this would be strictly possible. But can we suppose that whoever assumed the name had the boldness to address his apocryphal work to the "seven churches" which stood in near relations with the apostle? Or if we deny these relations, as Scholten does, we fall into a still greater difficulty; for then we must admit that the composer, with unparalleled fatuity, in writing to churches that had never known the apostle, represents him as having been at Patmos, close by

---

[1] See Canon of Muratori, lines 70–72, and stichometry of the *Codex claromontanus* in Credner, *Gesch. der neutest. Kanon*, p. 177.

Ephesus, — in fact, so near, and so dependent on its port, that if he did go there it must have been by way of Ephesus, — as acquainted with their nearest secrets, and as holding full authority over them. Would these churches, which (as Scholten holds) well knew that John had never been in or near Asia, have let themselves be taken in by so crude a pretence? One thing stands out clear in any hypothesis, — that the Apostle John was for some years the head of the churches in Asia.[1] This being granted, it is hard not to admit that he was really the author of this book; for, since its date is precisely fixed, we find no room for forgery. If the apostle was living in Asia in January, A. D. 69, or had merely been there, the first four chapters are unthinkable as the work of another hand. Supposing (as Scholten does) that he died at the beginning of this year, which does not seem to have been the fact, we do not escape the difficulty. The book is written as if the revelator were still alive; it is to be circulated at once among the Asiatic churches; if the apostle were dead the fraud would be too glaring. What would they have said at Ephesus in February, at receiving such a book, claiming to be from an apostle whom they knew to be no longer living, and whom (as Scholten thinks) they had never seen?

The book itself, on a closer view, rather confirms than weakens this opinion. The Apostle John seems, next after James, to have been the most ardent of the Judaising Christians, while the Apocalypse breathes a bitter hatred against Paul and all who were lax in keeping the Jewish Law. The book strikingly reflects the violent and fanatical temper of this apostle (see below, chap. xv.). It is indeed the work of that "son of thunder," that stormy Boanerges, who would have forbidden the use of his Master's name to any outside the narrow circle of the disciples; who, if he could, would have rained fire and brimstone upon the inhospitable Samaritans. The description of the celestial Court, with its material splen-

---

[1] See Appendix at the end of this volume.

dour of thrones and crowns, is indeed that of one who, when young, had aspired to sit with his brother on thrones at the right and left of the Messiah-King. The writer of the Apocalypse has his mind engrossed by the two objects, Rome (chaps. xiii.–xviii.) and Jerusalem (chaps. xi.–xii.). He appears to have seen Rome, with its temples, statues, and lavish imperial idolatry; and we may easily suppose that John journeyed thither in company with Peter. What regards Jerusalem is yet more striking. The writer constantly returns upon "the beloved city," thinks only of her, is familiar with the sufferings of the church there during the Jewish revolt, as we see in the fine image of the woman and her flight into the wilderness (xii. 13–17): we feel that he had been a pillar of this church, an enthusiastic devotee of the Jewish party. The tradition of Asia Minor seems, just so, to have kept the memory of John as that of a rigid Judaiser. In the Paschal controversy, which so vexed the Church during the latter half of the second century, the churches in Asia rely chiefly on the authority of John in celebrating Easter on the fourteenth of Nisan, according to the Jewish law. Polycarp in 160 and Polycrates in 190 appeal to the same authority to defend their antique custom against the innovators who, relying on the Fourth Gospel, insisted that Jesus, "the true passover," did not eat the paschal lamb with his disciples the night before his death, and who transferred the feast to the day of the resurrection.[1]

The language of the Apocalypse is a further reason for ascribing the book to a member of the church at Jerusalem. It is wholly different from that in the other New Testament books. It was doubtless written in Greek,[2] but in Greek moulded upon Hebrew, — Hebrew in its style of thought, hardly to be understood and felt by those ignorant of Hebrew. Besides sacramental terms (ix. 11, xvi. 16) and "the number of the beast," which are in Hebrew, like forms appear in every

---

[1] See Euseb. v. 24.

[2] Thus, "I am the Alpha and the Omega." The weights and measures are Greek.

line.¹ The writer is surprisingly saturated with the prophetic writings and earlier apocalypses; clearly, he knows them by heart. He is familiar with the Greek version of the [Jewish] sacred books; but in his citations the Hebrew text comes into his mind.² How different from the style of Paul, Luke, the writer of "Hebrews," or even the Synoptics! Only a man who had passed years at Jerusalem, in the schools about the Temple, could be so steeped in the Scripture, or share so keenly the passions and hopes of that rebellious people, with its hatred of Rome.

Another point not to be overlooked is that the Apocalypse has some features kindred with those of the Fourth Gospel and the Johannine epistles. Thus, the expression "the Word of God" (xix. 13), so characteristic of the Fourth Gospel, is first found here. The image of "living waters" is common to the two.³ The expression "Lamb of God" in the Fourth Gospel (i. 29, 36) recalls the frequent designation of Christ as "Lamb" in the Apocalypse. Both apply to the Messiah the words "me whom they have pierced" (Zech. xii. 10), and translate it in the same way (i. 7; xix. 37),—a rendering which differs from the Septuagint, but answers to the Hebrew. I by no means infer that the two books are from the same hand; but it is significant that the Gospel (which surely has some connection with the Apostle John) shows in its style and imagery something akin to a book which there are strong grounds for attributing to that apostle.

Church tradition has hesitated upon this point. Even in the middle of the second century the Apocalypse seems not to

---

¹ Note especially i. 4, where the Greek translation of *Jehovah* is undeclined [ὁ ἦν: like "I Am hath sent me."].

² He adopts several expressions of the LXX., even when inaccurate: as "tabernacle of witness" for *assembly*; Almighty (i. 8 : παντοκράτωρ) for "Jehovah of hosts." The phrase, "He shall rule them (ποιμανεῖ) with a rod of iron" (Ps. ii. 9), several times quoted, is taken from the LXX. rather than the Hebrew ["break them"], doubtless because it was so employed in the Christian Messianic exegesis.

³ xxi. 6, xxii. 1, 17; John iv. and x.

have had the importance we might expect for a composition which had been given out as a solemn manifesto from the pen of an apostle. It is doubtful whether Papias accepted it as the writing of John. He, like the author of the Apocalypse, was a millenarian; but he seems to have held this doctrine from "unwritten tradition." If he had cited this book in proof, Eusebius would have said so, eager as he was to gather every evidence from that ancient writer as to the apostolic record. Nor is the testimony of Andrew or of Aretas[1] clear upon this point. The author of the "Shepherd of Hermas," it would seem (Vis. iv., Sim. ix.), knew and imitated the Apocalypse; but it does not follow that he regarded it as a work of the apostle. Justin Martyr, about the middle of the second century, first plainly asserts that authorship (Tryph. 81); but he came forth from none of the great churches, and is accordingly of slight authority as to tradition. Melito, who commented on certain passages of the book, Theophilus of Antioch, and Apollonius, who used it freely in their polemics,[2] seem to have had the same opinion of it with Justin. The same may be said of the Canon of Muratori.[3] After A. D. 200 the general opinion is that the "John" of the Apocalypse is really the apostle. Irenæus (*Adv. Hær., pass.*), Tertullian (*Adv. Marc.* iii. 14, iv. 5), Clement of Alexandria (*Strom.* vi. 13; *Pæd.* ii. 12), Origen (*Matt.* xvi. 6; *Joh.* i. 14, ii. 4; cf. Euseb. vi. 25), Hippolytus (*Philos.* vii. 36) have no hesitation. Still, the contrary opinion is constantly upheld. To those who parted more and more widely from the early Judaic Christianity and millenarianism, the Apocalypse was a dangerous book, impossible to defend, unworthy of an apostle, contain-

---

[1] Bishops of Cæsarea in Cappadocia, of the fifth and sixth centuries.

[2] See Euseb. iv. 24, 26; v. 18; Jerome, *De viris illustr.* 24; Melito, *De var.* (*sub fine*). It may be asked if the name "John" in Eusebius is not an explanation added by the historian. But, as he puts in relief the passages which throw doubt on the genuineness of the Apocalypse, we may infer that he did not add the name without the authority of the writers mentioned.

[3] Lines 47, 48, 70-72; the latter passage, however, seems to show a tendency to regard it as apocryphal.

ing prophecies that were never fulfilled. Marcion, Cerdo, and the Gnostics rejected it wholly;[1] the "Apostolic Constitutions" omit it in their canon (ii. 57, vii. 47); the old Syriac version (*Peshito*) has it not. The opponents of the Montanist reveries, such as the priest Caius (Euseb. iii. 28)[2] and the Alogi (Epiph. li. 3, 4, 32–35) claimed to find it the work of Cerinthus. Finally, in the latter half of the third century, the Alexandrian school, in hostility to the millenarianism revived by Valerian's persecution, criticised the book with excessive rigour and undisguised dislike; Dionysius, the bishop, proved completely that it could not be by the author of the Fourth Gospel, and brought into vogue the theory of John the Elder.[3] In the fourth century the Church was divided in opinion (Euseb. iii. 24; Jer. Epist. 129). Eusebius, though doubtful, is on the whole unfriendly to the theory that it was written by the son of Zebedee. Gregory Nazianzen and almost all the Christian scholars of his time refused to see an apostle's handiwork in a book so sharply opposed to their taste, their notions of apologetics, and their prejudice as scholars. We may say that, if this party had had control, the Apocalypse would have been put in the same rank with the "Shepherd" and the *Antilegomena*, of which the Greek text is almost wholly lost. Happily, it was too late for such exclusion to prevail. Thanks to able opposition, a book containing bitter attacks on Paul was kept side by side with Paul's own writings, making up a volume supposed to proceed from one and the same inspired source.

Now, has this obstinate protest, making so marked a feature in Church history, any great weight in the view of independent criticism? We cannot say. Certainly Dionysius was right

---

[1] Tert. *Adv. Marc.* iv. 5; *Hær.* 6.

[2] Doubts as to this passage are removed by the fragment of Dionysius Alex. in Euseb. vii. 25, and by what Epiphanius says of the Alogi. The rendering "*as if* he were a great apostle" is inadmissible (Comp. Theodoret, *Hær. fab.* ii. 3).

[3] Euseb. vii. 25. The question had probably been discussed by Hippolytus. See list in *Corp. inscr. Gr.* 8613, A. 3.

in maintaining that the same hand could not have written both the Fourth Gospel and the Apocalypse. But, in face of that dilemma, the modern critic gives a different answer from that of the third century. The genuineness of the Apocalypse is far more probable than that of the Gospel; and, if we must assign any share to a supposed "John the Elder," that share is far likelier to be the Gospel and epistles. What motive had the opponents of Montanism in the third century, or those Christians of the fourth, educated in the Greek schools of Alexandria, Cæsarea, and Antioch, to deny that the Apocalypse was really the work of the Apostle John? Was it a tradition or memory preserved in the churches? Not at all. Their reasons were purely those of *a priori* dogma. First, if the Apocalypse should be ascribed to the apostle, it was almost impossible for a man of sense and learning to admit the genuineness of the Fourth Gospel, and to doubt this would be thought an attack upon Christianity itself. Besides, the supposed visions of John seemed to be a source of errors ever renewed, — of a perpetual recrudescence of Judaic Christianity, wild prophecy, and rash millenarianism. What reply could be made to the Montanists and similar mystics, who were consistent believers in the Apocalypse? or to those troops of enthusiasts who rushed upon martyrdom, intoxicated by the wild poetry of that old book of the year 69? The only reply could be that this book, the fountain-head of all their delusions, was not the work of an apostle. The reason that led Caius, Dionysius, and so many others to deny that the Apocalypse was from John was precisely that which leads us to the opposite conclusion. The book is Judæo-Christian, Ebionite; it is the work of an enthusiast drunk with hate against the Roman empire and the pagan world; it forbids all reconciliation with that empire and that world; its messianic doctrine is purely material; it affirms the thousand years' reign of saints and martyrs; it asserts the end of the world to be close at hand. These reasons — in which reasonable Christians, following the direction of Paul, and later of the Alexandrian school, found unanswerable difficulties — are for us the marks of antiquity and of apostolic genuineness. We are not frightened at Ebionism or Montanism; as simple historians, we assert that the adherents of these sects, rejected by the "orthodoxy" of their time, were the true successors of Jesus, of the Twelve, and of "the household of the Master." The rational direction which Christianity has followed, through a moderated *gnosis*, the belated victory of the Pauline school, and above all the ascendency of such men as Clement of Alexandria and Origen, should not make us forget the circumstances of its origin. The delusions, impossibilities, materialising views, paradoxes, monstrosities, which shocked Eusebius when he read the old Ebionite and millenarian writers like Papias, were the real primitive Christianity. That the dreams of these lofty enthusiasts might become a religion capable to live, men of good sense and fine intelligence — such as the Greeks who became Christians in the third century — must take in hand the task of those old visionaries, to modify, chastise, and prune it of its overgrowth. In this task of theirs, the most authentic monuments of the early childlike simplicity became embarrassing testimony, which they tried to thrust back into oblivion. That happened which always happens at the origin of a religious movement, which we notice in particular during the first century or two of the Franciscan Order: the founders were overmastered by the new-comers; the true successors of the fathers soon came to be "suspects" and heretics. Hence, as we often have occasion to insist, the favourite scriptures of the Ebionite and millenarian Judæo-Christianity — "Enoch," "Baruch," "Assumption of Moses," "Ascension of Isaiah," the fourth Esdras, the "Shepherd of Hermas," the "Epistle of Barnabas" — were better preserved in Latin or Oriental versions than in the Greek text. Hence, too, the more or less complete loss of the Greek text of Papias and Irenæus. The "orthodox" Greek Church has always shown itself extremely intolerant of such books, and has systematically suppressed them.

Thus the reasons for ascribing the Apocalypse to the Apostle John remain strong; and I think that those who shall read this history will be struck at the way in which everything is made clear and connected in this view. But, in a world where notions of literary property were so different from ours, a work might belong to an author in various degrees. Did the Apostle John himself write the manifesto of A. D. 69? This we may surely doubt. It is enough for my theory if he knew it, approved it, and allowed it to circulate in his name. Thus we should explain the first three verses, which seem to be from another hand than the Seer's; as well as passages like xviii. 20 and xxi. 14, which lead us to think of a different pen. So in Ephesians ii. 20 we feel sure that an amanuensis or an imitator has come between us and Paul. We have to be on our guard against the abuse made of apostolic names to give currency to apocryphal compositions.[1] Many things in the Apocalypse are ill adapted to an immediate disciple of Jesus.[2] We are surprised to find one who was of the inner circle in which the gospel was wrought out exhibiting his former friend as a glorified Messiah, sitting on God's throne, ruling the nations, — so wholly different from him of Galilee that the Seer trembles at sight of him and "falls at his feet as dead" (i. 17). One who had known the real Jesus would scarcely, even at the end of six and thirty years, have undergone such a mental revolution. Mary of Magdala, on beholding the risen Jesus, exclaims, "My Master!" while John, on seeing the heavens opened, must find him whom he loved transformed into the dread Messiah. It is no less surprising to see from the pen of one of the chief figures in the gospel idyll a composition purely artificial, a mere copy, showing in every line a cold imitation of the ancient prophetic visions. The picture of the Galilæan fishermen given us by the Synoptics by no means represents to us men of the study, diligent readers of old books, pedantic rabbins. Is the picture by the Synoptics, then, the false one? and was the company that gathered about Jesus a good deal more pedantic, more scholastic, more like the

---

[1] Compare the evidences from Caius and Dionysius of Alexandria in Euseb. iii. 28.

[2] Compare i. 12 with ver. 9, 19, 20; vi. 9; xx. 4; xxii. 8.

Scribes and Pharisees, than one could possibly gather from Matthew, Mark, and Luke?

If we admit the view I have suggested, — that John rather adopted the Apocalypse than wrote it with his own hand, — we have the further advantage of accounting for the limited reception of the book during three quarters of the century following its composition. Very likely the author himself, after the year 70, — seeing Jerusalem taken, the Flavian emperors firm on their throne, the Empire reconstructed, and the world persisting to exist in spite of the three-and-a-half years' term he had allowed it, — checked the circulation of his work. The Apocalypse, in fact, did not reach its highest importance till near the middle of the second century, when millenarianism became a point of dispute in the church; when, especially, persecutions again gave to outcries against "the Beast" their meaning and their fitness, — as we see in the letter of the churches of Lyons and Vienne in Eusebius (v. 1, 10, 58). The fortune of the Apocalypse was thus bound up with the alternations of peace and conflict in the Church. Each persecution gave it new currency; when the persecution was stayed, its true day of peril came, and it had nearly been banished from the canon as a misleading and seditious pamphlet.

Two traditions which I have accepted as plausible in this volume — the coming of Peter to Rome, and the residence of John at Ephesus — have been the subject of much controversy, and are discussed in an appendix. I have there considered Scholten's recent treatise on the apostle's abode in Asia, with the attention due to all the writings of this eminent Dutch critic. The conclusions to which I have come (which, however, I hold as merely probable) will, no doubt, — like the use I have made of the Fourth Gospel in writing the "Life of Jesus," — move the scorn of a young, self-confident school, in whose eyes every point is proved so that it be negative; a school that peremptorily taxes with ignorance those who do not accept its exaggerations on sight. I beg the thoughtful, serious reader to believe that I have enough respect for him to neglect nothing that may serve in the search for truth in the line of study

I undertake. But it is my maxim that history is one thing and disquisition is another. History cannot be well taken in hand until erudition has heaped up whole libraries of memoirs and critical essays. But, when history comes to be disengaged from this scaffolding, all it owes the reader is to point out the original source on which each statement rests. In these volumes devoted to the beginnings of Christian history, the notes fill a third of the page; but if I had been obliged to add the bibliography, citations from modern authors, and detailed discussions of the views held, they would have covered at least three-quarters. True, the method I have followed assumes the reader to be familiar with the results of critical study in the Old and New Testaments, a claim which few of my countrymen can make. But how many works of value could there be, if a writer must first be sure of a public to understand him fully? I say, too, that even one with no knowledge of German, if he is acquainted with what has been written in our language upon the subject, can perfectly well follow my argument. The excellent collection of essays in the *Revue de théologie* (published till recently at Strasburg), is an encyclopædia of modern exegesis, not relieving us, it is true, from the duty of exploring the German and Dutch scholars, but for half a century reporting all great discussions of theological erudition.[1] I have always insisted that Germany has earned lasting glory by founding the science of biblical criticism, with the researches appertaining thereto; and this, with sufficient emphasis to be above the charge of ignoring the obligations I have a hundred times acknowledged. German exegesis has its faults, which ever so liberal a theologian cannot avoid; but the patience, persistency, and good faith it has displayed are worthy of all praise. Many a noble building-stone has Ger-

---

[1] This and the succeeding paragraph contain the author's personal acknowledgments to between thirty and forty eminent scholars, and critics of the modern schools. As these lists, however, were written nearly twenty years ago, they would be an insufficient guide for more recent explorers in a field whose bounds are so rapidly extending, and hence they are omitted here. — ED.

many added in the intellectual structure of mankind; but, among them all, biblical science is, perhaps, that which has been chiselled with the greatest care, and which bears most completely the stamp of the workman's hand.

I would here record my special gratitude to those accomplished Italian scholars, who were my inestimable guides throughout a recent journey in Italy. It will appear in the following pages at how many points this journey touched the topics it treats. Though no stranger to Italy, I was athirst to greet once more that land so full of memories, the richly endowed mother of every new intellectual birth. According to Rabbinical tradition, there was at Rome, during the long eclipse of beauty which we call the Middle Age, an ancient image, kept in a secret spot, so beautiful that the Romans would come by night to kiss it stealthily. Of such embraces, 'twas said, Antichrist was born.[1] This child of the marble image was verily a son of Italy. All the great protests of man's conscience against the extravagances of Christendom came of old from the bosom of this land; and from this they will come again in future time.

I will confess that my delight in history, the singular joy in beholding the spectacle displayed on the theatre of the world, has especially entranced me in this volume. I have had such joy in writing it that I ask no other reward than I have found in the task itself. Often have I reproached myself for taking so much pleasure in my study, while my unhappy country was wasting in long agony; but my conscience is clear of blame. When in the elections of 1869 I solicited the votes of my fellow-citizens, all my placards bore conspicuously this inscription: "No Revolution! no War! War would be as fatal as Revolution." In September, 1870, I implored the enlightened minds of Germany and Europe to reflect on the frightful peril that menaced civilisation. During the siege of Paris, in November, I risked great unpopularity by advocating an Assembly, with powers to treat for peace. In the elections of 1871, I

---

[1] Buxtorf, *Lexicon Chald.*, etc., p. 222.

replied to the overtures made me, "Such a charge can be neither sought nor refused." When order was restored, I bestowed all my attention upon the reforms which I considered most urgent for the salvation of the State. I have done what I could. We owe it to our country to be frank with her; we need employ no flatteries or tricks to win her to accept our service or accord with our views.

Moreover, while this volume is primarily addressed to inquirers and men of taste, it will, perhaps, teach more than one lesson. Here we shall see crime carried to its height, and protest lifted against it in accents saintly and sublime. Such a sight will have its religious use. I believe as fully as ever that religion is not a mere illusion of our nature; that it answers to something objectively real; that he who follows its inspirations is the truly inspired man. To simplify religion is not to undermine it, but often, rather, to make it strong. The little Protestant sects of our day, like Christianity at its birth, are here to prove it. The great error of Romanism is to think that we can contend against the advance of materialism with an intricate dogmatic system, burdening ourselves more heavily each day with some fresh marvel.

The people will henceforth endure only a religion without miracle; but such a religion might yet be a living one if those who have the care of souls would accept the degree of positivism that has gained a hold on the mental temper of the working class; and if, reducing dogma to its lowest terms, they would make worship a means of moral training and helpful co-operation. Above the Family, beyond the State, mankind needs the Church. The stability of the American Union, with its amazing democracy, is found only in its innumerable sects. If (as we may suppose) Ultramontane Catholicism can no longer win back to its temples the population of great cities, personal effort must create those little centres where the poor and weak may find instruction, moral help, friendly guidance, sometimes material aid. Civil society — call it village, district, province, state, or fatherland — owes something to the betterment of the individual; but it acts only within strict limits. The family owes more; but it is often weak, sometimes wholly helpless. Associations formed upon a moral foundation can alone bestow on every man that comes into the world a living bond uniting him with the Past, duties toward the Future, examples to be followed, a heritage of Virtue to be received and handed down, a tradition of Self-sacrifice which he has to carry on.

NOTE ON THE LATER CRITICISM OF THE APOCALYPSE.

THIS portion of Renan's great work was completed about the year 1872. At that time there was a wide if not universal consent of opinion among scholars on the three main points of his exposition: that the Apocalypse expresses the mind of an extreme Jewish party in the Christian Church; that it was written during, or just before, the terrors of the Jewish war of A. D. 68-70; and that its most characteristic and obscure predictions refer personally to Nero, and to the current popular expectation that, after his real or supposed death, he would be for a time restored to power. These points are fully illustrated in chapter xvi. of the present volume. The question of a possible plurality of authorship appears to have been hardly so much as raised.

Of other points remaining unresolved, the following are most important: an early Christian tradition ascribing the work to the time of Domitian, about twenty-five years later than the date here assumed; numerous passages or phrases which appear to express doctrinal conceptions of the second century; and, in particular, a seemingly irreconcilable duality of conception, — the Jewish Messiah, vengeful and triumphant, being here and there set aside for the Christian Redeemer under the image of a Lamb slain in sacrifice for the sins of his people, while a rigid Jewish partialism gives way to the promise of a world-wide salvation. It has also to be noticed that the clear references to Nero are all contained in a single broken passage — chapters xi.-xiv.; xvii., xviii. — which is strictly an episode, interrupting what is otherwise the regular unfolding of a celestial drama.[1] The most complete exhibition of the points above

---

[1] In this episode the scene is transferred from heaven to earth, and is full of literary wealth and passion, quite remote from the bare symbolism of the celestial visions. Here we have the true Hebraic temper: "faith in the perpetuity of the Temple; hope of the return of Israel to God and his final deliverance; a human Messiah, born of the Israelitish theocracy, and caught up to heaven to escape the wrath of the Dragon, — a Messiah without cross or death; the return of Moses and Elias [the two olive-trees and candlesticks]

enumerated, accessible in English, is given by Dr. Martineau in "The Seat of Authority in Religion" (1890), pages 217-237.

Two attempted solutions of the questions thus raised are all that need to be considered here. The first is that of Daniel Voelter (Tübingen, 1882), advocating a plurality of authorship, as modified by Eberhard Vischer in an essay of very great ability, published in 1886.[1] It may be stated, in a general way, thus: At some later period of distress in the Christian Church, — presumably in the time of Domitian, the date assigned by Harnack (1896), — there came into the hands of some Christian teacher of authority a Hebrew document, which proved to be a book of visions composed during the extreme agony of the Jewish people in 69 or 70. This he translated (the translation being strongly tinged with the original Hebrew colouring), freely interspersing passages to adapt it to the needs and temper of his own day, and prefixing an introduction, with letters to the seven churches, their form and symbolism being shaped upon the Hebrew original. In this — with a few passages added here and there, down to A. D. 135 — we have the "Apocalypse of John."

Vischer's essay opened up a new field of discussion, which is already occupied by a considerable literature, on a topic that had seemed "exhausted and going to sleep." To this discussion a defence of the single authorship, by M. Bovon, in the Lausanne *Revue de Théologie* (on the ground of the general identity of eschatological views among Jews and Christians) is perhaps the most notable single contribution. A modified view by M. Sabatier, referred to on page 12, defends with great skill and charm the general unity of style and composition in the Apocalypse as a whole, but makes a marked exception of the episode just spoken of, in chapter xi. and the succeeding chapters. This, it holds, was adopted bodily by the Christian writer of the time of Domitian, to be pondered, like the obscure predictions of "Daniel," as a divine oracle, "bitter" and hard to understand, — "the last cry of distress, vengeance, and hope, of the expiring Jewish nation." — ED.

in chapter xi.; a severe and jealous monotheism; a passion of vengeance against the enemies of the Jewish people; triumph and savage joy at the sight of desolated Rome; material splendours of the New Jerusalem." These are contained in the "little book" of chapter x., — the figure under which this episode is introduced. (Sabatier, *Les Origines de l'Apocalypse de Saint Jean*.)

In Gunkel's *Schöpfung und Chaos* (Göttingen, 1895), it is maintained that the entire episode of the Dragon is a Babylonian myth, adopted very early into the Hebrew apocalyptic imagery. In this view the "number of the Beast" (666) has its equivalent in the Hebrew, ההום קדמוניה = "primeval chaos."

[1] *Die Offenbarung Johannis, eine Jüdische Apokalypse in Christlicher Bearbeitung*, Leipzig, pp. 137. It contains an Appendix by Professor Harnack, and the full Greek text of chapters iv.-xxii. 5, containing the assumed original document, and marking in the type twelve or more supposed interpolations.

ANTICHRIST.

CHAPTER I.

PAUL IN PRISON. — A. D. 61.

IT was a strange time; never, perhaps, had mankind passed through a more extraordinary crisis. Nero was just entering on his twenty-fourth year. The head of this wretched youth, whose mother's crime had put him on the throne of the world at seventeen, was growing completely crazed. Many symptoms had long caused anxiety in those who knew him. His was a mind prodigiously given to display; an evil nature full of hypocrisy, levity, and vanity; an incredible compound of distorted intelligence, profound malice, and self-love both cruel and suspicious, and a refinement of craft without parallel. Such he was by nature. Still, it needed special circumstances to make of him that monster who has no second in history, and who finds his like only in the reports of criminal pathology.[1] The school of crime in which he had grown up — the necessity which that wicked woman almost laid upon him, to enter on the scene by an act of parricide — made him early conceive the world as a shocking comedy in which he was the chief actor. At the present moment

---

[1] See the reflection in Pausanias, vii. 17: 3.

he has completely forsaken his masters, the philosophers; he has slain almost all his kindred; he has brought the most shameful extravagances into fashion; Roman society, in great part, following his example, has gone down to the last depth of depravity. Antique hardness of heart was coming to its height; a truer popular instinct was beginning to react against it. About the time when Paul entered Rome, this was the chronicle of the day: —

Pedanius Secundus, prefect of Rome, a man of consular rank, had been assassinated by one of his slaves, who might well plead extenuating circumstances in his favour. By the law, every slave who had been under the same roof with him when the crime was committed must be put to death. Of these wretches there were near four hundred. When it was learned that this atrocious butchery was really to take place, the slumbering sense of justice in the vilest of the people was shocked. There was a riot; but the Senate and the Emperor decreed that the law must take its course.[1]

Among these four hundred innocents slaughtered in the name of a hateful law, there may have been more than one Christian. The bottom of the pit of iniquity was now reached; to go on must be to go upward. Certain moral indications of a strange sort had appeared in the higher ranks of Roman society.[2] Four years before, there had been much talk of a high-born lady, Pomponia Græcina, wife of Aulus Plautius, the first conqueror of Britain.[3] She was charged with

---

[1] Tac. *Ann.* xiv. 42.
[2] Tertull. *Apol.* 1.
[3] See Borghesi, *Works*, i. 17-27; Ovid, *Pontica*, i. 6, ii. 6, iv. 9; Tac. *Agric.* 4.

"outlandish superstition." She always dressed in black, and never relaxed in her austerity of manner. This melancholy was ascribed to shocking memories, especially the death of her near friend, Julia, daughter of Drusus, who perished at the hand of Messalina. One of her sons seems also to have been the victim of one of Nero's most enormous crimes;[1] but Pomponia evidently bore in her heart a profounder grief, and, it may be, a mysterious hope. According to old custom, she was referred to the tribunal of her husband, who assembled their kindred, investigated the charge as a family matter, and pronounced her innocent. This noble lady lived long after, safe in her husband's protection, always sad, always held in honour. She seems never to have told her secret.[2] Who knows whether what superficial observers took for melancholy was not a deep peace of soul, calm meditation, a resigned looking forward to death, scorn of a society at once silly and malevolent, the unspoken joy of a heart that renounces pleasure? Who knows whether Pomponia Græcina was not the first saint in the world of rank, the elder sister of Melania, Eustochia, and Paula?[3]

This strange condition of things, while it exposed the church at Rome to political storms, gave to it, although small in numbers, an importance among the

[1] Sueton. *Nero*, 35.
[2] Tac. *Ann.* xiii. 32.
[3] The Gens *Pomponia Græcina* is thought by some to have held for several centuries high rank in the Church at Rome. The name seems to have been found in the cemetery of St. Calixtus (inscription of the third or fourth century doubtfully restored: Rossi, *Roma sotteran.* i. 306; ii. 360; inscr. tav. 49, 50, No. 27). The identifying of Pomponia Græcina with the *Lucina* whose memory clings to the oldest Christian burial-places seems more than doubtful. There was only one Lucina, of the third century.

first. Rome, under Nero, was not in the least like a provincial city. Every one who looked for a great career must go to it. In coming thither Paul himself had been guided by a clear intuition. His arrival there was an event in his life second only to his conversion. He felt that he had reached the zenith of his apostolic career, and doubtless recalled the dream in which, after one of his days of conflict, Christ appeared to him, saying, "Be of good cheer, Paul; for as thou hast testified of me in Jerusalem, so must thou bear witness also at Rome." [1]

As soon as they came near the walls of the eternal city, the centurion Julius conducted his prisoners to the prætorian barracks, built by Sejanus near the *via Nomentana*, and put them in charge of the "captain of the guard" (*præfectus prætorianus*).[2] Those who appealed to the emperor, on entering Rome, were held as the emperor's prisoners, and as such confided to the imperial guard.[3] There were usually two prætorian prefects; at this time there was but one.[4] Since A.D. 51, this high charge had been in the hands of the noble Afranius Burrhus,[5] who a year later atoned by a grievous death for the crime of seeking to do good by a compact with evil. With him Paul doubtless had direct communication; though it may be that the humane treatment given to the apostle was due to the influence which that upright and good man shed about him. Paul was put in military guard; that is,

---

[1] Acts xxiii. 11; comp. xix. 24; xxvii. 24.

[2] Acts xxviii. 16; Phil. i. 13; Suet. *Tiberius*, 37.

[3] Pliny, *Epist.* x. 65; Josephus, *Antiq.* xviii. 6: 6, 7; Philostratus, *Sophistæ*, ii. 32.

[4] Tillemont, *Hist. des empereurs*, i. 702.

[5] See Josephus, *Antiq.* xx. 8: 9.

in keeping of an officer of the military stores (*frumentarius*),[1] to whom he was chained, but not painfully or constantly. He was allowed to live in quarters hired at his own charge, probably near the barracks, where any might come freely to see him,[2] and here he waited for two years the hearing of his appeal. Burrhus died in March, A. D. 62, and was succeeded by Fenius Rufus and the infamous Tigellinus, the partner of Nero's debauchery, and the agent of his crimes. Seneca, from this time on, kept aloof from public affairs, and Nero had no other counsellors than the Furies.

The relations of Paul with the faithful in Rome had begun, as we have seen, during his abode at Corinth. Three days after his arrival he wished, according to his custom, to come in contact with the chief *hakamim* (wise men). The Christian body in Rome had not been formed in the Jewish synagogue, but of believers from abroad, who had landed at Ostia or Puteoli, and gathered in a church which had little to do with the various synagogues of Rome. Owing to the vastness of the city, and the multitude of strangers who met in it,[3] there was little common acquaintance, and quite opposite ways of thinking might prevail there without ever coming into touch. Paul, then, followed the same course here as in his first and second missions in the

---

[1] Acts xxviii. 16, 20; comp. "Saint Paul," p. 156; Jos. *Ant.* xviii. 6: 7; Seneca, *De tranq. animæ*, 10. *Frumentarii* were attached, apparently, to every corps (Renier).

[2] Acts xxxiii. 16, 17, 20, 23, 30. Phil. i. 7, 13, 14, 17, 30. Col. iv. 3, 4, 18. Eph. ii. 1; iii. 1; vi. 19, 20.

[3] The Jewish population may have been some twenty or thirty thousand, counting women and children (Jos. *Ant.* xvii. 11: 1; xviii. 3: 5. Tac. *Ann.* ii. 85). The well-known passage in Cicero (*pro Flacco*, 28) implies about that number.

towns where he planted the faith. He sent to invite several chiefs of the synagogue to visit him. To these he set forth the situation in the most favourable light, assuring them that he neither had done nor wished to do anything against his people; that he strove for the "hope of Israel;" that is, faith in the resurrection. The Jews replied that they had never heard of him, or received any message from Judæa that spoke of him, and invited him to explain his views; "for," said they, "we hear that the sect you tell us of is everywhere spoken against." A time was set for the discussion, and a large number of Jews gathered in the little room which made his dwelling to hear him. The discussion lasted almost a whole day, Paul setting forth the texts of Moses and the Prophets which, as he thought, proved Jesus to be the Messiah. A few assented, the larger number remained incredulous. The Jews of Rome prided themselves on their exact observance of the Law:[1] here was not the place for him to succeed. The meeting broke up in loud dispute; in anger he quoted a passage of Isaiah (vi. 9, 10), very familiar to Christian preachers,[2] on the wilful blindness of those hardened men who shut their eyes and stop their ears so as neither to see nor hear the truth. He ended, says the account, with the usual threat of offering the kingdom of God, rejected by the Jews, to Gentiles who would more readily accept it.

His mission among the pagans was, in truth, far more successful. His prison-cell became the centre of an ardent apostolate. During the two years of his

---

[1] Φιλέντολοι (lovers of the commandments). See "Saint Paul," pp. 104–107.

[2] Matt. xiii. 14; Mark xiv. 12; Luke viii. 10; John xii. 40; Rom. xi. 8.

captivity he was never once molested in his work.¹ Some of his disciples continued with him, among them Timothy and Aristarchus;² Luke must have left him, as Paul does not send his greeting to the Philippians. His friends seem, by turns, to have shared his imprisonment.³ The progress of conversion was remarkable.⁴ The apostle wrought miracles, it was said, controlling spirits and the heavenly powers,⁵ which accounts we may compare with the legend of Simon Magus. Paul in prison was thus more effective than when in free activity. His chains, which he dragged to the prætor's court, and displayed with a sort of pride,⁶ were eloquent in themselves. At his example, inspired by his courage in captivity, his disciples and other Roman Christians grew bold in speech.

At first they found no obstacle.⁷ Even Campania and the cities near Vesuvius received (perhaps from the church at Puteoli) the germs of Christian faith, which here found the ordinary condition of its growth, a soil of Judaism to receive it.⁸ Strange conquests were brought about. The pure life of the faithful was

[1] Acts xxviii. 30, 31 ; Phil. 7.
[2] Phil. i. 1; ii. 19; Col. iv. 10; Philem. 24.
[3] Col. iv. 10 ; Philem. 13, 23.   [4] Phil. i. 12.
[5] Rom. xv. 18, 19.   [6] Phil. i. 13.
[7] Phil. i. 14.
[8] Garrucci, *Bull. archeol. napol.*, new series, ann. 2, p. 8; Rossi, *Bull. di archeol. crist.* 1864, p. 69, 92; Zangemeister, *Inscr. pariet.* No. 679. For the Jews at Puteoli, see Minervini, *Bull arch. napol.* new ser. ann. 3, p. 105; at Pompeii, Garrucci, as above, pp. 8, 68. On the various eastern or southern populations at Puteoli, see "Saint Paul," p. 114; Mommsen, *Inscr. napol.* No. 2462 ; Fiorelli, *Inscr. Lat.* (museum of Naples), Nos. 691, 692, 693; Minervini, *Mon. ant. ined.* i. (Naples, 1852), 40–43, App. vii–ix; *Zeitschr. der d. m. G.* 1869, 150 *et seq.*; *Journ. asiat.* Apr. 1873. Comp. Gervasio (*Mem. d. Accad. Ercolan.* vol. ix.; Scherillo, *La venuta di S. Pietro in Napoli* (Naples, 1859), pp. 97–149. See Tertull. *Apol.* 40.

a powerful charm, which won many a Roman dame:[1] the better families, indeed, still retained an unbroken tradition of modesty and nobility of character in their ladies. The new sect had disciples even in Nero's household,[2] and perhaps among the Jews also, who were numerous in the lower ranks of service,[3] — for example, the Jewess Acme, waiting-maid of Livia; the Samaritan Thallus, freedman of Tiberius[4]—and among the slaves and freedmen enrolled in societies or clubs (*collegia*), whose condition touched the meanest and the highest, the most brilliant and most squalid.[5] Vague hints would lead us to suppose that Paul had relations with members or freedmen of the Annæan house.[6] It

[1] As we see in the Acts of Peter reported by the pseudo-Linus.

[2] Phil. iv. 22. Cf. *Philosoph.* ix. 12; Gruter, 642, 8; Cardinali, *Dipl.* p. 221, No. 410. According to Chrysostom (i. 48, ii. 168, ix. 349, xi. 673, 722, ed. Montfaucon), Astorius [an Arian of Cappadocia, in the fourth century], p. 168 (ed. Combefis); Theophylact (in 2 Tim. iv. 16), Glycas (*Ann.* p. 236, Paris ed.), communications of Paul with one of the women, and with a favourite servant of Nero's court, are to be traced in the Acts of Peter and Paul. Comp. the apocryphal "Passions" of these apostles, ascribed to St. Linus, in *Bibl. patrum maxima*, ii. 67 *et seq.*; the Acts of St. Tropez in *Acta SS. Maii.* p. 6 (note the expression *magnus in officio Cæsaris Neronis*, and comp. Gruter, 599, 6; *Rhein Mus.* new ser. vi. 16); *Acta Petri et Pauli* (Tisch. *Acta apost. apocr.*) §§ 31, 80, 84, Paris MSS. There is no ground for identifying the legendary woman of the court with Acte, though the inscription 735 of Orelli is no objection, not being the epitaph of Acte, as supposed (Greppo, *Trois mémoires*, Paris, 1810, mém. 1, and additions).

[3] See below, p. 141, 142.

[4] Jos. *Antiq.* xvii. 5: 7; 18, v. 4; *Wars*, i. 33: 6, 7.

[5] Tac. *Hist.* ii. 92.

[6] The following inscription, seemingly of the third century, was discovered a few years ago at Ostia:—

D · M ·
M · ANNEO ·
PAVLO · PETRO
M · ANNEVS · PAVLVS
FILIO · CARISSIMO

(*Rossi, Bull.* 1867, 6 *et seq.* Cf. Dion. Alex. in Euseb. vii. 25: 14). There

is clear, in any case, that the distinction between Jew and Christian was well understood in Rome at this time by people of intelligence. Christianity seemed to them a separate "superstition," an outgrowth from Judaism, hating it and hated by it.[1] Nero, in particular, knew well enough what was going on, and regarded it with a certain curiosity. Already, perhaps, some of the Jewish intriguers about him stirred his imagination with the affairs of the East, and had promised him that kingdom of Jerusalem which was the dream of his last hours, his latest hallucination.[2]

We do not know with certainty the name of any member of the church in Rome at this time. A document of dubious value reckons, as friends of Paul and Timothy, the names of Eubulus, Pudens, Claudia, and that Linus whom later ecclesiastical tradition recorded as Peter's successor in the Roman

---

were many Peters in the third century (of Lampsacus, of Alexandria, etc.), and still more Pauls (of Samosata, etc.). In the fourth, the belief prevailed of relations of St. Paul with Seneca, suggesting an apocryphal correspondence (Jerome, *De vir. illustr.* 12; Aug. *Epist.* 153, to Macedonius, 14; pseudo-Linus, pp. 70, 71). The belief originated from a certain supposed likeness in doctrine (Tertull. *De anima*, 20). Paul, indeed, had relations with Gallio, Seneca's brother; but the slight interest felt by these enlightened men in popular superstitions (Acts xviii. 12-17) does not lead us to suppose that Seneca's curiosity was moved in the least regarding Paul. The law that Seneca, as consul in the latter half of A. D. 57 (Rossi, *Bull.* 1866, 60, 62), had to pronounce on Paul's appeal, rests on an erroneous chronology. In a lost book, *Contra Superstitiones*, Seneca spoke of Jews, not Christians (Aug. *De civ. Dei*, vi. 11). This prejudice against Jews would have ill disposed him towards Paul and the Christians if he had ever met them. Such a man could not have been Paul's disciple.

[1] A passage of Tacitus, preserved by Sulpicius Severus (Bernays, *Ueber die Kronik des Sulp. Sev.*, Berlin, 1861, 57), speaks of "these superstitions, though mutually hostile, yet proceeding from a common origin . . . Christians came from Jews." (Comp. Tac. *Ann.* xv. 44.)

[2] Suet. *Nero*, 40.

bishopric.¹ Nor have we any means of estimating, even approximately, the number of the disciples. They made, no doubt, but a small fraction of the Jewish population.²

All seemed to be going well; but the fiercely bitter party that had taken it in hand to fight Paul to the ends of the earth did not sleep. We have seen the emissaries of those eager conservatives hunting him, as it were, by scent on his trail, while in his travels by sea he left a long wake of hatred behind him. Shown under the baleful features of a man who teaches the eating of flesh sacrificed to idols, and the sharing of gentile works of uncleanness, he is pointed out to all men in advance, and marked as the object of vengeance. This is hard for us at this day to believe, but we cannot well doubt it, since Paul himself has told it.³ Even at this solemn and critical moment, he finds himself confronted by the basest passions. Adversaries — members of that Judæo-Christian sect, which now for ten years he had found everywhere in his path — mocked him with a sort of counterfeit preaching of the gospel. Envious, disputatious, hateful, they watched the occasion to oppose him, to embitter the griefs of his imprisonment, to stir up the Jews against him, to belittle the merit of his endurance. The good-

---

¹ 2 Tim. iv. 21. This verse served later as the ground of legends regarding the senator Pudens and his family. On the name Linus, see Le Bas (*Inscr.* iii. No. 1081). Greek names at Rome usually indicate slaves or freedmen (Suet. *Claud.* 25; *Galba*, 14; Tac. *Hist.* i. 13). The *cognomen gentilitium* alone of freedmen might be Latin. For Claudia, comp. Claudia Aster (below, p. 141, 142), Κλαυδία πιστή (inscr. at Rome, Orelli, i. 367). A Claudia is named among the freed people of Acte (Orelli, 735; Fabretti, *Inscr.* 124–126). On the names registered in Romans xvi. see "Saint Paul," Introd. lxv–lxx.

² See note 3, p. 35.   ³ Phil. i. 15–17; ii. 20, 21.

will, love, and honour exhibited toward him by others, their eagerly declared conviction that his chains were the glory and best vindication of the Gospel, sweetened to him all that bitter draught. In his own words, written at this time, —

What then? If only Christ be preached, whether in pretence or in truth, I rejoice in it and will rejoice. For I know that this will prove my salvation through your prayer and the aid of the spirit of Christ. This is my earnest expectation and my hope, that Christ shall be glorified whether by my life or death. For my life is Christ, and to me death is gain; so that if I live I have the harvest of my work, and which I would choose I do not know. Thus I am in doubt between the two: for my desire is to depart and be with Christ, which for me is far more to be desired; yet to remain among you is to render the better service.[1]

This greatness of soul gave him marvellous assurance, cheer, and strength. To one of the churches he writes, "If my blood must be sprinkled as a libation upon the sacrifice of your faith, I am glad and rejoice with you all; so do you rejoice and be glad with me."[2] Still he was more glad to believe in his own speedy acquittal; for he saw in it the triumph of the gospel and the opening to new labours. His thought, it is true, seems to turn no longer to the West; rather he would withdraw to Philippi or Colossæ to wait the Lord's appearing. Perhaps he had come to a better knowledge of the Latin world, and saw that outside of Rome and Campania, regions which immigration from the Levant had made much like Greece and Asia Minor, he would find extreme difficulty, if only in the language. As we may infer

[1] Phil. i. 18–24. [2] Phil. ii. 17, 18.

from a hint of Dion Cassius (lx. 17), he perhaps knew a little Latin, but not enough for effective speech. Jewish and Christian proselyting in the first century made little advance in really Latin towns; it was restricted to such cities as Rome and Puteoli, where Greek was widely diffused by constant arrivals from the East. Paul's purpose had been sufficiently carried out: the gospel had been preached in both the Grecian and the Roman world;[1] in the noble hyperbole of prophetic speech, it had reached "the uttermost parts of the earth,"[2] and been "fully preached" to all nations under heaven.[3] What he had now in mind was to declare the word freely in Rome,[4] then return to the churches in Macedonia and Asia,[5] and wait patiently with them, in prayer and ecstasy, for the coming of Christ.

Few years in the apostle's life were happier than these.[6] Great comfort came to him from time to time, while he had nothing now to fear from the malevolence of the Jews. His poor prison cell was the centre of a surprising activity. The insane profanities of Rome — its spectacles, debaucheries, and crimes, — the infamies of Tigellinus, the intrepidity of Thraseas, the shocking fate of the innocent Octavia, the death of Pallas — such tragedies touched not these pious enthusiasts. "The fashion of this world is passing by," said they. The grand vision of a divine future made them blind to the bloody filth through which they walked. In truth, the prophetic word of Jesus was coming to fulfilment. Amid the outer darkness where Satan

---

[1] Acts xxiii. 11; Col. i. 23.
[2] Acts i. 18.
[3] Rom. xv. 19.
[4] Col. iv. 3.
[5] Phil. i. 26; ii. 24.
[6] Phil. i. 7.

reigns as king, amid its weeping and gnashing of teeth, is set the little paradise of the elect, where they dwell in their secluded realm, radiant with light and azure, the kingdom of God their Father. But what a hell without! How dreadful is the abode in the kingdom of the Beast, "where their worm dieth not and the fire is not quenched"!

One of the great joys of Paul at this time, apparently not long after his arrival at Rome,[1] was the coming of a message from his beloved church at Philippi, the first he had established in Europe, the home of so much devoted affection. The wealthy Lydia, whom Paul calls his "true yokefellow" (iv. 3),[2] would surely not forget him. Epaphroditus, the church's messenger, brought a sum of money (ii. 25), a relief which Paul greatly needed, considering the costs of his present situation. He had always excepted that church from his usual rule of taking no gift from his converts, and received this bounty gladly. The tidings it sent were cheering, tidings of entire harmony, troubled only by some small difference between two deaconesses, Euodia and Syntyche, whom he seeks to conciliate (i. 27; iv. 2). Vexations from certain "adversaries," which had brought about a few arrests, served only to show the constancy of the true believers (i. 28–30; cf. Acts xvi. 23). That heresy of the Judæo-Christians, the assumed need of circumcision, had assailed without dividing them (iii. 2, 3). Some ill examples of worldly and self-indulgent Christians, of whom he writes with

---

[1] Phil. i. 13; ii. 28.

[2] This interpretation of the word σύζυγος, which Renan supposes to mean "wife," seems to be set aside by the masculine gender of the adjective. Comp. "Saint Paul," 148, 149, where it appears that one tradition holds that Paul was married. — ED.

tears (iii. 18, 19), appear not to have discredited the church. Epaphroditus stayed some time with Paul, and fell into a sickness due to his devotion, of which he nearly died; and an eager desire now came upon him to revisit Philippi, to calm his friends' anxiety. Paul accordingly bade him good speed (ii. 25, 26), giving him a letter for the faithful at Philippi, full of tenderness, written by the hand of Timothy.[1] He had never expressed in so loving phrases his heartfelt affection for those churches of his founding, so wholly good and pure.

He congratulates them, not only on their belief in Christ, but on having suffered for his sake. Those of them who are in prison should be proud to endure the same treatment that they have seen inflicted on their apostle, and that he now endures. They are like a little group of God's children in a corrupt and perverse generation, like lights in a world of darkness (i. 29, 30; ii. 14–16). He warns them against the example of others less perfect, that is, those not yet free from Jewish prejudice (iii. 15–19). The teachers of "circumcision" are spoken of with great disdain:

Have an eye to the dogs, the evil-doers, and those who mutilate themselves. We are the real "circumcised," we, who worship God in the spirit, who put our glory and trust in Christ, not in the flesh. If I chose to make boast in differences of the flesh, I could do it with better right than any other, — of pure Israelite blood, circumcised when a week old, of the tribe of Benjamin, a Hebrew of the Hebrews,

---

[1] This epistle, in its present form, has been supposed to be made up of two, the former ending with the words, "rejoice in the Lord" (iii. 1), which in the preamble to the second is omitted. The words "to write the same things" seem to refer to an earlier letter; and Polycarp (*Ad Phil.* 3) speaks of several written by Paul to the Philippians.

a strict legal Pharisee, in zeal a persecutor of saints, without blame in whatever concerns the keeping of the Law. But all this I hold as nothing and as filth, since I have found the transcendent knowledge of Christ. To gain this I have lost all else. I have exchanged all merit of my own, from keeping of the Law, for that which alone God regards, the life of faith in Him, — that which comes from faith in Christ, the power of his resurrection, the sharing of his sufferings, and taking upon myself the image of his death, if in any manner I may share also his rising from the dead. Not that I have yet attained this, or am already perfect; but I press on. Forgetting what is behind and reaching forth to what is before me, I strive toward the goal for the prize of victory in the race. This is the mind that should be in those who are full-grown men. Our citizenship is in heaven, whence we expect our Saviour Christ, who will transfigure our wretched body to the likeness of his glorious body, by virtue of that Divine decree which has put all things under his control. Therefore, brothers beloved and longed for, my joy and crown, so stand fast in the Lord, my dearly beloved.[1]

Above all, he urges them to harmony and obedience. The way of life he has shown them, the example he has given of Christianity in practice, is the true one; yet each believer has his own revelation, his special inspiration, which also is from God (iii. 15). He prays his "true yokefellow" to reconcile Euodia and Syntyche, and aid them in their service of charity to the poor (iv. 2, 3). He bids them to rejoice, "for the Lord is at hand" (iv. 4, 5). His thanks for the gift sent him from the rich ladies of Philippi are a model of right feeling and genuine piety: —

I have had great joy in the Lord at this late blossoming out of your care for me: you had thought of it before, but

[1] Chap. iii. 2–iv. 1.

had no opportunity. It is not that I am in need; for I have learned to be content with what I have. I know how to live in penury or in abundance; I have learned, wherever I am, and in whatever condition, to be full or famished, to abound or to suffer want. I can do anything in Him who strengthens me. But it was well done of you to share in my distress. It is not the gift I think of, but the rich gain that may come to you. I have all I need, and more, since I have received from Epaphroditus the gift you sent, fragrant as incense, a sacrifice of sweet odour, dear and acceptable to God.[1]

He urges humility, which makes each of us hold the rest in honour; charity, which makes us, like Christ, think more of others than of ourselves. Jesus had in himself the possibilities of complete divinity; he might, if he would, have shown himself in heavenly splendour during his earthly life: but then the method of his salvation would have been reversed. Therefore he laid aside his native glory, to appear in "the form of a servant." Thus, to the world's eye, seen outwardly, he appeared only a man. "He humbled himself, making himself subject to death, even the death of the cross; and this is why God has exalted him, and given him a name above every other name, since it is His will that at the name of Jesus every knee should bend, in heaven, on earth, or in the world below, and every tongue confess him Lord, to the glory of God the Father" (ii. 1–11).

Jesus, as we see, was in Paul's thought increasing in dignity from day to day. Paul does not as yet make him the equal of God; he believes rather in his divine nature, and regards his earthly life as the carrying-out of a divine plan which is effected by his coming "in

[1] Chap. iv. 10–18.

the flesh." Imprisonment had on Paul the effect which it commonly has on strong souls, exalting them to a lofty pitch, and effecting in them profound revolutions of thought. He hopes soon to send Timothy to the Philippians with fresh instructions (ii. 19–23), though it is doubtful if this purpose was ever carried out. At all events Timothy must have speedily returned to him, as he was at hand when the epistles to the Colossians and Philemon were written. Luke seems also to have been for a short time absent, since his name does not appear in "Philippians," as it does in the two later epistles.

CHAPTER II.

PETER AT ROME. — A. D. 61.

PAUL'S imprisonment and entrance into Rome, — a triumph in the view of the disciples, — with the opportunity given by his residence in the capital of the world, left no peace to the Judaising party. To them Paul was a sort of stimulant, an active rival, whom they were ever complaining of, yet eager to imitate. Peter, in particular, always divided between admiration of his bold associate and the tasks imposed on him by his personal followers, spent his life — which also had its own many trials, as Clement of Rome tells us [1] — in copying Paul's career, in following him at a distance, in holding after him the strong positions which might insure success to their common work. About A. D. 54, probably by Paul's example, he established himself at Antioch. The report of Paul's arrival in Rome, which reached Syria and Judæa in the course of the year 61, might well suggest to him also the thought of a journey to the West.

He seems to have come with quite an apostolic company. First, his interpreter, John Mark, whom he called his son, was his usual companion.[2] The Apostle

---

[1] 1 *Ad Cor.* ch. v.
[2] Col. iv. 10; Philem. 24; 1 Pet. v. 13. Comp. Euseb. ii. 15; iii. 39; Iren. iii. 1: 1; Tertull. *Adv. Marc.* iv. 5; Clem. Alex. in Euseb. vi. 14; Origen, *id.* vi. 25; Epiph. li. 6; Jerome, *Epist.* 150, 11. One Mark Peter, probably a Christian, appears at Bostra, A. D. 278 (Waddington, *Inscr.* 1909).

John, as I have more than once observed, seems also to have commonly been with him;[1] and we have reason to think that Barnabas may have shared the journey: he was probably the writer of Hebrews, who evidently had been in Rome.[2] Finally, it is quite possible that Simon Magus went on his own account to the capital of the world, drawn by the attraction it had for all chiefs of sects, — as the Gnostics of the second century, — charlatans, magicians, and wonder-workers.[3] To the Jews the journey to Italy was easy and common. The

---

[1] Acts i. 13; iii. 1, etc.; iv. 13, 19; viii. 14; John xxi.; Gal. ii. 9. The horror felt at the massacres of A. D. 64 in Rome is so vivid in the Apocalypse that the writer may well have witnessed them, or at least have been in Rome (chs. xiii., xvii.). Patmos may have been chosen for the scene of these visions, as the last port of landing on the way from Rome to Ephesus, as will appear when I come to speak of the Apocalypse. I will speak later of the tradition concerning John at the Latin gate. The Fourth Gospel, it is true, was not written by John; yet we may note the passage in ch. xxi. 15-23 (see "The Apostles," chap. ii.), which was doubtless written by some one intimate with Peter, and a witness of his death.

[2] See Introd. p. 11.

[3] Justin, *Apol.* i. 26, 56; Iren. i. 23: 1; Hippol. *Phil.* vi. 20; *Constit. Apost.* vi. 9; Euseb. ii. 13, 14. (Justin and Irenæus, it is true, often rest on strangely mistaken evidence.) The presence of Simon at Rome is the base of the apocryphal Acts of Peter (Tisch. *Acta apost. apocr.*, p. 13; comp. *Recogn.* ii. 9; iii. 63, 64), which was at first an Ebionite scripture. Eusebius (ii. 14) admits the main fact, to which Irenæus seems to refer. The way in which the writer of "Acts" (viii. 24) speaks of Simon, leaving a possibility of his conversion, seems to suppose him to be yet living. The passage in Tacitus (*Ann.* xii. 52) does not contradict the presence of Simon in Rome (comp. *id.* xiv. 9; *Hist.* i. 22). The injurious use of Simon's name in the second century, as an *alias* for Paul, does not disprove either his existence or his having gone to Rome. It may be noted that the *mathematici* (astrologers), the *Chaldæi*, and the γόητες (magicians of every sort), were never so abundant at Rome as now: Tac. *Ann.* xii. 52; *Hist.* i. 22; ii. 62; Dion Cass. lxv. 1; lxvi. 9; Suet. *Tib.* 36; *Vitell.* 14; Juv. vi. 542; Euseb. *Chron.* (Domitian, *Ann.* 9); Zonaras, *Ann.* vi. 5.

historian Josephus[1] was at Rome, in A. D. 62 or 63, to obtain the liberation of certain Jewish priests — very holy persons, who would eat nothing "unclean," and so lived on nuts and figs when away from home — whom Felix had sent to answer to the emperor for some unknown charge. Who were these priests? Had their business nothing to do with that of Peter and Paul? In lack of evidence, we are free to think as we will on all these matters. The fact itself, on which modern Catholics rest the very base of the structure of their faith, is far from being certain.[2] Still, as I think,

---

[1] *Life*, 3.

[2] It is quite sure that Peter was not at Rome when Paul wrote "Romans" (comp. Dion. of Cor. in Euseb. ii. 25). Paul never interfered with churches of the "circumcision" (Gal. ii. 7, 8; 2 Cor. x. 16; Rom. xv. 18–20), and there were none in Rome when he went there, as is shown by Acts xxviii. 17–20. The reckoning of Eusebius (ii. 14; *Chron. Claud.* 2) and Jerome (*De vir. illustr.* 1) as to Peter's arrival in Rome is thus erroneous. But nothing disproves his coming later, and certain hints make this likely: — 1. A tradition of the second century (Euseb. ii. 15, 25; iii. 1; vi. 14; Ignat. *Ad Rom.* 4; Iren. iii. 1: 1; 3: 3; Tert. *Scorp.* 15; *Præscr.* 36; Κήρυγμα Παύλου, in sequel to Cyprian's Works, p. 139, ed. Rigault), not wholly without weight, though confused with manifest errors, and evidently implying an *a priori* intention to make the "prince of the apostles" founder of the church at the world's capital, as was also falsely claimed for that of Corinth; 2. The undoubted fact that Peter died in a form of martyrdom hardly likely except at Rome (see chap. viii., below); 3. The epistle 1 Peter, dated at Rome ("Babylon"), which is strong evidence, even if written by some other hand, which would have employed that date to give it further credit; 4. The legend which prevailed at Rome, sound in substance, that Peter followed everywhere in the footsteps of Simon Magus (i. e., Paul), and came to Rome to strive against him: Περίοδοι and Κήρυγμα Πέτρου, also Π. καὶ Π. κήρυμα, cited by Heracleon and Clem. Alex.; Lipsius, *Römische Petrussage*, 13; Hilgenfeld, *N. T. extra Can. rec.* iv. 52; Euseb. ii. 14; Hippol. *Phil.* vii. 20; *Const. Apost.* vi. 9; comp. Syriac Κήρυγμα: Cureton, *Anc. Syr. doc.* 35–41. — As to localities in Rome attached to this legend (the house of Pudens, etc.), they are worthless, though the *via nomentana*, mentioned as the place of his baptising, is a very ancient Christian centre. (See Bosio, *Roma Sott.* (1650), 400–402; Rossi, *id.* i. 189; *Bull.* 1867, 37, 48, 49; *Acta SS. Maii*,

the "Acts of Peter," told by the Ebionites, were fabulous only in details. The main idea in these "Acts"— that Peter goes through the world following Simon Magus to refute him, carrying the true gospel which is to confound the doctrine of the impostor,[1] "following him as light the darkness, as knowledge ignorance, as healing sickness"—is a true one; though we must substitute Paul for Simon, and, instead of the bitter hate expressed by the Ebionites for the preacher to the gentiles, imagine mere difference of opinion between the two apostles, excluding neither sympathy nor fellowship in the essential thing, the love of Jesus. In this journey, undertaken by the old Galilæan disciple in Paul's footsteps, we may well admit that Peter, following closely, touched at Corinth, where he already had a considerable party,[2] and greatly confirmed the Jewish Christians. Thus the Church there could afterwards claim to have been founded by both the apostles, and, by a trifling error of dates, maintain that they had been there together, and went thence in company to meet their death in Rome.[3]

What were the relations of the two apostles while in Rome? Certain testimonies would lead us to think that these were quite friendly.[4] We shall soon find Mark, Peter's amanuensis, on the way to Asia, with a

---

iv. 299: Pud. and Prax.; *Acta SS. Jan.* ii. 7: Marcell.) The inscription in *Journ. de Naples*, Mar. 17, 1870, *Il trionfo della Chiesa cattolica*, is a gross fraud. (See Appendix.)

[1] Hom. Clem. ii. 17; iii. 59.
[2] 1 Cor. i. 12; iii. 22; ix. 5.
[3] See Dionysius of Corinth in Euseb. ii. 25. (The text is uncertain and obscure.) Origen, Eusebius, Epiphanius, and Jerome speak of Peter's preaching in Asia Minor, on the very insufficient evidence of 1 Pet. i. 1.
[4] Comp. Κήρυγμα Παύλου in *De non iterum bapt.*, l. c.

kind word from Paul;[1] and besides, the Epistle of Peter (so-called, and quite probably genuine) is largely indebted to those of Paul. Two well-established points are to be kept in view throughout this history: first, that a deep line of division — deeper than has ever since marked off any schism in the Church — separated the founders of Christianity, while the dispute between them, after the fashion of the time, was extremely bitter;[2] and, the second, that even in their lifetime a loftier thought united these hostile brethren, in anticipation of that grand union which it was the Church's office to bring about after their death. This twofold aspect is often to be found in religious movements. To understand these divisions we must also take into account the hot and sensitive temper of the Jews, apt to sudden violence of speech. In these little pious groups there are continual quarrels and reconciliations; there are sharp words with no sundering of good-will. One is for Peter, one for Paul; but these divisions are of not more account than those within our own scientific schools. Paul has in this regard an excellent maxim,[3] which we may render, "Let each abide in the form of instruction he has received,"—an admirable rule, which the Roman Church in later time has not always kept. Faithfulness to Jesus was enough; "confessional" divisions were, so to speak, a simple question of antecedents, independent of the personal qualities of the believer.

It is, however, a matter of importance — one which

[1] Col. iv. 10.
[2] See in Jude and in the Apocalypse (chaps. ii. and iii.) the fanatical traits ascribed to John. Also 2 John 9, 10; Iren. iii. 3, 4; and the bitter phrases to be found on every page of Paul's writings.
[3] Rom. vi. 17.

would lead us to think that a good understanding never came about between the two apostles — that, in the memory of the generation following, Peter and Paul are heads of two opposing parties in the Church; and that the writer of the Apocalypse, almost immediately after their death (at least that of Peter), is, of all the Judæo-Christians, the most bitter against Paul, even excluding him from the number of the apostles (xxi.14).[1] Paul regarded himself as the leader of the converted pagans, wherever they might be. This was his understanding of the arrangement made at Antioch; but the Judæo-Christians evidently took it otherwise. This party, which had always been strong at Rome, no doubt was much reinforced by the coming of Peter, who became its head, and head of the church there, — a rank to which the unique dignity of this city gave singular importance. As we see throughout the Apocalypse, the part played by Rome had in it something providential. Owing to a certain reaction against Paul, Peter, as leader of the opposition, came to be more and more regarded as chief of the apostles.[2] "Chief of the apostles in the capital of the world!" — the combination struck the fancy of the more impressible. What could be more telling? Thus was already formed that wide association of ideas which for a thousand years and more was to control the destinies of humanity. The names Peter and Rome became inseparable: Rome is the predestined capital of Latin Christianity; the legend of Peter, the first Pope, is already sketched, though it will need four or five centuries for its full development. Rome, at least,

---

[1] Compare "Saint Paul," chap. xiii. near the end
[2] See the letter of Clement to James in the Clementine Homilies, 1.

had no longer any doubt, from the day when Peter set his foot there, that this day fixed its destiny, and that the poor Syrian who then entered its gates established a possession to last for ages.

The moral, social, and political situation was becoming more strained from day to day. Everywhere were heard tales of prodigies and disasters.[1] The Christians, as we see in the Apocalypse, were more affected by these than any others: the idea that Satan is the god of this world struck deeper root among them.[2] The public spectacles seemed to them devilish, — not that they ever attended them, but heard of them in common talk. An Icarus, who in the great wooden amphitheatre pretended to float in the air, but fell to the ground close to Nero's seat, spattering him with blood,[3] struck their fancy greatly, and gave the main incident in their legend of Simon Magus. Crime at Rome touched the last limits of the infernal sublime; and, whether from love of mystery or for precaution against the police, it became customary to speak of the city under the name of Babylon.[4]

This ill-dissembled antipathy for a world they did not know became a characteristic mark of Christians. "Hatred to mankind" (*odium humani generis*) was the popular summary of their doctrine.[5] Their apparent

---

[1] See Tac. *Ann.* xiv. 12, 22; xv. 22. Suet. *Nero*, 36, 39; Dion Cass. lxi. 16, 18; Philost. *Apoll.* iv. 43; Seneca, *Quæst. nat.* vi. 1; Euseb. *Chron. Nero*, ann. 7, 9, 10.

[2] See 2 Cor. iv. 4. Eph. vi. 12. John xii. 31; xiv. 30.

[3] Suet. *Nero*, 12. See below, p. 59.

[4] See 1 Pet. v. 13; Apoc. chs. xiv.–xviii.; *Carm. Sibyll.* v. 142, 158. The Jews were accustomed to apply to modern things symbolic names taken from their sacred books: thus "Edom" signified both Rome and the empire (Buxtorf, *Lex. Chald.*, etc., s. v. אדום); and the name "Cuthite" was applied both to Samaritans and to pagans.

[5] Tac. *Ann.* xv. 44 (cf. *Hist.* v. 5); Suet. *Nero*, 16.

melancholy was an insult to "the felicity of the age;" their belief in the approaching end of the world was a denial of the official optimism, which declared that all things were becoming new. The marks of abhorrence with which they passed the temple-fronts seemed to hint that they had it in mind to destroy them by fire.[1] These old sanctuaries of the Roman religion were very dear to those of patriotic feeling; to insult them was to insult Evander, Numa, the ancestors of the Roman people, and the trophies of its victories.[2] The Christians were charged with all misdeeds; their worship was regarded as a superstition, sombre, baleful to the empire; many a horrid or shameful tale went about regarding them; the most enlightened believed in these tales, and regarded those whom they accused as capable of every crime.

Those of the new religion gained few adherents except in the lower classes. Well-bred people avoided speaking of them by name, or did so with an apology: "whom the vulgar called Christians," says Tacitus. But their progress among the people was astonishing: you might call it an inundation, when the water, long dammed up, burst its dikes, to use the historian's phrase. The church at Rome was an entire population (*multitudo ingens*). Court and town began to talk of it as a serious thing; its advance made for a time the news of the day. Conservatives thought with a kind of terror of the cesspool of filth which they imagined in the low grounds of the city; they spoke with rage of evil weeds that could not be rooted out, which sprang up as fast as they could be torn away.

---

[1] 1 Pet. iv. 4; Tac. *Hist.* v. 5: *pessimus quisque, spretis religionibus patriis.*
[2] Tac. *Ann.* xv. 41, 44; *Hist.* v. 5.

"A race of men of a new and wicked superstition," says Suetonius. "This sort of people," says Tacitus, "will always be outlawed, and will always stay among us;" "often checked, but most abundant in growth," adds Dion Cassius.[1]

Popular malice invented impossible crimes to be charged against the Christians. They were made responsible for every public disaster; they were accused of preaching revolt against the emperor, and inciting an insurrection of slaves.[2] In common opinion the Christian came to be what the Jew was at times in the Middle Age, — the scapegoat of every calamity, a man who thinks only of mischief, a poisoner of springs, an eater of children's flesh, a kindler of conflagrations.[3] At every fresh crime, the slightest hint would cause a Christian to be arrested, or even put to torture. The mere name was often enough to lead to his arrest. If he was seen to hold aloof from pagan sacrifices, he was insulted.[4] The age of persecution was already begun, to last, with brief intervals, till the time of Constantine. In the thirty years since the religion was first preached, only Jews had been its persecutors; against them it had been defended by the Romans, who were now its persecutors in their turn. The terror and the hate spread from the capital to the provinces, and evoked the wildest outrage.[5] With this

---

[1] See Suet. *Nero*, 16. Tac. *Hist.* i. 22; *Ann.* xii. 52. Dion Cass. xxxvii. 17.

[2] Rom. xiii. 1-5; 1 Pet. ii. 13-18.

[3] Tac. *Ann.* xv. 44; Suet. *Nero*, 16; Seneca, in St. Augustine's *Civ. Dei*, vi. 11; 1 Pet. ii. 12, 15; iii. 16. 2 Pet. ii. 12.

[4] 1 Pet. iv. 4.

[5] 1 Pet. i. 6; ii. 19, 20; iii. 14; iv. 12-14; v. 8-10. Jas. ii. 6. Tertull. *Ad nationes*, i. 7.

were mingled atrocious jestings: the walls of the places where the Christians met were covered with insulting or filthy inscriptions against the brethren and sisters.¹ The fashion of representing Jesus as a man with an ass's head was perhaps already adopted.²

No one doubts now that these charges of crime and infamy were calumnies. We have numerous reasons to believe that the Christian leaders gave not the least ground for the ill-will which was presently to bring upon them such brutal atrocities. All the party leaders in the Christian community were agreed as to the attitude to be held towards the Roman authorities. In theory, these magistrates might be regarded as ministers of Satan, since they were protectors of idolatry and the props of a world given over to Satan;³ but in practice they were treated with entire respect. The Ebionite faction alone shared the exalted temper of the Zealots and other Jewish fanatics. Towards the State the apostles appear to have been conservative and legiti-

---

¹ Rossi, *Bull. di arch. crist.*, 1864, 69, 70.

² M. Rossi (*id.* p. 72) thinks he has read on the walls of a building in Pompeii which seems to have served for Christian gatherings: *Mulus hic muscellas docuit* (see Zangemeister, *Inscr. pariet.* 2016). Comp. the graven stone published by Stefanone (*Gemmæ*, Venice, 1646, tab. 30), representing an ass posing as school-teacher before a group of children bent in obeisance (republished by Fr. Münter, *Primordia eccles. Afric.*, Hafn. 1829, p. 218; and by F. X. Kraus, *Das Spott-crucifix vom Palatin*, Vienna, 1869, transl. by Ch. de Linas, Arras, 1870). The museum of Luynes (Bibl. nat. cab. des antiques, terra cotta, 779) has a tablet from Syria representing Jesus caricatured as a little man in a long gown, holding a book, with a big ass's-head, long ears, and eyes to which it is sought to give a leering and mystical expression. Comp. also the [well-known] grotesque crucifix of the Palatine (Garrucci, *Il crocifisso graffito*, Rome, 1857; Kraus-Linas, as above; *Comptes rendus de l'Acad. des inscr.*, 1870, 32–36). See Tertull. *Apol.* 16; Minut. Felix, 9, 28; Celsus in Origen, *Contra Celsum*, vi. 31.

³ Luke iv. 6; John xii. 31; Eph. vi. 12.

mist. Far from urging the slave to revolt, they insist on his submission to his master, however stern and harsh, as if he were serving Christ in person; and this not under compulsion, to escape chastisement, but by conscience, because God so wills. God himself stands behind the master. Slavery was so far from seeming to them against nature that Christians held slaves, even Christian slaves.[1] We have seen Paul restrain the impulse towards a political rising, in A. D. 57, urging upon the faithful in Rome, and doubtless many other churches, submission to "the powers that be," whatever their source, and laying down the maxim that he who bears the sword [the military police] is a servant of God, to be dreaded only by the wrong-doer. Peter, on his part, was the most placid of men; we shall soon find the rule of submission to the powers taught in his name, almost in the very words of Paul.[2] The school that later gathered about John held the same view as to the divine origin of sovereignty.[3] The leaders dreaded nothing more than to see their followers mixed up in illegal acts, whose odium would fall back upon the entire body.[4] The language of the apostles at this supreme moment was the language of supreme prudence. A few wretches put to torture, a few slaves under the lash, would seem to have broken out in insults, calling their masters idolaters, and threatening them with the wrath of God.[5] Others, zealous to excess, declaimed aloud against the pagans, reproaching them with their vices; but their more sensible

---

[1] 1 Pet. ii. 18. Col. iii. 22, 25; iv. 1. Eph. vi. 5–9, with the episode of Onesimus.
[2] 1 Pet. ii. 13, 14.   [3] John xix. 11.
[4] 1 Pet. ii. 11, 12; iv. 15.   [5] 1 Pet. ii. 23.

brethren wittily called them "bishops (overseers) of the outsiders" (ἀλλοτριοεπίσκοποι). Cruel mishaps befell some of these intermeddlers; but the sober directors of the body, far from applauding them, would tell them, plainly enough, that they had got only what they deserved.[1]

The condition of the Christians was rendered harder by all sorts of perplexities which there is not evidence enough to enable us to disentangle. The Jews were very influential with the emperor and Poppæa.[2] The diviners (*mathematici*), among the rest one Balbillus of Ephesus, thronged about the emperor, and gave him atrocious counsels, under pretence of exercising that part of their skill which consisted in turning aside strokes of ill-fortune and evil presages.[3] The legend of Simon Magus brings his name into this circle of sorcerers, and may possibly have some foundation in fact, though very doubtful.[4] The writer of the Apocalypse says much of a "false prophet," who is represented as an ally of Nero, a wonder-worker who makes fire fall from the sky, who makes graven images live and speak, and marks men with "the mark of the Beast."[5] It may be that Balbillus is here meant; still, it is noticeable that the prodigies of the false prophet in the Apocalypse are much like the jugglery ascribed

---

[1] 1 Pet. iv. 15.   [2] See below, pp. 141, 142.
[3] Suet. *Nero*, 34, 36, 40; Tac. *Hist.* i. 22.
[4] See the Pseudo-Clementine *Homilies*, ii. 34; *Recogn.* i. 74; iii. 47, 57, 63, 64; "Acts of Peter" (spurious), Tisch. 3931; "Linus" in *Bibl. max. patrum*, ii. 67; "Marcellus" in Fabricius, *Cod. apocr. N. T.*, iii. 635 *et seq.*; "Abdias," i. 16, 17; *Const. apostol.* vi. 9; Iren. i. 23: 1; Euseb. ii. 14; "Hegesippus," *De excid. Hieros.* iii. 2; Epiphan. xxi. 5; Arnobius, *Adv. gentes*, ii. 13; Philastr. *Hær.* 29; Sulp. Sev. ii. 28, etc. Comp. Rossi, *Bull.* 1867, 70, 71.
[5] Apoc. xiii. 14–17; xvi. 13; xix. 20.

to Simon in the legend.[1] The emblem of a monster that spoke like a dragon and had "two horns like a lamb," designating the false prophet (xiii. 11), is far better suited to a false Messiah like Simon of Gitton than to a mere conjurer. And besides, the tale of Simon cast down from the air is not unlike an accident which happened in the Circus under Nero to an accrobat who played the part of Icarus.[2] The constant practice of the Apocalypse to speak in enigmas makes such a reference very obscure; but we shall not err if we look sharply behind every line of this strange book for allusions to the pettiest incidents or anecdotes of Nero's reign.

Further, the heart of the Christian body was never more burdened, more palpitating, than now. The disciples believed themselves to be in a transitory state, of very brief duration. Each day they looked for the appearing of their Lord in judgment. "He is coming! Yet one hour! He is close at hand!" Such was the common speech among them.[3] The martyr-spirit — the thought that a martyr glorifies Christ by his death, and that this death is a victory — was already diffused everywhere.[4] To a pagan, on the other hand, the flesh of Christians seemed the natural prey of the tormentor. A very popular play of this time, called "Laureolus," exhibited the chief actor (a sort of hypocritical knave) as crucified upon the stage amid the plaudits of the

---

[1] *Recogn.* ii. 9; *Philos.* vi. 20; *Const. Apost.* vi. 9.

[2] Suet. *Nero*, 12; Dion Chrys. Or. xxi. 9; Juv. iii. 78–80. Comp. *Recogn.* ii. 9. Juvenal speaks of the false Icarus as a Greek. (See p. 54.)

[3] Phil. iv. 5; Jas. v. 8; 1 Pet. iv. 7; Heb. x. 37; 1 John ii. 18.

[4] Phil. i. 20; John xxi. 19. Comp. the expression of Caius, "trophies" of the apostles [referring to the martyrdom of Peter and Paul] in Euseb. ii. 25.

spectators, and devoured by a bear. This was before Christianity was brought to Rome; it was exhibited [under Caligula] in A.D. 41; but it seems to have been applied to the Christian martyrs, and the diminutive *Laureolus*, answering to *Stephanos* ["wreath"], might invite such comparisons.[1]

[1] Suet. *Caius*, 57; Juvenal, viii. 186, 187; Martial, *Spectacula*, 7.

CHAPTER III.

THE CHURCHES IN JUDÆA. — A. D. 62.

The hostility encountered by the Christian community in Rome, perhaps also in Greece and Asia Minor, was felt as far as Judæa.[1] But here the persecution had other grounds. The wealthy Sadducees, the Temple aristocracy, showed extreme bitterness against the pious poor, and blasphemed the name of Christian.[2] About this time there was circulated a letter of James, "servant of God and of the Lord Jesus Christ," addressed "to the twelve tribes of the Dispersion."[3] This is one of the finest pieces of early Christian literature, recalling now the Gospels, now the serene and placid wisdom of Ecclesiastes: especially the parable of the Tongue in chapter iii. is a charming fragment in the old Hebrew spirit. Its authorship is doubtful, as it must always be in such cases, considering how many letters were in circulation of supposed apostolic origin.[4] The party of Jewish Christians, accustomed to appeal at will to the authority of James, may have ascribed to him this manifesto, in which the motive clearly is to withstand innovators.[5] If James had any share in it,

---

[1] James i. 2–4, 12; iv. 9; v. 7, 8. Both this epistle and that of Peter begin with an exhortation to patience.

[2] *Ibid.* ii. 6, 7; v. 1–6.   [3] See chap. v. *post.*

[4] 2 Thess. ii. 2.

[5] Comp. Rom. iii. 27, 28; iv. 2–5; v. 1, with James ii. 21–24.

at least it was not drafted by his hand. It is uncertain whether he knew Greek, his mother tongue being Syriac;[1] while this epistle is much the best piece of writing in the New Testament, its Greek being pure and almost classic, as is also that of Jude. Apart from this, it agrees perfectly with what we know of James's character. The writer is surely a Jewish Rabbi; he holds strongly by the Law; he uses the word "synagogue;"[2] he is an opponent of Paul. The epistle is in tone like the Synoptics, which, as we shall see hereafter, proceeded from the family of Jesus, whose head was James, "the Lord's brother." And still, Jesus is mentioned in it by name only twice or thrice, and then simply as the Messiah, with none of the lofty flights of hyperbole already multiplied by the ardent imagination of Paul.

James — or the Jewish moralist who speaks with the authority of his name — brings us at once into the humble love-feast of the persecuted brethren. Let them rejoice in the trials of their faith; for when put to the proof faith yields patience, and patience is the condition of all perfect work; he who endures the test will receive the crown of life.[3] But our teacher's heart is full of the contrast between rich and poor. Some rivalry must have arisen at Jerusalem between the brethren favoured and those cast down by fortune; and the poor complained of the exactions of the rich with their sumptuous pride, groaning among themselves.[4] To this class-bitterness he makes the following appeal: —

---

[1] Euseb. *Demonstr. evang.* iii. 5, 7.
[2] James ii. 2, rendered "assembly;" in v. 14, ἐκκλησία.
[3] James i. 2–4, 12.   [4] *Ibid.* iv. 11; v. 9.

Let the brother that is humble reflect on his high privilege, and the rich on his frail condition, for wealth shall pass like the flower of the field.[1] . . . Brothers, let there be no respect of persons in the faith of our glorious Lord, the Christ. Suppose a man come into your synagogue with a gold ring, dressed in fine apparel, and there come in a poor man in shabby clothing, and you say to one, " Sit comfortably here," and to the other, " Stand out there, or here below my footstool:" is not that making distinctions among brethren, and judging with wicked thoughts? My dear brothers, listen: has not God chosen the poor of the world to make them rich in faith, heirs of the kingdom which He has promised to those who love him? And yet you have scorned the poor! Do not rich men lord it over you, and drag you before the law-courts? Do they not thus insult that noble name which is given to you all alike?[2]

Pride, corruption, brutality, luxury among the wealthy Sadducees, had, in fact, come to their worst excess.[3] Women would buy even the high-priest's office from King Agrippa with gold for their husbands.[4] Martha, daughter of Boëthus, one of these simoniacs, when she went to see her husband in state, had a carpet spread from her house-door to the sanctuary.[5] Thus the priesthood was wonderfully degraded. These secular priests were ashamed of the holiest duties of their office. The rite of sacrifice became repulsive to these dainty gentlemen, condemned thus to tasks of butcher and flesher! Some of them would put on silk

---

[1] James i. 9–11.   [2] *Ibid.* ii. 1–7.

[3] Babyl. Talm. *Ioma,* 9 a, 35 b; Derenbourg, *Hist. de la Palestine,* 234–236.

[4] For example, Martha, daughter of Boëthus, for Jesus (Joshua), son of Gamala. Mishna, *Jebamoth,* vi. 4; Babyl. Talm. *id.* 61 a; *Ioma,* 18 a; Jos. *Antiq.* **xx.** 9: 4, 7; Derenbourg, 248, 249.

[5] Midrash *Eka,* i. 16.

gloves, so as not to spoil the delicacy of their hands by the touch of victims. The whole talmudic tradition — just as the Gospels and the Epistle of James do — shows us the priests of these last years before the ruin of the Temple as gluttonous, luxurious, hard-hearted towards the poor. The Talmud has a fabulous list of what was needed to maintain the high-priest's table, — not to be taken literally, but as evidence of the common opinion. Four cries, said tradition, went forth from the confines of the Temple: the first, "Go forth from hence, sons of Eli, for you defile the Temple of the Eternal;" the second, "Go forth from hence, Issachar of Kaphar-Barkai, who, having care only for yourself, profane the victims holy to the Lord" (that is, by wearing silk gloves when engaged in sacrifice); the third, "Open ye, O gates, that Ishmael may come in, the son of Phabi, disciple of Phinehas, that he may fulfil the office of the priest;"[1] the fourth, "Open ye, O gates, that John may come in, the son of Nebedæus, disciple of gluttons, to gorge himself with victims."[2] A sort of chant, or curse upon the priestly houses, was current in the streets of Jerusalem, which ran thus: —

> Plague be upon the house of Boëthus —
> A plague upon them by reason of their clubs!
> Plague be upon the house of Hanan (Annas) —
> A plague upon them by reason of their plots!

---

[1] The allusion is to the son of Eli, who made profit for himself from the sacrifice [1 Sam. ii. 14], not to the model priest of the time of Moses [Num. xxv. 7]. Phinehas the son of Eli is not, it is true, a legendary person; his brother Hophni has as good claim to remembrance as he; but the name may have been chosen for a play of words [the name meaning "brazen-mouth"]. See Derenbourg, 233, 234, note.

[2] Babyl. Talm., *Pesachim*, 57 a; *Kerithoth*, 28 a.

> Plague be upon the house of Cantheras —
> A plague upon them by reason of their shames (*kalams*)!
> Plague be upon the house of Ishmael son of Phabi —
> A plague upon them by reason of their fists!
> These are high-priests; their sons are treasurers;
> Their sons-in-law overseers; their slaves beat us with clubs![1]

It was open war between these wealthy pontiffs, friends of the Romans, seizing fat offices for themselves and their kindred, and the poor priests upheld by the people. Bloody quarrels broke out daily. The shameless insolence of the pontifical families went so far as to send and seize from the threshing-floors tithes that belonged to the upper priesthood, beating those who resisted, and reducing to misery the poorer clergy.[2] Conceive the wrath of the pious man, the Jew-democrat, rich in the promise of all the Prophets, when thus abused in the Temple — his own house! — by the insolent lackeys of these self-indulgent and unbelieving priests! The Christians gathered about James made common cause with these poor victims, holy men (*hasidim*) as they too were, and held in favour by the people. Beggary came, as it were, to be a virtue and a mark of patriotism. The rich were friends of the Romans; great wealth, in fact, depended on Roman favour, so that one could hardly prosper but by a sort of apostasy and treason. To hate the rich became a mark of piety. The saints (*hasidim*) must needs starve, or else work on those haughty structures of the Herodians, in which they saw only a pompous display of vanity; and so they considered

---

[1] Tosifta, *Menachoth*, s. f.; Babyl. Talm. *Pesachim*, 57 a; Derenbourg, 233 *et seq.*

[2] Jos. *Antiq.* xx. 8: 8; 9: 2.

themselves victims of the infidels, while "poor man" passed as a synonym for "saint."[1] Listen to the following: —

And now, you rich men, weep and wail for the wretchedness that is coming upon you! Your riches are rotten; your clothing is moth-eaten; your gold and silver are tarnished, and the rust of them will testify against you [that your guilt is of long standing], and will eat into your flesh like fire. You have been heaping up wealth in these last days [when the end of all things is close at hand]. See! the wage of the workmen who have mown your fields, which you have kept back from them, cries out, and the complaint of your reapers has reached the ears of the Lord of hosts! You have lived in luxury and wantonness on the earth; you have fattened yourselves [like cattle] for the day of slaughter; you have condemned — you have destroyed — the honest man who offered no resistance.[2]

In these strange pages we see the simmering of that spirit of social revolution which in a few years was to bathe Jerusalem in blood. Nowhere else is that feeling of aversion for the world which was the soul of primitive Christianity expressed with such energy as here. "To keep himself unspotted from the world"[3] is the supreme precept; "the friendship of the world is enmity with God;"[4] every natural desire (ἐπιθυμία) is a vanity, an illusion, a seed of death.[5] The end is so near! Why fall out with one another? Why go to law with one another? The true judge is near, standing at the door.[6]

Come now, you who say, "To-day or to-morrow we will go to the city close by, and stay there a year, trading and making

---

[1] See "Life of Jesus," chap. xi. [2] James v. 1–6.
[3] Ibid. i. 27. [4] Ibid. iv. 4.
[5] Ibid. i. 14; iv. 1. [6] Ibid. iv. 1; v. 7–9.

profit," — not knowing what will happen to-morrow; for what is your life? it is a vapor that appears a little while and then vanishes, — instead of saying, "If the Lord will and we are alive, we will do this or that."[1]

When he speaks of humility, patience, mercy, the exaltation of the poor, the joy of those who mourn, James seems to have had in memory the very words of Jesus.[2] Still, as we see, he holds close to the Law.[3] A whole paragraph of his epistle[4] is devoted to warning the faithful against Paul's doctrine of salvation by faith and the worthlessness of works: in this he shows himself an Ebionite.[5] A phrase of his[6] directly contradicts one in Romans.[7] Contrary to the apostle of the gentiles,[8] the apostle of Jerusalem[9] insists that Abraham was saved by works, and that "faith without works is dead." "The devils also believe," but they are not saved. Departing from his usual moderation, James here calls his opponent an "empty man."[10] In one or two other places[11] we may find an allusion to debates already dividing the Church, which a few centuries later crowd the history of religious opinion.

A spirit of lofty piety and touching charity filled this church of the saints. "Religion pure and undefiled," said James, "is to watch over the fatherless

---

[1] James iv. 13-15. Comp. Luke xii. 15-21.
[2] *Ibid.* ii. 8; iv. 6-10; v. 7, 8.
[3] *Ibid.* ii. 10, 11; iv. 11.   [4] *Ibid.* ii. 14-20.
[5] See Hippolytus, *Phil.* vii. 34; x. 22.   [6] James ii. 24.
[7] Rom. iii. 28.   [8] *Ibid.* iv. 1-5.
[9] James ii. 22-24.
[10] *Ibid.* ii. 20. Compare the saying of R. Simeon, a contemporary of James: *Pirké Aboth*, i. 17.
[11] *Ibid.* i. 22-25; v. 19, 20.

and widows in their distress."[1] The power of healing sickness, chiefly by anointing with oil,[2] was considered as of common right among the faithful.[3] The use of oil, with prayer, in cases of sickness, has always been a favourite Semitic practice, and is still found among the Arabs; even non-believers acknowledged this as a special gift among the Christians.[4] The elders were thought to have this gift in the highest degree, and thus came to be a sort of spiritualist doctors; and the practice was held in much esteem by James himself. In this we find the germ of most of the Catholic sacraments. Confession of sins, long practised among the Jews,[5] was considered an excellent means of pardon and healing,—two things held inseparable in the belief of that time.[6] Thus:—

If any one among you is suffering, let him pray; if any one is cheerful, let him sing; if any one is sick, let him call the elders of the church, and let them pray, anointing him with oil in the name of the Lord: the prayer of faith will heal the sick, and the Lord will restore him, and if he has committed sin it will be forgiven. Confess your faults to one another, and pray for one another, that you may be cured. The prayer of a just man, when in earnest, has great power.[7]

---

[1] James i. 27. [2] *Ibid.* v. 14.
[3] Comp. Gregory of Tours, i. 41.
[4] See the accounts of healings wrought by *minim* of Caphar-Nahum (Christians) in the Talmud. The Healer is almost always James (Jacob of Caphar-Shekania, of Caphar-Naboria, of Caphar-Hannania), and the healing is in the name of Jesus, son of Pandera (Midrash *Koheleth*, i. 8; vii. 26; Babyl. Talm. *Aboda zara*, 27 b; Jerus. Talm. *id.* ii. 40 d; *Shabbath*, xiv. s. f. These traditions refer to the first century. Comp. "Life of Jesus," 448, note 2.
[5] 2 Sam. xii. 13; Lev. v. 1; Ps. xxxii.; Jos. *Antiq.* viii. 5: 6; Mishna, *Ioma*, iii. 9; iv. 2; vi. 3.
[6] Matt. iii. 6; Mark i. 5; Acts xix. 18; "Life of Jesus," 261.
[7] James v. 13–16.

The apocryphal books of visions, vividly expressing the popular religious passions, were eagerly received among this little group of Jewish enthusiasts.[1] Rather, they sprang up side by side with it, almost in its very heart, so that it is often hard to distinguish them in quality from the genuine New Testament writings.[2] These little books, of yesterday's birth, were seriously taken as the very words of Enoch, Baruch, or Moses. The strangest notions about hell, the rebel angels, the wicked giants who caused the Flood, flowed out widely, having their chief source in the books of Enoch.[3] In all these fables there were vivid allusions to the events of the day. The prophetic Noah, the pious Enoch, incessantly predicting the Deluge to men incapable of understanding, who all the while go on eating, drinking, marrying, and heaping up riches,[4] — who are they but seers of these latter days, vainly warning a frivolous generation, that will not acknowledge the end of all things to be near? A new chapter, a period of life beneath the earth, is now added to the legend of Jesus. The question is raised, What did he do during the three days he passed within the tomb?[5] They would have it that in this interval he went down among the shades, giving battle to Death where were the "spirits in prison" of the rebellious and unbelieving, preaching to the phantoms and the demons, and opening the way

---

[1] Jude 6, 9, 14, 15; 1 Pet. iii. 19, 20.

[2] See "Life of Jesus," 41, 42.

[3] 1 Pet. iii. 19, 20, 22; Jude 6, 9; Rev. xx. 7; 2 Pet. ii. 4, 11; Enoch, ch. vi. *et seq.*; comparing Gen. v. 22; vi. 1, 2: Stephen of Byzantium, s. v. Ἰκόνιον.

[4] Luke xvii. 26, 27.

[5] For the first hint of the working of imagination in this direction, see Acts ii. 24, 27, 31.

for their deliverance.[1] This notion was essential in order that Jesus might be the universal Saviour in the full meaning of the term: thus Saint Paul accepts it in his later writings.[2] These fictions, however, did not find their way into the Synoptics,—no doubt because that part of the canon was already closed when they sprang up. They remained, as it were, floating in the air, outside the gospel texts, and took shape long after in the apocryphal work called the "Gospel of Nicodemus."[3]

But the special task of the Christian conscience was wrought in the silence of Judæa and the neighbouring region. The Synoptic Gospels grew up, as it were, limb by limb, as a living organism completes itself little by little, and reaches its perfect unity under its mysterious law of growth. At the date now had in view, was there any existing written text of the acts and words of Jesus? Had the apostle Matthew—if it was he—drawn up in Hebrew the discourses of his Master? Had Mark—or whoever wrote under that name—put in writing his notes upon that life?[4] It may be doubted. Paul, at all events, had no such document in hand. Had he perhaps an oral, or what we may call mnemonic, tradition of those words? One

---

[1] 1 Pet. iii. 19, 20, 22; iv. 6. Justin. *Tryph.* 72 (interpolated from Jeremiah); Iren. iii. 20: 4; iv. 22: 1; 27: 2; 33: 1, 12; v. 31: 1; Tert. *De anima*, 7, 55; Clem. Alex. *Strom.* vi. 6; Orig. *c. Cels.* ii. 43; Hippol. *De Antichristo*, 26. The attempts of Protestant critics to impugn this ancient Christian myth are an offence to true criticism.

[2] Phil. ii. 10; Col. i. 20; Eph. i. 10; iv. 9. See also Rom. xiv. 9; Herm. *Shep.* Simil. ix. 16; Clem. Alex. *Strom.* ii. 9; vi. 6.

[3] In Part Second, not earlier than the fourth century. Comp. Symbol of Sirmium, in Socr. *Hist. Eccl.* ii. 37.

[4] Papias (Euseb. iii. 39). That the Gospel of Luke did not as yet exist is sufficiently clear from 1 Pet. ii. 23, compared with Luke xxiii. 34.

may infer such a tradition for his account of the eucharist;[1] perhaps for the crucifixion; possibly a hint of the resurrection;[2] but not for the maxims and parables: as to the supper, he most nearly follows Luke. In his view Jesus is an expiatory victim, a superhuman being, — one risen from the dead, not a moralist. His citations of Jesus' words are vague, and not such as the evangelists put in his mouth.[3] The apostolic epistles, other than those of Paul, give no evidence that any such written memorial had yet appeared.

The inference would seem to be that certain narratives — as of the Supper, the Crucifixion, the Resurrection — were repeated from memory in words that admitted little variation. A passage like that regarding the Supper, for example, exhibits a likeness, such as that of the story of the crucifixion in the Fourth Gospel, to that in the Synoptics. The main features of the Synoptic narrative were probably shaped out already — though, as just noted, it makes no mention of the legend of Jesus in the world below, which must have appeared about A. D. 60; but, while the apostles lived, books that claimed to fix the tradition, which was in their sole keeping, would have had no chance of acceptance.[4] And besides, why write the life of Jesus? He is just now coming back. A world on the eve of perishing needs no new books. When the witnesses are dead, then it will be time enough to fix in writing a figure which is fading from men's memories every

---

[1] 1 Cor. xi. 23-26.   [2] *Ibid.* xv. 3-7.

[3] See 1 Thess. iv. 8, 9; v. 2, 6. Gal. v. 14. 1 Cor. vii. 10, 12, 25, 40; xiii. 2. 2 Cor. iii. 6. Rom. xii. 14, 19. Acts xx. 35 proves nothing.

[4] Irenæus (iii. 1) says that Mark did not write till after the death of Peter.

day. So with the St. Simonists in our day: at the death of Enfantin works on the origin of the sect and its founder's life began to appear; while in his lifetime such writings would not be allowed, as too damaging to his personal importance. On this point the churches of Judæa and the vicinity had a great advantage; since the knowledge of Jesus' words was far more widespread and accurate here than elsewhere. In this regard we note a difference between the epistles of James and Paul. This little composition of James is pervaded by a certain evangelic fragrance; we seem to hear in it at times the very echo of the words of Jesus; in it the atmosphere of Galilæan life is keen and fresh.[1]

We have no historical account of missions sent out directly from the church at Jerusalem. Its very principles would hardly lead it to spend its strength in such work. In general, there were few Ebionite or Judæo-Christian missions. The narrow spirit of the *Ebionim* would permit only envoys "of the circumcision." As we gather from the picture traced in the writings of the second century, — perhaps exaggerated, but at any rate faithful to the local spirit, — the Judæo-Christian preacher was watched with a suspicious eye; his antecedents were looked into; he was forced to undergo certain tests, with a six years' novitiate, as we see in the first words of the Clementine homilies;[2] he must have regular papers, making a formal confession of faith, in conformity with that

---

[1] See James i. 6, 27; ii. 1–4, 8, 10, 13; iv. 11, 12, 13–17; v. 12; and especially v. 14, 15, conforming so strictly with the Galilæan view of healing and pardon; also the exaltation of poverty and hatred of riches.

[2] See "Saint Paul," chap. x.

of the apostles at Jerusalem. Thus handicapped, a fruitful apostleship was a thing impossible; under such conditions Christianity would never have been preached. Even those whom James sent forth seem to have been much more busied with overthrowing Paul's foundations than in building on their own account. True, the churches of Bithynia, Pontus, and Cappadocia, which appear just now beside those of Asia and Galatia,[1] were not the work of Paul; but no more, it would seem, were they the work of Peter or of James: doubtless they were founded by that nameless preaching of the faithful which is most efficacious of all. It is my opinion, on the other hand, that Batanæa, Hauran, Decapolis, and generally the whole region east of Jordan, which presently became the centre and citadel of Jewish Christianity, were evangelised by adepts of the church at Jerusalem. On this side, the limit of Roman domination was quickly reached. Now the regions of Arabia lent no ear to the new doctrine, and lands subject to the Parthian kings (Arsacidæ) were scarce open to movements coming from the Roman domain. The range of apostolic geography is very narrow. The first Christians never dream of the barbaric or the Persian world; that of Arabia hardly has an existence for them. The missions of Thomas among the Parthians, Andrew among the Scythians, and Bartholomew into India, belong to legend. Christian imagination in the early time turns little to the East; the aim of apostolic pilgrimage is to the farthest West. Paul, as we have seen, looks beyond Italy toward Spain,[2] while in the Orient the missionaries appear to regard the goal as already reached.

[1] 1 Pet. i. 1.   [2] Rom. xv. 24, 28.

THE CHURCHES IN JUDÆA.   75

Was the name of Jesus heard during the first century at Edessa? Was there at this time near the upper Euphrates (Osrhoene) a Christianity of Syrian speech? The fables that surround the cradle of that church do not allow us to speak with certainty.[1] It is likely, however, that the close relations of Judaism in this quarter — recalling the stay of the [Assyrian] royal family of Adiabene at Jerusalem [and the conversion of Queen Helena to Judaism (about A.D. 18), mentioned by Josephus] — served in the propagation of Christianity. Samosata and Commagene early had men of learning who were members of the Church or at least friendly to it.[2] This region of the Euphrates, in any case, received the faith from Antioch.[3]

The clouds that gathered on the eastern horizon

---

[1] The regular list of bishops of Edessa begins about A. D. 300. (See Assemani, *Bibl. Or.* i. 424 *et seq.*) Cureton ("Ancient Syriac Documents," pp. 23, 61, 71, 72 : Lond. 1864) is full of anachronisms and contradictions. All that concerns the apostolate of Thaddæus (or Adæus, which is only a variation of that name) and the Christianity of King Abgarus (Abgar Uchamas) is apocryphal and fabulous. The false Leboubna of Edessa in Cureton (*ib.* 6–23; cf. 108–112); the same, tr. from Armenian (pub. by Alishan, Venice, 1868), and in Langlois (Hist. of Armenia, i. 313; cf. Cureton, 166). Comp. Moses of Khorene (*Hist. of Arm.* ii. 26–36); Faustus of Byzantium, iii. 1; Geneal. of St. Greg. 1 (Langlois, vol. ii.); Euseb. I. 13; ii. 1; Assemani, i. 318; iii. 289, 302, 611; Nicephorus, ii. 7, 40; St. Ephrem, *Carm. nisib.* 138 (ed. Bickell); Lequien, *Oriens chr.* ii. 1101, 2. The acts of the martyrs Sherbil and Barsamia, sufferers under Trajan (Cureton, 41–72; cf. *Acta Sanct.* Jan. ii. 1026), are of little value. The Syriac *Peshito* belongs to the end of the second century. Bardesanes, it is true [d. A. D. 223], assumes an established Christianity of some duration.

[2] Letter of Mara, son of Serapion, in Cureton: *Spicil. Syr.* 73, 74, of date about A. D. 73.

[3] The false Leboubna, in Cureton, 23; in Langlois, 325. Edessa, and even Seleucia on the Tigris, at first acknowledged the ecclesiastical supremacy of Antioch: Assemani, ii. 396 ; iii. (pt. 2) DCXX.; Lequien, *Or. christ.* ii. 1104, 5.

checked the advance of these Christian preachings. The prudent administration of Festus could do nothing to stay the disease preying on the heart of Judæa. Brigands, zealots, assassins, impostors of every sort, swarmed everywhere. One deceiver, after twenty others, offered safety and deliverance from their woes to all who should follow him into the desert. Those who went were slaughtered by Roman soldiers;[1] but nobody was cured of trust in false prophets. Festus died in Judæa, early in A. D. 62, and Nero sent Albinus as his successor. At the same time Herod Agrippa the second deprived Joseph Cabi of the pontificate, which he bestowed upon Hanan, son of the Hanan (or Annas) who had been the chief agent in the crucifixion of Jesus. This was the fifth of the sons of Hanan who held that dignity.[2]

The younger Hanan was haughty, stern, and bold. He was the flower of Sadduceeism, the complete expression of that cruel and inhuman sect, which did its best to make the exercise of authority insupportable and hateful. James, "the Lord's brother," was well-known in Jerusalem as a bitter advocate of the poor, a prophet of antique mould, loud in invective against the rich and powerful.[3] Hanan resolved that he should die. In the absence of Agrippa, and before Albinus had arrived in Judæa, he summoned the court

---

[1] Jos. *Antiq.* xx. 8: 10; *War*, ii. 14: 1.

[2] Jos. *Antiq.* xx. 9: 1. Josephus in his "Jewish War" (iv. 5: 2) speaks with much praise of the younger Hanan; but we note in this work a tendency to exalt those who were slain by the revolutionists in Jerusalem. The "Antiquities" are more trustworthy on this point.

[3] James v. 1–6. This paragraph may possibly have been published in Jerusalem as a sort of prophecy: ver. 4 (the "cries" of the labourer) seems an allusion to a fact told by Josephus in *Antiq.* xx. 8: 8; 9: 2.

of Sanhedrim, and brought before it James with some other saints. They were accused of violating the Law, and condemned to death by stoning. The authority of Agrippa was needful to the assembling of the Sanhedrim,[1] and that of Albinus was legally essential to the sentence; but the furious Hanan set himself above all rules. James was stoned near the Temple; and, since there was delay or difficulty in carrying out the sentence, his head was crushed by a fuller with his beating-club. He was, it is said, ninety-six years old.[2]

The death of this holy man had the worst effect throughout the city. The devout Pharisees, strict observers of the Law, were deeply incensed. James was universally honoured, as one of those men whose prayers have greatest weight. It is said that a "Rechabite" (probably an Essene), or, as some say, Simeon, son of Cleopas, nephew of James, cried out as he was stoned, "Hold! what are you about? Will you kill the just man who prays for you?" A passage of Isaiah,[3] as then understood, was applied to him. "'Let us crush the righteous man,' say they, 'because he displeases us;' that is why the fruit of their works is consumed." Elegies in Hebrew were composed upon his death, full of allusions to Scripture passages and to his name, *Obliam*: traces of these may be found in Hegesippus. Almost the whole population joined in inviting King Agrippa to put bounds to the high-

---

[1] As appears in the phrase χωρὶς τῆς ἐκείνου γνώμης, the word ἐκείνου seeming to refer to the king — an explanation best suited to what we know of the government of that day.

[2] Jos. *Antiq.* xx. 9: 1; Hegesippus in Euseb. ii. 23; iv. 22. Clem. Alex. *id.* ii. 1; Epiphan. lxxviii. 14. The story of Hegesippus is legendary in its details.

[3] Isaiah iii. 10.

priest's audacity. Albinus, already on his way from Alexandria, learned the crime of Hanan, to whom he sent a threatening letter, afterwards deposing him. So Hanan held the office for only three months. The disasters which presently fell upon the nation were regarded by many as a judgment upon that murder.[1] The Christians saw in the event a "sign of the time," a proof that the final catastrophe was near.[2]

A sort of strange insanity, in fact, prevailed in Jerusalem. Anarchy was at its height. The zealots, though decimated by executions, were masters of the situation. Albinus, no way a man like Festus, sought only to make profit by connivance with the bandits.[3] On every side were seen prognostics of some unheard-of calamity. Towards the end of the year a man named Jesus, son of Hanan, a sort of Jeremiah risen from the dead, began to roam through the streets by day and night, crying, "A voice from the East! a voice from the West! a voice from the four winds! a voice against Jerusalem and the Temple! a voice against the bridegroom and his bride! a voice against all the people!" He was scourged with whips, but repeated the same cry. He was beaten with rods till his bones were laid bare, but at every blow he repeated with a woful voice, "Woe, woe to Jerusalem!"[4] He was never seen to speak with any one; but he went on still repeating, "Woe, woe, to Jerusalem!" without ever assailing those who beat him, or thanking those who gave him

---

[1] Josephus and Eusebius, as above. For the addition made by Origen to the passage in Josephus, see "Saint Paul," p. 80, note.

[2] In Matt. xxiv. 9; Mark xiii. 9; Luke xxi. 12, 13, we may perhaps trace allusions to the death of James.

[3] Jos. *Antiq.* xx. 7; *War*, ii. 14: 1.

[4] Jos. *War*, vi. 5: 3.

alms. And so he went on until the siege, his voice seeming never to be weakened.

If this Jesus, son of Hanan, was not a disciple of Jesus, at least his prophetic cry was the true expression of what was deepest in the Christian conscience. Jerusalem had filled up her measure. The city that killed the prophets and stoned the messengers sent to her, scourging one and crucifying another, is henceforth the Accursed City. About this time were composed those brief books of visions, which some ascribed to Enoch[1] and others to Jesus, showing a striking likeness to the outcries of Jesus, son of Hanan.[2] These fragments were later adopted in the text of the Synoptics, and exhibited as the discourses spoken by Jesus in his last days.[3] Perhaps the watchword was already sounded, to forsake Judæa and flee to the mountains.[4] At least the Synoptics are stamped deeply with the marks of this anguish; it abides in them as a birthmark, indelibly imprinted. With the gentle maxims of Jesus are mingled the colouring of a sombre apocalypse and the forecasting of a troubled and anxious fancy. But the calmer temper of the Christians shielded them from that madness which distracted others of their people, who shared with them their messianic dreams. For them the Messiah was already come. He had lived in the wilderness; he had ascended to heaven after the lapse of thirty years. The impostors or enthusiasts who sought to draw the

---

[1] Comp. Epist. of Barnabas (Gr. text) 4, 16, with Matt. xxiv. 22; Mark xiii. 20. See "Life of Jesus," p. 42, note.

[2] Especially the "voice against the bridegroom," compared with Matt. xxiv. 19; Mark xiii. 17; Luke xxi. 23.

[3] Matt. xxiv. 3–31; Mark xiii. 3–20; Luke xxi. 7–28.

[4] Matt. xxiv. 16; Mark xiii. 14; Luke xxi. 21.

people after them were false Christs and false prophets.[1] The death of James, and perhaps of some others,[2] led them, also, more and more to divorce their cause from that of Judaism. An object of hate to all, they found comfort in the precepts of Jesus. He, as many held, had foretold that amid these many trials not a hair of their head should perish.[3]

The situation was so full of peril, it was seen so clearly that they were on the eve of a catastrophe, that no immediate successor to James was set at the head of the church in Jerusalem.[4] The other "brothers of the Lord" — Judas, Simon, and Cleopas — continued to be of highest authority in the community. After the war, as we shall see, they served as a rallying-point to all the faithful in Judæa.[5] Jerusalem had now but eight years to survive; and, long even before the fatal hour, the volcanic outburst drove far away the little group of pious Jews that had become bound together in the memory of Jesus.

[1] Compare Jos. *Antiq.* xx. 8: 6, 10, with Matt. xxiv. 5, 11, 23, 26; Mark xiii. 6, 21, 22; Luke xxi. 8.
[2] "Certain others," says Josephus, *Antiq.* xx. 9: 1. But it is not sure that these "others" were Christians.
[3] Luke xxi. 18, 19. [4] Euseb. iii. 11.
[5] Euseb. iii. 11; iv. 5, 20, 22 (according to Hegesippus). *Constit. apostol.* vii. 46.

CHAPTER IV.

LATEST ACTS OF PAUL. — A. D. 62, 63.

MEANWHILE Paul had to undergo in prison the delays of an administration thrown out of gear by the sovereign's extravagances and his infamous surroundings. He had with him Timothy, Luke, Aristarchus, and, by some accounts, Titus, while Tychicus had lately rejoined him. A certain Jesus (a Jew surnamed Justus),[1] one Demetrius or Demas (an uncircumcised proselyte, apparently from Thessalonica),[2] and Crescens, of whom we know little, shared his captivity and his work.[3] Mark — who, by my theory, had come to Rome with Peter — appears to have made friends again with the one whose early apostolic work he had shared, and from whom he had parted in sharp contention,[4] and served him, probably, in his communications with Peter.[5] At any rate, Paul was just now on ill terms with the Christians "of the circumcision," judging them to have little friendliness toward him; and declared[6] that he had no good fellow-workers among them.

---

[1] For this name as used among the Jews compare *Corp. inscr. Græc.* No. 9922; *Bereshith rabba,* § 6.

[2] Col. iv. 11, comparing ver. 14.

[3] Col. i. 1; iv. 7, 10, 11, 14. Philem. 1, 24. Eph. vi. 21. 2 Tim. (apocr.) iv. 9–12.

[4] Acts xx. 39.

[5] Col. iv. 10; Philem. 24; 2 Tim. iv. 11; 1 Pet. v. 13.

[6] Col. iv. 11.

Among these new circumstances, in the imperial capital where all opinions met and mingled, great changes were now wrought in the thought of Paul, — changes which make his writings of this period widely different from those composed during his second and third missions. Christian doctrine was fast unfolding inwardly. In a few months of these fruitful years, theology made more advance than afterward in centuries. The new doctrine was finding its balance, and, as it were, making itself scaffoldings and props on every side for its firmer support. One might compare it to an organism at a critical stage of evolution, which puts forth a limb, transforms an organ, trims away a superfluity, so as to attain an harmonious life; that is, a condition in which the living creature may freely put forth reflex action, giving it consistence and support.

The flame of a consuming activity had hitherto left Paul no leisure to reflect on the lapse of time, or to discover that Jesus tarried long in his appearing; but these weary months of captivity turned his thoughts in upon themselves. He was now, too, growing old, — " such a one as Paul the aged;"[1] a certain sadness of advancing years succeeded to the heat of his passionate youth. Reflection pushed its way into consciousness, forcing him to round out his thought and reduce it to a system. From a man of action, he became a mystic, a theologian, a speculative thinker. The eagerness of absolute conviction, unable to take a single step backward, could not prevent his wondering, now and then, why the sky did not open sooner, or the last trump already sound. His faith was not shaken, but it craved other grounds of support. His idea of the Christ changed

[1] Philem. 9.

accordingly. His inward vision is not so much the Son of Man appearing in the clouds, holding judgment at the general resurrection; but of a Christ exalted in his own divinity, in substance and act one with God. To him the resurrection is no longer in the future; it has already come to pass.[1] If a man changes once, he keeps on changing; one may be at the same time the most impassioned and the most advancing of men. Certain it is that the grand images of the final revelation and the resurrection — once so familiar to Paul, found in some shape on every page of his letters of the second and third missions, and even in that to the Philippians[2] — are far less prominent in the later epistles of his captivity.[3] Here their place is taken by a theory of the Christ, conceived as a sort of divine person, much like the Logos-theory, which later took its final form in the writings ascribed to John.

A like change is observable in the style. The epistles of his captivity have more ample flow, but lose something of nerve. The thought is less vigorously handled. The diction greatly differs from that of the earlier period. The favourite expressions of the Johannine School — light, darkness, life, love, and the like — become dominant.[4] We already find traces of the eclectic philosophy of the Gnostics. Justification by Jesus is no longer the living question; the dispute of faith and works seems reconciled in the unity of Christian life, which combines both grace and knowledge.[5] Christ, now the central being of the universe,

---

[1] Col. ii. 12; iii. 1; but see 2 Tim. ii. 18.
[2] Phil. i. 6; ii. 16; iii. 20, 21; iv. 5.
[3] Col. iii. 4.
[4] Col. i. 12, 13; iii. 4. Eph. v. 8, 11, 13. Comp. Phil. ii. 16.
[5] Col. i. 10; iii. 9, 10; Eph. ii. 8–10. Here we have the phrase, "not

harmonises in his deified personality the two rival Christologies. The genuineness of these writings has been contested, not without grounds; still, the argument in its favour is so strong,[1] that I prefer to attribute the variance of style and thought to a natural advance in Paul's manner. His earlier and doubtless genuine writings have in them the germ of this later style. In certain relations the terms "Christ" and "God" are almost interchangeable: Christ exercises the offices of divinity; like God, his name is invoked in prayer; he is the essential mediator of approach to God. In the warmth of the disciples' attachment to Jesus any theory [of divinity], held in any part of the Jewish world, might be referred to him. Suppose a man to appear in our day who answered to all the diverse demands of our democracy: to one, his partisans would say, "You are for organised labour, and *he* is organised labour;" to another, "You are for moral independence, and *he* is moral independence;" to a third, "You are for co-operation, and *he* is co-operation;" to a fourth, "You are for solidarity, and *he* is solidarity."

The new theory of Paul, as found in Colossians and Ephesians, may be summed up somewhat thus:—

This world is the kingdom of darkness, that is, of Satan and his infernal hierarchy, who fill the spaces of the air. The realm of saints, on the other hand, is the kingdom of light. The saints are what they are, not by their own merit (for before Christ, all were enemies of God), but by the merits of Christ, the Son of God's

of works," no longer "works of the law" (as in Gal. ii. 16), which would be hardly intelligible to a Greek.

[1] See Introduction to "Saint Paul," p. 6.

love, which He freely transfers to them. The blood of his Son, shed upon the cross, blots out their sin, reconciles every creature with God, making peace reign in heaven and on earth. The Son is the visible image of the Invisible, the first-born of the creation; all was created in him, through him, and for him,—things in heaven and on earth, visible and invisible, thrones, powers, and dominions.[1] He was before all things, and all exist in him. He and the Church make one body, of which he is the head. As he has always held the first rank in all things, so he holds it in the resurrection, which goes before the general resurrection. The fulness of divinity dwells bodily in him. Thus, he is a true divinity to man, a sort of first agent of the creation, intermediate between God and man,—as Philo calls the Word "a god to us the imperfect."[2] Whatever monotheism says of the relations of man to God may be said, in Paul's theology, of the relations of man to Jesus.[3] Veneration for him, which in James does not go beyond *dulia* or *hyperdulia*,[4] extends with Paul to a true *latria*, such as no Jew had ever paid to a man of woman born.[5]

This mystery, prepared by God from everlasting, is now in the fulness of time revealed to his saints of the last days. The time is come when every one must in his own degree fulfil the work of Christ: his work is

---

[1] Orders of the angels; see Rom. viii. 38; 1 Cor. xv. 24; 1 Pet. iii. 22; *Testam. of the Patriarchs*: Levi, 3 *et seq.*

[2] *Leg. alleg.* iii. 73.

[3] The uncertainty of the text in Col. ii. 2 prevents any argument from it.

[4] James i. 1.

[5] By the Catholic distinction, *dulia* signifies the worship paid to saints, *hyperdulia* that to the Virgin, *latria* that to God alone. — ED.

fulfilled by suffering, and thus suffering is a privilege in which we should rejoice and boast. The Christian, as a fellow-worker with Jesus, is like him filled with the fulness (πλήρωμα) of God.¹ Jesus in his resurrection has bestowed his own life upon all. The wall of separation, which the Law set up between God's people and the gentiles, Jesus has taken away; from the two reconciled portions of mankind he has made a new humanity; all the old hatreds he has slain on the cross. The letter of the Law was as the note of a debt which mankind could not pay, but Jesus has cancelled it by nailing it to the cross. Thus the world made by him is a world wholly new; he is the corner-stone of the temple built by God for his own worship. The Christian is dead to the world, buried with Jesus in the tomb; his "life is hid with Christ in God." Until Christ shall appear and unite him in his own glory, he "mortifies his body," by the extinction of his natural desires, by taking in everything the course opposite to nature, stripping away "the old man" and putting on "the new man," made new in the image of his Maker. In this view there is no longer Greek or Jew, circumcised or uncircumcised, barbarian, Scythian, slave, or freeman; Christ is all, and in all. The saints are those to whom by free gift God has made application of the merits of Christ, and whom he thus predestined to the divine adoption before the world was. The Church is one, as God himself is one. Its work is the building-up of the body of Christ; the final purpose of all things is the realising of the perfect Man, the complete union of Christ with all his members,— a condition in which he will be in truth the head of a humanity made anew

---

[1] Col. ii. 10; Eph. iii. 19; John i. 16.

after his likeness, receiving from him motion and life by a series of organs joined together in due subordination. The powers of darkness in the air about us struggle to prevent this fulfilment. There will be a terrible conflict between them and the saints, and a season of affliction; but, armed with the gifts of Christ, the saints will triumph.

Doctrines such as these were not wholly original. They were, in part, those of the Jewish Egyptian school, notably those of Philo. Christ, thus become a divine "hypostasis," is the Logos of the Jewish Alexandrian philosophy, the *mem'ra* of the Chaldaic paraphrases, archetype of all things, by whom all things were created.[1] The powers of the air, to which the empire of the world has been given, these strange hierarchies celestial and infernal,[2] are those of the Jewish cabbala and the Gnostics. The mysterious *pleroma*, the final purpose of Christ's work, is much like the divine *pleroma* placed by the Gnostics at the summit of the universal scale. The gnostic and cabbalist theosophy, which we may regard as the mythology of monotheism, and which we seem to find hinted in Simon of Gitton,[3] appears in the first century with all its essential fea-

---

[1] Philo, *De prof.* 2, 19, 20, 26; *Vita Mosis*, ii. 42; *De mundi opif.* 4-8; *De conf. ling.* 14, 19, 28; *De migr. Abr.* 1, 2; *De somniis*, i. 13, 37, 41; ii. 37; *De monarchia*, ii. 5; *Quod Deus immut.* 6, 36; *De agr. Noe*, 2; *De plant. Noe*, 2, 4; *Legis alleg.* i. 18; iii. 34, 59-61; *De cher.* 11, 35; *De mundo*, 2, 3; *Quis rer. div. hæres*, 26, 38, 42, 44, 48; *De post. Caini*, 35; fragm. in Euseb. *Præpar. evang.* vii. 13; John of Damascus (Mangey, ii. 655).

[2] Philo, *De somn.* i. 22; Testament of the twelve patriarchs: *Levi*, 3; *Benj.* 3; Mishna, *Aboth*, v. 6; Babyl. Talm., *Beracoth*, 6 a; *Tanhouma*, § *Mishpatim;* Ialkout on Job, § 913; Plutarch, *Quæst. Rom.* 14; Iamblichus, *De myst. Ægypt.*, ii. 3; Test. of Solomon, in Fabricius, *Cod. pseud. V. T.*, i. 1047; 1 Pet. iii. 22; Ignat. *Ad Trallianos*, 4, 5.

[3] Acts viii. 10.

tures. To throw over to the second century, on system, all the documents in which traces are found of such a theory, is very rash. The same thing, in germ, was in Philo and in primitive Christianity. The theosophic conception of Christ came necessarily from the messianic conception of the Son of Man, when it once became evident, after long waiting, that the Son of Man did not return. In the most incontestably genuine of Paul's epistles there are certain features which lack little of being as advanced as those in the writings of his captivity. Thus, Satan is called "the god of this world."[1] Hebrews, written before A.D. 70, shows the same tendency to place Jesus in the realm of abstract speculation.[2] All this will appear very clearly when we come to speak of the Johannine writings. With Paul, who had not himself known Jesus, this metamorphosis of the idea of Christ was in a way inevitable. While the school which held the living tradition of the Master created the Jesus of the Synoptics, the enthusiast, who had never seen but in his dreams the Founder of his faith, transfigured him more and more into a super-human being, a sort of metaphysical First Principle, that may never have appeared in life.

This transfiguration, moreover, did not come to pass in the thought of Paul alone. The churches he had founded advanced in the same direction with him. Especially those of Asia Minor were carried by a certain force of interior growth to the most exaggerated views upon the divinity of Jesus. This we may easily understand. For the fraction of Christendom which grew up from the familiar conversations by the sea of Galilee, Jesus would always remain the beloved Son of God

---

[1] 2 Cor. iv. 4: cf. John xii. 31.   [2] Heb. i. 5–8.

whom they had seen walking among men with the charm of his presence and his kindly smile; but when his name was heard among the people of far-away Phrygia, where the speaker himself professed never to have seen him, and to have known nothing of his life on earth,[1] what could those good and simple-minded hearers think of him who was thus proclaimed? What image could they form of him? Was it as a wise man, — a teacher, of attractive personality? It was not so that Paul set forth his character. He was, or seemed to be, quite ignorant of the historic Jesus. Was it as the Messiah, the Son of Man, about to appear in the clouds in the "great and dreadful day of the Lord?"[2] These images were strange to the gentiles, and implied knowledge of the Jewish scriptures. Evidently the figure that would oftenest present itself to these pious provincials was that of an incarnation, — a god in human form walking on the earth, — just as Paul himself was taken to be at Lystra.[3] This notion was very familiar in Asia Minor; not long after this, Apollonius of Tyana made profitable use of it. To reconcile such a view with the doctrine of one God, only one way lay open: to conceive Jesus as a divine *hypostasis* clothed in flesh, a sort of double of the one God, taking human form for the fulfilment of a divine plan. We must bear in mind that we are no longer in Syria. Christianity has passed from Semitic soil to the charge of races intoxicated with imagination and mythology. The prophet Mahomet, whose legend is so purely human among the Arabs, becomes to the Shiites of Persia and India a completely supernatural being, a sort of Vishnu or Buddha.

[1] 2 Cor. v. 16.   [2] Mal. iv. 5.   [3] Acts xiv. 12.

Certain relations of the apostle at this time with the churches of Asia Minor gave him the opportunity to set forth the new form which his thought had taken. The pious Epaphroditus (or Epaphras), teacher and founder of the church at Colossæ, and head of the churches on the borders of the Lycus, came to him bearing a missive from them.[1] Paul had never been in this valley, but his authority there stood high.[2] He was regarded as the apostle of that region, and every one there felt bound to put faith in him.[3] Learning of his captivity, the churches of Colossæ, Laodicea on the Lycus, and Hierapolis deputed Epaphras to visit him in prison,[4] comfort him, assure him of the attachment of the faithful, and probably offer him a gift in money, of which he might be in need.[5] His report of the zeal of these new converts gave Paul great joy;[6] their faith, love, and hospitality were admirable; but in these Phrygian churches Christianity was taking a strange turn. Away from contact with the chief apostles, withdrawn from all Jewish influence, and mostly made up of pagan converts, they inclined to mingle their Christian faith with Greek philosophy and local superstitions.[7] In the quiet little town of Colossæ, amid the noise of its cascades and foaming eddies, in front of Hierapolis and its dazzling mountain,[8] the belief in Christ's full divinity grew from day to day. Phrygia,

---

[1] Col. i. 7, 8; ii. 1; iv. 12-16.
[2] *Ibid.* ii. 1, 5; Eph. iii. 2; iv. 21.
[3] Philem. 19.   [4] *Ibid.* 23.
[5] Col. i. 7, with the reading ὑπὲρ ὑμῶν.
[6] Col. i. 4, 9; Eph. i. 15.
[7] Col. ii. 4, 8. See Eph. ii. 19-22; iii. 1-7; iv. 17, 22. This epistle is probably addressed to the churches of the Lycus valley.
[8] See "Saint Paul," chap. xiii.

as we remember, was a country of original religious genius. Its mysteries had, or claimed to have, a lofty symbolic meaning. Some of the rites there practised had a likeness to those of the new faith.[1] For Christians with no religious tradition of their own, who had gone through no such initiation into monotheism as the Jews, there must be strong inducement to connect the new dogma with the old symbol which came to them here as a heritage from very ancient time. They had been devout pagans before adopting the Syrian opinions; and in adopting them would probably not think they were breaking formally with their past. And then, what man really religious ever wholly renounces the traditional teaching in whose shelter he has first felt the presence of the infinite, or does not seek some reconciliation, hopeless as it may be, between his old faith and that to which the advance of his thought has brought him?

In the second century the demand for compromise came to be extremely urgent, and brought about a fully developed Gnosticism. Like tendencies at the end of the first century, as we shall see, filled the church at Ephesus with restless agitation. Cerinthus and the writer of the Fourth Gospel set out from the same postulate, — that the soul of Jesus was a celestial being distinct from his earthly manifestation.[2] About A. D. 60, Colossæ was touched with the same disturbance. A theosophy compounded of native beliefs,[3] an

---

[1] Garrucci, *Tre sepolcri* (Naples, 1852), and *Les mystères du syncrétisme phrygien*, in the *Mél. d'Arch.* of Cahier and Martin, iv. 1 *et seq.*

[2] Iren. *Adv. hær.* i. 26: 1.

[3] See canons 35, 36 of the Council of Laodicea; Theodoret on Col. ii. 17, 18.

Ebionitish Judaism,[1] philosophic notions,[2] and points taken from the doctrine newly preached, was ably set forth.[3] A worship of uncreated Æons, a highly developed scheme of angels and dæmons, — in a word, Gnosticism with its arbitrary practices and its materialised abstractions, — began to prevail;[4] and, by its deceitful seductions, undermined the Christian faith in its most vital and essential parts. Mingled with this were unnatural abstinences, morbid self-denials, a show of austerity refusing to the body its rights,[5] — in a word, all those aberrations of the moral sense which in the second century produced the Phrygian heresies (Montanist, Pepuzian, Cataphrygian) which allied themselves with the various forms of mystical frenzy that still survive in the dervishes of our day. Thus every day appeared in sharp contrast the difference between Christians of pagan and those of Jewish antecedents. Christian mythology and metaphysics sprang up in the churches of Paul's founding. Born of polytheistic ancestry, converts from paganism found the idea of a god becoming man very simple and easy; while to the Jews the notion of incarnate deity was something blasphemous and abhorrent.

Paul wished to keep Epaphras, whose service might be of use to him,[6] and decided to reply to the Colossians by sending Tychicus of Ephesus, charging him with messages to the churches in Asia.[7] The most convenient route for him to follow was to land at Ephesus or

---

[1] Col. ii. 11, 12, 16-23.
[2] *Ibid.* 8.   [3] *Ibid.* 4, 8.
[4] Col. i. 16; ii. 10, 15, 18. Eph. i. 21; vi. 20. Comp. 1 Tim. i. 4; vi. 20. Epiphan. xxi. 2; Tert. *Præscr.* 33; Iren. i. 31: 2.
[5] Col. ii. 18, 22, 23.   [6] *Ibid.* iv. 12, 13
[7] *Ibid.* 7, 8; Eph. vi. 21, 22; 2 Tim. iv. 12.

Miletus, and proceed by the valleys of the Mæander and the Lycus. Thus he might visit the several Christian communities, give them news of Paul, carry personal messages as to his relations with the authorities, which it might be imprudent to put in writing, — a precaution which may be noted in several of the epistles and elsewhere,[1] — and deliver to each the letters specially addressed to them.[2] Those which were closest together were bidden to share their letters, reading them by turns in their assemblies.[3] Tychicus might, besides, take with him a sort of Encyclical, modelled upon Colossians, and meant for those to whom he had no special message to deliver. The preparation of this circular letter seems to have been left to some disciple or amanuensis, acting under Paul's instructions, or from a copy by his hand.[4] The Epistle to the Romans seems also to have had this character, as a circular letter.[5]

The letter addressed under these conditions to the Colossians has come down to us. The doubts as to its genuineness I have considered in a former volume. It was dictated to Timothy,[6] and signed by Paul, with the postscript, "Remember my bonds."[7] The circular letter, unaddressed, which Tychicus was to deliver on the way, seems to be the same that we have in

---

[1] Cf. 1 John 12 ; 2 John 13.

[2] Col. iv. 13, 16. Laodicea and Hierapolis are so near together that a single letter may have served them both (see iv. 13). If Laodicea alone is named (as in iv. 16), it is because that is rather nearer to Colossæ.

[3] Col. iv. 16.

[4] It is noticeable that Ephesians does not contain at its close (vi. 21) the name of Timothy. It differs, further, in style from Paul's ordinary writing, and even from the special style of Colossians.

[5] See "Saint Paul," Introduction.

[6] Col. i. 1. [7] *Ibid.* iv. 13.

"Ephesians." Certainly, it was not written for the church at Ephesus, — since it is addressed only to converted pagans,[1] — a church that Paul had never seen,[2] to which he had nothing special to say. The ancient copies gave in the address no name of the church it was meant for;[3] the final words[4] are indeterminate; the Vatican and Sinaitic manuscripts have a like peculiarity, the words, "in Ephesus"[5] being written by a later hand, while in that of Vienna (67) these words are erased. It has been supposed to be really that addressed to the Laodiceans at the same time with Colossians.[6] I have given elsewhere[7] the reasons which lead me, against this view, rather to regard it as the circular letter above described. Tychicus, as he passed by his native city, Ephesus, may have shown a copy to the elders, and they may have kept it as a precious document for instruction; nay, it may have been this very copy that served when the collection of Paul's epistles was made up, whence came the title it is known by at this day. So "Romans" is known to us by the name of the most important of the churches that had received it. What we do know, is that Ephesians is an imitation, or paraphrase, of Colossians, with additions taken from other, and perhaps some lost, letters of Paul.

Ephesians, along with Colossians, makes the best exposition of Paul's views toward the close of his

[1] Eph. ii. 11, 19; iii. 1; iv. 17, 22.
[2] *Ibid.* i. 15; iii. 2; iv. 21.
[3] Basil, *Contra Eunom.* ii. 19; Jerome on Eph. i. 1.
[4] Eph. vi. 23, 24. [5] *Ibid.* i. 1.
[6] *Ibid.* iv. 16. This was the opinion of Marcion : Tertull. *Adv.* Marc. v. 11; Epiph. xlii. 9, 11; cf. Canon of Muratori, ll. 62, 63.
[7] See Introduction to "Saint Paul."

career. These two have for the last period of his life the same value that Romans has for the great era of his apostleship. The thought of the founder of Christian theology has here arrived at its clearest expression. We recognise in them that final task of spiritualising to which great minds submit their thought just before their end, beyond which nothing lies but death.

Surely Paul was right in contending against that perilous disease Gnosticism, which was before long seriously to menace the human reason. Against this chimerical "worshipping of angels"[1] he sets his Christ, above all that is not God himself.[2] We are still indebted to him for the last attack he delivered against the circumcision, the vain practices, and the prejudices of the Jews.[3] The moral he draws from his transcendent conception of the Christ is in many ways deserving of admiration. But — good heavens! how he goes beyond all bounds! How this audacious scorn of reason, this brilliant praise of madness, this storm of paradox — how it leads the way to the defeat of that perfect reason which shuns extremes! The "old man," so roughly attacked by Paul, will strike back; he will assert himself as not deserving such anathema. All that Past, stricken by an unjust sentence, will again in the "Renaissance" become a principle of new life for the world, starved by Christianity to the last degree of inanition. In this sense Paul will prove to have been one of the most dangerous foes of civilisation. His half-thoughts will have been so many defeats of the human spirit. When that spirit shall triumph, he

---

[1] Col. ii. 18.
[2] *Ibid.* i. 16; ii. 10, 15; Eph. i. 21; vi. 12.
[3] Col. ii. 11, 12, 16, 23; Eph. ii., iii.

will pass away. The triumph of Jesus will be the extinction of Paul.

"Colossians" ends with conveying the kind words and wishes of their saintly and devoted catechist, Epaphras, enjoining therewith an exchange of letters with them of Laodicea.[1] With Tychicus, bearer of the correspondence, Paul associates as messenger one Onesimus, whom he calls "a faithful and dear brother.[2] The story of Onesimus is a touching one. He had been a slave of Philemon, one of the chief men in the church at Colossæ; he robbed his master, ran away, and went to hide in Rome. Here, perhaps through his countryman Epaphras, he came to know Paul, who made a convert of him, induced him to return to his master, and made him companion of Tychicus on the journey. To calm the apprehension which this poor boy might feel, Paul dictates to Timothy a note for Philemon, — a little masterpiece in its kind, — which he puts into the runaway's hand. Thus he writes: —

Paul, a prisoner of Jesus Christ, and Timothy his brother, to our dear friend and fellow-labourer Philemon, to our sister Appia, and to our comrade in arms Archippus, and to the church that is in your house: grace and peace to you all from God our Father, and Christ Jesus our Lord: —

I thank my God, making mention of you in my prayers, hearing of your love and faith to the Lord Jesus and all his saints, that your fellowship in the faith may be effectual, to the knowledge of that great blessing which we have in Christ. For I have great joy and comfort in your love, because the very heart of the saints has rest in you, my brother. And thus, while I might make bold in Christ to enjoin it on you

---

[1] Col. iv. 12, 13.

[2] *Ibid.* 9, with Philemon, throughout. Onesimus was a slave's name (Suet. Galba, 13).

as a duty, yet I choose rather to urge it upon you for love's sake,—the more, that I am now an old man, and in prison for Christ. I call upon you for my own child, born to me here in prison—my son Onesimus,[1] who was once unhelpful to you, but now very helpful to you and me. I have sent him back to you; and pray you to receive him as the child of my own heart. I would, indeed, have kept him with me, that he might serve me in your stead here in my gospel-prison; but I would not do it without your knowledge, lest I might take your kindness by force, and not of your own free will.

It may be, indeed, that he left you for a time on purpose that you might take him back for good,[2]—no longer as a bondman, but better than that, a dear brother: very dear to me, but how much more to you, both in his own person and in the Lord! If then you hold me as a partner, receive him as if it were myself; and if he wronged you once, or owes you any debt, charge it to my account.

And here Paul takes the pen, so as to make his letter a real note of credit, and adds these words:—

I Paul write this with my own hand. I will pay the debt, without making any account of what you owe me,—namely, your own soul. Yes, my brother, let me have "help" of you in the Lord, and do you comfort my heart in Christ.

Here he proceeds again to dictate:—.

I have written to you sure of your consent, and knowing that you will do over and above what I say. But make ready to receive me as a guest; for I hope that through your prayers I may receive hospitality of you. Epaphras, my fellow-prisoner, Mark, Aristarchus, Demas, and Luke, my fellow-labourers, salute you. The grace of our Lord Jesus Christ be with the spirit of you all.

---

[1] This name means "helpful."

[2] Probably an allusion to Levit. xxv. 46, a fruitful text of rabbinic disputations.

We see that Paul indulged in singular illusions. He thought himself to be on the point of deliverance; he was already forming fresh plans of travel, and saw himself at the heart of Asia Minor,[1] among the churches that revered him as their apostle, and yet had never heard him. John Mark too was preparing to visit Asia, probably on some behest of Peter. The churches in Phrygia had already been advised of his speedy arrival. In the letter to the Colossians Paul inserts a new recommendation concerning him.[2] The air of this recommendation is rather cool. Paul was afraid that the old differences between them, and still more Mark's close relations with the party of Jerusalem, might embarrass his friends in Asia, and that they might hesitate about receiving a man whom till now they had had reason to distrust. Such misunderstandings he would prevent, and hence directed his own churches to receive Mark in case he passed their way. Mark, too, was a nephew of Barnabas,[3] whose name was dear to the Galatians, and could not have been unknown in Phrygia, Colossæ being only some forty leagues from Antioch in Pisidia, in the province of Galatia. We do not know the result. A severe earthquake had just devastated all the valley of the Lycus. The rich Laodicea was built up again from its own resources,[4] but Colossæ could not recover; it almost

---

[1] We find similar hints in Acts xix. 21; Rom. xv. 23, 24; Phil. i. 25; ii. 24. It may be that Paul, to revive the interest of his disciples in these churches, would speak of these intended journeys even when there was but slight chance of them.

[2] Col. iv. 10; cf. 1 Pet. v. 13.

[3] Col. iv. 10.

[4] Tac. *Ann.* xiv. 27; cf. Apoc. iii. 17, 18. See "Saint Paul," chap. xiii.

disappears from the list of churches (having, as Waddington remarks, no coinage of its own), and the Apocalypse, in 69, makes no mention of it. Its significance in Christian history passes over to Laodicea and Hierapolis.

Paul's apostolic activity consoled him for the sorrows which assailed him from every side. He reflected that he suffered for his beloved churches; he looked on himself as the victim who opened to the gentiles the doors of the household of Israel.[1] Still, in the later months of his imprisonment he felt something of despondency and loneliness.[2] Already, while writing to the Philippians,[3] in contrasting the conduct of his dear and faithful Timothy to that of some others, he had said, "Every man seeks his own, and not the interest of Christ." Timothy alone seems never to have called forth any complaint from this severe taskmaster, embittered and hard to please. We may not suppose that Aristarchus, Epaphras, or Jesus called "the Just," had abandoned him; they are, indeed, numbered among the faithful in Colossians and Ephesians. But several of them may have been away at once. Titus was on a mission;[4] others, who owed everything to Paul,—especially some from Asia, among them Phygellus and Hermogenes,—ceased to visit him.[5] Thronged as he once was, he was now left almost alone, shunned by the Jewish Christians,[6] while Luke was at times his only companion.[7] His disposition, always

---

[1] Col. i. 24; Eph. iii. 1.

[2] Col. iv. 11. 2 Tim. i. 15; ii. 17, 18; iii. 1-7, 13; iv. 3, 4, 6-16. The latter epistle is not Paul's, but it may show marks of his hand.

[3] Phil. ii. 21.   [4] 2 Tim. iv. 10.   [5] *Ibid.* i. 15.

[6] The most plausible rendering of Col. iv. 11; cf. Tit. i. 10.

[7] 2 Tim. iv. 11.

somewhat sombre, grew more harsh; it was, indeed, not easy to live in his company. Thus he cruelly felt the ingratitude of men. Every word he is supposed to have written at this time is full of discontent and bitterness,—the whole of Second Timothy, for example. The church at Rome was closely allied with that at Jerusalem, and, for the most part, made up of Jewish converts. Jewish orthodoxy was strong at Rome, and must have made an obstinate fight against him. The heart of the aged apostle was bruised, and he longed for death.[1]

If we had to do with one of a different temperament and another race, we should try to conceive of Paul, in these last days, as coming to the conviction that he had spent his life for a dream, as renouncing all the sacred Prophets for a book he had hardly looked into till now,—Ecclesiastes, a delightful book, the only one of so kindly temper ever written by a Jew,—and as declaring that the happy man is he who, having lived till old age in content with the wife of his youth, dies without having lost a child.[2] A trait characteristic of the great men of Europe is that, at certain hours, they yield to the argument of Epicurus; while still in the ardour of their activity they are seized with a deep weari-

---

[1] That noble passage, "I am now ready to be offered; I have fought a good fight," etc. (2 Tim. iv. 6–8), though held by many to be from Paul's own pen, appears to be contradicted by the plans of travel he was constantly forming. It would not appear that he had ever, in his prison, had so clear a presentiment of his approaching end as this would show.

[2] A Greek inscription at Beyrout reads thus:—

Θάρσει· τέθνηκας γὰρ ἀπενθήτοις ἐπὶ τέκνοις,
Ζώουσαν προλιπὼν ἣν ἐπόθεις ἄλοχον.

Courage: thou diest with thy children yet unmourned,
And leavest living still thy well-beloved spouse.

(*Mission de Phénicie*, p. 347.)

ness of life, and when at the summit of success doubt whether the cause they serve is worth the sacrifice it has cost. Many, at the height of action, will confess to themselves that the day they begin to be wise will be the day when, free from all care, they contemplate and enjoy the peace of Nature. Few, at least, wholly escape these vain regrets. There is hardly a priest, a monk, or a devotee, who does not at fifty bewail his vow, though he still keep true to it. We scarce conceive a hero without a touch of scepticism; we approve the virtuous man who says now and then, "I have found thee, Virtue, but a name." For he who is too sure of the reward of virtue has no great merit; his good deeds then seem to be merely a good investment. Jesus was himself no stranger to this subtile sentiment; more than once his divine charge seems to have weighed heavily upon him. But, surely, it was not so with Paul. He never had his agony of Gethsemane; and that is one reason why we find him less dear to our hearts. While Jesus had in their loftiest degree the qualities that put him in the highest rank of men, — I mean the gift of a certain buoyancy in his task, of being on a level above it, and not allowing himself to be wholly possessed by it, — Paul was not quite free from the defect which pains us in our sectaries: he believes, if I may so express myself, ponderously. We should choose to see him now and then sitting, like ourselves, weary at the wayside, with a keen sense of the vanity of sharply defined opinions. Marcus Aurelius, the most august representative of our European race, second to none in virtue, did not even know what fanaticism meant. It is not so in the East. Our Western race alone is capable of realising virtue without faith, of combining doubt with hope. Those strong Jewish souls, given over to the terrible intensity of their nature, exempt from the dainty vices of the Greek and Roman civilisation, were like powerful springs always under tension. Even to the end, Paul doubtless saw before him the imperishable crown laid up for him, and like a racer strained the harder as he neared the goal — if we may take the words wrongly ascribed to him[1] as a sort of historic romance in perfect keeping with his spirit and his situation in these last days. He had, too, his intervals of consolation. Onesiphorus of Ephesus, when he came to Rome, found him out, and without shrinking from his prison cell, waited on him and refreshed his heart;[2] while Demas, on the other hand, tired of his unbending severity, left him,[3] so that, as we see, Paul always treats him with a certain coldness.[4]

Did Paul appear before Nero, or rather, the council to which his appeal was made?[5] It is almost certain that he did.[6] Hints (of doubtful value, it is true) speak of a "first defence," at which no friend stood by him, from which he came off successfully, strong in the grace that upheld him; so that he compares himself to one who has been "delivered from a lion's mouth,"[7] — still,

---

[1] 2 Tim. iv. 6–8.   [2] *Ibid.* i. 16, 18.   [3] *Ibid.* iv. 9.
[4] Col. iv. 14, "and so does Demas."
[5] See Dion Cassius, liii. 22.
[6] The writer of Acts, in fact, knew how the case was. He would not have put in Paul's mouth (xxiii. 11; xxvii. 24) a prophecy of what he knew never came to pass. The words, "bear witness" ($\mu\alpha\rho\tau\upsilon\rho\tilde{\eta}\sigma\alpha\iota$), in the former passage, denote a public and formal testimony — as we see by comparing the two clauses of the verse. The same term in Clem. Rom. on 1 Cor. i. 5, compared with Luke xxi. 12, seems to refer to appearing before Nero's council: cf. 1 Pet. ii. 13–17.
[7] 2 Tim. iv. 16, 17.

however, being kept a prisoner.[1] It is probable that his case was dismissed with acquittal at the end of two years of imprisonment.[2] The Roman authority had no apparent interest in condemning him for a sectarian dispute in which it felt no concern. There is, besides, strong reason for believing that before his death he undertook another course of journeys and preachings, — not, however, in those districts of Greece and Asia which were the scenes of his former ministry. The writer of Acts, who surely knew the truth about his later life, would not have lent him language[3] that expressly denied this truth.

Five years before this time, a few months before his arrest, in writing from Corinth to the disciples in Rome, Paul had spoken[4] of his intention to go into Spain. He did not wish, he said, to remain as a teacher among them, but only to stay a little while and enjoy the sight of them on his way to remoter parts. Thus his visit at Rome was to be incidental to a distant ministry, which seems to have been his real object. During his long stay there, however, he seems at times to have changed his purpose as to a journey

---

[1] 2 Tim. i. 8.

[2] Acts xxviii. 30. The language of Acts xxviii. 31 would be strange if Paul had been put to death at the end of the two years. On the other hand, it may be urged that if he had been acquitted the writer — always eager to prove the Romans favourable to Christianity, which was lawful under certain legal precedents — would not have failed to say so, and to continue his account. I shall show hereafter that Clement of Rome, Second Timothy, and the Canon of Muratori assume journeys of Paul subsequent to his captivity. (Comp. Euseb. ii. 22; Jerome, *De viris ill.* 5; Euthalius in Zaccagni, *Coll. monum. vet. eccles. Gr.* p. 531 *et seq.*) These are weak testimonies, no doubt, since they rest on no direct tradition, and imply a theory which assumes the genuineness of "Timothy" and "Titus."

[3] Acts xx. 25.   [4] Rom. xv. 24, 28.

in the West. To the Philippians,[1] and to Philemon at Colossæ,[2] he expresses the hope of visiting them; but this, it is clear, he never did.[3] What, then, was his course on leaving prison? It is natural to suppose that he carried out his first plan, and set out upon his journey as soon as he could. Some strong reasons would lead us to believe that he effected his purpose of going to Spain.[4] This journey had in his mind a high doctrinal importance, and he strongly set his heart upon it.[5] It was his earnest wish that he might report the glad tidings as having reached the extreme West; and so prove the gospel promise to have been

---

[1] Phil. i. 25–27.   [2] Philem. 22.

[3] Acts xx. 25: "Ye shall see my face no more."

[4] 1. The so-called Canon of Muratori, composed at Rome late in the second century, speaks of this as a well-known fact (ll. 37, 38: see the reading of Laurent, *Neutest. Stud.* 108–110, 200). — 2. Clement of Rome (*Epist.* i. 5) says that Paul preached "to the limit of the West," which, written at Rome, can hardly signify Rome itself. True, in the apocryphal epistle of Clement to James at the beginning of the "Homilies," which also was written at Rome, still stronger expressions are used as to Peter, who yet, in the writer's view, had never been farther than Rome (chap. i.). Paul, too (Rom. xvi. 26), asserts that the mystery of Christ has been revealed "to all nations;" though he himself in the same epistle (xv. 19) says that he has preached it only as far as Illyria, — an expression which must be further restricted by 2 Cor. x. 14, 16, where he does not speak of having gone farther west than Corinth. — 3. The follower of Paul who wrote 2 Timothy, thought that after leaving prison he completed his mission by going to all lands yet unvisited (iv. 17), which journeys were not taken towards the East (Acts xx. 25; cf. Epiph. xxvii. 6; Athan. *Epist. ad Drac.* pt. 1; Chrysost. vii. 725; xi. 724; Theodoret in Phil. i. 25; 2 Tim. iv. 17; Hippol. of Thebes, *De duod. apost.* (Gallandi, *Bibl. patrum*, xiv. 117). All these prove little, since they rest, not on tradition, but on an inference from Rom. xv. 28. Eusebius knows nothing of such an episode. In general, the story of Paul's journey to Spain fell into disfavour in the Church opinion of the third and the fourth centuries, because of an *a priori* preference for the view that Peter and Paul died together as martyrs at Rome, which that journey appeared to contradict.

[5] See Ignatius, *Ad Rom.* 2.

fulfilled, since it had been carried to the very ends of the world.[1] This is not the only case in which the extent of his travels was exaggerated in his mind.[2] It was a common belief among the faithful that before Christ's reappearing the kingdom of God must have been preached everywhere.[3] In the apostles' way of speaking, to preach it in a single city was enough to claim that it had been spoken through that country; to preach it to ten persons in a city would justify them in saying that that city had heard it.

If Paul went as far as Spain, he doubtless went by sea. It is just posssible that some port in the south of Gaul received the impress of his footstep. In any case, there remains no appreciable result of that problematic journey to the West.

[1] Revel. xiv. 6. Comp. Melito, *De veritate*, p. xl, 18, 19; *Spicilegium Sol.* vol. 2.
[2] See "Saint Paul," end of chap. xvii.
[3] Matt. xxiv. 14: "This gospel of the kingdom shall be preached in all the world for a witness unto all nations, and then shall the end come."

CHAPTER V.

NEARING THE CRISIS. — A. D. 63.

At the close of Paul's imprisonment we lose at once the guidance of the Acts and the Epistles. We fall into a deep night, in sharp contrast to the clear historic light of the last ten years. The writer of Acts stops short, no doubt to avoid the need of telling the hateful acts of that Roman power which he has treated with such marked respect, and has taken so many occasions to exhibit as favourable to the Christians.[1] This blank silence makes us quite unsure of the events we should most like to know. Happily, Tacitus and the book of Revelation throw a bright ray upon this deep night. Up to this time, Christianity has been the secret of those humble folk to whom it has been their one source of gladness; it is now about to burst upon the stage of history with a clap of thunder whose echoes are far and long.

The apostles, as we have seen, relaxed no effort to moderate the passion of their brethren, stirred by the outrages of which they were the victims. This effort did not always succeed. At sundry times Christians had been condemned, and it had been possible to assert that their sentence was the penalty of some crime or misdemeanour. The rule for such cases — what we may call "the martyr's code" — is laid down by the apostles with excellent good sense. "Is one condemned for

---

[1] See Introduction to "The Apostles."

bearing the name of Christian? Happy is he;[1] Jesus himself has said, 'Ye shall be hated of all men for my name's sake.'"[2] But, to be entitled to count that hate a privilege, one must be without reproach. About this time — partly to calm undue excitement, to check acts of insubordination against public authority, and also to assert his own right of counsel to all the churches — Peter, in imitation of Paul, thought good to write a circular letter of instruction to the Christian bodies of Asia Minor, Jewish and pagan converts alike. Epistles were the order of the day; they served not merely the purpose of correspondence, but made a special form of literature, a class by itself, of little religious treatises.[3] Paul, as we have seen, followed this course in his imprisonment. Each of the apostles, after his example, would have his own epistle, a sample of his style and manner of instruction, containing his favourite maxims, — or, if he did not, others did it for him. This new style of epistle, later called "catholic," did not assume a special message to any one in particular; but it was its writer's own word, his sermon, his ruling thought, his theological "brief" in eight or ten pages. Scraps of phrases might be taken from the homiletic common stock, which by constant borrowing had lost their label, and belonged to nobody.

Mark had just returned from Asia Minor,[4] whither he had gone by Peter's commission, with a note of introduction from Paul;[5] and his journey was perhaps the occasion of a good understanding between the two.

---

[1] 1 Peter iv. 14.

[2] Matt. x. 22; xxiv. 9. Mark xiii. 13. Luke xxi. 12, 17.

[3] See Introduction to "Saint Paul;" and, for the genuineness of 1 Peter, pp. 4, 5, *ante*.

[4] 1 Pet. v. 13.   [5] Col. iv. 10.

It had, further, put Peter in touch with the Eastern churches, and gave him a certain right to address them on points of doctrine. Mark, as usual, served him as amanuensis and interpreter in the drafting of his letter, for we may doubt whether Peter could speak or write either Greek or Latin, his own tongue being Syriac.[1] Mark stood in relations with both Peter and Paul, and this may explain the borrowings in Peter's epistle from the writings of Paul; or, if we are to infer that the writer was Silvanus or Silas,[2] Paul's companion at Philippi, our argument is still stronger. At all events Peter, or his amanuensis, or whoever wrote in his name, had before his eyes both Romans and Ephesians,[3] which are the two "catholic" epistles of Paul, — true circular letters, distributed everywhere. The church at Rome may have had a copy of Ephesians, a recent document, a sort of general formulary of his faith, addressed to a group of churches, and was still surer to have one of Romans. But Paul's other writings, which were more of the nature of private letters, can hardly have been known there. A few less characteristic passages in Peter seem to have been taken from James.[4] Peter had held something of a neutral position in the apostolic controversies; and was he not

---

[1] Euseb. *Demonstr. evang.* iii. 5, 7.

[2] 1 Pet. v. 12.

[3] Comp. 1 Pet. i. 1, 2 with Eph. i. 4–7; —— i. 3: Eph. i. 3; —— i. 14: Eph. ii. 3; Rom. xii. 2; —— i. 21: Rom. iv. 24; —— ii. 5: Rom. xii. 1; —— ii. 6–10: Rom. ix. 25, 32, 33; —— ii. 11: Rom. vii. 23; —— ii. 13: Rom. xiii. 1–4; —— ii. 18: Eph. vi. 5; —— iii. 1: Eph. v. 22; —— iii. 9: Rom. xii. 17; —— iii. 22: Rom. viii. 24; Eph. i. 20; —— iv. 1: Rom. vi. 6; —— iv. 10, 11: Rom. xii. 6–8; —— v. 1: Rom. viii. 18; —— v. 5: Eph. v. 21-24. See Introd. to "Saint Paul."

[4] Comp. 1 Pet. i. 6, 7 with Jas. i. 2; —— i. 24: Jas. i. 10, 11; —— iv. 8: Jas. v. 20; —— v. 5, 9: Jas. iv. 6, 7, 10.

glad of the opportunity to make James and Paul speak, as it were, by one mouth, and so show that the difference between them was only on the surface? As a pledge of friendly feeling, would he not make himself the spokesman of the Pauline ideas — softened, it is true, and without the essential cap-stone of salvation by faith? It is more likely, however, that he knew his own slender literary faculty, and made no scruple of appropriating to his own use the pious phrases which were constantly repeated about him, and, though from different sources, did not formally contradict one another. Happily for him, he seems all his life to have been a very commonplace theologian, and we must not look in his writings for any consistent system.

The radical difference in the habitual point of view between Peter and Paul appears in the first line of the epistle: "Peter, an apostle of Jesus Christ, to the *exiles of the Dispersion* in Pontus, Galatia," etc. Such expressions are wholly Jewish. To the Palestinian mind the family of Israel was made up of two parts, — those who did and those who did not dwell in the Holy Land; those who did not (*Toshabim*) are comprised under the general name of the Dispersion (*Galoutha*). To Peter and to James (i. 1), the Christians, even of pagan origin,[1] are so completely a part of the people of Israel that every church outside of Palestine belongs in their view in the list of "exiles." Jerusalem is the only spot on earth where the Christian can be really at home.[2]

The Epistle of Peter, in spite of its poor style (much

[1] Thus, 1 Pet. i. 14, 18; ii. 9, 10; iii. 6; iv. 3 are evidently addressed to pagan converts.
[2] 1 Pet. ii. 11, 12.

more like Paul's than that of James or Jude), is a touching fragment, reflecting admirably the state of the Christian mind toward the end of Nero's reign. If it is not his own writing (a supposition which the great number of spurious apostolic writings in circulation requires me to mention), at least its composer has faithfully caught the spirit of that time, and it is curiously parallel in many places with the Apocalypse.[1] It is pervaded by a gentle sadness, a resigned confidence. The last days are close at hand.[2] Before them will come trials, from which the elect will come forth purified as by fire. Jesus, whom the faithful love and believe in, never having seen him, will soon appear and fill them with joy. Foreseen by God from all eternity, foretold by the prophets, the mystery of Redemption has been effected by his death and resurrection. The elect, called to a new birth in his blood, are a people of saints, a spiritual temple, a royal priesthood, offering spiritual victims. Thus:—

Beloved, I call upon you as aliens and exiles, to maintain an honourable bearing among the gentiles, keeping yourselves free from carnal desires that war against the soul; so that while men speak against you as ill-doers, they may look upon your honourable works and praise God in the day of his visitation. Be subject by the Lord's help to every ordinance of man: to the Emperor, as sovereign; to governors, as commissioned by him to the punishment of those who do evil and the honour of those who do well. It is God's will that by your right conduct you put to silence the ignorance of foolish men; as freemen, not holding your freedom as a cloak of malice, but as bondmen of God. Honour all men; love the brotherhood; fear God; honour the emperor. If house-servants, be

---

[1] See 1 Pet. iv. 7, 14, 15, 16; v. 13.
[2] *Ibid.* i. 7, 13; iv. 7, 13; v. 1, 10.

submissive to your masters with all dread,—not only to the good and indulgent, but also to those of crooked temper. It is a privilege to suffer pain for one's faith through his conscience toward God, suffering unjustly. For what glory is it if you endure being punished for a fault? but if you endure suffering when you have done well, that is a grateful thing in the sight of God. That is the very thing you were called to; for Christ, too, suffered for your sake, leaving you an example that you should follow in his steps. He did no wrong, and no deceit was found in his mouth; when insulted he did not retort with insult, or threaten when he suffered wrong, but left his defence to Him who judges justly.[1]

The ideal of Christ's Passion — the touching picture of his suffering without anger or complaint — wrought thus early, as we see, a powerful effect upon the Christian conscience. We may doubt whether the story of it was already written. This story grew from time to time by the addition of new incidents: thus the passage in this epistle (ii. 23) seems to show that the prayer of Jesus for his tormentors [2] was not known to the writer. But the main features of it were fixed in the memory of the faithful, and stood before them as perpetual admonitions to long-suffering. One of the leading thoughts among them was that "the Messiah must needs suffer."[3] Jesus, or a true disciple of his, appeared to their imagination under the form of a lamb, brought dumb to the slaughter. This tender lamb, slain in its early days by cruel men, clung to their hearts; they lavished upon it thoughts of pitying affection, a loving tenderness like that of Mary Magdalen at the sepulchre. The innocent victim, with the knife

---

[1] 1 Pet. ii. 11-23.
[2] "Father, forgive them." Luke xxiii. 34.
[3] *Ibid.* xxiv. 26; Acts xvii. 3; xxvi. 23.

plunged in its bleeding flesh, drew tears from all who heard the tale. The expression "Lamb of God," as applied to Jesus, was already in use,[1] and was closely connected with the idea of the paschal lamb.[2] One of the profoundest symbols of Christian art existed in germ in these two images. Such an appeal to fancy, which so touched Saint Francis of Assisi as to draw tears, came from that noble passage of the second Isaiah,[3] which describes the ideal Hebrew Prophet, the "man of sorrows," as a lamb led to the slaughter, or "a sheep that before her shearers is dumb."

This pattern of humble submission Peter would make the rule of conduct in every rank of the Christian community. The elders must govern their flock with gentleness, avoiding all air of command; the younger must submit themselves to the older; above all, the woman, who may not preach, must by the modest charm of her piety be the chief missionary of the faith: —

And do you wives be in like manner submissive to your husbands, so that, if any of them are not persuaded by the word, they may, without the word, be won by beholding your pure and modest life. And your adorning, let it be not the outside braiding of the hair, or wearing of golden ornaments or rich garments, but the hidden beauty of the heart, the indestructible charm of a calm and gentle spirit which is precious in the eye of God. For so those holy women of old, whose hope was in God, adorned themselves, and were dutiful to their own husbands — like Sarah, whose true daughters you

---

[1] See 1 Pet. i. 19; ii. 22-25; Acts viii. 32; John i. 29, 36; Rev. (throughout); Epist. Barn. 5.

[2] John xix. 36; Justin, *Tryph.* 40.

[3] Chap. lii. 13–liii. 12. [The passage is given in full in the "Life of Jesus," pp. 82, 83.]

are as long as you do well and give way to no idle terror (πτόησιν); for she was submissive to Abraham, and called him "my lord." You men, too, deal with your wives considerately, as becomes the stronger or more intelligent towards the weaker, giving them honour as joint-heirs with you of the grace of life. And in fine, be all united in mind, compassionate, with brotherly love, warm-hearted, thinking modestly of yourselves. Do not give back evil for evil, or taunt for taunt; but return words of kindness. For who will do you harm if you follow the example of the good? But even if you suffer for well-doing, count that, too, a privilege.[1]

Hope of the kingdom of God, declared by Christians, gave occasion to misunderstandings,[2] the pagans supposing that they spoke of a political revolution just about to take place. Hence, says Peter, —

Have an answer always ready for any that demand a reason for your hope, but give it with modesty and deference, strong in your good conscience; so that those who speak unjustly of you as criminals may be put to shame. It is better to suffer for right-doing, if God wills it so, than for wrong-doing.[3] Long enough have you wrought the will of the pagans, when you lived in debauchery, wantonness, drunken excesses, revellings, banquetings, and wicked service of false gods. And now they think it strange that you do not plunge into the same excess of profligacy with them, and vilify you, — for which they will give account to One who stands ready to judge the living and the dead.[4] The end of all is drawing near! —

Dear friends, do not be amazed at the fire that is kindled to try you, as if some strange thing had befallen you; but be glad that you are to have a share in Christ's suffering, so that in the revealing of his glory you may rejoice with great joy. But let not one of you suffer as a murderer, or thief, or male-

---

[1] 1 Pet. iii. 1–14.
[2] As we see from Hegesippus in Euseb. iii. 20.
[3] 1 Pet. iii. 15–17.   [4] *Ibid.* iv. 3–7.

factor, or one who spies into another man's affairs. If any one suffers as a Christian, let him not be ashamed, but let him thank God that he shares that name; for the time is come for judgment to begin from God's house, and if it comes to us first, how will it be with those who have not obeyed his gospel? If it is a hard thing to save the good, what will the case be of the impious and wicked? Let those, then, who suffer by God's will in their well-doing, commit their lives to him as a faithful Creator.[1] Humble yourselves, under the strong hand of God, that he may lift you up in his good time. Be sober and keep awake; your adversary, the false accuser, roams about like a roaring lion, seeking whom he may devour. Stand firm against him, strong in the faith; for you know that the same things you endure are suffered also by the brotherhood through the world. After a little suffering, the all-gracious God will fully restore you, strengthen and establish you. His is the glory and strength in every age.[2]

If this epistle is Peter's own, as I am glad to think, it does all credit to his good sense, uprightness, and candour. In it he asserts no authority; speaking to elders, he calls himself a fellow-elder.[3] He puts himself forward only because he has been a witness of Christ's suffering, and hopes to share the glory that will presently be revealed. The letter was carried into Asia by one Silvanus, no doubt the same with the Silvanus or Silas who was Paul's companion, as we may infer from the words "as I suppose" near the close.[4] In this case he was selected as one already known to the disciples in Asia Minor through his journey there with Paul. To these distant churches Peter sends the greetings of Mark in a form which assumes that he too is not a stranger to them.[5]

[1] 1 Pet. iv. 12–19.   [2] *Ibid.* v. 6–11.   [3] *Ibid.* ver. 1.
[4] *Ibid.* ver. 12.   [5] 1 Pet. v. 13; cf. Col. iv. 10.

The letter ends with the customary salutations. The church in Rome is indicated by the words "elect at Babylon." The sect was closely watched. Too plain a letter, if intercepted, might bring disastrous consequences. To put any suspicions of the police on a false track, Peter chose to indicate Rome by the name of the old capital of Asiatic impiety, whose symbolic meaning would be well understood, and would presently furnish, in the Apocalypse, the main theme of an entire poem.[1]

[1] See Euseb. ii. 15: 2; comp. Rev. xiv. 8; xvi. 19; xvii. 5; xviii. 2, 10, 21; *Carm. Sibyll.* v. 142, 158; Midrash, *Shir hasshirim* rabba, i. 6; Commodian, *Instr.* acrost. xli. 12; Apocalypse of Esdras, i. 1, 28, 32. It is unlikely that Babylon on the Euphrates is meant in 1 Pet. v. 13. Christianity in the first century did not reach out in the direction of Babylonia. Moreover, a few years before the date of this epistle, the Jews had been expelled from Babylon, and had even been compelled to abandon Seleucia and Ctesiphon for Nehardea and Nisibe (Josephus, *Antiq.* xviii. 9: 8, 9). In the third century there were no longer any *minim* at Nehardea (Babyl. Talm. *Pesachim*, 56 a). Such symbolic names are extremely common amongst the Jews (Esther iii. 1, 10; viii. 3, 5; Rev. xi. 8). In like manner Rome is sometimes called "Nineveh" (Buxtorf, *Lex. chald.* col. 221); the Roman empire is "Edom;" the Christians are "Cuthim," and the Slavs, "Chanaan." (See chap. ii., *ante.*)

CHAPTER VI.

CONFLAGRATION OF ROME. — A. D. 64.

THE violent madness of Nero at length reached a crisis in the most shocking catastrophe which the world had ever known. An invincible necessity had put all power at that time into a single hand, — that of the heir of Cæsar's great legendary name. Any other rule was then impossible. Commonly the provinces found themselves well content under it; but yet it hid an enormous danger. If the Cæsar of the day should lose his wits, if all the veins in his poor head, disturbed by a power till then unheard-of, should burst at once, there followed insanity without a name: the world was given over to a monster. There was no way to drive him out: his German guard, having everything to lose if he should fall, raged furiously about him; the wild boar, driven to bay, showed his tusks and fought with desperation. In Nero's case, it was a thing at once frightful and grotesque, imposing and absurd. As he was, in his way, a man of letters, his insanity took in the main a literary turn. The dreams of all ages, all poems, all legends, — Bacchus and Sardanapalus, Ninus and Priam, Troy and Babylon, Homer and the stale poetry of the day, — danced a chaotic dance in one poor brain. It was the brain of a wretched artist, who took himself very seriously, to whom chance had given the power to realise all his vagaries.[1] Imagine, then, a man about as level-headed as the heroes in a drama of Victor Hugo, — one to figure in a carnival, a mixture of madman, dunce, and actor, — clothed with resistless power, and charged with the administration of the world. He had not the black-hearted malignity of Domitian,[2] the love of wickedness for its own sake; nor was he a monster of extravagance, like Caligula. He was a painstaking stage-hero, an operatic emperor, music-mad, trembling before the pit, and making that tremble too,[3] — what a commonplace citizen of our day would be, crazed by the reading of modern poets and fancying himself bound in every-day life to imitate the characters of some romantic fiction.[4]

Now, government is eminently a practical matter. Romanticism in it is wholly out of place. It is at home in the world of art, but in the world of action it is quite the opposite. In the education of a prince, it is fatal above all things. In this view, Seneca did his imperial pupil much more harm by his bad literary taste than good by his fine philosophy. Seneca was a man of brilliant parts, of talent beyond the common, — a man much to be respected in spite of more than one blot, but completely spoiled by a declamatory and literary vanity, incapable of sound feeling or of reasoning except in formal phrases. By dint of training his pupil to express things he had never thought, and to put together strings of sublime words in advance of any meaning, he made of him a thin-skinned comedian, a vile rhetorician, spouting sentiments of humanity

---

[1] Suet. *Nero*, 20, 49.   [2] *Ibid.* 20, 39; Jos. *Antiq.* xx. 8: 3.
[3] Suet. *Nero*, 23, 24.
[4] "*Han d'Islande*" and "*Les Burgraves*," the titles of a tale and a drama of Victor Hugo. — ED.

when he was sure of having listeners. The old pedagogue saw deeply into the evil of the time, his pupils' and his own, when he exclaimed, in one of his sincere moments, "We are sick with a flux of words" (*Litterarum intemperantia laboramus.*[1]).

These absurdities in Nero seemed harmless at first; the trained ape watched himself a while, and kept the posture which his masters had taught him. He displayed no special cruelty till after the death of his mother Agrippina; but that vice soon possessed him wholly. Hereafter, every year is marked by some new crime. Burrhus disappears, and everybody thinks he was put to death by Nero; the innocent Octavia passes away from the world, steeped in calumny; Seneca keeps in his retreat, expecting arrest at any hour, brooding upon dreaded tortures, hardening his thought by meditation on the scourge and axe, exerting himself to prove that death is a deliverance.[2] When Tigellinus is master of everything, the revel is at its height. Every day Nero proclaims that Art is the only thing to be taken seriously; that all virtue is a lie; that the real gentleman is he who shamelessly avows his shame; that the great man is he who can intelligently abuse all, ruin all, squander all.[3] A man of virtue is to him a hypocrite, a conspirator, a dangerous fellow, above all, a rival to himself; and when he discovers in any man some shocking turpitude that seems to prove his theory, he feels a new delight. The political dangers that grow from inflation, and that vile spirit of rivalry which was from the beginning the worm at the root of Latin civilisation, begin to be laid bare. This third-

---

[1] Letters to Lucilius, cvi. 12.   [2] See *Consolatio ad Marciam*, 20.
[3] Suet. *Nero*, 20, 29, 30; Dion Cassius, lxi. 4, 5.

rate actor has succeeded in giving himself the power of life and death over his auditory; this amateur poet can threaten with torture those who do not applaud his verse. A monomaniac, tipsy with a glimmer of literary fame, who turns the fine sayings he has learned by heart into cannibal jests,—an ugly-tempered street-Arab, bidding for cheers from would-be wits of the pavement,—such is the sovereign under whom the empire groans. Extravagance like this had never been seen before. Oriental despots, terrible but austere, did not break out into these crazy fits of laughter, these debauches of diseased artistry. Caligula's madness had been short-lived; it was but a fit, and at bottom he was a jester with a modicum of real wit. But Nero's insanity, on the contrary, which in general was only silly, was now and then frightfully tragical. Most shocking of all it was to see him, in his own declamatory style, make stage-play of his remorse, turning it into capital for his poetry. In his melodramatic fashion, he would cry out that he was haunted by the Furies, and would spout Greek verses on the guilt and the torture of parricides. Some evil deity seemed to have created him in jest, in order to entertain himself with the horrid masquerade of a human creature in which every spring should creak,—the hideous spectacle of an epileptic world, like what we might imagine of a riotous dance of apes on the Congo, or the bloody orgies of a king of cannibals.

At such a spectacle, all the world seemed to be taken dizzy. A club was got up by certain detestable bucks, called "the Knights of Augustus," who made it their business to cheer all the emperor's mad pranks, and contrive for him farces suited to night prowlers of the streets.¹ In due time, we shall find an emperor a graduate of this school.² A dirty flood of ill-flavoured imaginations, shallow fancies, jests meant for comic, a sickening slang like that in our cheapest newspapers, discharged itself over Rome and made a fashion there.³ Caligula had already invented this baleful style of imperial stage-hero; and Nero ostentatiously took him for a model.⁴ It was not enough to drive chariots in the circus, to rasp his throat as a public singer, and make provincial tours on the operatic stage:⁵ he must exhibit himself fishing with golden nets drawn in by purple cords;⁶ or himself placing in the theatre his cliques to lead the applause; or assigning to himself all the prizes of the old Greek games; or planning festivities such that the like was never heard of; or playing upon the stage in parts without a name.⁷

These insane freaks were in great part due to the wretched taste of the time, and the extravagant rank assigned to the declaimer's art, which aimed at the prodigious, and revelled in monstrosities.⁸ In a word, there was everywhere lack of sincerity; a style without savour, like Seneca's in his tragedies; capability to paint feelings that are not felt; the art of talking like a man of virtue without being one. For the grand style we find the loud and big; art is utterly dispro-

---

[1] Pliny, *Hist. Nat.* xiii. 22: 43. [2] Suetonius, *Otho*, 2.

[3] Tacitus, *Ann.* xiv. 14–16. See in Suetonius specimens of Nero's jests, to show the sort of pleasantry he affected. Comp. Tac. *Ann.* xiv. 57; Dion Cass. lxii. 14; lxiii. 8.

[4] Suet. *Nero*, 30.

[5] Tac. *Ann.* xv. 33, 34; Suet. *Nero*, 20, 22, 24, 25.

[6] Euseb. *Chron. Ann.* 6 of Nero.

[7] Suet. *Nero*, 11, 20, 21, 23–25, 27, 30; Tac. *Ann.* xv. 37 *et seq.*; Dion Cass. lxi. 17–21; lxii. 15.

[8] Juvenal, *Sat.* i. *ad. init.*; Martial, *Spectacula*.

portioned; it is the age of colossal statues, of materialising art, theatrical, falsely pathetic, of which we have a masterpiece in the *Laocoön*,[1] — an admirable statue, no doubt, but in posture too like a leading tenor vociferating a solo, all the real emotion being from the bodily pain it shows. People were no longer satisfied with the purely moral suffering in the *Children of Niobe*, radiant with beauty; they craved an image of physical agony, and took delight in it, as the seventeenth century enjoyed the realistic sculpture of Puget.[2] Capacity of sensation was exhausted; the essential thing in Art had come to be such coarse devices as the Greeks would have scarce admitted in what was meant only for the popular eye. The people were literally crazed with spectacles, — not serious exhibitions, or ennobling tragedies, but sensational plays and fantastic shows. A degraded taste for "living pictures" had come in vogue. It was no longer enough for the imagination to enjoy the exquisite creations of the poets. The old myths must be represented "in the flesh," whatever might be in them most ferocious or obscene; people went into ecstasy before the actors' attitudes and groups, seeking in them the effects of statuary. The shout of fifty thousand spectators, crowded in one vast bowl, and mutually heated, was so intoxicating a thing that the sovereign himself would envy the charioteer, the singer, or the actor; the glory of the circus or the theatre

---

[1] Without pretending to decide on the date of this famous group, we may note that about this time it came to be regarded as a masterpiece without rival. See Pliny, *Hist. Nat.* xxxvi. 5: 4; Overbeck, *Die antiken Schriftquellen zur Gesch. der bild. Künste*, 391, 392; H. Brunn, *Gesch. der griech. Künstler*, i. 469, 495 *et seq.*

[2] Whose most famous work represented the athlete Milo, caught in the cleft of an oak, and attacked by a lion. — ED.

was the most glorious of all. Not one of the emperors who had a single weak spot in his head could withstand the temptation to gather wreaths from these lamentable games. Caligula had left on the stage the little wit he ever had, and would pass whole days in the theatre among the idlers;[1] and at a later day Commodus and Caracalla contested with Nero the palm of insanity. Laws had to be enacted to forbid senators and knights entrance upon the arena, to wrestle like gladiators or fight against wild beasts. The prize-ring came to be the centre of life, — as if the rest of the world were made only to furnish forth a Roman holiday. New devices were constantly brought forward, each more extravagant than the last, composed and directed by the imperial conductor. The people went from one festival to the next; their talk was only of the last day's spectacle, while waiting for the one promised them to-day;[2] and they ended with a sincere attachment to a prince who made their life an endless bacchanal. We cannot doubt the popularity which Nero won by these shameful means; it is proof enough that after his death Otho could gain the sovereignty by reviving Nero's memory, by imitating him, and by reminding men that he too had been one of the exquisites of his company.

It cannot be said, in strictness, that the poor wretch was void of heart, or of all feeling for the good and beautiful. Far from being incapable of kindliness, he would often show himself "a good fellow;" and it was just this that made him cruel, for he craved to be

---

[1] Suet. *Caius*, 18.
[2] See Martial's "Epigrams," especially the *Liber de Spectaculis*, which at some points may be likened to our cheap newspapers.

loved and admired for his own sake, and was angry with those who did not feel so towards him. His nature was jealous, sensitive, and an act of petty treason would put him beside himself. His deeds of vengeance were mostly — as with Lucan and Vestinus — against those admitted to his nearer circle, who had taken advantage of the familiarity he encouraged to tease him with their wit; for he had a sense of his own absurdities, and was afraid of letting them be seen. His chief ground of hating Thraseas was that he could not win his love,[1] and Lucan's grotesque citation of a bad half line was his destruction.[2] Without ever denying himself the services of one Galvia Crispinilla,[3] he was really fond of several women; and these women — Poppæa, Acte — loved him. After Poppæa's death, brought about by his brutality, he had a sort of sensual remorse almost pathetic: he was long under the dominion of a tender sentiment, and sought for anything that resembled her, hunting even for inanimate substitutes.[4] Poppæa, on her part, had a regard for him which so distinguished a woman would not have confessed for an ordinary man. A lady of the court, in the highest society, skilled in enhancing the attractions of rare beauty and supreme elegance[5] by the arts of a studied modesty, she kept in her heart through all her crimes a religious instinct which inclined

---

[1] "I wish Thraseas [whom he put to death a little after] was but as great a lover of me as he is a most upright judge." Plutarch's "Political Precepts," in his *Morals* (Engl. transl. v. 128). Comp. Tac. *Ann.* xv. 68; xvi. 22; Dion Cass. lxii. 26.

[2] Suet., fragm. of *Lucani vita:* "*Sub terris tonuisse putes.*"

[3] *Magistra libidinum;* Tac. *Hist.* i. 78; comp. Dion Cass. lxiii. 12.

[4] Dion Cass. lxii. 28; lxiii. 12, 13; Plin. xxxvii. 3: 12.

[5] Tac. *Ann.* xiii. 45. See her bust in the Capitol (No. 17) and that in the Vatican (No. 408).

her toward Judaism.[1] Among women, Nero seems to have been very susceptible to a charm that comes from a certain mingling of piety and coquetry. Those alternations of freedom in manner with a proud reserve, — that way of never going abroad except with face partly veiled (*ne satiaret adspectum, vel quia sic decebat*), — her winning speech, above all, that touching regard for her own beauty, such that when once her mirror showed her a few specks she fell into a womanish fit of desperation, and wished to die,[2] — all this strongly impressed the fancy of the young debauchee, on whom the show of modesty had the force of a mighty illusion. We shall soon see how Nero, playing his part as Antichrist, created, as it were, a new artistic sense, and was the first to gloat over the spectacle of Christian maiden modesty unveiled. Poppæa, at once voluptuous and devout, held him in a mood of like emotions. The conjugal reproach which caused her death[3] seems to show that even in her closer relations with Nero she never quite lost a certain pride which was manifest in their first intimacy.[4] As for Acte, if she was not a Christian, as has been thought, at least she was not far from being one. She was a slave of Asiatic birth, — that is, from a country with which the Christians at Rome had daily intercourse. It has often been observed that the handsome freedwomen

---

[1] Josephus (*Antiq.* xx. 8: 11) says that she was "pious" (θεοσεβής); cf. *Life*, 3. What Tacitus (*Ann.* xvi. 6; *Hist.* v. 5) says of her funeral wholly conforms to this (comp. Pliny, xii. 18: 41); and he notes her inclination to diviners (*Hist.* i. 22).

[2] Dion Cass. lxii. 28.

[3] Suet. *Nero*, 35. "She reproached him for returning late from his charioteering."

[4] Tac. *Ann.* xiii. 46.

who had most admirers were much given to Oriental religions; while Ovid, Propertius, and the pictures at Pompeii show how much the Iris-worship was in fashion in that social class. Acte always kept her simple tastes, and never quite withdrew herself from the little slave-circle she had belonged to.[1] She first made part of the Annæan family, about which we have seen the Christians group and gather; and under the influence of Seneca she played, in the most appalling and tragic circumstances, a part which, slave as she was, we can call by no other name than honourable.[2] This poor child,[3] humble, gentle, shown on many monuments as surrounded by a group of people bearing names almost Christian,—Claudia, Felicula, Stephanus, Crescens, Phœbe, Onesimus, Thallus, Artemas, Helpis,[4] —was the first love of Nero when a youth. She was faithful to him till death; and we shall see her again at Phaon's villa, piously discharging the last duties to that poor corpse from which all else shrank in horror.

And, strange as it may seem, it is yet conceivable that women may have loved him. He was, if you will, a monster, a creature of absurdities, ill made-up, a misshapen product of nature; but he was not a vulgar monster. One might say that destiny, by an odd caprice, had chosen to realise in him that monster figured by the logicians as the "goat-stag,"—a being of two natures, queer, incoherent, generally hateful, but in some moods pitiable. An emotional woman will be governed more by sympathy and personal liking than by strict rules of moral judgment; a trifle of good

[1] Tac. *Ann.* xiii. 46. [2] *Ibid.* 13; xiv. 2.
[3] *Ibid.* xiii. 12, 13, 46; Suet. *Nero,* 28; Dion Cass. lxi. 7.
[4] Fabretti, *Inscr.* 124–126; Orelli, 735, 2885; Henzen, 5412, 5413.

looks, with good-nature ever so violently distorted, will be enough to turn her indignation into pity. She is, above all, indulgent toward an artist intoxicated by his art, a Byron, slave to his fancy, who frankly puts in practice his poetic creed. When Acte laid Nero's bloody corpse in the tomb of the Domitii, she doubtless wept over the profaning of natural gifts known to her alone; and at the same hour, as we may believe, more than one Christian woman named him in her prayers.

Though of inferior talent, he had some of an artist's gifts: he carved and painted well; his verses were good, spite of a certain schoolboy emphasis,[1] and, whatever may have been said, the verses were his own, — Suetonius saw his autograph drafts of them, filled with erasures.[2] He was the first to discover the superb landscape of Subiaco, and made himself a charming summer-retreat there. His understanding was clear and keen in the observation of natural objects; he had a fondness for experiments, new inventions, and works of ingenuity;[3] he wished to understand the causes of things, and detected very shrewdly the tricks of pretended magic, as well as the hollowness of the religions of the day.[4] The biographer just cited has told how the passion for a singer's vocation was roused in him.[5] He owed his instruction to Terpnos, the most famous harpist of his time. He was seen passing whole nights by the music-master's side, studying his manner, absorbed in listening, panting in suspense, intoxicated,

---

[1] Suet. *Lucan.*   [2] Suet. *Nero*, 52.
[3] Seneca. *Quæst. nat.* vi. 8; Pliny, xi. 49: 109; xix. 3: 15; xxxvii. 3: 11.
[4] Suet. *Nero*, 56; Pliny, xxx. 2: 5; Pausanias, ii. 37: 5.
[5] Suet. *Nero*, 20.

eagerly inhaling the air of that new world open to him at the touch of a great artist. This, too, was the source of his disgust for the Romans, who were in general poor judges in matters of art; and of his liking for the Greeks, whom alone he thought competent to appreciate him, and for the Orientals, who would split their throats in loud applause. From this time forth the only glory he would admit was the glory of an artist. A new life woke in him. His rank as emperor he no longer thought of; to deny his genius was high treason; the enemies of Rome were those who did not join in the applause.

His affectation of being master of fashion in everything was certainly ridiculous; still, we must own there was more state-policy in it than we might think. The emperor's first duty — such was the baseness of the time — was to amuse the people. Above all else the sovereign must be a great organizer of festivals; the head entertainer must be brought to pay his debt in person — as we see by the complaints made against Galba.[1] Many of the extravagances charged against Nero were blamable only from the point of view of the old Roman manners and the strict code of deportment that had hitherto prevailed. That masculine society was offended at seeing the emperor in an embroidered dressing-gown at an audience of the senate; or in scandalous undress at a military review, without a belt, and with a muffler about his neck to protect his voice.[2] True Romans were justly indignant at the invasion of Oriental fashions; but, inevitably, the older and more outworn civilisation prevailed over the younger in

[1] Suet. *Galba*, 12, 13.
[2] Dion Cass. lxxiii. 13, 20, 25; Suet. *Nero*, 51.

virtue of its very corruption. Antony and Cleopatra[1] had dreamed long ago of an Oriental empire; Nero himself[2] had listened to hints of a royalty like that, and, when driven to bay, his thought was to apply for the governorship of Egypt. Every year, from Augustus to Constantine, shows us some new step of advance in the conquest of the Latin by the Greek.

We must remember, too, that insanity was "in the air." If we except that admirable core of aristocratic society which came to the throne with Nerva and Trajan, the ablest men made, as it were, a game of life — such levity was in the general mind. The one who represents and sums up the quality of the time — the "honest man" in this reign of transcendent iniquity — is Petronius.[3] He gave the day to sleep, the night to business and amusement. He was not one of those fast-livers who ruin themselves in vulgar debauchery, but a voluptuary thoroughly versed in the science of pleasure. The natural ease and free play of his speech and acts gave him a most winning air of frankness. While proconsul in Bithynia, and afterward as consul, he showed the finest talent of administration. When he returned to vice, or the affected display of it, he found his way to the inmost circle of Nero's court, and came to be sovereign judge of taste, — *arbiter elegantiarum;* nothing was delightful or in good form without his verdict. The base Tigellinus, who ruled by depravity and malice, dreaded a rival, his own superior in the arts of pleasure, and succeeded in destroying him. Petronius had too high self-respect to contend with this despicable wretch; but still he

---

[1] Horace, *Od.* i. 37. [2] Suet. 40; Tac. *Ann.* xv. 36.
[3] Tac. xvi. 18–20.

would not quit life too abruptly. After opening his own veins he closed them again; then opened them anew, chatting of trifles with his friends and listening to their talk — not on the immortality of the soul and philosophic theories, but of songs and ballads; taking just that time to reward certain of his slaves and chastise others; and so, reclining at his table, he fell asleep. This all-accomplished sceptic, of cool and polished style, is the probable author of a romance (the *Satyricon*) of wonderful spirit and point, and at the same time of a refined dissoluteness, which makes a perfect mirror of Nero's time. Not every one who will can be king of fashion. There is a mastery in the elegances of life, below the realm of science or morality. The banquet of the universe would lack completeness if the world were full only of fanatics, iconoclasts, and virtuous heavyweights.

It may not be denied that the taste for art was keen and sincere among the men of this evil time. Few things of beauty were now made, but the finest of elder time were eagerly sought. Petronius, an hour before he died, broke in pieces a murrine vase, that Nero might not own it.[1] Objects of art were held at fabulous prices; Nero was madly fond of them.[2] Ravished by the idea of grandeur, but with the worst judgment possible, he schemed fantastic palaces, and vast cities like Babylon, Thebes, or Memphis. The imperial dwelling on the Palatine — the old house of Tiberius — had been quite a modest one, essentially a private house till the reign of Caligula, as we find in recent excavations. Caligula, who is to be regarded as the founder of a school in government in which Nero has

[1] Pliny, xxxvii. 2: 7.   [2] Suet. *Nero*, 47.

been too easily held to have no master, considerably enlarged it;[1] and Nero, affecting to find himself crowded in it, jested without stint at his predecessors who had been content with so narrow quarters. He accordingly blocked out in cheap materials a residence as big as a Chinese or Assyrian palace, calling it a "transitional" structure, which he intended soon to make permanent. It was a whole world in itself. With porches three miles long, parks that made a pasturage for flocks, enclosures fenced in for solitude, lakes amid a perspective of fantastic towns, with vineyards and forests, it covered a space vaster than the Louvre, Tuileries, and Champs-Élysées put together,[2] reaching from the Palatine to the gardens of Mæcenas on the summit of the Esquiline, near where is now the church of St. Eusebius. It was a real fairy-land, in which the engineers, Severus and Celer, had surpassed themselves. Nero wished to carry out his plan in such fashion that it should be called the "Golden House." He was amused by talk of insane undertakings that should make his name immortal.[3] Above all, his mind was filled with schemes about Rome, which he wished to rebuild from bottom to top, and have it called Neropolis.

Rome, for a century past, was coming to be the wonder of the world, equalling in grandeur the ancient capitals of the East. Its edifices were solid, strong, and handsome; but the streets looked mean to people of fashion, for the rage was every day more and more for structures essentially vulgar, built for ornament,

---

[1] Suet. *Caius*, 22.
[2] Suet. *Nero*, 31; Tac. *Ann.* xv. 39, 42; Pliny, xxxiii. 3: 16; xxxvi. 15: 24.
[3] Suet. 16, 31; Tac. xv. 42, 46; Pliny, iv. 4: 5; xv. 6: 8.

aiming at general effect, such as delights a cockney's eye, and hunting up a thousand petty fancies unknown to the ancient Greeks. Nero was the leader of this fashion. The Rome of his imagination was something like our new Paris, — an artificial city, built to order of the higher powers, aiming in its plan to catch the admiring eye of strangers and provincials. The young madcap intoxicated himself with these tasteless and unsound plans. He longed, too, for the sight of something strange, — some great showy spectacle, worthy of an artist; something that would stand as a monument to mark the era of his reign. "Till my day," he would say, "no one knew on what a scale a prince can work."[1] All these inward promptings of a disordered fancy seemed to take form in an astounding event which had momentous consequences affecting the subject of our story.

The incendiary mania is contagious, and is often on the verge of a true insanity; and hence there is great peril in waking it in weak brains where it may be slumbering. It was characteristic of Nero that he could not resist a fixed idea, however criminal. The Burning of Troy — a game he used to play in childhood[2] — took complete and terrible possession of his fancy.[3] One of the pieces represented in one of his festivals was the *Conflagration* of Afranius, in which an outburst of flame was exhibited on the stage.[4] In one

---

[1] Suet. *Nero*, 37.

[2] Such games were much in fashion at the time. See Dion Cassius, xlviii. 20; liv. 26; Suet. *Jul.* 39; *Aug.* 43; *Tib.* 6; *Caius*, 18; *Claudius*, 21; *Nero*, 7; Servius, *ad Æn.* v. 602; Persius, i. 4, 51.

[3] Suet. *Nero*, 7, 11, 22, 47; Tac. *Ann.* xv. 39; Dion Cass. lxii. 16, 18, 29.

[4] Suet. *Nero*, 11.

of his fits of self-willed fury against fortune, Nero cried out, "O happy Priam, who could see with his own eyes the destruction of his empire and his capital city both at once!"[1] On another occasion, hearing recited a Greek verse from the *Bellerophon* of Euripides, to this effect:

"When I am dead let earth and fire mingle!"

"No, not that," said he, "but while I am alive!"[2] It is no doubt an exaggeration to say that Nero set fire to Rome purely to have a repetition of the Burning of Troy;[3] for, as will appear, he was away from the city when the fire broke out. Still, the tradition is not without ground; for that demon of corrupt drama, which had laid hold upon him, was — as with scoundrels of every time — a principal agent in the shocking crime.

On the nineteenth of July, A. D. 64, a fire broke out at Rome with extraordinary violence,[4] beginning near the *Porta Capena*, in that part of the *Circus Maximus* near mounts Palatine and Cœlius. This district contained numerous shops full of combustible matters, in which the flames spread with prodigious rapidity. Thence it swept round the Palatine, devastated the *Velabrum*,[5]

---

[1] Dion Cass. lviii. 23; lxii. 16.

[2] Suet. 38; Dion Cass. lviii. 23.

[3] Euseb. *Chron. Ann.* 65; Orosius, vii. 7. The saying reported by Dion Cassius (lxii. 16) was spoken, no doubt, in a rolling volley of literary paradoxes, and should not be too strictly taken. Conversations among bright wits, reported by servants or dull people listening at the keyhole, may undergo strange transformations.

[4] Tac. *Ann.* xv. 38–44, 52; Suet. *Nero*, 31, 38, 39; *Vesp.* 8; Dion Cass. lxii. 16–18; Pliny, xvii. 1: 1; Euseb. *Chron. Ann.* 65; Orelli, *Inscr.* 736, which seems quite genuine. Sulp. Severus (ii. 29) closely follows Tacitus; Orosius (vii. 7) chiefly Suetonius.

[5] The Temple of Hercules, spoken of by Tacitus (*Ann.* xv. 41), was on the site of the present church of St. Anastasius; the *Regia* and temple of Vesta were also at the foot of the Palatine.

the Forum, and the *Carinæ* (the consular quarter spoken of by Suetonius). It then ran over the hills, did great damage on the Palatine,[1] and went down into the hollows, where it fed for six days and seven nights upon the close-packed quarters pierced by crooked lanes. A vast mass of stone buildings at the foot of the Esquiline (at the foot of the present street St. John Lateran) checked the conflagration for a while; then it rekindled and lasted three days more. Many of the population perished. Of the fourteen "regions" composing the city, three were wholly destroyed, seven others were reduced to blackened ruins. Rome was a city prodigiously close-built, with a population extremely dense: we may compare it to certain districts of Naples, where the poor live in the open air and only go indoors to sleep, eight or ten in a room. The disaster was frightful, such as had never before been seen.

Nero was at Antium when the fire broke out, and did not return to the city till it came near his temporary palace. It was impossible to do anything to stay the flames. The imperial houses of the Palatine, the "transitional" house itself, with the outlying buildings and the entire quarter thereabout, were buried under the ruins.[2] Nero evidently made no great effort to save his own dwelling. He was transported with the sublime horror of the spectacle. It was afterwards said that, mounted upon a tower, he gazed at the

---

[1] Tac. *Ann.* xv. 39, 41; Dion Cass. lxii. 18. The temple of Jupiter Stator was on the Palatine. The fire probably caught upon the hill by the strip (a sort of isthmus) which, near the Arch of Titus, joins the Palatine level with the *Summa Sacra Via.*

[2] For the extent of the conflagration see Noël des Vergers, art. *Nero*, in *Nouvelle biogr. générale*, xxxvii. 728-730.

conflagration; and that here, in stage costume, lyre in hand, he sang the destruction of Troy, in the impressive measure of the antique elegy.[1]

That was a legend, which grew out of a series of exaggerated rumours of the time. But a universal belief, from the very first, held that the conflagration had been ordered by Nero, or at all events started by him afresh when it was just dying out.[2] Persons of

[1] The story, as told by Tacitus (xv. 39), says nothing of this circumstance, while he speaks, it is true, of a rumour that Nero during the fire sang the ruin of Troy "in his private theatre." This, if true, could only have been at Antium — which greatly hurts the story. Tacitus evidently mentions the report without believing it. The accounts of Suetonius and Dion Cassius do not agree in details: one puts the scene on the Esquiline, the other on the Palatine. The incident was derived, no doubt, from the poem called *Troica*, composed by Nero, and publicly recited by him the next year, which carried a double meaning like Lucan's *Catacausmos Iliacus*, written about this time (Dion Cass. lxii. 29; Servius, *ad Æn.* v. 370; *Georg.* iii. 36; Persius, i. 123; Statius, *Silv.* ii. 7: 58-61; Juv. viii. 221; Petronius, p. 105). The scandal of such allusions struck the public, and caused it to be said that "Nero played the lyre over the ruins of his country." (The expression *patriæ ruinis* is in Tac. xv. 42.) Thus the phrase became an anecdote, and — as a legend commonly grows from a true saying and a right feeling, converted into fact with some violence done to time and place — the song *Troica* was referred to the time of the catastrophe. The story was a hard one for those who like Tacitus knew that Nero was then at Antium, and thus, to make it more consistent, they assumed it to be "in his private theatre;" while those who did not know that he was at Antium through the greater part of the burning carried the tale to Rome, each choosing the most effective spot. What is now shown as the so-called *torre di Nerone* dates from the Middle Age.

[2] Suetonius (*Nero*, 38), Dion Cassius (lxxii. 16), and Pliny (xvii. 1: 1), state this positively; Tacitus (xv. 38) expresses no opinion, but farther on (xv. 67) says that "the conflagration" was charged to Nero as a notorious crime. In his last days, says Suetonius (*Nero*, 43). he wished to burn Rome again. In such reports, no doubt, something is to be allowed to popular gossip or ill-will. What makes the charge a grave one is that it is hard to see how so enormous a fire could have made headway in a city like Rome, mostly built of stone, without some outside help. An inscription of Orelli, No. 736, shows the exceptional character of the conflagration. The great fires in the times of Titus and Commodus were nothing like it.

Nero's household were thought to have been seen setting fire at various spots; in some localities these were men pretending to be drunk, and it seemed to spring up of itself in many places at once. Tales were told of men having been seen while it was burning — soldiers and watchmen appointed to extinguish it — who would put the brands together for fresh burning, and hinder the efforts made to confine the flames; and this with a threatening mien, as if they were set to execute official orders. Possibly they were criminals, who made things worse in the hope of plunder. Great stone structures near the emperor's palace, where he wanted more ground, were demolished as in a time of siege or assault; and, where the fire started afresh, it began with buildings that belonged to Tigellinus. Suspicion was further strengthened by the fact that, when the fire was over, under pretence of clearing off the ruins at his own expense, to leave the ground free to its owners, Nero undertook to carry away the rubbish, so effectively that no one was allowed to go near. It was still worse when they saw him making a handsome profit from the general disaster; when they saw the new palace, Nero's "Golden House," long the plaything of his insane fancy, rising on the site of his old "transitional" residence, widened out by spaces which the conflagration had swept clean.[1] He had designed, they thought, to clear the ground for this new palace, to make an excuse for the reconstruction he had long set his heart on, and to secure funds for it by seizing on the ruins of the conflagration; in short, to satiate that crazy vanity which made him long for a new Rome to build, that it might date from him and bear his name.

[1] Suet. *Nero*, 31, 38.

Everything goes to show that this was no calumny. The true thing about Nero is hardly ever the likely thing. Needless to say that, with all the resources of his power, there were simpler ways to get the ground he wanted than to burn it clean. The emperor's power, looked at one way, might seem boundless; but in another direction it quickly found its limits, when it ran against the habits or prejudices of a people excessively conservative of its religious landmarks. Rome was full of sanctuaries, holy places, shrines, buildings, which no statute of conveyance could possibly put out of sight. The mighty Julius, and other emperors besides, had found their plans of public improvement, especially as to rectifying the channel of the Tiber, crossed by this hindrance. To carry out his mad schemes, a conflagration furnished the only means Nero could employ. The condition of things was like that in Constantinople and other great Moslem towns, where improvements are cut short by mosques and clerical edicts. In the East, conflagration is but a weak expedient; since, after it is over, the soil itself remains sacred as a sort of inalienable patrimony of true believers. But at Rome, where sanctity belonged to the building, not the ground, the course taken proved effectual. A new Rome, with straight wide streets, was soon rebuilt on the emperor's plans, helped out by the bounties which he offered.

It was an insult to every honest man in the city. The choicest antiquities of Rome, houses that had belonged to famous captains of old, still decorated with the spoils of triumph, objects the most revered, trophies, antique votive tablets, temples of highest sanctity, everything visible that told of the ancient Roman worship, had gone out of sight. The city was, as it were, clad in mourning for its old memories and sacred legends. In vain would Nero relieve at his own charge the miseries he had caused; in vain point out that, taking all into the account, it was a mere process of cleansing and sanitation, — that the new city would be far better than the old. No true Roman would believe him. All for whom a city is something more than a pile of stones were cut to the heart; a blow was struck at the nation's conscience. This temple, built by Evander — that other, by Servius Tullius — here, the sacred precinct of Jupiter Stator — Numa's palace, the religious home of the Roman people — those monuments, telling of so many victories; those masterpieces of Hellenic art, — how repair the loss of those? What, in comparison with them, were these sumptuous displays, these vast monumental avenues, these endless architectural straight lines? There were expiatory ceremonies without number; the Sibylline Books were explored for oracles; ladies of rank offered many a propitiatory sacrifice. But there remained the secret sense of a crime, a sacrilege; and Nero began to discover that he had gone too far.

CHAPTER VII.

THE CHRISTIAN MARTYRS.

A TRULY infernal thought now entered the heart of Nero. He looked the world over to see whether there were not somewhere wretches even more hateful than he to the towns-people of Rome, on whom the guilt of the conflagration might be made to fall. He bethought him of the Christians. The abhorrence they had shown for the temples and edifices most venerated by the Romans made it easy to think of them as the authors of a calamity that had swept away those sanctuaries. Their air of sadness in presence of these monuments appeared an insult to the nation. Rome was a very pious city; and one who condemned its worship made himself quickly known. We have to remember that some Jewish purists went so far that they would not touch a coin that had an effigy, and deemed it as great a crime to look upon or carry a graven image as to sculpture one; while others refused to pass through a city-gate decorated with a statue.[1] All this challenged the popular contumely and ill-will. Perhaps the language of Christians about the final conflagration,[2] — their gloomy prophecies, their persistently repeating that the world would soon end, and end by fire, — helped

---

[1] *Philosophumena*, ix. 26. *Non Cæsaribus honor:* Tac. *Hist.* v. 5.
[2] Comp. *Carm. Sibyll.* iv. 172 (of about A. D. 75); 2 Pet. iii. 7-13.

make them likely to be taken for incendiaries. It may even be granted that some of the believers had rashly given ground for the charge that they were willing to justify their oracles, at all cost, by an earthly conflagration that should serve as a prelude to celestial flames. What propitiatory act, at all events, could be more effective than that these enemies of the gods should perish by a death of torture? Gazing on their horrid torments, the people would say, "Ah, so it is: they are the guilty ones." We must bear in mind that public opinion held the most hateful deeds charged against them to be things fully proved.[1]

Far from us be the thought that the pious followers of Jesus were in any manner guilty of the charges laid against them; let us only admit that general opinion might be misled by appearances. Though they did not kindle the flame, unquestionably they rejoiced at it.[2] They desired the existing condition of things to be at an end, and they predicted it. In the Apocalypse[3] the prayers of the saints bring fire upon the earth, with earthquakes. During the disaster the attitude of the Christians must have seemed equivocal; some of them, no doubt, failed to show reverence or sorrow at the burning of a temple, or perhaps did not hide a certain satisfaction. We may fancy one of their conventicles just across the Tiber, and hearing them say to one another, "Is not that just what we foretold?" There is often danger in being too true a prophet. "If we chose to avenge ourselves," said Tertullian, "one night and a few torches would be enough."[4] The Jews were often charged with being

[1] Tac. *Ann.* xv. 44.
[2] Rev. xviii.
[3] *Ibid.* viii. 3–5.
[4] Tertull. *Apol.* 37.

incendiaries because of their living apart.[1] The same crime was one of the "atrocities clinging to the name,"[2] which went into the definition of "Christian."

Accordingly, without being in the least guilty of that catastrophe, the Christians might be held, so to speak, as "accomplices in will." Within four years and a half, we shall find in the Apocalypse an anthem on the burning of Rome, of which more than one feature is doubtless borrowed from the horrors of this summer. The destruction of Rome by fire was, indeed, a Jewish and Christian dream. Still, it was only a dream. These pious sectaries were unquestionably well content to see in vision the saints and angels applauding in heaven what they regarded as a righteous judgment.

It is hard to believe that the idea of accusing the Christians of the July conflagrations came of itself to Nero. Doubtless, if he had known these good brethren nearly, he would have heartily hated them. Naturally, they could not appreciate his merit in posing thus as a leading actor in front of the stage filled by the high life of the day; and what particularly enraged Nero was failure to recognize his talent as an actor of supreme merit. But he had, no doubt, only heard them spoken of; he had never come in personal touch with them. Who could have suggested the execrable thought? It is likely that suspicions had been started in more than one section of the city.[3] The sect, by this time, was well known in the official world, and was much talked about.[4] Paul, as we have seen, had

---

[1] They were accused, A. D. 67, of trying to burn Antioch (Jos. *Wars*, vii. 3: 2–4).

[2] Pliny, *Epist.* x. 97.   [3] Dion Cass. lxii. 18.

[4] Tert. *Apol.* 5.

friends among persons belonging to the service of the emperor's palace.[1] Among the promises made to Nero by certain persons, a very remarkable one was that, in case he were deprived of the empire, he would hold dominion in the East, and in particular the kingdom of Jerusalem.[2] Messianic ideas among the Jews at Rome often took shape as vague hopes of a Roman empire in the East; as we find that Vespasian was afterwards aided by these fancies.[3] From the accession of Caligula to the death of Nero, Jewish cabals never ceased at Rome.[4] Jews had greatly aided in bringing the family of Germanicus to power and sustaining it. Whether through the Herods or other intriguers, they beset the palace, often to the ruin of their enemies.[5] King Agrippa the younger had been very influential under Caligula and Claudius; when in Rome, he played the part of a man of consequence. Tiberius Alexander, again, held very high positions;[6] while Josephus is rather favourable to Nero, whom he considers to have been slandered, ascribing his crimes to his bad surroundings. Poppæa, according to him, was a woman of piety, favourable to the Jews, supporting the claims of their zealots, and adopting some of their rites. He knew her in the year 62 or 63, got from her the pardon of Jewish priests under arrest, and retained a grateful recollection of her.[7] We find a touching epitaph of a

---

[1] Phil. iv. 22.   [2] Suet. 40; Tac. xv. 36.
[3] Tac. *Hist.* i. 10; v. 13; Suet. *Vesp.* 4; Jos. *Wars*, iii. 3: 9; Bab. Talm. *Gittin*, 56 a.
[4] Note how prominent are the Jews in Martial, Persius, and Juvenal; especially in Persius, v. 179 *et seq.*
[5] Jos. *Antiq.* xviii., xix., xx.
[6] *Acad. of Inscr.* etc. Mém. xxvi. p. 294 *et seq.*
[7] *Antiq.* xx. 8: 3, 11; 11: 1; *Wars*, iv. 9: 2; *Life*, 3. See ch. ii. *ante.*

Jewish Esther, born at Jerusalem, a freedwoman of Claudius or Nero, who enjoined on her friend Arescusus to allow no inscription on her gravestone contrary to the Law, — for example, the letters D. M.[1] There were at Rome Jewish actors and actresses;[2] under Nero this was an easy way to come near the emperor. Mention is made of Alityrus, a Jewish mimic actor, a favourite with Nero and Poppæa; it was by him that Josephus was introduced to the empress.[3] Nero, hating everything Roman, liked to turn to the East, to surround himself with Orientals,[4] and keep up intrigues in that quarter.[5]

Is all this enough to build a theory upon? May we, perhaps, trace to the hatred of Jews for Christians that ferocious caprice which exposed the most harmless of men to the most monstrous cruelties? It looks ill for the Jews, at all events, that their private interviews with Nero and Poppæa were just when the emperor conceived his hateful scheme against the Christians.[6] Tiberius Alexander, in particular, a man sure to detest the saints, was then at the height of favour.[7] Why should the Romans, who commonly confounded Jew and Christian, make just now so sharp

---

[1] Mommsen, *Inscr. regni Neap.* No. 6467 (do not mind Garruci's remarks in *Cimitero*, 24, 25: I verified the inscription at Naples). For the name *Aster*, see Renier, *Inscr. de l'Alg.* No. 3340.

[2] It has been wrongly inferred from the marks on the sarcophagus-cover of the Jewess Faustina (Lapi, *Epit. Sev.* 177, 8; *Corp. inscr. gr.* No. 9920) that she was an actress.

[3] *Life*, 3.

[4] See Tacitus, *Hist.* ii. 95, for special instances.

[5] See Tac. *Ann.* xv. 36; Suet. *Nero*, 31, 36, 40, 47; *Carm. Sibyll.* v. 146.

[6] There is an unlikely surmise of jealousy between Poppæa, who favoured the Jews, and the dubiously Christian Acte.

[7] *Wars*, ii. 15: 1.

distinction between them?[1] Why should the Jews, towards whom the Romans felt the same moral antipathy and religious prejudice as to the Christians,[2] be just now untouched by calumny? Punishment inflicted on Jews would have been just as good an expiation. Clement of Rome,— or the writer (certainly a Roman) of the epistle ascribed to him,— in a passage alluding to the massacres of Christians ordered by Nero, explains them in a characteristic way very obscure to us: all these horrors, he says, are "the result of jealousy,"[3] — evidently meaning interior divisions and animosities among members of the same fraternity. Hence a suspicion rises, strengthened by the undoubted fact that, until the destruction of Jerusalem six years later, the Jews were the real persecutors, and spared no effort to exterminate the Christians.[4] A tradition current in the fourth century had it that both the death of Paul, and also that of Peter, in the persecution of A. D. 64, were induced by the conversion of a concubine and a favourite of Nero;[5] while another tradition refers it to the defeat of Simon Magus.[6] With one of so lawless fancy as Nero anything is credible. Possibly the selection of Christians for slaughter may

[1] Tert. *Apol.* 21. Seneca makes no distinction; to him Christians have no separate existence. See Aug. *De civ. Dei*, vi. 11.

[2] Comp. Tac. *Ann.* xv. 44; *Hist.* v. 5, as corrected by Bernays after Sulp. Severus (*Ueber die Chronik v. Sulp. Sev.*) p. 57.

[3] διὰ ζῆλον: *Ad Cor.* 3, 5, 6.

[4] This appears everywhere in Acts. Comp. "Acts of Polycarp," 17, 18; and observe the phrase, *licet contrarias sibi*, in the address of Titus: Sulp. Sev. (Tacit.) ii. 30: 6.

[5] See note, p. 46, *ante*.

[6] "Acts of Peter and Paul," 78; Pseudo-Marcellus, Pseudo-Linus, Pseudo-Abdias, i. 18; Pseudo-Hegesippus, iii. 2; Gregory of Tours, *Hist. eccl.* i. 24.

have been a mere caprice of the emperor or of Tigellinus.[1] Nero needed no outside pressure to form a scheme so monstrous as to set at naught all laws of probability.

The first arrests were of a number of persons suspected of belonging to the new sect, who were "packed together," says Clement, in a prison which was itself a torture.[2] They confessed their faith, which may have been taken as a confession of the charge. These arrests were followed by many others.[3] The greater part of the accused seem to have been proselytes, who kept the terms of the decision given[4] at Jerusalem.[5] It is not to be supposed that true Christians denounced their brethren; but papers may have been seized, or half-initiated neophytes may have been broken down by torture. There was surprise that so great a multitude had accepted these gloomy doctrines; and the sect was spoken of with terror. Every man of sense saw the evidence of their guilt to be extremely weak; "their true crime," it was said, "is hatred of mankind" (*odium humani generis*). Though convinced that the conflagration was Nero's crime, many sober Romans saw in that cast of the net by the police a shrewd device to deliver the city from a deadly pest. Tacitus shows some pity,[6] but is still of this opinion. Suetonius[7] rates it among the creditable acts of Nero that he

---

[1] This latter would involve Poppæa. See Tac. *Ann.* xv. 61.

[2] Clem. Rom. *Ad Cor.* i. 6; "Shepherd" of Hermas, i. vis. 3: 2.

[3] *Multitudo ingens*, says Tacitus (*Ann.* xv. 44). Equivalent expressions are in Clem. Rom. *Ad. Cor.* i. 6, and Rev. vii. 9, 14.

[4] Acts xv.

[5] Rev. xii. 17, which seems to refer to the Roman horrors of A. D. 64.

[6] Tac. *Ann.* xv. 44.

[7] Suet. *Nero*, 16.

put the followers of "the new and baleful superstition" under these frightful tortures.

These tortures were indeed something frightful. Never had such refinements of cruelty been seen. Almost all those under arrest were of the lower orders (*humiliores*), people of no account. The punishment of these wretches, held guilty of treason or sacrilege, consisted in being cast out to wild beasts or burned alive in the amphitheatre, with the accompaniment of cruel scourgings.[1] One of the most shocking traits of Roman manners was to make a festival of public executions, and popular games of butchery.[2] Persia, in moods of fanaticism and terror, had known frightful displays of torture, and more than once had felt a sort of gloomy delight in them; but never, until the Roman dominion, had any gone so far as to seek public sport in such horrors, or a subject of laughter and applause. The amphitheatres, which at this time were of wood, had become the scene of executions, while the courts furnished victims to the arena. Condemned criminals were forwarded to Rome from all parts of the world to furnish material for the circus and popular entertainment.[3] Add to this a savage exaggeration of the criminal code, so that petty offences were punished with death, and a multitude of judicial errors resulting from defective criminal procedure, and we see how distorted

---

[1] Paul, *Sentent.* v. 39: 4; Ulpian, *Digest.* xlviii. 13; comp. Heb. x. 33; Jos. *Wars*, vii. 3: 1; Mart. *Polycl.* 11–13; Tert. *Apol.* 12; Lact. *De mort. persecut.* To die in the circus was the penalty for criminal slaves (Petronius, p. 145). See also "Shepherd" of Hermas, i. vis. 3: 2; and the Acts of the martyrs of Lyons (in Euseb. v. 1: 38), and of Africa, § 18 (Ruinart, p 100).

[2] Philo, *In Flac.* 10; Jos. *Wars*, viii. 3: 1; Suet. *Nero*, 12.

[3] See Martyrdom of St. Ignatius: εἰς τέρψιν τοῦ δήμου.

were all notions on the subject. The victims were regarded as rather unfortunate than guilty; in the mass, they were even held to be mostly innocent (*innoxia corpora*).[1]

To the barbarity of the torment was now added the indignity of derision. The victims were kept for a holiday, to which was no doubt given an expiatory character. Few days of such distinction were enjoyed at Rome. The "morning's sport," devoted to combats with wild beasts,[2] beheld a strange procession. The condemned, clad in skins of beasts, were thrust upon the arena, where they were torn to pieces by bloodhounds; others were crucified;[3] others, again, wrapped in garments steeped in oil, pitch, or resin, were fastened to stakes, and reserved to illuminate the scene by night; these living torches were fired as twilight came on. Nero opened for the spectacle his magnificent gardens beyond the Tiber, now the site of the *Borgo*, with the square and basilica of Saint Peter's (the "Black Meadow" of the Middle Age). Here was a circus, begun by Caligula and continued by Claudius, bounded by an obelisk brought from Heliopolis, the same which now stands in the middle of the *Piazza*.[4] The spot had

---

[1] Manil. *Astron.* v. 6: 6; comp. the mediæval notions attached to the words *marturiare*, and the like.

[2] Seneca, *Epist.* 7; Suet. *Claud.* 34; Martial, x. 25; xiii. 95; Tert. *Apol.* 15. Comp. Ovid, *Met.* xi. 26; Virgil (*redeunt spectacula mane*); Orelli, 2553, 4. The martyrs of Carthage (§ 47) partake their last meal at night.

[3] The reading in Tacitus, *aut flammandi atque*, has been questioned (see Bernays, *Chron. des Sulp. Sev.* 54, 55, n.), but on no sufficient ground; the second *aut*, however, may be superfluous. *Flammandi* (= *ut flammarentur*) is right [or it may be read as a present passive participle].

[4] Suet. *Claudius*, 21; Tac. *Ann.* xiv. 14; Pliny, xvi. 40: 76; xxxvi. 11: 15. This circus is the *naumachia* (sea-fight) spoken of in the "Acts of

before this been the scene of torchlight slaughter, when Caligula, as he passed in his chariot, ordered a number of ex-consuls, senators, and ladies of rank to be beheaded.[1] It may have seemed an ingenious device to substitute bodies of living men and women, wrapped in blazing raiment, for flames kindled upon pillars to illuminate the scene. As a mode of punishment, this way of burning was not new; it was the ordinary sentence of incendiaries, and was called the "shirt of torment" (*tunica molesta*);[2] but it had never before been used for the lighting of a public square. By the blaze of these hideous torches, Nero — who had brought these night-races into fashion — displayed himself in the arena, sometimes mingling among the people in jockey-costume, sometimes driving his chariot, and bidding for applause. Still, there were here and there signs of pity. Even some who thought the Christians guilty, and admitted the punishment to be deserved, were filled with horror at these barbarous sports. Good men would have wished that only the public benefit should be regarded, in purging the city of dangerous criminals, but that there should be no appearance of making them a sacrifice to one man's bloodthirsty cruelty.[3]

Peter." Comp. Platner and Bunsen, *Beschr. der Stadt Rom.* ii. 1: 39. The obelisk, formerly in the sacristy, was removed by Sixtus V.

[1] Sen. *De ira*, iii. 18.

[2] Juvenal, i. 155, 6; viii. 233–5; Martial, *Epig.* x. 25: 5 ; comp. Sen. *De ira*, iii. 3. Notice the condition of "burning" (*uri*) in gladiatorial contracts in Hor. *Sat.* ii. 7: 58; Petron. p. 149 (Bücheler); Sen. *Epist.* 37.

[3] Tac. *Ann.* xv. 44; Suet. *Nero*, 16; Clem. Rom. *Ad. Cor.* i. 6; Tert. *Apol.* 5 (citing official documents); *Ad nat.* i. 7; *Scorp.* 15; Euseb. ii. 22, 25; Chron. *Nero*, *Ann.* 13; Lact. *De mort. persec.* 2; Sulp. Sev. *Hist. Sacra*, ii. 29; Orosius, vii. 7; Greg. Tur. i. 24; George Sync., *Chron.* p. 339. Echoes of this persecution and allusions to its cruelties are found

Women and maidens were forced to bear a part in these horrible sports, and the nameless indignities they suffered were made matter of public jesting.[1] It was the custom under Nero that the condemned should represent in the amphitheatre parts in mythological tales involving the actor's death. These abominable melodramas, in which mechanical skill was employed with prodigious effect,[2] were something new. Greece would have been amazed at a proposal so to employ ferocity for theatrical effect, and make a fine art of torture. The unhappy wretch was dragged into the arena, richly attired as a god or hero devoted to death; and then, in his torment, he exhibited some tragic scene of a story consecrated by sculptors and poets.[3] At one time, it might be Hercules, raving in torment on Mt. Œta, tearing off the poisoned shirt of Nessus, a tunic of flaming pitch; at another, Orpheus, rent in pieces by a bear; or Dædalus, hurled from the sky and devoured by beasts; or Pasiphaë, assaulted by the bull; or Attys, son of Crœsus, slain with a javelin[4] — possibly an error for Adonis, torn by a boar; or at times there would be horrible masquerades, in which men were clad in red mantles as priests of Saturn, and women as priestesses of Ceres with frontlets on their brows; or, again, there were dramatic scenes, in which

in Rev. vi. 9–11; vii. 9–14; xii. 10–12, 17; xiii. 7, 10, 15, 16; xiv. 12, 13; xvi. 6; xvii. 6; xviii. 24; xx. 4; Heb. x. 32–34; "Shepherd" of Hermas, i. vis. 3: 2; *Carm. Sibyll.* iv. 136; v. 136, 385; Matt. xxiv. 9 (?). It will presently appear that Revelation is a direct outgrowth of Nero's persecution. The inscription in Orelli (730) is false.

[1] Clem. Rom. i. 6.   [2] Mart. *Spect.* xxi.

[3] Martial, *Spect.* v. (cf. Suet. *Nero*, 12; Apul. *Metam.* i. 10); *id.* viii., xxi.; Tert. *Apol.* 9, 15; *Ad. nat.* i. 10. The *tunica molesta* was generally used in representing Hercules on Mt. Œta (Juv. viii. 235; Mart. x. 25: 5).

[4] Herodotus, i. 23.

the actor was really put to death, like Laureolus;[1] or, perhaps, tragic deeds like that of Mucius Scævola.[2] At the close of the entertainment Mercury, with a wand of red-hot iron, would touch each body to see if it should stir; while lackeys in masks, personating Pluto or Orcus, dragged out the corpses by the feet, knocking in the head any that might still show signs of life.[3]

Christian ladies of the highest rank must have their share in these horrors. Some played the part of the Danaïds, and others that of Dirce.[4] It is hard to see how the story of the former could furnish the due picture of horrors; for the punishment exhibited,[5] assigned by all mythology to those guilty maids, was scarcely cruel enough to please Nero and the frequenters of his shows. Perhaps they marched in file, bearing urns,[6] and as each passed, she received the fatal blow from an actor disguised as Lynceus;[7] or perhaps Amymone, one of the number, was seen chased by a satyr and assailed by Neptune;[8] or it may be that these wretched maidens exhibited in succession the whole series of the punishments of Tartarus, and died after hours of torment. Representations of the world below were then in fashion. A few years before (A. D. 41), some Egyptians and Nubians came to Rome,

---

[1] See end of chap. ii., *ante*.

[2] Martial, *Epig.* viii. 30; x. 25.

[3] These scenes have been described at length in the powerful and tragic tale of *Quo Vadis*, by H. Sienkiewicz. — ED.

[4] Clem. Rom. i. 6.

[5] Pausanias, x. 31: 9, 11; Mus. Pio-Clem. iv. tab. 36.

[6] Mus. Pio-Clem. ii. 2; Guigniaut, *Relig. de l'Ant.* pl. 606 *a*. Comp. *Bulletino dell' Inst. di corr. arch.*, 1843, 119–123.

[7] See Schol. on Eurip. *Hec.* 886; Servius on *Æn.* x. 497.

[8] Hygin, *Fabulæ*, 169; see below, p. 156.

and had great success in exhibitions by night, displaying by order the horrors of Tartarus,[1] in conformity with pictures existing at Thebes, particularly those on the tomb of Sethi I.

Regarding the torment of Dirce, there can be no doubt at all. A well-known colossal group in the museum at Naples is that of the Farnese Bull, in which Amphion and Zethus are fastening Dirce to the horns of a wild bull, which will drag her through the rocks and briers of Cithæron.[2] This poor piece of Rhodian sculpture, taken to Rome in the time of Augustus, was an object of universal admiration.[3] What finer subject for that brutal style of art brought into vogue by the cruelty of the time, which consisted in turning famous sculptures into living pictures? An inscription and a fresco at Pompeii seem to prove that this dreadful scene was often exhibited in the arena, when a woman was to suffer death.[4] Fastened by the hair, naked, to the horns of a wild bull, these poor creatures were exposed to the wanton gaze of a ferocious mob. Some of the Christian women immolated thus were feeble of body,[5]

---

[1] Suet. *Caius*, 57.

[2] *Real Museo Borbonico*, xiv. tab. iv. v.; Guigniaut, pl. 728, 728 *a.*; Gargiulo, i. No. 1-3; iii. No. 23. Comp. *Mem. della R. Acad. Ercol.* iii. 386 *et seq.*; iv. pt. 1; vii. 1 *et seq.*; Raoul-Rochette, *Choix de peint. de Pompei*, pl. xxiii. 277-288; *Ann. de l'Inst. de corr. arch.* xi. (1839), 287-292; Helbig, *Wandgemälde*, 1151, 2, 3; Jahn, *Arch. Zeit.* 1853, No. 36, etc.

[3] Pliny, xxxvi. 5:4. See Brunn, *ubi supra*, p. 129, n. 3.

[4] See Apuleius, *Metam.* vi. 127; Lucian, *Lucius*, 23; *Memorie, etc.*, vii., plate in the first paper, apparently showing the torture as a spectacle. Also Hygin, *Fab.* 8; and comp. the martyrdom of Blandina, exposed (at Vienne) in a net to a bull, and of Perpetua and Felicitas (at Carthage) exposed in like manner to a maddened cow (Euseb. v. 1; "Martyrs of Africa," § 20).

[5] Clem. Rom. i. 6.

though of courage superhuman; but that beastly crowd had eyes only for the torn side and the mangled breast.

Nero was, without doubt, present at these spectacles. As he was near-sighted, he used to put to his eye on such occasions a concave lens of "emerald,"[1] which served him as an eye-glass.[2] He liked to exhibit his connoisseurship in matters of sculpture; it is said that he made brutal remarks on his mother's dead body, praising this point and criticising that. Living flesh quivering in a wild beast's jaw, or a poor shrinking girl, screening herself by a modest gesture, then tossed by a bull and cast in lifeless fragments on the gravel of the arena, must exhibit a play of form and colour worthy of an artist-sense like his. Here he was, in the front row, on a low balcony,[3] in a group of vestals and curule magistrates, — with his ill-favoured countenance, his short sight, his blue eyes, his curled light-brown hair, his cruel mouth, his air like a big silly baby, at once cross and dull, open-mouthed, swollen with vanity,[4] while brazen music throbbed in the air, turned to a bloody mist. He would, no doubt, inspect with a critic's eye the shrinking attitudes of these new Dirces; and I imagine he found a charm he had never known before in the air of resignation with which these pure-hearted girls faced their hideous death.

These shocking scenes were long remembered. Even in the time of Domitian, when an actor suffered

---

[1] The term "emerald" — σμάραγδος — was probably given, according to Liddell and Scott, to "all greenish crystals," or to glass. — Ed.

[2] Pliny, xxxvii. 5: 16.   [3] Suet. *Nero*, 12.

[4] See portraits of the Capitol, Vatican, Palatine, and Louvre; cf. Pliny, xi. 27: 54.

death in playing his part,—especially a Laureolus, actually dying on the cross,—they remembered these votive offerings (*piacula*) of Nero's day, and thought this was another incendiary of Rome.[1] The slang-terms *sarmentitii* or *sarmentarii* ("faggot-men"), and *semaxii* ("half axle-men"),[2] and the popular cry, "Christians to the lions!" seem to date from this time.[3] Nero, with a sort of artist-touch, had stamped infant Christianity with an indelible mark; the bloody scar (*nævus*) on the forehead of the martyr-church will never be effaced.

Those of the brethren who were not tortured had, in a way, their share in the torture of the rest by the sympathy they felt and the pains they took to visit them in their chains. This dangerous privilege they often bought at the price of all their goods; so that the survivors of the crisis were many of them wholly ruined. This they hardly thought of; they looked only for durable riches in heaven, and would say among themselves, "Yet a little longer, and he that is to come will come."[4]

Such was the prelude to that wonderful poem of Christian martyrdom,—this epic of the amphitheatre, which was to last two hundred and fifty years, and give birth to the ennobling of woman and the redemption of the slave by such episodes as the following: Blandina on the cross, dazzling the eyes of her companions, who saw in this pale and gentle slave-girl the image of the crucified Redeemer; Potamiena, protected against insult

---

[1] Mart. *Spect.* vii. 10; Juv. viii. 133-235.

[2] The stakes to which they were bound when burned were probably wrecks of chariots broken in the races. For these terms, see Tertullian.

[3] Tert. *Apol.* 14, 40.   [4] Heb. x. 32-34.

by the young officer who led her forth to execution; the mob stricken with horror when it saw the bleeding bosom of Felicitas; Perpetua in the arena, binding up her own hair, torn and disordered by wild beasts, lest "in her hour of glory" she might seem to be in mourning. Legend tells how one of these saintly maidens, on her way to the scene of torture, met the pitying eye of a youth touched by her beauty; and, wishing to leave him a mark of remembrance, gave him the kerchief that covered her bosom, fired by which token, the youth ran an instant after upon his martyrdom: such was the dangerous charm of these bloody scenes at Rome, Lyons, or Carthage! The joy of these sufferers in the amphitheatre grew contagious, just as did the resignation of the "victims" in the Reign of Terror. The imagination of the time conceived of the Christians as, first of all, obstinate to suffer: the token they are known by is their desire for death.[1] To check excess of eagerness for martyrdom required the most dreaded of threats, the charge of heresy, with expulsion from the Church.

The blunder of the educated classes in the empire, in evoking this feverish exaltation of spirits, cannot be too severely censured. To suffer for one's belief is so sweet a thing that this alone is enough to win men to believe. More than one sceptic has been converted by no better reason than that. In the East there have even been impostors who would lie for the mere pleasure of lying, and of suffering for the lie. There

---

[1] *Moriendi contemptus*, says Tacitus (*Hist.* v. 5). He, it is true, applies it to Jews, not Christians, though he well knows the difference. What Epictetus and Aurelius say of Galilæans applies also to the fanatics of the siege. See "The Apostles," p. 235, n.

is no sceptic who does not view the martyr with a certain envy, grudging to him that supreme joy of a positive belief in something. A secret instinct impels us to stand with "them which are persecuted." Whoever thinks to arrest a religious or social movement by measures of repression, proves his complete ignorance of the human heart, and testifies that he understands nothing of the true method of political action.

What has happened once may happen again. Tacitus would have turned aside in wrath if he could have been shown the future of those Christians whom he thought of as ignoble wretches. High-born Romans would have cried out if some looker-on, gifted with a spirit of prophecy, had dared say to him: "These incendiaries will be the saviours of the world." Here is the everlasting refutation of conservative dogmatism: it is an incurable twist of conscience, a secret perversity of judgment. Wretches flouted by all decent people have come to be saints of the earth. It were not well that such revolutions of opinion should be frequent. The safety of human society demands that its verdict should not be too often set aside. Ever since the condemnation of Jesus, ever since martyrs have found gain to their cause by revolt against the law, there has always been a tribunal of private appeal against the charge of social guilt. Every convicted offender can say, "Jesus too was condemned; the martyrs were held to be dangerous criminals, whom society was well rid of; and yet centuries have confessed that they were right." A hard hit for those ponderous assertions by which society would make out its foes to be lacking at once in common-sense and common virtue!

Since the day when Jesus breathed his last on Calvary, the most solemn date of all Christian history was that — about the first of August in the year sixty-four — when the festival of death was held in Nero's gardens. A structure is solid in proportion to the amount of virtue, sacrifice, and self-devotion that has gone into its foundation. Fanatics are the only real founders. Judaism endures to this day because of the intense frenzy of its prophets and men of zeal; Christianity, because of the boldness of its first witnesses. That orgy of Nero was the bloody baptism which marked Rome as the martyr-city, destined to a place of its own in Christian history, and to be the second holy city. Thus the Vatican Mount came to be held by conquerors of a sort never known till then. The brainless creature who held the helm of the world did not see that he was helping to lay the foundation of a new social order, was signing for the future a charter, written in vermilion, that would be held good at the end of eighteen centuries. Rome, guilty of all that innocent blood,[1] became like Babylon, a sacramental and symbolic city. On that day Nero took a position of the first rank in Christian history. That miracle of horror, that wonder of iniquity, was a manifest sign to all. One hundred and fifty years later Tertullian cries out: "Yes, we are proud that our outlawry was spoken by such a man! Understand him well, and you shall see that it is high honour to have been condemned by Nero."[2] The expectation had already gone abroad that, before the true Christ should come, would be the coming of a sort of infernal Christ,

---

[1] Rev. xviii. 24; xix. 2.
[2] *Apol.* 5; *Ad. nat.* i. 7; comp. Sulp. Sev. ii. 28.

who would be at all points the opposite of Jesus.[1] It was no longer to be doubted: the ANTICHRIST, the Prince of Evil, did exist. This was the monster with a human face, made up of cruelty, deceit, shamelessness, and pride, which ran through the world as a Knight of Folly, casting light on his triumphs in the chariot-race from torches of human flesh, getting drunk with the blood of saints, or even worse. Suetonius has described a monstrous game devised by Nero, which we are tempted to think had to do with Christians: youths, men, women, and maidens were bound naked to stakes in the arena, when a wild beast, rushing out of the den (*cavea*), spent his rage on their living flesh, while the freedman Doryphorus (an infamous creature of Nero's, to whom he pretended to be married) seemed to beat off the beast,— Nero himself, disguised in a wild beast's skin.[2] The name of Nero is discovered: we shall find it as "the Beast." Caligula was the Anti-God; Nero is the Anti-Christ. The figure in the Apocalypse is conceived. The Christian maiden, fastened to a stake and exposed to the filthy approaches of the Beast, bears with her into all coming time that frightful image.

On this day, too, by a strange contradiction, was evolved that lovely paradox which has made for centuries, and still constitutes in part, the best thing in man's life. It was an hour registered in heaven, when

---

[1] See "Saint Paul," chap. ix.

[2] Doryphorus ("spearman") was probably a stage-name. He is called Pythagoras by Tacitus (*Ann.* xv. 37) and Dion Cass. (lxii. 28; lxiii. 13, 22; but see lxi. 5). See Suet. *Nero*, 29, and the above passages of Dion Cassius; and comp. Tac. xv. 44; Clem. Rom. *Ad Cor.* i. c. 6. Especially note the part assigned to Nero, under the name "the Beast," comparing Heb. x. 33; *Carm. Sibyll.* v. (cir. A. D. 140), 385, 386.

womanly purity, till now so scrupulously hidden from the world's eye, appeared in open daylight before fifty thousand spectators, unshamed as the marble figure in a sculptor's studio, in the form of a maiden about to die. This was the revealing of a secret unknown to antiquity, the clear announcement that simple modesty is in itself a beauty and a delight. We have already seen that great enchantress called Imagination, who from age to age transforms the ideal of womanhood, toiling incessantly to set above the pride of beauty the charm of modesty, — Poppæa herself reigned only by assuming its outer shape, — and of resigned humility, wherein was the triumph of the gentle Acte. Wonted to lead his own age in ways of the unknown, Nero, it would seem, had a foretaste of this sentiment, and, in his artist-extravagances, discovered the secret charm that is found in Christian art. His affection for Acte and for Poppæa shows that he was capable of the finer emotions. And, as all that came into his hands tended to the monstrous, he would set before his eyes the vision of his dreams. At the centre of his crystal lens was pictured a maiden figure,[1] as of the heroine carven on an antique cameo; and the shrinking form of the girl-martyr, winning the applause of this friend of Petronius, this master-artist, who perhaps saluted the dying maid with some favourite line of a classic poet, became a rival to the self-conscious loveliness of the Grecian Aphrodite. When with brutal hand the jaded world tore away the veil of Christian modesty, that it might find a new sensation in the martyr's agony, the

---

[1] In the original, *L'image de l'aïeule de Cymodocée*, Cymodoce being the heroine of Chateaubriand's *Les Martyrs*, supposed to have suffered in the persecution of Diocletian. — Ed.

poor child might perhaps think to herself, "I too am beautiful!" This was the first budding forth of an art entirely new. A new type of beauty, to be developed in Christian ages, sprang into being under the eye of Nero, owing the revelation of its magic to the crime which, by rending its robe, disclosed its virgin purity.

CHAPTER VIII.

DEATH OF PETER AND PAUL. — A. D. 64.

WE do not certainly know the name of any Christian who perished in the shocking events of August, A. D. 64. Those arrested were new converts, and little known to one another. Those holy women who had amazed the Church by their constancy have left no name. They are spoken of in Christian tradition only as "the Danaïds and the Dirces."[1] But the memory of the places remained, living and profound. The circus or *naumachia*, — afterwards conceived as a palace of Nero,[2] — the two bounds, the obelisk, a terebinth, which served as rallying-points of memory to the early Christian generations (see below), became the foundation of a complete ecclesiastical topography, which ended in the consecration of the Vatican mount, and its designation to a religious future of the highest importance.

Although the affair had been confined to the city of Rome, and although Roman opinion was by all means to be propitiated, — exasperated as it was by the great fire, — yet the atrocity set on foot by Nero could not fail to find an echo in the provinces, and to stir up in them a revival of persecution.[3] The churches of Asia Minor,

---

[1] Clem. Rom. *Ad Cor.* i. 6.
[2] Becker, *Handb. d. röm. Alt.* i. 671; Lipsius, *Röm. Petrussage*, 104, n.
[3] Suetonius (*Nero*, 16) and Tertullian (*Ad nat.* i. 7) speak of it only in general terms.

especially, were severely tried,[1] the pagan population of this region being quickly roused to fanaticism.[2] Some were imprisoned at Smyrna.[3] One Antipas was a "faithful martyr" at Pergamus,[4] though the writer's habit of employing symbolic names, or anagrams, makes the name uncertain; he seems to have suffered near the famous temple of Æsculapius, perhaps in a wooden amphitheatre not far distant, on some holiday.[5] Pergamus was the only city of Asia Minor, excepting Cyzicus, where there were regular gladiatorial combats, which were under the direction of a priesthood.[6] There was no positive law forbidding the profession of Christianity,[7] which, however, put one out of the protection of law. Such terms as *hostis, hostis patriæ, hostis publicus, humani generis inimicus, hostis deorum atque hominum*, written in the statute, indicate enemies of society in general, against whom, says Tertullian,

---

[1] Rev. i.–iii.; vi. 11; xx. 4 (referring to "them which were beheaded," which was not the case in Rome). If the writer was not himself in Rome, his fervid temper shows that the persecution was very sharp in Asia Minor; he was also a "companion in tribulation" (i. 9). But my opinion is that he was in Rome during the events referred to.

[2] See Martyrd. of Polycarp, 3, 4, 12; Acts xix. 23–28.

[3] Rev. ii. 9, 10; *Mart. Polycarp.* 17, 18.

[4] Rev. ii. 13.

[5] See Mem. of the Acad. of Berlin, 1872, 48–58.

[6] Galen, xiii. p. 600; xviii. pt. 2, p. 567 (ed. Kuhn).

[7] Commodian, *Carm.* xl., xli.; Euseb. ii. 25; *Chron. ann.* 13 Nero; Lact. *De mort. pers.* 2; Sulp. Sev. *Hist. sacr.* ii. 28, 29; Orosius, vii. 7, and Euthalius in Zaccagni, p. 532, give the same account. Rossi (*Bull.*, etc., 1864, pp. 69, 92 *et seq.*; 1865, 93) thinks he saw a charcoal inscription on the wall of an inn at Pompeii, containing hints of bloody jests of the populace against the Christians; but the inscription has disappeared (Zangemeister, *Inscr. pariet.* 679), and Rossi's explanation of it is dubious (see *Comptes rendus de l'Acad.* 1866, 189); the scrawl, containing the word VINA, refers to charges of wine. In any case it cannot be older than A. D. 78 or 79, for such inscriptions do not last long. Tertullian (*Apol.* 40) says there were no Christians in Pompeii before 79.

every man becomes a soldier.¹ Thus the mere name "Christian" was a crime;² and, as the judge had absolute discretion in deciding on such offences,³ the life of every disciple, from this day forth, was at the mercy of magistrates excessively hard-hearted, and full of the bitterest prejudice against them.⁴

We may, probably enough, connect the deaths of Peter and Paul with the incidents narrated above.⁵ A strange fortune has brought it about that the disappearance of these two is wrapped in mystery. It is certain that Peter suffered martyrdom,⁶ and it is hardly to be supposed that it was elsewhere than at Rome:⁷ in that case, it was at Jerusalem or Antioch, each of them equally unlikely; while the only known incident that seems to throw light on his death is that told by Tacitus.⁸ Strong reasons lead us to believe that Paul too suffered in Rome. The expression of Clement

---

[1] *Apol.* 2, 25, 35, 37; *Ad Scap.* 4; Cod. Theod. l. 3, 6, 7, 9; *de Maleficis et mathematicis* (ix. 18). Comp. Acts of Cyprian's martyrdom, § 4 (Ruinart, *Acta sincera*, 217).

[2] 1 Pet. iv. 14; Matt. x. 22; xxiv. 9; Mark xiii. 13; Luke xxi. 12, 17.

[3] Digest l. 6, *ad legem Juliam peculatus* (xlviii. 13; *ib.* l. 4, § 2).

[4] Paul, *Sentent.* v. 29: 1; Luke xxi. 12 is written under the fresh impression of these judicial cruelties.

[5] So Eusebius (*Chron.*), agreeing with Clem. Rom. i. 5, 6, and confirmed by Rev. xviii. 20: see Euthalius, 532; Geo. Syncellus, 339.

[6] John xxi. 18, 19, comp. with xii. 32, 33; xiii. 36 (passages written, without question, before A. D. 150, and the stronger because they allude to the fact as well known); 2 Pet. i. 14; Can. of Murat. ll. 36, 37; Clem. Rom. i. 5; Dion. of Corinth, and Caius priest at Rome, in Euseb. ii. 25; Tert. *Præscr.* 36, *Adv. Marc.* iv. 5; *Scorp.* 15. Comp. also Luke xxii. 32-34, with John xiii. 36-38, and the Canon of Muratori; also, Macarius Magnes, iv. 4 (unpublished).

[7] See Rev. xviii. 20.

[8] Tac. *Ann.* xv. 44. Read carefully Clem. Rom. *Ad Cor.* i. 5, 6 (ed. Hilgenfeld). The "great multitude of the elect," with the Danaïds and Dirces, surely died at Rome ; and these martyrs were gathered in heaps (συνηθροίσθη) with Peter and Paul.

($\mu\alpha\rho\tau\nu\rho\eta\sigma\alpha\varsigma$: see Acts xxiii. 11) does not of itself assert death by violence; but such (apart from the parallel with Peter) is the sense obviously implied.[1] We may, then, refer his death, as well as Peter's, to the events of July and August, A. D. 64.[2] Thus was sealed in death the reconciliation of these two souls, one so strong and the other so true; thus, by the authority of legend (which is to say divine) was estab-

---

[1] Comp. Euseb. ii. 25 (Dionysius and Caius); Tertull. (l. c.); Ignatius, Eph. 12 (wanting in the Syriac); Commodian, *Carm.* 821.

[2] The leading authority is Clem. Rom. i. 5, 6; this epistle was certainly written at Rome not many years after the apostles' death (ch. 5), probably 93 to 96, establishing a link between the martyrdom of Peter, of Paul, of the "great multitude," and of the Danaïds and Dirces, by the expression "with these men were gathered," etc. (implying a "batch" of victims hurriedly and violently seized), and the motive of "jealousy" assigned. Now it is clear that the "great multitude," with the Danaïds and Dirces, suffered in Nero's persecution. The account in Eusebius tells us that Peter and Paul died in Rome about the same time. This testimony, it is true, is weakened by what is said of Peter's apostolate at Corinth, and his travels along with Paul, with the evident motive to give him a place as apostle to the gentiles. Tertullian (*Præscr.* 36; *Adv. Marc.* iv. 5), and Commodian (*Carm.* v. 821), also unite the two apostles in their death. See Iren. *Adv. hær.* iii. 1: 4; 3: 3; Euseb. ii. 22, 25; iii. 1; *Chron. ann.* 13; Lact. *De mort. pers.* 2; *Inst. div.* iv. 21; Jer. *De vir. ill.* 5; Euthalius, (Zaccagni, *Coll. mon. vet. eccl. gr.* 532); Sulp. Sev. *Hist. sacr.* ii. 29; Bede, *De vet. temp.* 303 (Giles). The entire Roman tradition, — Caius in Eus. ii. 25; *Liber pontif.* (Bianchini, art. Peter and Cornelius, note the contradictions); Acts of Peter and Paul (*Bibl. max. patrum*, ii. 69 c.); *Acts*, etc. (Tischendorf, § 84); do. of Peter (Bosio, *Roma sott.* 74, etc.), — puts the martyrdom and burial of Peter in Nero's circus, with minute indications of the spot, — that is, just where these atrocities took place (see Platner and Bunsen, ii. 1: 39–41). Finally, the opinion that Peter was crucified head downward sufficiently answers to Tac. xv. 44; while the opinion that the two apostles suffered on the same day got footing without contradiction (Labbe, *Concil.* iv. 1262; Jer. *De vir. ill.* 5). Prudentius, Augustine, and others, hold that they died on the same date a year apart. Eusebius and Jerome, from theory, not tradition, set the date in A. D. 68. See Tillemont, *Mem.* i. *n.* 40, on Peter; Zonaras, xi. 13; Land, *Anecd. Syr.* i. 116.

lished the touching brotherhood of two men, whom party feeling had set each against the other, but who, we may believe, were superior to party feeling, and were always friends. The great legend of Peter and Paul, who, like the twin founders of the ancient city, laboured together for its later glory,[1] having in human history a significance not unlike that of Jesus, dates from the day when, according to tradition, they suffered death together. Nero was herein the unconscious but most effective agent in founding historic Christianity; for it was he who laid the corner-stone of the holy city.

As to the manner of the apostles' death, we have clear evidence that Peter was crucified.[2] Old texts say that his wife was crucified with him, and that he saw her led to execution.[3] A story generally received in the third century held that he requested to be crucified head downward, as being unworthy to die in the same way as Jesus.[4] A characteristic thing in the horrors of this time was the pains taken to devise new and horrid

---

[1] See Clement of Rome, Dionysius of Corinth, Caius, and Tertullian as above cited; the "preaching of Paul," cited in Lact. *Inst. div.* iv. 21, and in the work, *De bapt. non iter.*, in the sequel to Cyprian (ed. Rigault, 139); Ignatius, *Ad Rom.* 4; Iren. iii. 1: 4; iii. 2, 3; Tert. *Præscr.* 23. Note, too, the inscription (p. 46, note *ante*) M. ANNÆO PAVLO PETRO, in which *Petrus* must be a Christian *adnomen* (but see Orelli, 516, 5455). For sculptured monuments, see Rossi, *Bull.*, 1864, 81; 1866, 52; Martigny, *Dict.* 537, 538.

[2] John xxi. 18, 19 (cf. xii. 32, 33; xiii. 36); Tert. *Adv. Marc.* iv. 5; *Præscr.* 36; *Scorp.* 15; Euseb. ii. 25; Lact. *De mort. pers.* 2; Orosius, vii. 7. Tacitus speaks of some who were *crucibus adfixi*. Emendations suggested in this passage (Bernays, *Ueber die Chron.*, etc.) would set aside the mention of simple crucifixion; but Sulp. Severus (ii. 29), who nearly copies Tacitus (a better text than ours), agreeing with Hermas, i. vis. 3: 2, expressly gives *cruces* (σταυρούς) in the account.

[3] Clem. Alex. *Strom.* vii. 11.

[4] *Acta Petri et Pauli*, c. 81 (cf. Pseudo-Linus, 69, 70); Euseb. iii. 1 (following Origen); *id. Demonstr. evang.* iii. 5; Jer. *De vir. ill.* 1.

modes of torture; and it is possible that Peter was exposed to the crowd in that shocking attitude. Seneca[1] speaks of cases where tyrants have been known thus to reverse the posture of their victims; and Christian piety may have seen a mystical refinement[2] in what was only an executioner's strange caprice.[3] Possibly the words of the Fourth Gospel, "Thou shalt stretch forth thy hands, and another shall gird thee, and carry thee whither thou wouldest not,"[4] allude to some peculiarity in the mode of Peter's death.[5] Paul, as a freeman born, was beheaded.[6] Probably he had a formal trial,[7] and was not included in the summary condemnation of the Christian victims. Timothy, as would appear, was arrested with him and detained in prison.[8]

Early in the third century there already existed near Rome two monuments, bearing the names of the apostles Peter and Paul. That of Peter was at the foot of the Vatican hill; that of Paul, on the road to Ostia. In rhetorical phrase they were called the "trophies" of the two apostles;[9] and they were probably *cellæ* or *memoriæ* consecrated to their names. Such memorials existed in public before the time of Constantine, as we learn from Eusebius;[10] and we have a right to

[1] *Consol. ad Marciam*, 20.   [2] Rufinus, tr. of Euseb. iii. 1.
[3] Euseb. as above.   [4] John xxi. 18.
[5] The "girding" was not essential, or even customary. The passage in the Gospel of Nicodemus (pt. 1, A. ch. 10) refers to a very modern conception as to the crucifixion of Jesus.
[6] Tert. *Præscr.* 36; *Scorp.* 15; Euseb. ii. 25; Lact. *De mort.* 2; Orosius, vii. 7; Euthalius (in Zaccagni), 427, 522, 531–37; cf. Paul, *Sent.* v. 29: 1.
[7] Clem. Rom. i. 5; see note 6 on p. 161, *ante*.
[8] Heb. xiii. 23 (but see p. 177, below).
[9] Caius in Euseb. ii. 25. The construction of a *memoria* of Peter on the Vatican by Anencletus (*Lib. pontif.* "Anenclet.") is legendary. See Lipsius, *Chron. der röm. Bischöfe*, 269; cf. Bianchini's text.
[10] *Vita Const.* ii. 40.

suppose them at this time to be known only to the faithful, — though of the publicity of Christian burial-places there is no doubt.[1] Possibly they were only the terebinth of the Vatican, long associated with the name of Peter, and the pine of the Salvian waters, about which, by some traditions, were gathered the memories of Paul.[2] Later on, these "trophies" became the tombs of the two apostles. About the middle of the third century two bodies were found, held in universal veneration as theirs,[3] which seem to have come from the catacombs on the Appian Way, where there were Jewish cemeteries.[4] In the fourth century these bodies lay

---

[1] See Rossi, *Rom. sott.* i. 209, 210.

[2] *Acta*, etc., 80 (ed. Tisch. p. 35, n.), p. 162, n., *ante*. Still, these waters are too far from the basilica of St. Paul *fuori i muri* to allow identification.

[3] *Kalendarium liberianum*, 3 kal. Jun. (*Abh. der kön. sächs. Gesch.*, phil.-hist. Classe, i. 632); Inscr. of Damasus (Gruter, ii. 1163); *Lib. pontif.* (Bianchini and Lipsius); art. *Petrus, Cornelius, Damasus*, and all but two from Linus to Victor (this book is self-contradictory). All that concerns the transfers made by St. Cornelius is very obscure. If he only restored the bodies to their first resting-place why were they ever taken away? The reason given in the case of Peter (Lampr. *Heliogr.* 23) is very weak, and as to Paul there is none. The nearness of the Jewish cemetery *Vigna Randanini* makes me think that the two bodies in question were taken by Cornelius from the catacombs by the Appian Way, when the Decian persecution made care for martyrs' remains a religious duty, and stirred the zeal of the faithful Lucina, who was satisfied with very little proof, or even perhaps could not deny herself some little pious frauds. Thus we explain the traditions as to the stay of the bodies in the catacomb of St. Sebastian, — the *catacumbas* (κατὰ τύμβους : Marchi, *Mon. delle arti crist. prim.* 199-220). See *Lib. pontif.*; Bede, *De temp. rat.* 309 (ed. Giles); Acts of St. Sebastian, and others (Bosio, 247, 248, 251-256, 259, 260); *Acta SS. Jan.* ii. 258, 278; Gruter, 1172, No. 12; Rossi, i. 236, 240-242; *Catal. imp. rom.* (Roncalli, *Vet. lat. scr. chron.*, Padua, 1787, ii. 248). Some MSS. of the *Acta P. et P.* give data for reconciling conflicting accounts. Tisch. *Acta apost. apocr.* 38, 39, n.; Lips. *Die Quellen der röm. Petrussage*, 99; Mabillon, *Liturg. Gall.* 159; Greg. I. *Epist.* iv. 30; Acts of Mar Scherbil, in Cureton, *Anc. Syr. Doc.* 61 *et seq.*

[4] There are two, about three hundred yards apart, north and south,

on the site of the two "trophies."[1] Over them were built two churches, of which one was replaced by the present St. Peter's, while the other, St. Paul's, outside the walls, retained its essential features down to our time.[2]

It is possible that the "trophies" so venerated about the year 200 really marked the spots where the two apostles suffered. Paul, it is not unlikely, lived in his last days on the Ostian road, in the region lying outward from the Lavernal gate.[3] The shade of Peter, on the other hand, ever flits in the legend about the foot of the Vatican, the gardens and circus of Nero, especially about the obelisk,[4] — the circus guarding the memory of the martyrs of that date, among whom, in lack

---

on the ground from which, according to tradition, the bodies were taken. (Rossi, 1867, 3, 16). This would show that the place (*cata-tumbas*), where the graves of the two apostles were in the third century supposed to be, was part of a vast Jewish underground cemetery, at the bend of the Appian Way toward St. Sebastian. Here was the place of Christian burial in the first three centuries (Rossi, vol. ii.).

[1] Eusebius (ii. 25) uses the term "cemetery" (place of rest) to denote the place of burial, implying that Caius means the same thing by "trophy." The Roman tradition generally holds that both the apostles were buried near the spots where they died (Bosio, 74, 197), often confounding, in the case of martyrs, the place of burial with that of execution (Hegesippus in Euseb. ii. 23: 18; *Lib. pont. s. v. Peter* and *Cornelius; Acta*, etc., § 84). This tradition, however, probably arose from the circumstance that, after the bodies were removed and the churches built, it was claimed that the sacred relics had always been there (Euthalius in Zaccagni, 522).

[2] It was destroyed by fire in 1827, and afterwards replaced by the existing monumental structure.

[3] *Kal. lib.* l. c.; *Lib. pont.* l. c.; *Acta*, etc., 80. The basilica of St. Paul, built on the site indicated, no doubt took the place of Caius's "trophy." A later opinion held that Paul was beheaded two miles farther on, near the *Aquæ Salviæ* or *Ad guttam jugiter manantem* (now "St. Paul of the three fountains"), one of the most striking spots on the Campagna: Greg. I. *Epist.* xiv. 14; *Acta*, etc., 80 (in some MSS.); *Acta Junii*, v. 435.

[4] Bosio, 74; Lips. 102.

of clearer knowledge, the tradition would fain include Peter. I, however, prefer to think there was some ground of fact,[1] and that the old site of the obelisk in the sacristy of St. Peter's, marked by an inscription, — not the *Montorio*, which has no claim, — shows very nearly the spot where the frightful spectacle of the crucified apostle glutted the mob's cruel gaze.

It is hardly to be supposed that the bodies so held in reverence were really those of the apostles. True, the custom of protecting the memory of the martyrs' tombs is very ancient in the Church;[2] but about the years 100 and 120 there was at Rome a great development of legend touching these two apostles, in which was wide scope for pious assertion. It is next to incredible that the bodies of the martyred victims could have been recognised and claimed in the days following those awful butcheries. In the hideous mass of human remains, — bruised, burned, trampled, dragged by hooks into the "place of spoils," and then cast into pits,[3] — all marks of identity would be lost. Remains of victims were no doubt often recovered by authority from the executioners;[4] but, even supposing, as we may, that brethren would be found to brave death in

---

[1] See note, p. 162.   [2] Euseb. ii. 23: 18.

[3] By chance the name of one Primitivus has been preserved as the officer who directed this shocking business, whose epitaph is on the tomb where he rested along with the trainer Claudius, the net-fighter Telesphorus, and Claudius Agathocles, surgeon of the morning games, all (as appears) Nero's slaves or freedmen (Orelli, 2554). The passionless marble adds, "Light be the earth upon you!" We have the epitaph of another surgeon of the games, Eutychus, also a slave of Nero, and his wife Irene (*id.* 2553). It is noticeable that all these officers of the arena have the same names as those known among the Christians, great numbers having come from Asia.

[4] Digest, *De cadaveribus punitorum*, xlviii. 24 (1, 2); Diocl. and Max. Cod. Just., constit. 11, *De religiosis et sumptibus funerum* (ii. 44).

search of the precious relics, they would, most likely, instead, have been sent to join the piles of the dead.[1] For several days, as we find in Tacitus, the mere name "Christian" was a death-sentence. But this is of small account. If the basilica of the Vatican does not really cover Peter's tomb, at least it marks for our memory one of the holiest spots of Christendom. The open space where the bad taste of two centuries ago built a theatrical circular colonnade is a second Calvary. Even if it was not the scene of Peter's martyrdom, here at least, we cannot doubt, suffered the Christian Danaïds and Dirces.

If, as we may believe, John came to Rome with Peter, we may find plausible ground for the old tradition that tells how he was cast into a cauldron of boiling oil near the later site of the Latin gate,[2] apparently for the name of Jesus.[3] We are led to think that he witnessed, and suffered in, the Neronian persecution. The Apocalypse is the cry of horror uttered by a witness who has lived in "Babylon," who has known the Beast, has seen the bloody corpses of his martyred brothers, and has himself felt the touch of death.[4] The wretches

---

[1] The tradition of such recoveries at this time by a lady named Lucina involves a confusion of date. She is represented (*Lib. pontif.*) as an adviser of Pope Cornelius in 252; and her legendary task extends to Diocletian's persecution, A. D. 405–409; Acts of St. Sebastian (*Acta Jan.* ii. 258, 278).

[2] Tert. *Præscr.* 36 (see Jer. *in Matt.* xx. 23; *Adv. Jovin.* i. 26; Euseb. vi. 5). Tertullian does not fix the spot, but a Roman tradition apparently refers to that mentioned above (Platner and Bunsen, iii. 604). There are other examples of plunging into boiling oil (Euseb. vi. 5). The Latin gate was in the wall of Aurelian (date 271); there was none of that name in the old wall. See pseudo-Prochorus, ch. 10, 11 (Latin tr.).

[3] Rev. i. 9, a conclusive testimony, even if not written by John himself. Polycrates speaks of him as "martyr and teacher" (Euseb. iii. 24 : 3; v. 24: 3), — though this may be taken from the text in "Revelation."

[4] Rev. i. 9; vi. 9; xiii. 10; xx. 4.

condemned to serve as torches by night must first be plunged in oil or other inflammable substance (boiling or not); and John was possibly devoted to the same torment as his brethren, and destined to illuminate the night-festival of the Latin Way — then saved, by hazard or caprice. In this quarter befell incidents in the horrors of those dreadful days. The southern part of Rome — the *Porta Capena,* the Ostian, Appian, and Latin ways — forms a region where the story of the infant Church in the days of Nero seems to gather.

Jealous destiny has ordained that, on many a point which stirs our lively curiosity, we may never emerge from the shadow which hides the birth of legend. Questions touching the death of the apostles Peter and Paul are met, I repeat, only by more or less probable conjectures. The death of Paul, in particular, is wrapped in thick darkness. Expressions in the Apocalypse, written about 68 or 69, would incline us to think that the writer supposed him to be still living.[1] Very likely his end was wholly unknown. If he took the journey to the West which some passages speak of, shipwreck, sickness, or accident may have taken him from the sight of men. The Canon of Muratori mentions the "passion" of Peter, but not that of Paul, while it speaks of "Paul's journey from Rome into Spain" as the last act of his life; and to this view the passage of Clement (i. 5) would easily fit. He no longer had about him the shining group of his disciples; the details of his death would remain unknown; and later legend would fill out the blank, keeping in view the rank of Roman citizen given him in "Acts," and at the same time the desire of the Christian heart to keep true the

---

[1] Rev. ii. 2, 9; iii. 9.

parallel between him and Peter. There is something that mocks us, it is true, in the mystery that shrouds this stormful apostle's death. It might be interesting to dream of Paul doubting, shipwrecked, abandoned, betrayed by his own, solitary, stricken with the disenchantment of old age. It would flatter us to know that the scales fell from his eyes a second time. Our gentle incredulity would have its mild revenge if the most dogmatic of men had passed away saddened, desponding — let us rather say, tranquil — on some shore or highway of Spain, saying, "I, too, have gone astray." But this is allowing too much to mere conjecture. It is certain that neither apostle was living in the year seventy; they did not behold the ruin of Jerusalem, which would have impressed Paul so profoundly. In the sequel of our history, then, I will assume that the two great champions of Christian thought disappeared at Rome during the awful tempest of sixty-four. The death of James was a little more than two years earlier. Of the "pillar-apostles" John only now remained. Other friends of Jesus still survived at Jerusalem, but forgotten, and, as it were, lost in the on-coming gloom of that storm-cloud into which Judæa was plunged for many years.

In another volume I shall show in what manner the Church completed the reconciliation of Peter and Paul, of which their death had only sketched the outline. Its full success was at that cost. Seemingly, the Jewish Christianity of Peter and the Hellenic Christianity of Paul could not be allied; but each was needful, that the work of the future might be made complete. The one represents the conservative spirit, without which nothing can be solid; the other represents movement and advance, without which nothing can be alive. Life is the resultant of a struggle between two opposing forces. Death is as sure from the lack of all revolutionary breath as from the too great stress of the revolutionary spirit.

CHAPTER IX.

AFTER THE CRISIS. — A. D. 64, 65.

THE consciousness of a community of men is like the consciousness of one man. Every impression that exceeds a certain degree of energy leaves in the brain a trace which is like a wound, and keeps it long, if not always, under the spell of an hallucination or fixed idea. The bloody episode which has been described had equalled in horror the most frightful dreams of which a sick brain is capable; and it haunted the Christian imagination for many years, making it the prey of a sort of vertigo, tormenting it with monstrous dreams, so that a cruel death seemed the fate in store for all the faithful.[1] But is not this very thing the surest sign that the last great day draws near? The souls of the victims of the Beast are conceived as waiting beneath God's altar for the holy hour, and "crying with a loud voice for vengeance."[2] The angel of God appeases them, bidding them to be at rest, and wait yet a little longer, for the time is near when their brethren appointed to slaughter will be slain in their turn. Nero will take care of that. He is the infernal monster to whom God will yield up his power for a season while the catastrophe draws near, who will then appear as a terrifying sign in heaven on the evening horizon of the latter day.[3]

---

[1] Rev. vi. 11.   [2] *Ibid.* vi. 9, 10.
[3] See Cyprian, *De exhort. mart.*, preface.

The air was as it were steeped everywhere with the martyr-spirit. Nero's court seemed filled with a disinterested hate of goodness. From end to end of the Mediterranean it was a death-struggle of right and wrong. That hard Roman world had declared war on piety in every form; and piety was driven to forsake a world given over to treachery, cruelty, and debauch. Every good man was in peril, for Nero's malignant jealousy against virtue had reached its height. The task of philosophy was to fortify its votaries for torture. Seneca, Thraseas, Barea Soranus, Musonius, Cornutus, —all have undergone, or will soon undergo, the consequences of their bold protest. Death by the executioner seems the natural fate of virtue.[1] Even the sceptic Petronius, because he is a gentleman, cannot live in a world ruled by Tigellinus. A touching echo from the victims of this Terror has come to us in inscriptions from an island of religious exile, whence no one might return.[2] In a sepulchral grotto near Cagliari,[3] a family of exiles (perhaps worshippers of Isis)[4] has left to us a touching and almost Christian plaint. As soon as these unfortunates arrived in Sardinia, the husband fell sick in the pestilential air of the island; the wife (Benedicta) besought the gods that she might be taken in his place, and her prayer was heard.

Such a story made clear the futility of massacre. A movement in a narrow aristocratic circle may be stopped by a few executions; but not so a popular movement, which needs not chiefs or learned teachers.

---

[1] Seneca, Letters to Lucilius, *passim*.
[2] Tac. *Ann.* ii. 85.   [3] *Corp. inscr. gr.* 5759.
[4] As may be inferred from the name, or rather epithet, *Benedicta*, and the sculptures of the grotto.

A garden where flowers are cut up by the root perishes; but a mown meadow sprouts more vigorous than before. Thus Christianity, far from being checked by Nero's wanton cruelties, put forth a sturdier growth than ever. Wrath waxed hot in the heart of the survivors; and the one thought with them all was how they might come to be masters of the pagans, and rule them with a rod of iron, as they deserved.[1] A conflagration far more dreadful than that with which they were falsely charged should destroy that city of iniquity, which had become the temple of Satan. The doctrine of the final destruction of the world by fire struck deeper root day by day. Fire alone could purge the earth of the crimes that soiled it; fire alone seemed the right and fit end of such a mass of horrors.

Most of the Christians at Rome who had escaped the massacre no doubt forsook the city.[2] For ten or twelve years the church there was thrown into extreme confusion, opening a wide door to legend. Still the life of the community was not completely broken off. The Seer of the Apocalypse, in December of 68 or the following January, enjoins upon his people to "come out of" the wicked city.[3] Even allowing its share to prophetic fiction, it is hard not to infer from these words that the church in Rome soon recovered its importance. Only the leaders quitted for good a place where their ministry could for a season bear no fruit.

The province of Asia Minor was the one part of the Roman world where life was most endurable for Jews.

---

[1] Rev. ii. 26, 27.

[2] So we infer from Heb. v. 11–14; xiii. 24. They probably made up those "away from Italy" (οἱ ἀπὸ τῆς Ἰταλίας) addressed in this epistle.

[3] Rev. xviii. 4.

Between the Jews of Rome and those of Ephesus there was constant intercourse, as we have seen in the case of Aquila and Priscilla. Hither the fugitives now fled, and Ephesus became the spot where the effect of the Neronian persecution was most keenly felt. Here was concentrated the animosity against Rome; and here, within about four years, was delivered the tremendous invective by which the Christian conscience answered back to the atrocity of Nero.

There is nothing improbable in assuming that among the Christian leaders who escaped from Rome was included the apostle whom we have seen following so closely the footsteps of Peter. If there is any truth in the stories of what happened (as was afterwards believed) near the Latin gate, we may suppose that John, escaping as by miracle, left the city at once, and in that case he would naturally take refuge in Asia. His residence at Ephesus may be a matter of doubt, like most incidents in the lives of the apostles; still, it is not a thing unlikely in itself, and I incline rather to accept than to reject it.[1]

[1] The chief argument is from the Apocalypse. If this was written by John the apostle, the case is clear. If by one who wished it to be taken as his work,—supposing him in that case to have died before 68, as we could hardly admit a forgery in his lifetime,— we are struck by the circumstance that the vision is represented as at Patmos, a stopping-place for those going to or returning from Asia. It is especially to be noted that the apostle is made to address the churches in Asia as having a certain authority among them, and knowing their inner life. What would have been the effect of the first three chapters on those who knew that he had never been at Patmos or among them? Dionysius of Alexandria (Euseb. vii. 25) saw this clearly, and assumes that the writer can have been no other than one of the apostles who had been in Asia. The alternative is that the writer was another man of the same name with the apostle,—the unlikeliest theory of all.

Direct evidences of John's abode in Ephesus are from the last quarter

The church at Ephesus was mixed, a part being of Pauline, a part of Judæo-Christian faith. The latter must hold the ascendency, now at the arrival of the Roman colony, particularly if it brought a personal follower of Jesus, a teacher from Jerusalem, one of those eminent leaders before whom Paul himself would bow. Since Peter and James were gone, John was the only surviving apostle of the first rank; he had come to be the head of all the Judæo-Christian churches; he was held in extreme deference; it was the general belief — he himself had said it — that Jesus had a special love for him. Many a tale was founded upon this fact; and for a time Ephesus was the centre of Christian life, while Rome and Jerusalem were almost forbidden abodes, through the fury of the time.

There was soon warm contention between the dominant party, having at its head "the disciple whom Jesus loved," and the group of proselytes gathered by Paul, which spread to all the Asiatic churches.[1] The air was filled with declamations against the Balaam who had sown scandal among the sons of Israel, — had taught them they might associate with the heathen

of the second century, — Apollonius: Euseb. v. 18; Polycrates, bishop of Ephesus (note this): *id.* iii. 31; v. 24; Irenæus, ii. 22: 5; iii. 1: 1; 3: 4; 11: 1; v. 26: 1; 30: 1, 3; 33: 4; Letter to Victor: Euseb. v. 24; and especially the letter to Florinus in Euseb. v. 20 (testimony of great weight, of genuineness hardly to be doubted, since Waddington has fixed the martyrdom of Polycarp at Feb. 23, 155 : *Mém. de l'Acad. des inscr.* xxvi. 233); Clem. of Alex. *Quis dives*, 42; Orig. *in Matt.* xvi. 6; Opp. ii. 24 (ed. Delarue); Dion. of Alex.: Euseb. vii. 25; Euseb. iii. 1, 18, 20, 23, 31, 39; v. 24; *Chron. ann.* 98; Epiph. lxxviii. 11; *Mart. of Ignatius*, i. 3; Jer. *De vir. ill.* 9; *Adv. Jov.* i. 26; *ad Gal.* vi. The silence of Papias (Euseb. iii. 39, with *Chron. ann.* 98), of Hegesippus, and the so-called letters of Ignatius, is a serious point, as is also the very old confusion between John "the apostle" and "the elder." See Appendix.

[1] *St. Paul*, chap. xiii.

without guilt, or marry the heathen women. John, on the other hand, was more and more looked on as a Jewish high-priest (ἱερεύς). Like James, he wore the gold plate on the forehead (πέταλον).[1] He was the Teacher; he even, perhaps from the incident of the boiling oil, came to be called Martyr.

Among the fugitives who came from Rome to Ephesus, Barnabas appears to have been included (see below). Timothy was in prison at this time, — we know not where, perhaps at Corinth,[2] at any rate not far from Ephesus, — but was set free after a few months. As soon as Barnabas knew of his release, seeing that quiet was restored, he bethought him of returning to Rome with Timothy, whom he had known and loved in the company of Paul.[3] The apostolic group, scattered by the persecution of 64, now aimed at reconstruction. The school of Paul was the weaker, being without its head, and sought to rest on the solider portion of the Church. Timothy, accustomed to yield, had little force after Paul's death; while Barnabas, who had always held a middle path between the parties, never once offending against charity, came to be the gathering centre for the fragments after the great wreck. This admirable man was thus a second time the restorer of Jesus' work, the good genius of harmony and peace.

In circumstances like these, as I think, was composed a work bearing a title not easy to explain, "the Epistle to the Hebrews." It would seem to have been

---

[1] Polycrates in Euseb. iii. 31: 3; v. 24: 3. The same is attributed to Mark in apocryphal documents (A. de Valois in note on Euseb. v. 24: p. 191); see Suicer, *Thes. eccl.* (*s. v.* πέταλον); "St. Paul," 307.

[2] Heb. xiii. 23.   [3] *Ibid.* xiii. 19, 23.

written at Ephesus by Barnabas, and addressed to the church at Rome (whence that church seems to have been always better informed than others of its authorship),[1] in the name of the little community of Italian Christians in the capital of Asia. By its intermediate position, at the meeting-point of various tendencies that had not so far been well harmonised, this epistle rightfully belongs to that man of reconciling temper, who often prevented those diverse tendencies in the young community from coming to open quarrel. The opposition between churches of Jewish and pagan origin seems, in this little treatise, to be resolved, or rather lost, in an overflowing flood of transcendental metaphysics and placid charity. As I before remarked, a taste for *midrashim*, or little treatises in epistolary form, had become well established. Paul had put his whole thought into "Romans," and "Ephesians" had been the maturest expression of his later doctrine. "Hebrews" appears to be a document of this class. No Christian book so much resembles the works of the Jewish school at Alexandria, especially the little tracts of Philo. Apollos had already tried his hand at the same task, and has even been thought to be the author of "Hebrews." Paul, while in prison, had greatly delighted in him. Alexandrinism, an element foreign to Jesus, was gradually winning entrance into Christian thought: we shall presently find this influence dominant in the so-called Johannine writings. In "Hebrews," Christian theology takes a form much like that we have found in the later style of Paul. The theory of the Divine Word (*Logos*) is rapidly unfolding.

[1] See Introduction. The first epistle of Clement, written at Rome about 95, is full of reminiscences of "Hebrews."

Jesus becomes more and more "the second divinity," the *metathronos* or Associate, the First-born on God's right hand, inferior to Him alone. Under existing circumstances, the writer expresses himself only in veiled words. We feel that he dreads to compromise the bearer of his letter, and those to whom it is sent: hence, perhaps, the vague title "Hebrews," and the absence of personal greetings or signature. A painful weight burdens him; his secret distress betrays itself in hints brief and deep.

God, he says, having in former time conveyed his will to men by his messengers the prophets, has in these last days employed the ministry of his Son, by whom he made the worlds ($a\hat{\iota}\hat{\omega}\nu as$),[1] and who sustains all by his word. This Son, the reflection of the Father's glory, and the image of His essence, whom it was the Father's pleasure to make heir of all things, became the ransom of sins in his manifestation to the world, and is now returned to sit in heavenly regions on the right of the Most High,[2] in rank superior to angels. The Mosaic law was announced by angels,[3] containing only the shadow of good things to come; while ours was delivered by the Lord himself, with proofs by signs, wonders, miracles, and gifts of the Holy Spirit, being given down to us in a sure manner by those who heard it direct from him. Through Jesus all men have been made sons of God. Moses was a

---

[1] $A\iota\grave{\omega}\nu$ is taken here in the sense of the Hebrew *ôlam* (Phœn. *oulom*, Arab. *âlam*), serving as transition to the Gnostic *Æons*.

[2] An early example of the cabbalistic style. Comp. Matt. xxvi. 64.

[3] Gal. iii. 19; Acts vii. 53. The theology of the time (as we see in Greek and Chaldean versions of the Old Testament and in Josephus) used the term "angels" in speaking of the visible manifestations of Deity, as in Deut. xxxiii. 2.

servant; Jesus is the Son, and is our especial High-Priest of the order of Melchizedek,[1] — an order far higher than the Levitical, which it has abolished, and enduring forever. Thus: —

He, indeed, is such a high-priest as we require, — holy, without sin or blot, apart from sinners, exalted above the heavens, who need not, like other priests, offer sacrifice daily for his own sins, and then for those of his people. The old law appointed as high-priests men liable to error; the new law has revealed the Son, established for eternity. . . . Thus we have a high-priest who sits in heaven at the right hand of the throne of God, as a minister of the true sanctuary and the true tabernacle which the Lord has built. Christ is the high-priest of blessings to come. . . . If the blood of bulls and goats, or ashes of a heifer, sprinkled on the unclean, sanctify them so as to give them purity of the flesh, how much more shall the blood of Christ, which he himself, a victim without blemish, has offered to God, purify our conscience from dead works! . . . For this end he is the mediator of the new testament: now, that there may be a testament (or will), the death of the testator must first be proved, since a will has no effect so long as the testator lives; and the original stipulation must be made good by blood. . . . By blood everything is made legally clean; and without the shedding of blood there is no expiation.[2]

We are, then, sanctified once for all by the sacrifice of Jesus, who will appear a second time to save those who look for his coming. The sacrifices of old never attained their end; they must be continually renewed. If the sacrifice of Atonement[3] must be repeated every year on a fixed day, does not that prove that the blood of victims had no [lasting] power? Instead of these

---

[1] Heb. iv. 14–16.   [2] *Ibid.* ix. 11–22.
[3] Levit. ch. xvi.

continual burnt-offerings, Jesus has made his own one offering, which makes the others needless. Thus there is no longer any question of sacrifice for sin.[1]

The writer deeply feels the dangers that menace the Church. Before his eyes is an unbroken prospect of suffering. His thought is filled with the tortures endured by the prophets and the martyrs of Antiochus in the days of the Maccabees.[2] The faith of many is weakening; and toward such weakness his words are stern: —

It is impossible that those who have once been enlightened, who have received the heavenly gift and shared the Holy Spirit, who have tasted the precious word of God and the blessing of the world to come, and then have fallen away, so as to crucify the Son of God afresh so far as is in their power, — it is impossible that they should be brought again to repentance. Soil which yields only thorns and thistles is accounted bad and worthy to be cursed, and must be burned over with fire. . . . God surely is not unjust, and he will not forget your good deeds, or the love you have shown to his name by serving his saints, as you have done and still do. Increase your zeal to the end, that your hopes may be fulfilled; and follow the example of those who by faith and perseverance have conquered the promised heritage.[3]

Some of the members were already growing negligent in attending the assemblies of the Church.[4] The writer asserts that these assemblies are of the very essence of the faith: it is here that the disciples exhort, rouse, and keep watch on one another; and in this they must be the more faithful as the last great day approaches: —

[1] Heb. ix. 23-28. [2] *Ibid.* xi. 32-40; xii. 1-11.
[3] *Ibid.* vi. 4-12. [4] *Ibid.* x. 25.

If we sin wilfully after we have received knowledge of the truth, as there is no more any sacrifice for sin henceforth, we have only to look in terror for the fiery judgment which will swallow up the unfaithful. It is a dreadful thing to fall into the hands of the living God![1] ... Remember the past days, when, after you were enlightened, you endured many a painful conflict, when some of you were exposed in the open theatre[2] to torment and outrage, or again when you were companions of those who so suffered. In fact, you have shown your fellow-feeling for those in chains (δεσμίοις), and have gladly suffered the plundering of your goods, knowing that you have treasures both glorious and enduring. Be brave, that you may obtain the reward promised you! Yet a little, a very little time, and he who shall come will come.[3]

Faith sums up the temper of the Christian soul.[4] Faith is the resolute looking forward to that which is promised, and firm assurance of that which is not seen. Faith is what created the great men under the old law, who died without having received the promised blessing, having only foreseen and hailed it from afar, confessing themselves strangers and pilgrims on the earth, always looking for a better country, a heavenly one, which they did not find. Here the writer recites the examples of the ancient worthies, — Abel, Enoch, Noah, Abraham, Sarah, Isaac, Jacob, Joseph, Moses, and "the harlot Rahab" : —

And what more? for the time would fail me to tell of Gideon, Barak, Samson, Jephthah, David, Samuel, and the Prophets, — who by faith subdued kingdoms, dispensed judg-

---

[1] Heb. xi. 26-31.

[2] Θλίψεσιν θεατριζόμενοι may, it is true, be a metaphor; still, I prefer to regard it as an allusion to the horrid spectacles of Nero's circus. A similar passage in Hermas (vis. iii. 2) surely refers to these tortures (see *post*, p. 306, note 3).

[3] Heb. x. 32-37.   [4] *Ibid.* ch. xi.

ment, obtained promises, stopped the mouth of lions, quenched the fury of fire, escaped the edge of the sword, recovered their strength from sickness, were mighty men of war, putting to flight the invasions of the enemy. . . . Some were beaten to death with clubs,[1] not consenting to release, but choosing before life a better resurrection; others suffered mocking, scourging, chains, or the dungeon; or were stoned, sawn asunder,[2] questioned by torture, or died by stroke of the sword; or went about clad in sheepskins and goatskins, destitute, afflicted, tormented, — of whom the world was not worthy! or they wandered in deserts and mountains, in dens and caves of the earth.

All these holy men, though fixed in their faith, did not witness the fulfilment of the promise; for God has reserved some better thing for us, not choosing that without us their work should be complete. Since, then, we are surrounded by so great a cloud of witnesses, let us persevere in the struggle that is still before us, looking always to Jesus, the founder and finisher of our faith! You have not yet resisted unto blood in your conflict against evil![3]

The writer then explains to the confessors that the sufferings they endure are not a punishment, but should be received as a fatherly discipline, such as one administers to a child, a pledge of his own tenderness. He urges them to guard against a temper of levity, like Esau's, bartering their heavenly inheritance for an earthly and short-lived privilege. He returns for the third time upon his favourite thought, that, after a fall involving the desertion of Christianity, there is no longer a chance for return.[4] Esau, too,

---

[1] Τυμπανίζω (to beat as a drum), one of the tortures of the Maccabæan time.

[2] The traditional death of Isaiah.   [3] Heb. xi. 32-xii. 4.

[4] *Ibid.* xiii. 16, 17, 25; comp. vi. 4-6; x. 26, 27, — passages which later played a great part in the Montanist and Novatian controversies.

sought to reclaim his father's blessing, but in vain, spite of his remorse and tears. We see that in the Neronian persecution there were some who fell away through weakness,[1] who after their apostasy would have desired to return; and this teacher would have them repelled. What blindness, he urges, is like the Christian's, who shrinks or denies when he has once come near "the holy mount Zion, and the city of the living God, the heavenly Jerusalem, the chorus of ten thousand angels, God the eternal Judge, the church of his first-born, the spirits of the just made perfect,[2] and Jesus the mediator of the new covenant, — and has been purified by a holier blood than that of Abel?"[3]

The writer ends by recalling to his readers those of their brethren who were still in the Roman dungeons;[4] above all, the memory of their spiritual leaders who are no more, — those great founders who have declared to them the word of God, and whose death was a triumph for the faith. Let them consider the end of those holy lives, and they will be strengthened.[5] Let them guard against false doctrines, especially those which make holiness consist in useless ritual forms, such as distinctions of food.[6] Here we find the disciple or friend of Paul. In truth, the whole epistle, like all of Paul's, is a long demonstration of the complete annulment of the Mosaic law. To bear the shame of Jesus, — to withdraw from the world, since "here we have no abiding city, but seek one which is to come," — to obey our leaders in the Church, paying them due

---

[1] Cf. Matt. xxiv. 10.

[2] The "first-born," and those "made perfect," are the sufferers in the recent persecution.

[3] Heb. xii. 18–24.　　　　[4] Ibid. xiii. 3.

[5] Ibid. xiii. 7.　　　　[6] Ibid. xiii. 9; cf. ix. 10.

respect, and making their task easy and pleasant, "since they watch over souls and must give account of them," — this is the rule of practice. No writing, perhaps, better shows the mystic dignity of Jesus expanding until at length it completely fills the Christian conscience. Not only is he the Logos by whom the worlds were made, but his blood is the universal ransom, the seal of a new alliance. The author is so full of this thought that he makes false readings in order to find it everywhere. Thus, in the Greek copy of the Psalms,[1] the two letters τι in the word ὠτία ("ears") were a little blurred; now, reading these as μ, and taking in the final σ of the word before, he made out σῶμα ("body"), which gives an excellent messianic sense: "Sacrifice and offering thou didst not desire, but *a body* hast thou prepared for me. Then I said, Behold, I come," etc.[2]

Strangely enough, in the Pauline school the death of Jesus is far more significant than his life. The precepts announced beside the Lake of Galilee have no interest for this school, which seems hardly to have known them. In the foreground it sees the sacrifice of Jesus, who devotes himself to atone for the sins of the world. This strange conception, put afterwards in the sharpest relief by Calvin, wrenched Christian theology far indeed from the early evangelical ideal! The Synoptic gospels, which are the really divine element in Christianity, have nought to do with the work of Paul. We shall soon see them budding forth from

[1] Ps. xl. 6. He can have known little of any tongue but Greek: see e. g., his argument on διαθήκη ["testament"], considered as equivalent to to *berith* ["league," in ix. 15-17].

[2] Heb. x. 5, — where the Hebrew sense is, "ears hast thou bestowed upon me."

that little humble household which still preserved in Palestine the true tradition of the life and the person of Jesus.

But the truly admirable thing in early Christian history is this: that those who tried most obstinately to draw the car of progress the wrong way were the ones who served best to make it advance. The epistle to the Hebrews marks just the point, in the religious development of mankind, where sacrifice disappears, which till then had made the very essence of religion. For the primitive man, God is an all-powerful being, whom man must propitiate or else bribe. Thus sacrifice arose from fear, or else from interest. To win his deity, the worshipper offered him a gift such as might move him,—a fine bit of meat, rich fat, a bowl of *soma* or wine: says Juvenal, "*tenui popano corruptus Osiris.*"[1] Disasters and diseases were thought to be inflictions sent by an angry God; and it was imagined that by putting some one else in place of the person threatened the wrath of the higher power might be turned away; possibly, said they, the god may even be satisfied with an animal, if it is useful, innocent, and good. God was judged by the pattern of man. Even to-day, in some parts of Africa and the East, the native thinks to win the favour of a stranger by killing a sheep at his feet, wetting his boots with the blood, and serving the flesh as food; and, just so, it was once thought that the Divine nature must be impressed by the offering of an object, particularly if the worshipper deprived himself of something really valuable. Until the great transformation wrought by the prophets of the eighth century before Christ, the idea of sacrifice

[1] *Sat.* vi. 541.

among the Israelites was not much higher than that of other tribes. A new era began when Isaiah cried out in Jehovah's name, "Sacrifice is an abomination to me; I delight not in the blood of bullocks, lambs, or goats!" The day he wrote these noble words (about 740 B. C.), Isaiah was the true forerunner of Christianity. On that day it was determined that, of the two rival claimants for the veneration of ancient tribes, the hereditary priest or sorcerer, and the inspired book, thought to contain secrets of the Divine mind, the latter would control the future of religion. The sorcerer (*nabi*) of the Semitic tribes became the "prophet," or sacred orator of the people, devoted to the advance of social justice. While the sacrificer (priest) continued to vaunt the efficacy of slaughter, so profitable to him, the prophet dared to announce that the true God cares far more for justice and mercy than for all the "bullocks" in the world. Enjoined, however, by antique ritual, which it was hard to set aside, and sustained by the self-interest of priests, sacrifice continued to be the law in ancient Israel. Toward the time at which we are now arrived, even before the destruction of the third Temple, the importance of this rite had lessened. The scattered condition of the Jews led them to regard as a secondary thing an office that could be performed only at Jerusalem.[1] Philo had declared that religious worship consisted mainly in pious hymns, to be sung rather with the heart than with the lips; and ventured to say that such prayers were of more worth than sacrifice.[2] The Essenes held the same view.[3] Paul, in "Romans"

---

[1] See Acts xxiv. 17.
[2] *De plant. Noe*, 25, 28–31. Comp. Theophrast. *De pietate*.
[3] Jos. *Ant*. xviii. 1: 5; Philo, *Quod omnis probus liber*, 12.

(xii. 1), declares that religion is a service of pure reason (λατρεία λογική). "Hebrews," in unfolding the view that Jesus is the true high-priest, and that his death as a sacrifice abolished all others, struck the last blow at bloody offerings. Christians, including those of Jewish origin, gradually ceased to regard themselves as bound to legal sacrifices, or else gave place to them only as a concession. The leading idea of the Mass — the belief that the sacrifice of Jesus is incessantly renewed in the ritual act of the Eucharist — is already perceptible, but in a very obscure distance.

CHAPTER X.

THE REVOLT IN JUDÆA. — A. D. 66.

THE state of exaltation through which the Christian mind was passing was soon disturbed by events taking place in Palestine, that made the visions of the wildest seers look reasonable. A feverish crisis, which can be compared only to that which raged in France during the Revolution, or to that in the Paris of 1871, took entire possession of the Jewish nation. These " maladies divine," for which the ancient healing art confessed itself powerless, seemed to have become the every-day condition of the Jews. One would have said that, being determined on excess, they wished to go as far as human passion could carry them. This strange race, which seems made on purpose to defy alike him who blesses and him who curses, was for four years in a convulsion, in presence of which the historian, divided between admiration and horror, must pause, with such emotion as he feels when confronted with anything mysterious and unaccountable.

The causes of this crisis were of old standing, and the crisis itself was unavoidable. The Mosaic Law was the work of Utopian enthusiasts, weakest of men in political judgment, possessed by a powerful socialist ideal; and, like Islam, it barred out, absolutely, any civil society running parallel to the religious society. This Law seems to have taken the formal character in which we find it, during the seventh century before Christ; and, even without the Assyrian conquest, it would have blown to pieces the petty monarchy of the house of David. Ever since the dominating control assumed by the prophetic class, the kingdom of Judah — embroiled with all its neighbours, possessed by a standing rage against Tyre, in deadly feud with Edom, Moab, and Ammon — was no longer capable of life. A people devoted to religious and social problems is doomed as a political society. The day when Israel became "a peculiar treasure to Jehovah, a kingdom of priests, a holy nation,"[1] it was ordained not to be a people like any other. You cannot pile together contradictory destinies; a superior quality is always balanced against some grave defect.

The Persian empire gave to Israel a little rest. This vast feudal system, tolerant to all diversities of province, very like the caliphate of Bagdad or the Ottoman empire, made a condition in which the Jews found themselves most at ease. The Egyptian (Ptolemaic) domination, of the third century B. C., seems also to have been quite kindly towards them. But it was not so with the sovereigns of Syria, the Seleucidæ. Antioch had become the centre of an active Grecian propaganda; Antiochus Epiphanes thought himself bound to establish everywhere the image of Olympian Jove as a sign of his own power. Then broke forth the first great Jewish revolt against the pagan civilization. Israel had patiently endured the blotting out of its own political existence since Nebuchadnezzar; but it kept no bounds when its religious institutions were in danger. A race in general unmilitary was seized with a fit of heroism.

---

[1] Exod. xix. 5, 6.

Without a regular army, without generals, without military skill, it defeated the Seleucids, maintained its revealed right, and created a second era of independence. But the Asmonæan monarchy was ever undermined by profound interior vices; it lasted but a century. The destiny of the Jewish people was not to found a separate nationality. These people dreamed of something broader than the nation; its ideal is not the City, but the Synagogue, the free congregation. It is the same with Islam, which has created an immense empire, but has destroyed every nationality among the peoples whom it has subdued, and leaves to them no other fatherland than the mosque and the monastery.

We often call such a social state by the name "theocracy." And we are right, if we mean by this that the central thought of the Semitic religions and of the empires that have grown from them is the sovereignty of God, conceived as sole Lord of the world and universal King. But with these peoples theocracy does not mean the reign of priests. The priest, properly so called, plays a feeble part in the history of Judaism or of Islamism. Power belongs to the representative of God, — to him whom God inspires, to the prophet, the holy man, the one who has received a mission from heaven, and who proves his mission by miracle or by success. In lack of prophet, power belongs to the revealer of visions, to the writer of apocryphal books ascribed to ancient prophets, to the teacher or interpreter of the Law, to the leader of the Synagogue, and still more to the head of the Family, who is guardian of the sacred trust, and transmits it to his children. Civil power, or royalty, has little to do with such a social constitution, which never works better than when its subjects are scattered, as tolerated aliens, throughout a great empire having no uniform administration. Judaism is naturally submissive, since it has within itself no resource of military power. We see the same thing among the Greeks of our own day: the Greek communities in Trieste, Smyrna, and Constantinople are far more flourishing than the petty kingdom of Greece; because these communities are relieved from the stress of political agitation, which is sure to ruin a race full of energy, that is put prematurely in possession of political independence.

The Roman dominion, established by Pompey in Judæa in the year 63 B. C., seemed at first to satisfy well some of the conditions of Jewish life. It was not at this time the practice of Rome to assimilate in its political system the nations successively annexed to it. The right of peace and war was taken from them, and Rome enforced little more than control over the larger questions of their politics. Under the degenerate successors of the Asmonæans, and under the Herods, the Jewish nation retained a quasi-independence, which ought to have been enough for it, since its religious institutions were scrupulously respected. But the inner crisis of the people was too violent. After passing a certain stage of religious fanaticism, man is uncontrolable. It must also be said that Rome tended constantly to make its power more heavily felt in the East. The petty subject royalties, at first maintained, disappeared from day to day, and the provinces were merged in an imperial power pure and simple. From the year 6 A. D., Judæa was ruled by governors (*procuratores*) subject to the imperial governors-general (*legati*) of Syria, and having at their side the parallel power of the

Herods. Such a mode of rule was unworkable, as became more clear from day to day. The Herods found little honour among men really patriotic and devout. Roman ways of administration, however reasonable in themselves, were abhorrent to the Jews. In general, the Roman power showed the utmost regard for the pettiest scruples of the nation.[1] But this was not enough. Things had come to such a pass that nothing could be done without touching upon some question of the canon. Positive religions, like Islamism and Judaism, do not admit any divided authority. If they have not absolute rule, they complain of persecution. If they find themselves protected, they become exacting, and try to make life unendurable to all other worships. This is clearly seen in Algeria, where the Israelites, knowing themselves to be protected against the Moslems, treat them intolerably, and keep the authorities eternally busied with their mutual complaints.

Doubtless there was wrong on both sides, as I freely admit, in the hundred years' experiment made by Roman and Jew to live together, which issued in so dreadful a catastrophe. Several of the governors were thoroughly bad men;[2] others may have been hard, abrupt, driven to exasperation by a religion that thorned them, whose grand future they knew nothing of. It would have needed perfection itself not to be exasperated by that narrow and haughty temper, that hostility to Greek and Roman culture, that ill-will to all mankind, which a surface-knowledge took to be the

---

[1] See an inscription discovered by Mr. Ganneau: *Rev. arch.* Apr.-May, 1872; *Journal Asiatique*, Aug.-Sept., 1872.

[2] See the proverb on the justice rendered at Cæsarea: Midrash, *Esther*, 1 (init.).

essence of a Jew. Besides, what could a magistrate possibly think of subjects always trying to accuse him before the emperor, and to form cabals against him even when he was perfectly in the right? In that deep hate which now these more than two thousand years has prevailed between the Jews and the rest of mankind, which party was first to blame? The question should not be so put. In such a case, all is at once action and reaction, cause and effect. Those barrings-out, those chained gateways of the Ghetto, that distinctive gabardine, — these things are all wrong; but who first insisted on them? It was those who thought themselves defiled by contact with the "gentiles;" those who demanded for themselves to be kept apart in a community by themselves. Fanaticism wrought the chains, and fanaticism has been redoubled by the chains, hate engendering hate. There is but one way of escape from this vicious circle: it is to abolish the source of hate, — that mischievous separation, first sought and desired by the sects, which afterwards became their reproach. Regarding Judaism, France in our century has solved the problem. By throwing down all legal barriers built about the Israelite, it has taken away what was narrow and exclusive in Judaism — its peculiar customs and its sequestered life — so completely that within two or three generations a Jewish family, settled in Paris, has almost ceased to lead a Jewish life.

It would be unfair to reproach Romans of the first century for not having done the same thing. Between the Roman empire and Jewish orthodoxy there was radical hostility. In this hostility Jews were oftenest insolent, quarrelsome, and aggressive. The idea of equity in common, which the Romans had with them in germ, was hateful to strict observers of the Law (*Torah*), who asserted a morality wholly at odds with a society purely secular, untouched by theocracy, like that of Rome. One was the founder of the State, the other of the Church. Rome created an administration rational and worldly; the Jews attempted to inaugurate the kingdom of God. There was an irrepressible conflict between this narrow but fruitful theocracy and the most absolute proclamation of the secular State that was ever made. The Jews had their law built on a foundation wholly different from the Roman right, and at bottom irreconcilable with it. Until they had been unmercifully checkmated, they could not be satisfied with mere tolerance, believing as they did that in their keeping was the eternal Word, the secret of the building of a holy city. It was with them just as it is with the Moslems of Algeria to-day, whom our social structure, though infinitely superior, inspires only with abhorrence. Their revealed law, at once civil and religious, fills them with pride, and makes them powerless to accept a philosophic legislation founded on the one principle of men's mutual relations. Add to this a profound ignorance, which forbids them to make any estimate of the forces of the civilized world, and blinds them to the fatal issue of the war into which they would fain plunge with a light heart.

One circumstance had much to do with keeping Judæa in a state of permanent hostility against the Empire: namely, that the Jews took no share in military service. Everywhere else the legions were enlisted from among the men of the country; and thus, with armies numerically weak, the Romans held vast regions.[1] The soldier in Roman service and the people of the region were fellow country-men. It was not so in Judæa. The legions that held the country were recruited mostly in Cæsarea or Sebaste, towns at enmity with Judaism. Thus no common understanding could exist between the army and the people. The Roman force at Jerusalem was fenced off in barracks apart, as in a permanent state of siege.

Besides, the feelings held towards Rome by the various parties in the Jewish world were by no means alike. Apart from worldlings like Tiberius Alexander, who had grown indifferent to the old worship and were regarded as traitors by their fellow religionists, every one (it is true) was unfriendly to the foreign masters; but not all, by any means, were inclined to revolt. In this view, four or five parties may be distinguished in Jerusalem.[2]

First, the party of Sadducees and Herodians, the residue of the house and dependents of Herod, the great houses of Hanan and Boëthus in charge of the high-priesthood: these made a world of epicureans and sceptical voluptuaries, hated by the people for their pride, their ungodliness, and their wealth. This party, essentially conservative, had a warrant of its privilege in the Roman occupation, and, with no good-will toward the Romans, was steadily opposed to any revolution.

Second, the party of the middle-class Pharisees,— an honest party, made up of men of sense, steady, quiet, orderly, fond of their religion, keeping its forms scrupulously, devoutly even, but without imagination;

---

[1] See the curious discourse reported of Agrippa II. by Josephus, *Wars*, ii. 16 : 4.

[2] Josephus, *Wars*, ii. 16 : 4; *Life*, 3.

fairly intelligent, acquainted with the outside world, and seeing clearly that revolt could end only in the destruction of the nation and the Temple. Josephus is the type of this class, whose fate was that which seems to be always in store for the moderates in times of revolution, — impotence, inconstancy, and the supreme humiliation of appearing as traitors in the eyes of the majority.

Third, zealots of all sorts, — fanatics, armed partisans (*sicarii*), assassins, a strange mass of mendicant enthusiasts, reduced to extremest misery by Sadducee injustice and violence; men regarding themselves as the only heirs of the promise made to Israel, of the "poor man" beloved of God; feeding their zeal on prophetic visions such as "Enoch," and apocalypses of violence; believing that the kingdom of God was just about to be revealed; and who came at length to the intensest exaltation of which history makes mention.

Fourth, brigands, vagabonds, adventurers, desperate freebooters, sprung from the complete social disintegration of the country. This sort of men, mostly of Idumæan or Nabathæan origin, recked little of any religious motive; but they were fomenters of disorder, and were natural allies of the Zealots.

Lastly, pious dreamers, Essenes, Christians, Ebionim, quietly waiting for the kingdom of heaven, devotees gathered about the Temple, praying and weeping. Of these were the followers of Jesus; but they were still of so little account in the public eye that Josephus takes no note of them among the parties to the struggle, nor does Justus of Tiberias, who also wrote the story of Jewish War.[1] We see at once that in the

[1] Photius, *Biblioth.*, cod. 33.

day of peril these pious folk can only flee. The spirit of Jesus, full as it was of a divine power to withdraw man from the world and give him comfort, could not inspire the narrow patriotism of the fighter and the hero.

The fanatics would naturally hold the balance of power. The democratic and revolutionary vein of Judaism stood out among them in an appalling degree. They were convinced that all power has its root in evil; that royalty is a work of Satan, — which theory was but too well justified by the examples of sovereigns like Caligula and Nero, real devils incarnate; and they would rather be chopped to pieces than give the title of master to any other than God.[1] Imitating Mattathias, the first of Zealots, who killed a Jew whom he saw sacrificing to idols,[2] they avenged their God by dagger-strokes. Merely to hear one uncircumcised speak of God or the Law was provocation enough to seize on him unawares, and then offer him the choice of circumcision or death.[3] Claiming to execute those mysterious sentences which are left to the "hand of God," and holding themselves bound to put in effect the dreadful penalty of excommunication, which meant outlawry and death, as the Hebrew formula implies,[4] they made an army of terrorists, whose revolutionary temper was at boiling heat. It might be seen in advance that such men's distempered conscience, incapable to distinguish their own gross passions from a mood which their fanatic fury would count holy,

---

[1] Like Judas the Gaulonite. See "Life of Jesus," pp. 120–122.
[2] 1 Macc. ii. 27.   [3] *Philosophumena*, ix. 26.
[4] See *Journal Asiatique*, Aug.-Sept. 1872, p. 178; also Jos. *Wars*, ii. 8: 8; and compare the formulas בידי שמים, etc.

would go on to the last excess, and be checked at no degree of madness.

Minds were under the spell of a kind of permanent hallucination. Terrifying rumours were in circulation everywhere. Men dreamed only of signs and omens; the apocalyptic hue of Jewish fancy stained everything with a bloody halo. Comets, swords in the sky, battles in the clouds, light breaking forth of itself by night from the depth of the sanctuary, victims at the moment of sacrifice bringing forth a monstrous progeny,—these were the tales told with horror from mouth to mouth. One day the vast brazen gates of the Temple had flown open of themselves, and refused to close. At the Passover of A. D. 65, about 3 A. M., the Temple was for half an hour lighted as bright as day: some thought that it was on fire. Again at Pentecost, the priests heard a sound as of many persons in the interior, making hasty preparations as if for flight, and saying to one another, "Let us depart hence!"[1] All this was not reached till later; but the great disturbance of mind was itself the best of signs that something extraordinary was about to happen.

Messianic prophecies, more than anything else, roused among the people a resistless craving for excitement. One does not resign himself to a humble sphere when he is looking forward to royal power in the near future. For the multitude, all messianic theories were summed up in a single text, said to be taken from Scripture: "At that time a Prince shall come forth from Judah who shall have rule over all the earth."[2] In vain do

---

[1] Jos. *Wars*, ii. 22: 1; vi. 5: 3, 4; Tac. *Hist.* v. 13; Bab. Talm. *Pesachim*, 57 a; *Kerithoth*, 28 a; *Ioma*, 39 b.

[2] Jos. *id.* vi. 5: 4; Suet. *Vesp.* 4, 5; Tac. *Hist.* v. 13.

we reason against an obstinate hope. Evidence is helpless to contend with the chimera which a people has once heartily embraced with all its strength.

Gessius Florus had succeeded Albinus as governor of Judæa near the end of 64 or at the beginning of 65. He seems to have been a really bad man; and he owed his office to the influence of his wife Cleopatra, a friend of Poppæa.[1] The ill-feeling between him and the Jews soon rose to the topmost height of fury. The Jews wore him out by their testiness, their incessant complaining about trifles, and their disrespect for civil or military authority; but he, on his part, took delight in nagging them, and in doing it ostentatiously. On the sixteenth or seventeenth of May, 66, there was a brush between his forces and the populace, on some slight grounds; and Florus withdrew to Cæsarea, leaving only one cohort in the tower Antonia, — a very blameworthy course. An armed force should be in the town it holds, and, when there are signs of revolt, not leave it to the fury of its passions without first exhausting all means of resistance. If Florus had kept himself in the city, it is likely that the revolt would not have forced his hand, and the disasters that followed might have been avoided. When he was once out of the way, it was sure that the Roman army would not re-enter Jerusalem but through conflagration and slaughter.

---

[1] Jos. *Antiq.* xx. 11: 1; *Wars*, ii. 14: 2, 3. Josephus is certainly hostile to Florus, and writes with a bias to prove his point. His theory is: (1) that the war was forced upon the Jews by his excesses ("he compelled us to take up arms," etc.: *Ant.* xx. 11: 1); (2) that it was not the act of the nation, but of a band of robbers and assassins, who ruled the situation by terror. We must be on our guard against misstatements resulting from his theory. Tacitus, however (*Hist.* v. 9, 10), seems to agree with him regarding Florus, at least, throwing heavy responsibility on the procurators. Florus was from Clazomenæ.

Still, the retreat of Florus was far from bringing on an open break between the city and the Roman power. Agrippa II. and Berenice were now at Jerusalem. Agrippa honestly tried to keep down violence; all the moderates joined with him; and appeal was even made to the popularity of Berenice, in whom the popular fancy thought to find again her great-grandmother Mariamne, the Asmonæan princess. While Agrippa harangued the crowd from the colonnade, the princess showed herself on the palace-balcony, which looked down upon it. All was in vain. Men of sense might urge that war would be the sure ruin of the nation; but they were held to be men of little faith. Agrippa, in despair or else in terror, fled from the city, and withdrew to his estates in Batanæa. A troop of the more violent set out at once, and captured by surprise the fortress of Masada,[1] on the border of the Dead Sea, two days' journey from Jerusalem, and well-nigh impregnable.[2]

This was an act of open hostility. The conflict in Jerusalem raged more fiercely, day by day, between the peace-party and those clamorous for war, — the former composed of the rich, who had everything to lose in an overthrow; the other including, besides sincere enthusiasts, that penniless crowd of a city population to which a state of revolution offers the hope of gain by the mere upsetting of every-day conditions. The moderates leaned on the little Roman garrison, lodged in the tower Antonia. The high-priest was an obscure man, one Matthias, son of Theophilus.[3] Since

---

[1] Saulcy, *Voyage*, etc., i. 199; pl. 11-13; Rey, *Voy. dans le Haouran*, 284; pl. 25, 26.
[2] Jos. *Wars*, ii. 14-16.   [3] Jos. *Antiq.* xx. 9: 7.

the deposition of the younger Hanan, who had put the apostle James to death, it seems to have been the practice to select the high-priest outside the powerful houses of Hanan, Cantheras, or Boëthus. The real chief of the priestly party was the old high-priest Ananias, son of Nabadæus,[1] a man of wealth, energetic, unpopular because of his pitiless severity in pressing his own claims, especially hated from the insolence and rapacity of his lackeys. A son of this Ananias, Eleazar, led the party of action, — a circumstance not rare in revolutionary times, disproving the theory of Josephus, who asserts that the war party was made up only of robbers and young men greedy of plunder. Eleazar held the important post of captain of the Temple, and seems to have been a man of sincere religious enthusiasm. He carried to the extreme the principle that sacrifice might be offered only by and for Jews; and forbade the customary vows for the emperor and the prosperity of Rome.[2] All the youth were full of ardour; for religious fanaticism among Semitic peoples is most violent in the young, — with the Moslems, even in children of ten or twelve. Members of old priestly families, Pharisees, and reasonable men in general, of fixed habits, saw the danger. Teachers of authority were put forward, and consultations were held with Rabbis, and arguments were urged from canon law, but all to no effect; for it was clear that the lower class of priests were already making common cause with Eleazar and the Zealots.

The higher priesthood and the aristocracy, in despair of gaining any hold upon the populace, which was car-

---

[1] See "Saint Paul," ch. xix.
[2] Bab. Talm. *Gittin*, 56 *b;* Tosiphtha, *Shabbath*, 17.

ried away by mere surface excitement, sent to entreat Florus and Agrippa that they would make haste to crush the insurrection, pointing out to them that it would soon be too late. Florus, says Josephus, wished a war of extermination, which would wholly blot out the Jewish race from the earth; and would make no reply. Agrippa sent a body of three thousand mounted Arabs to relieve the party of order, who, with this body of horse, held the upper town, now the Armenian and Jewish quarter.[1] The "party of action" occupied the Temple and the lower town, now the Mussulman quarter, with the *mogharibi*, the *haram*, etc. Between them there was open war. On the 14th of August the revolutionaries, led by Eleazar and Menahem, — son of Judas the Gaulonite, who sixty years before had stirred up the Jews by proclaiming that the true worshipper of God can owe allegiance to no man, — stormed the upper town, burning the house of Ananias, with the palaces of Agrippa and Berenice. Agrippa's mounted Arabs, with Ananias, his brother, and all the men of mark who could join them, retreated to the highest grounds of the Asmonæan palace.

Next day the insurgents attacked the tower Antonia, which they took within two days, setting fire to it. They then attacked and stormed the upper palace (September 6), the Arab horsemen being allowed to depart, while the Romans shut themselves up in the three towers, Hippicus, Phasaël, and Mariamne. Ananias and his brother were slain.[2] As in all popular movements, discord soon broke out among the chiefs

[1] For the topography, see Vogüé, Van de Velde, Saulcy, Wilson (*Ordnance Survey*, 1864, 1865); with atlas (Menke, Smith, and others).

[2] Compare Acts xxiii. 2, 3.

of the victorious party. Menahem made himself insufferable by his pride as an upstart demagogue; and Eleazar, son of Ananias, enraged at the assassination of his father, followed him up and killed him. The remnants of Menahem's faction then took refuge at Masada, which, till the war ended, continued the outpost of the fiercest Zealots.

The Romans held out long in their three towers, and when reduced to extremities, bargained only for their lives. Safe conduct was promised them; but, as soon as they laid down their arms, Eleazar slew them all except Metilius, file-leader (*primipilaris*) of the cohort, who consented to be circumcised. Thus Jerusalem was lost to the Romans toward the end of September, 66, a little over one hundred [129] years after it was taken by Pompey. Fearing that retreat might be cut off, the Roman garrison in the fortress of Machærus surrendered. The stronghold of Kypros, overlooking Jericho,[1] fell also into the hands of the insurgents,[2] who probably at this time occupied Herodium.[3] The weakness shown by the Romans in these events is perplexing, and gives some colour to the opinion of Josephus, that Florus meant to force matters to extremities. It is true that the first steps of revolt have something about them bewildering, which makes them very hard to check, so that cooler heads prefer to let them alone, to perish of their own excesses.

Within five months the insurrection had thus got a formidable foothold. Not only had it mastered the city of Jerusalem, but, by way of the desert of Judah, it was in touch with the Dead Sea region, where it held every

[1] Ritter, *Erdkunde*, xv. 458, 459.
[2] Jos. *Wars*, i. 21: 9; ii. 17, 18: 6.   [3] *Ibid.* iv. 9: 5; vii. 6: 1.

stronghold, and thus lent a hand to the Arabs and Nabathæans, who were more or less openly enemies of Rome. Judæa, Idumæa, Peræa, and Galilee sided with the insurrection. In Rome, during this time, an odious tyrant gave over the empire to be administered by the most worthless and incapable agents. If the Jews had succeeded in gathering about them all the disaffected populations of the East, it was all over with the Roman dominion in that part of the world. Unhappily for them, the result was just the opposite: their revolt inspired the inhabitants of Syria with twice their fidelity to the empire. The hate they had enkindled in their neighbours was enough, during this period of paralysis to the Roman power, to stir up against them other enemies at least as dangerous as the legions.

CHAPTER XI.

MASSACRES IN SYRIA AND EGYPT. — A. D. 66.

A GENERAL word-of-command, as it were, seems just now to have run through the East, everywhere inviting great massacres of Jews. Jewish life was proving itself more and more to be incompatible with Greek or Roman life. Each of the two races sought to exterminate the other, and between them was no quarter. To understand the conflict, we must first have seen how far Judaism pervaded the entire eastern portion of the Empire. "They have invaded every city," says Strabo, "and it is hard to find a place in the world that has not received this tribe, or, more correctly, accepted its domination (ἐπικρατεῖται). Egypt, the land of Cyrene, and many others, have adopted their customs, scrupulously observe their rules, and find great profit in keeping their national laws. In Egypt they have legal residence, and a great part of the city of Alexandria is assigned to them: they have their ethnarch, who attends to their affairs, administers justice among them, oversees the execution of contracts and wills, just as if he were the chief magistrate of an independent State."[1] Two elements as opposite as fire and water could not mingle thus without constant danger of most awful explosions.

We must not lay these to the account of the Roman government. Massacres just as awful took place among

[1] Quoted by Josephus, *Antiq.* xiv. 7:2.

the Parthians,[1] where the situation and policy were quite different from those in the West. One of the glories of Rome is to have founded its empire on peace, and the suppression of local wars. Rome never practised that detestable method of government — one of the political secrets of the Turkish empire — which consists in setting the various mixed populations in subject countries against one another. As to massacre on religious grounds, the idea of it was as far as possible from the Roman mind. The Roman, unknowing of all theology, never understood the meaning of sect, or how there could possibly be division on so small a matter as speculative opinion. Besides, antipathy against Jews was so universal in the ancient world that there was no need of pressing it. This antipathy makes, as it were, a boundary-trench among men, which perhaps will never be filled. It results from something else than difference of race. It is the hate between different classes, or social offices, in mankind, — the man of peace, content with home-delights, and the man of war; the merchant or the shopman and the peasant or the noble. It cannot be without reason that unhappy Israel has been ever the victim of slaughter. When every nation and every age has persecuted you, there must needs be some motive behind. Down to our day the Jew has pushed his way everywhere, claiming the common right. But, in fact, the Jew would never stand upon common right; he would hold to his peculiar law; he insisted upon the privileges open to all, and his own exceptional privileges into the bargain. He claimed the advantages of nationality without being of any nation, or sharing the burdens and duties of a

[1] Jos. *Ant.* xviii. 9.

nation. No people could ever tolerate that. A nation is in essence a military structure; it is founded and sustained by the sword; it is the work of the soldier and the peasant; it is what Jews have aided in nothing to establish. This is the one great misunderstanding in regard to Israelitish demands. The tolerated foreigner may be of service to a country, but on condition that the country does not allow him to interfere in its affairs. There is no justice in claiming family rights in a house you have not built, — like a bird that appropriates another's nest, or a hermit-crab (called by fishermen "the thief"), which lodges in a cockle-shell.[1]

The Jew has rendered to the world so many good and so many ill services, that we can never quite do him justice. We owe him so much, and at the same time see his faults so plainly, that we are vexed at the sight of him. This everlasting Jeremiah, this "man of sorrows," always complaining, offering his back to the smiters with an exasperating patience, — this being, strange to all our instincts of honour, pride, glory, delicacy, or taste, — this man so unsoldierly, so unknightly, who cares nothing for Greece, Rome, or Germany, to whom we yet owe our religion so truly that he has the right to say to a Christian, "Thou art but an adulterated Jew," — this man has been set as a target to contradiction and antipathy: a fruitful antipathy, which has made one element in the progress of mankind! In the first century of our era, the world seems to have had a dim consciousness of what was going on. It

---

[1] Some doctors assert with simplicity that Israel's duty is to keep the Law, and then God makes the rest of the world work for him: Bab. Talm., *Berachoth*, 35 *b*.

saw its master in this awkward stranger — shrinking, timid, without dignity to the eye; but upright, virtuous, diligent, straightforward, endowed with modest merit; no soldier, but a good tradesman, a good-humoured and steady labourer. The Jewish household radiant with hope, the synagogue where brotherhood was so full of charm, were regarded with a wishful eye. Such humbleness of spirit, so calm an acceptance of persecution and ignominy, — so resignedly finding comfort for his exclusion from the great world in the privilege of his family and his church, — a placid gaiety like that which makes the Oriental peasant of our day find his bliss in his very inferiority, in the humility of that sphere where he is but the happier for the outward cruelty and scorn he suffers, — all this the aristocrat of old could view only with moods of profound ill-humour, which would sometimes end in acts of hateful brutality.

The first muttering of the storm was heard at Cæsarea [1] almost at the moment when the revolution was coming to its full triumph in Jerusalem. In Cæsarea the condition of Jews and Syrians, including all who were not Jews, was most full of difficulty.[2] In Syrian towns of mixed population Jews made the wealthier class; but their wealth, as before noted, was due in part to an unfair advantage, — exemption from military service. Greeks and Syrians, who furnished recruits for the legionary ranks, were exasperated at finding themselves crowded by men exempt from public burdens, who made profit by the tolerance they enjoyed.[3] Hence

---

[1] Jos. *Wars*, ii. 18: 1-8; *Life*, 6.
[2] Comp. Ialkout, i. 110; Midrash *Eka*, i. 5; iv. 21; Bab. Talm., *Megilla*, 6 a.
[3] Jos. *Antiq.* xx. 8: 7; *Wars*, ii. 13: 7.

were incessant disputes, and endless complaints were brought before the Roman magistrates. Orientals commonly make religion the ground of petty quarrels; the least religious of men become emulously devout as soon as it gives a chance to annoy a neighbour, as the Turkish functionaries of our day find it, when assailed with grievances of this nature. From the year 60, or thereabout, the fight between the two parties at Cæsarea had been going on without truce. Nero settled the pending questions against the Jews, but the feud was only embittered.[1] Petty acts of spite (or possibly mere oversights) committed by Syrians became wilful crimes when seen with Jewish eyes. Young men would threaten, and then fight; grown men would make appeal to Roman authority, which would commonly sentence both parties to the bastinado.[2] Gessius Florus acted in a humaner way: he would begin by getting pay from both parties, and then laugh at the complainants. A synagogue having a party-wall, a can or pitcher, or the remains of a few chickens found at the sanctuary door, which the Jews insisted were the remnants of a pagan sacrifice, were the town-talk at Cæsarea, just at the time when Florus came back fuming with rage at the insult that had been put upon him by the populace of Jerusalem.

A few months after, when it was learned that this populace had succeeded in driving the Romans from their walls, passion was very hot. War was openly declared between Jews and Romans, and the Syrians thought they might now slaughter their foes with impunity. In an hour twenty thousand had been

---

[1] Jos. *Ant.* xx. 8: 7–9; *Wars*, ii. 14: 4.
[2] Jos. *Ant.* xx. 8: 7; *Wars*, ii. 13: 7.

butchered; not a single one remained in Cæsarea. Florus, in fact, gave orders to seize and commit to the galleys all who had escaped by flight. The crime called out frightful reprisals.[1] The Jews formed bands and set out, on their part, to slaughter the Syrians in Philadelphia, Hesebon, Gerasa, Pella, and Scythopolis; they ravaged Decapolis and Gaulonitis; they set fire to Sebaste and Ascalon; they made ruin of Anthedon and Gaza. The villages were burned, and every one not a Jew was killed. The Syrians, in revenge, slew every Jew they met. Southern Syria was a field of slaughter; every town was divided between two armed bodies, making war on each other without mercy; the nights were full of terror. There were incidents of special horror. At Scythopolis, Jews joined with their pagan neighbours to fight invading Jews; and this alliance did not save them from being slaughtered in their turn by the Scythopolitans.

Butcheries of Jews were revived with fresh violence at Ascalon, Acre, Tyre, Hippos, and Gadara. Those left unslain were cast into prison. The scenes of madness that were taking place at Jerusalem led men to see in every Jew a sort of dangerous lunatic, whose acts of fury it was a duty to anticipate.

This epidemic of massacre reached as far as Egypt. Here the hatred of Jew and Greek went to its greatest length. Half of Alexandria was a Jewish city, making a sort of autonomous republic.[2] In fact, for some months the prefect of Egypt had been a Jew, Tiberius Alexander,[3] — an apostate, it is true, not at all likely

---

[1] Jos. *Wars*, ii. 18: 1; *Life*, 6, 55.

[2] Strabo in Jos. *Antiq.* xiv. 7: 2.

[3] *Mém de l'Acad. des Inscr.*, etc., xxvi. 296.

to indulge the fanaticism of his fellow-religionists. The revolt broke out on occasion of a gathering in the amphitheatre. The first affront, it would appear, was offered by the Greeks, and the Jews retorted savagely. Armed with torches, they threatened to burn the Greeks alive in the amphitheatre to the last man, — all amphitheatres being then built of wood. Tiberius Alexander tried in vain to calm the tumult: the legions had to be sent for; the Jews resisted, and a frightful massacre followed. The Jewish quarter, called the Delta, was literally packed with corpses, and the number of the dead was reckoned at fifty thousand.

These horrors continued for about a month. To the north, they stopped at Tyre, since beyond that the Jewish populations were not large enough to give offence. In fact, the cause was more social than religious. Wherever Judaism came into power, life was made intolerable to the pagans. We easily see that the successful revolt of the summer of 66 carried a season of terror to all towns of mixed population anywhere near Palestine or Galilee. I have often pointed out this singular quality of the Jewish people, that its nature tends to violent extremes, and the conflict of good and evil lives, if I may so say, in its very heart. No spite like Jewish spite; and yet in the soul of Judaism dwells the very ideal of kindness, self-sacrifice, and love. The best-hearted of men have been Jews; the cruellest and wickedest have also been Jews. Strange race, truly marked with the seal of God! — which could yield side by side — buds, as it were, from a single stem — the infant Church and the fierce fanaticism of the revolt at Jerusalem, Jesus and John of Giscala, the

Apostles and the assassin Zealots, the Gospel and the Talmud! Can we wonder if these mysterious birth-pangs were accompanied by rendings, by delirium, and by fever raging without example?

Christians were no doubt often included in these September massacres, though in general those kindly sectaries would be safeguarded by their mild and inoffensive conduct. Most of those in the Syrian towns were what were then called "Judaisers;"[1] that is, converts from the native population, not born Jews. They were regarded with distrust, but were not put to death, being considered a sort of half-breeds, strangers in their own country.[2] On their own part, in passing through these dreadful months, their eyes were fixed on heaven, and in every incident of the frightful tempest they seemed to behold a sign of the time destined for the catastrophe: "Learn a lesson from the fig-tree. When its shoots are tender and put forth leaves, then you know that summer is near. So, when you see these things come to pass, understand that He is at hand, that He is at the very door!"[3]

Meanwhile the Roman power was making ready to win back by force the city which it had imprudently let go. Cestius Gallus, the imperial Governor-General of Syria, was advancing from Antioch southward with a considerable army. Agrippa joined him as guide; auxiliary troops came in to him from the towns, whose ancient hate against the Jews made good the lack of

---

[1] Jos. *Wars*, ii. 18: 2.

[2] The phrase in Josephus seems somewhat confused: τοὺς ἰουδαΐζοντας εἶχον ἐν ὑποψίᾳ, καὶ τὸ παρ' ἑκάστοις ἀμφίβολον οὔτε ἀνελεῖν τις προχείρως ὑπέμενε, καὶ μεμιγμένον ὡς βεβαίως ἀλλόφυλον ἐφοβεῖτο.

[3] Matt. xxiv. 32, 33.

military skill. Cestius easily brought Galilee and the sea-coast to submission, and on the twenty-fourth of October he reached Gabaon (now *El-Jib*), a little more than six miles from Jerusalem.

With astonishing boldness the insurgents went out to attack him here, and gave him check. Such a thing would be inconceivable if we were to think of the rebel force as a pack of devotees, beggarly fanatics, and highway robbers. There was in it material more solid and soldierly: Monobases and Cenedæus, two princes of the royal house of Adiabene; one Silas of Babylon, an officer of Agrippa, who had joined the party of the nation; Niger of Peræa, a trained soldier; Simon, son of Gioras, who was then entering on his heroic but stormy career. Agrippa thought the moment favourable for a parley. Two of his envoys came to promise the insurgents full pardon if they would submit. A great part of the population were desirous to accept; but the party of Zealots killed the envoys, and a few persons, indignant at the outrage, were assaulted. This quarrel gave Cestius his opportunity. He set out from Gabaon, and encamped on a spot called Sapha, or Scopus ["the Lookout"], an important post a short hour's march northward from Jerusalem, within sight of the city and Temple. Here he remained three days, awaiting the result of his communications with the city. On the fourth day (October 30) he set his force in order for an advance. The defenders abandoned all of the New Town,[1] and withdrew to the Inner City, both upper and lower, and the Temple. Cestius

---

[1] The present Christian quarter, to the northwest, joined to the old city by Agrippa's wall. The boundary of Jerusalem, at the time of which I write, was the same as at present, only varying a little on the south.

entered without resistance, occupied the new town, the quarter of Bezetha (the northern suburb), and the wood-market, which he set on fire; then laid siege to the upper town, setting his lines of attack in front of the Asmonæan palace [below the northern slope of the Temple hill].

Josephus asserts that, if Cestius Gallus had seen fit to storm at once, the war would have been at an end, explaining his inactivity by intrigue, whose chief motive was Florus's money. It appears that some members of the aristocratic party could be seen on the wall, led by one of the Hanans, who called out to Cestius, offering to open the gates. No doubt he feared an ambush. During five days he vainly tried to storm the wall. On the sixth day (November 5), he attacked the defences of the Temple from the north. There was a terrible fight under the colonnades; the insurgents were already getting discouraged, and the peace-party were preparing to receive Cestius, when he abruptly sounded a retreat. If the story of Josephus is correct, this conduct is inexplicable. Possibly the historian, to make out his case against Florus,[1] exaggerates the advantage gained at first by Cestius upon the Jews, and disparages the real strength of the resistance. What we know is, that Cestius went back to his camp at Scopus, and set out the next day for Gabaon, sharply followed by the Jews. Two days after (November 8) he retreated, still pursued, as far as the descent at Beth-horon, about ten miles northwest from

---

[1] We must remember that his method is to throw upon Florus the responsibility for the excesses of the revolt, by representing him as the one who at first prevented its suppression, and foiled the efforts of the peace party.

the city, where he abandoned his baggage and took refuge, with some difficulty, at Antipatris.[1]

The incompetency of Cestius as shown in this campaign is astonishing. The evil rule of Nero must have greatly degraded all the service of the State, to make such things possible. Cestius did not long survive his defeat, and his death, soon after, was laid by many to his disgrace.[2] We do not know what became of Florus.

[1] Six miles from the coast, and ten miles northeast from Jaffa. See Jos. *Wars*, ii. 18: 9–19; *Life*, 5-7 (here Gessius should probably be Cestius); Tac. *Hist.* v. 10; Suet. *Vesp.* 4.

[2] Tac. *Hist.* v. 10.

CHAPTER XII.

VESPASIAN IN GALILEE; TERROR AT JERUSALEM. — A. D. 66-68.

WHILE the Empire underwent this bloody check in the East, Nero, driven from one mad crime to another, was all absorbed in his vain pretensions as an artist. With Petronius had disappeared everything that could be called taste, tact, or courtesy. Colossal self-love gave him a burning thirst to grasp at every sort of glory in the world; so that, says Suetonius, he was "the rival of any man who in any way could touch the fancy of the vulgar."[1] He pursued those who attracted public attention with a bitter jealousy; to succeed, in no matter what, came to be a crime against the State; it is said that he even tried to stop the sale of Lucan's works.[2] He aspired to such fame as never had been known, "eager for things incredible," says Tacitus.[3] Vast projects were revolving in his head, — to cut through the isthmus of Corinth, to dig a canal from Baiæ to Ostia, to discover the sources of the Nile.[4] He had long dreamed of a journey to Greece, — not from a serious wish to see the masterpieces of matchless skill, but with the odd ambition to compete in the games established in different places and carry away the prize.

---

[1] *Nero*, 53. [2] Tac. *Ann.* xv. 49. [3] *Ibid.* 42.
[4] We may infer from Seneca (*Quæst. nat.* vi. 8) that the centurions sent on this errand penetrated as far as the Great Lakes.

These contests were literally numberless. The founding of games in Greece was one form of public benefaction: as with the founding of our college prizes, any citizen of moderate wealth had in this a ready way to bequeath a name to later times.[1] The noble exercises, which so greatly added to the strength and beauty of the ancients and became the school of Greek art, had become — as the mediæval tournaments afterwards became — the business of professionals, who made a trade of running in the races and winning crowns. Instead of free-born youths handsome and well-bred, here were only odious and worthless fops or men trained to a profitable special skill. The prizes, which the victors wore as a sort of personal decoration, gave the vainglorious Cæsar many a sleepless night; and he was already dreaming of his return to Rome in triumph, with the very rare title of " all-round victor " ($περιοδονίκης$) in the complete cycle of the four established games.[2]

His passion for public singing amounted to insanity.[3] One of his reasons for wishing the death of Thraseas was that he did not sacrifice to the emperor's "heavenly voice."[4] In the presence of the Parthian king, his guest, he would display his skill in nothing but the chariot-race.[5] Lyric dramas were put upon the stage, in which he took the leading part, while the gods,

---

[1] See the inscription from Larissa in report of *Acad. des Inscr.*, session of July 1, 1870; also *Revue Archéol.*, July–August, 1872, p. 109.

[2] See *Comptes rendus de l'Acad. des Inscr.*, 1872, p. 114; Dion Cassius lxiii. 8, 20, 21.

[3] Suet. *Nero*, pass.; Dion Cassius, lxiii. 26, 27; Euseb. *Chron.* 64; *Carm. Sib.*, v. 140, 141.

[4] Tac. *Ann.* xvi. 22; Dion Cass. lxii. 26.

[5] Dion Cass. lxiii. 6.

goddesses, heroes, and heroines were masked and robed in his likeness or that of his favourite mistress. Thus he played as Œdipus, Thyestes, Hercules, Alcmæon, Orestes, Canace; he was seen on the stage in chains (golden), guided as if blind, imitating the gestures of a madman, or personating a woman in labour. One of his latest schemes was to appear naked in the theatre as Hercules, crushing a lion in his arms or killing him with a club: the lion, it is said, was already selected and in training, when Nero died.[1] To leave one's seat while he was singing was so grave a crime that the most ridiculous precautions were taken to do it secretly. In contests of skill he would blacken his competitors or try to put them out of countenance, so that the poor fellows would sing false on purpose to be put out of competition with him. Judges would encourage him, or humour his timidity. If this absurd display brought a flush to any one's brow or an expression of pain to any face, he would say that there were persons he suspected of partiality. Meanwhile he obeyed the rules of the prize-games like a school-boy, trembling before the umpires and the scourge-bearers, and paying money not to be whipped if he should blunder. If he made a miss that should have thrown him out, he would turn pale, and had to be told in a whisper that the blunder had never been noticed amidst the popular enthusiasm and applause. The statues of those who had worn the wreath before him were cast down, lest they should excite dangerous fits of jealousy in him. In the races care was taken that he should come in first, even if he fell out of his chariot; but sometimes he would allow himself to be beaten, on purpose that he might be sup-

---

[1] Suet. *Nero*, 53.

posed to play a fair game.¹ In Italy, as I said before, he had the mortification of owing his success to hired plaudits from a group, skilfully made up and well paid, that followed him everywhere. The Romans became to him intolerable; he called them clowns, and said that a self-respecting artist could desire only the applause of Greeks.

He set off on the journey so eagerly anticipated in November, 66. He had been only a few days in Achaia when he learned the defeat of Cestius. This war, as he now clearly saw, required a brave and experienced commander; but, above all, it must be a man whom he did not fear. These qualities seemed to meet in Titus Flavius Vespasianus. Vespasian was a grave and steady soldier, a man of sixty, who had always been fortunate in his campaigns, and was of too low birth to be suspected of high ambitions. He was just now in discredit with Nero for not having shown enough admiration of his fine voice; and when the message first came to him, calling him to the command of the army in Palestine, he supposed for a moment that it was a sentence to death. His son Titus soon joined him; and about the same time Mucian succeeded Cestius as imperial legate (or governor-general) of Syria. The three men who within two years were to control the destiny of the empire thus came together in the East.²

The boldness of the insurgents was exalted to the highest pitch by the complete victory they had gained over a Roman army commanded by an imperial legate. The more intelligent and better informed in Jerusalem

---

[1] Dion Cass. lxiii. 1, 8; Suet. *Nero*, 21–24, 53.
[2] Jos. *Wars*, Proëm, 8; ii. 41: 1; 3: 1; Suet. *Vesp.* 4; Tac. *Hist.* v. 10.

were downcast; they judged, on good grounds, that the final advantage could not but be with the Romans. The ruin of the Temple and the nation appeared to them certain,[1] and emigration began at once. All the Herodians, and all those in the service of Agrippa, went over to the Romans.[2] A large number of Pharisees, looking only to the observance of the Law and the peaceful future of Israel, of which they dreamed, held that they must submit to the Romans, just as they had before submitted to the kings of Persia and Egypt. They cared little for the nation's independence. Rabbi Johanan Ben Zakai, the most famous Pharisee of the time, lived apart from politics.[3] Many doctors probably at this time withdrew to Jamnia [or Jabneh, near the coast, and not far from Joppa], where they founded the Talmudic schools, which soon became so celebrated.[4]

Meanwhile massacres began again, and extended to parts of Syria, free till now of the bloody epidemic. At Damascus, every male Jew was slaughtered. Most of the women of that city professed the Jewish religion, and unquestionably there were Christians in their number. Care was taken that the massacres should be committed by surprise, and without their knowledge.[5]

The defenders of the city displayed prodigious energy, enlisting even the lukewarm to their aid. A council was held in the Temple to form a national government, to consist of the best men in the nation. As yet the moderates had by no means abandoned the contest. Whether they still hoped to guide the move-

---

[1] Jos. *Life*, 4.   [2] Jos. *Wars*, ii. 20: 1; *Life*, 6.
[3] Mechilta on Ex. **xx**. 22; Bab. Talm. *Gitin*, 56 a, b; *Aboth d. Nathan*, ch. 4; Midrash rabba on Eccl. vii. 11, and on *Eka*, i. 5.
[4] Derenbourg, *Hist.* p. 288.   [5] Josephus, as above.

ment, or had a secret hope such as one dallies with so fondly at a crisis, spite of all warnings of reason, they allowed themselves to be drawn to the front at almost every point. Men of great weight, many members of Sadducæan and priestly families, the higher ranks of Pharisees,[1] with the wise and upright Simeon ben-Gamaliel[2] at their head, joined the party of revolution. They acted under strict forms of law, recognising the supremacy of the Sanhedrim. City and Temple remained in the hands of the established authorities, — Hanan, eldest of the priesthood,[3] Joshua ben-Gamala, Simeon ben-Gamaliel, and Joseph ben-Gorion. Joseph and Hanan were named commissioners at Jerusalem; Eleazar, son of Simon, a demagogue without principle, whose personal ambition was rendered dangerous by the wealth he had acquired, was purposely set aside. Commissioners were also chosen for the provinces, all being moderate men except Eleazar, son of Ananias, who was sent to Idumæa. Josephus, afterwards of so brilliant repute as historian, was prefect of Galilee. Many among them were sober-minded men, who accepted their posts largely to aid in maintaining order, and with the hope of controlling the elements of anarchy which threatened to ruin everything.[4]

The excitement in Jerusalem was very great. The city resembled a camp, or a workshop of arms. On every side resounded the cries of young men in military drill.[5]

---

[1] The upper middle-class: Jos. *Life*, 5.

[2] Son of Gamaliel of the "Acts," and grandson of Hillel: Jos. *Life*, 38.

[3] Son of the high-priest who condemned Jesus: Jos. *Wars*, iv. 3: 7.

[4] Jos. *Wars*, ii. 20: 3; 22: 1; *Life*, 7. Josephus disguises the part he took in the revolt, representing himself as more moderate than he really was.

[5] Jos. *Wars*, ii. 21: 4.

Jews from the remote East, above all from Parthia, thronged thither, persuaded that the Roman dominion was now at an end.[1] They felt that Nero's reign would soon be over, and were convinced that the empire would perish with him, — an idea which we find also in the Apocalypse.[2] This last heir of Cæsar's name, plunged in shame and contempt, was to them as an evident sign. Seen from this point of view, the insurrection must seem far less insane than it looks to us, knowing as we do that the empire had strength yet left for several revivals. It might really be supposed that the work of Augustus was out of joint; at any moment the Parthians might be seen, in fancy, pouring over the Roman territories,[3] — and this would have happened, in fact, if various causes had not just then greatly weakened the Parthian power. One of the noblest visions in the book of Enoch is that in which the prophet sees a sword given to the sheep, and the sheep, thus armed, driving back the wild beasts, which in their turn take to flight.[4] Such was, in fact, the feeling of the Jews. For lack of military training, they could not see how deceitful was the success they had gained over Cestius and Florus. They stamped coins after the pattern of the Maccabees, having the figure of the Temple, or some Jewish device, with inscriptions in ancient Hebrew letters.[5] These coins,

---

[1] Jos. *Wars*, proëm, 2; vi. 6: 2; Dion Cass. lxvi. 4.
[2] See ch. xvi., *post*.
[3] Rev. ix. 14–21; xvi. 12–16; Jos. *Wars*, vi. 6: 2.
[4] Enoch, xc. 19 (Dillmann and the later editions).
[5] It is very hard to distinguish the coins of this first revolt from those of the second (A. D. 132), or of the Maccabees (see Madden's "Jewish Coinage," p. 154, which sums up all previous study, adopting, however, the theories of Levy, which are themselves very doubtful). We may fear

dated from the "year of deliverance," or of the "liberty of Zion," were at first without name, or with only that of Jerusalem; afterward they bore the names of party leaders, who held supreme power at the will of some one or other faction.[1] It may even be that in the first months of the revolt, Eleazar, son of Simon, who had in hand an enormous quantity of silver, ventured to coin money, giving himself the title of high-priest.[2] The amount, at all events, must have been considerable; it was called "money of Jerusalem," or "money of Danger."[3]

Hanan came to be more and more the head of the moderate party. He still hoped to bring the mass of the people to peace, and quietly endeavoured to check the making of weapons and to paralyse resistance while giving it the air of discipline. This is the most hazardous of games to play in a time of revolution; he was, in short, what revolutionists call a traitor.[4] In the eyes of enthusiasts he had the fault of seeing things too clearly; in the view of history he cannot be

---

that the subject can never be made quite clear; for in the earlier revolt the Asmonæan coinage may have been copied, or its own in the later. Every coin having either the figure or the inscription described in the text is one belonging to the earlier revolt, or else is an imitation of it; the latter revolt, in fact, never held possession of Jerusalem. In the earlier, the Roman coinage appears not to have been restamped, as it was afterwards (Madden, 171, 176, 203–205).

[1] Eleazar, son of Simon, and Simon, son of Gioras. We are not sure whether John of Gischala coined money (see Madden, 64, 173, 180, 182). Coinage is wrongly credited to Hanan and to Simeon, son of Gamaliel, who was a plain citizen, a doctor held in high respect, with no attribute of sovereignty whatever (Derenbourg, *Hist.*, etc., 270, 271, 286, 423, 424).

[2] Madden, 156, 161, 162; Jos. *Wars*, ii. 20: 3.

[3] Tosiphtha, *Maaser scheni*, 1; Jer. Talm. *id.* 1, 2; Bab. Talm. *Baba kama*, 97 b; *Bechoroth*, 50 a; *Aboda zara*, 52 b; Levy, *Gesch.* 126, 127.

[4] Jos. *Wars*, ii. 22: 1.

VESPASIAN IN GALILEE.   225

acquitted of having accepted the most false of positions, — that of making war without faith in it, merely because driven to it by ignorant fanatics. In the provinces there was horrible confusion. The districts to the south and east of the Dead Sea, wholly peopled by Arabs,[1] poured upon Judæa hordes of bandits, who lived by massacre and pillage. Under such conditions order was impossible; for to establish order, two things must be driven out which made the very strength of the revolution, — fanaticism and brigandage. A terrible situation, when the only choice is whether you will appeal to the stranger or to anarchy! In Acrabatene (a district lying between Judæa and Samaria) a young and brave partisan, Simon, son of Gioras, pillaged and tortured the rich.[2] In Galilee Josephus tried in vain to maintain something like a rational policy. One John of Gischala, a bold and tricky agitator, uniting an implacable disposition with a heated enthusiasm, managed to foil him at every point. As always happens in the East, Josephus was forced to enlist the brigands, under regular pay, as the price of general security from plunder.[3]

Meanwhile Vespasian went on with his preparations for the difficult campaign before him. His plan was to attack the insurrection from the north; to crush it first in Galilee, then in Judæa; to throw it back in some way upon Jerusalem; and, when he had packed its forces all about this central point, where crowding, famine, and factions were sure to bring about frightful

---

[1] The Nabathæan inscriptions are in Syriac, but their proper names are Arabic (*Obéis*, *Jamer*, etc.).

[2] Jos. *Wars*, ii. 22: 2; iv. 9: 3, 4.

[3] *Ibid.* ii. 20: 5–21; *Life*, 8, 9.

scenes, to wait; or, if that should not be enough, to strike one great blow. He went first to Antioch, where Agrippa came to join him with all his forces. Antioch had not yet had its massacre of Jews, — no doubt because a multitude of the Greeks living there had embraced the Jewish faith, — mostly in the Christian form, — and this deadened the mutual hate. But just at this moment the storm broke out. The wild charge of having plotted to set fire to the city brought on butcheries, followed by a sharp persecution, in which many Christians doubtless perished, confounded with the adherents of a faith that was no longer more than half their own.[1]

The expedition set out in March, 67, following the usual sea-coast road, and fixed its headquarters at Ptolemais (Acre). The first blow fell upon Galilee. Here the population were heroic. The little town of Judifat, or Jotapata,[2] just fortified, made an astonishing resistance. Not one of its defenders would survive. Pent up in a place without exit, they slew one another. "Galilæan" became another name for a sectarian fanatic, obstinately bent on death by his own choice.[3] Tiberias, Tarichææ, and Gamala surrendered, but not till after great slaughter. History gives few examples of a people so ground to pieces. The very waves of that quiet lake where Jesus had dreamed of the heavenly kingdom were stained with blood, while the shore was

---

[1] Jos. *Wars*, vii. 3: 3, 4.

[2] Now *Jefat*, *Tell Jefat*, or *Tell Jephta* (cf. Schultz, in *Zeitschr. der d. m. G.* 1849, 49, 50, 61; Ritter, xvi. 764; Robinson, iii. 105; Aug. Parent, *Siège de J.* (1866), p. 3; Neubauer, *Geog. du Talmud*, 193, 203, 204. *Gopatata* in Reland is an error of copy; *Jiphtah-el* (Josh. xv. 43) has nothing to do with it.

[3] See "The Apostles," p. 235, *n*. 4.

covered with putrefying corpses and the air poisoned with corruption. Crowds of Jews had taken refuge on boats, but Vespasian gave orders to kill or drown them all. The remnant of the able-bodied were sold as slaves; six thousand captives were sent to Nero in Achaia to the severest tasks in cutting through the isthmus of Corinth;[1] the aged were slaughtered. Almost the only one who escaped was Josephus, a man of no depth of nature, and always doubting the issue of the war, who surrendered to the Romans, and was soon on the best terms with Vespasian and Titus. All his ability as a writer has not sufficed to wash from his conduct a certain smear of baseness.[2]

The best of the year 67 was taken up with this business of extermination. Galilee never recovered from it. The Christians who were there doubtless took refuge beyond the lake, and the name of Jesus' birthplace appears no more in Christian history. Gischala held out to the last, but fell in November or December. John of Gischala, who had defended it with fury, escaped, and succeeded in reaching Judæa. Vespasian and Titus took winter-quarters at Cæsarea, preparing for the siege of Jerusalem in the following year.[3]

The great weakness of a provisional government organized for national defence is that it cannot survive

---

[1] Jos. *Wars*, iii. 10: 10; Lucian (or Philostratus), *Nero*, etc., 3. The Sibylline verses allude to this taskwork in v. 32, 138, 217; viii. 155; xii. 84. Comp. Philostratus, *Apoll.* v. 19.

[2] His "Life" (38, 39) gives a very poor explanation of the distrust felt towards him by the best men in Jerusalem. Justus of Tiberias (*Life*, 65) was very hostile to him.

[3] Jos. *Wars*, iii.–iv. 2; *Life*, 65, 74, 75 (greatly expanded by the historian's vanity); Tac. *Hist.* v. 10.

defeat. Constantly undermined by the more impatient, it falls as soon as it can no longer give to the fickle multitude that victory for the sake of which it was put in place. John of Gischala and the refugees from Galilee, coming into Jerusalem day after day with rage in their hearts, lifted again that cry of fury which was the life-breath of the revolution. Hot and panting, they gasped such words as these: "We are not beaten, but we want better posts. Why wear us out in Gischala and such wretched holes, when we have the metropolis to defend?" Said John of Gischala, "I have seen the Roman engines shivered to pieces against the walls of villages in Galilee. Unless they have wings they will never cross the defences of Jerusalem!" All the young people were for "war to the bitter end." Troops of volunteers take readily to plunder. Bands of fanatics, religious or political, are always much like highway robbers.[1] One must live; and a free-lance can scarce live at all except as a freebooter. That is why, at a time of national crisis, "brigand" is almost synonymous with "hero." A war party is always tyrannous. No country was ever saved by moderate coun-

[1] Barabbas, whom we infer from Mark (xv. 7) to be a member of some religious or political organization, is called by John (xviii. 4) "a robber." So the Vendeans were "brigands of the Loire." So, to a certain degree, we find the volunteers of the French Revolution,—noting that Josephus, to whom we owe the whole account, was a sort of Dumouriez. His hostility toward his political opponents breaks out constantly. To take his word for it, the firebrands were a mere wretched handful, answering to no national sentiment whatever. Tacitus and Dion Cassius state the whole thing differently. According to them, it was an entire population of fanatics. Josephus clearly wishes to lessen his country-people's guilt in the eyes of the Romans, and thinks to excuse them by belittling their patriotism and courage. We must remember, too, that the "Wars of the Jews" was submitted to Titus's inspection and received the official permit of Agrippa. At least, Josephus says so (*Life*, 65).

sels; for the first rule of moderation is to yield to circumstances, while heroism commonly consists in refusing an ear to reason. Josephus, eminently a man of order, is probably right in asserting that the resolve not to retreat was the act of a few enthusiasts, dragging after them, by main force, the body of quiet citizens, who would have desired nothing better than to submit. It is almost always so. If a nation has no dynasty — which at bottom is only a permanent and regulated terrorism — great sacrifices can be got from it only by means of terror. The body of a population are cowards at heart; but in times of revolution the coward does not count. Enthusiasts are always few; but they force the hand of the others by cutting off the chance of conciliation.[1] The rule in such situations is that power falls necessarily into the hands of the more ardent, and that politicians are fatally helpless.

In the presence of that burning fever, increasing every day, the position of the "moderates" (οἱ μέτριοι) was no longer tenable. The bands of pillagers, when they had stripped the country, fell back on Jerusalem; fugitives from the Roman arms came, one after another, to heap themselves upon the city, bringing famine with them. There was no effective authority. The Zealots reigned;[2] all those suspected of "moderantism" were slaughtered without mercy. Until now

---

[1] Note, in particular, what came to pass in Tiberias (Jos. *Wars*, iii. 9: 7, 8; *Life*, 65). Just so the Mussulman fanaticism is generally that of a minority, which dominates an entire population.

[2] The name "zealot" (Heb. *kanna*) had hitherto been used in a good sense. The terrorists of the revolt had claimed it to themselves, and made it nearly synonymous with "partisan" or "assassin" (*sicarius*). See Jos. *Wars*, iv. 3:9; viii. 8:1. On this word in the Talmud, see Derenbourg, 279, 281, 285, 475–8; Jos. *Wars*, ii. 13:3; *Ant.* xx. 8:5.

war and violence had stopped at the Temple limits. Now, zealots and robbers crowded pell-mell into the holy house. All rules of legal purity were forgotten. The courts were stained with blood, fouling men's feet as they walked.[1] In the eyes of priests, no crime was more awful. To the devout, it was the "abomination" foretold by Daniel, which would invade the sacred place just before the last days. The zealot, like all fighting fanatics, made no account of rites, which they subordinated to the really "holy work" of fighting. A crime hardly less atrocious was to change the order of the priesthood. Disregarding the privilege of the families from which the high-priest was commonly taken, they chose an ignoble branch of the sacerdotal stock, and resorted to the purely democratic method of choosing by lot.[2] This naturally produced strange results. The lot fell upon a rustic, who had to be dragged to Jerusalem and invested in his own despite with the sacred robes, and the pontificate was profaned by scenes of revelry. All serious-minded people — Pharisee and Sadducee, the Simeons ben-Gamaliel and Josephs ben-Gorian — were wounded in what they held most dear.

Such excesses at length impelled the aristocratic party of the Sadducees to attempt a reaction. With much ability and courage, Hanan sought to unite the better class of citizens and men of sense, to overthrow the monstrous alliance of fanaticism and impiety. The Zealots were close-pressed, and forced to take refuge in the Temple, which became a hospital for the wounded. To save the revolution, they now took the extreme

---

[1] Jos., *Wars*, iv. 3 : 6.
[2] Tosiphtha *Ioma*, 1 ; Sifra, on *Levit.* xxi. 10 ; Tanhouma, 48 *a*.

step of calling in the Idumæans, bands of robbers accustomed to every violence, who were roaming about Jerusalem. Their entrance was the signal for a massacre. All that could be found who belonged to the priestly caste were slaughtered. Hanan and Jesus, sons of Gamala, were exposed to frightful outrage: their bodies were cast out unburied, — a thing unheard-of among the Jews.

Thus perished the son of the man chiefly guilty of the death of Jesus. The Beni-Hanan remained to the last true to their part, — if I may say so, to their duty. Like most of those who try to build a dike to hold back the fury of fanatic sects, they were swept away; but they perished honourably. The last Hanan seems to have been a man of great ability;[1] for nearly two years he had maintained the struggle against anarchy. He was a true aristocrat, sometimes hard of heart,[2] but grave, filled with a genuine political sense, greatly respected, liberal in this, that he would have the nation governed by men of the better sort, and not by violent factions. Josephus does not doubt that, if he had lived, he would have obtained honourable terms of peace between Romans and Jews, and regards the day of his death as that of doom to the city of Jerusalem and the Jewish Commonwealth. At least, it was the end of the Sadducæan party, which was often haughty, selfish, and cruel, but the only representative of a policy at once reasonable and capable of saving the country.[3] To use the common expression, one

---

[1] Jos. *Wars*, iv. 5: 2.

[2] Comp. *Antiq.* xx. 9: 1; *Wars*, iv. 5: 2. These passages vary in some points, but no doubt refer to the same person (see *Wars*, iv. 3: 9).

[3] *Wars*, iv. 3–5: 2.

might be tempted to say that Jesus was "avenged" by the death of Hanan. It was those of Hanan's house who had said, before Jesus, "If things go on thus, the Romans will come and destroy both the holy place and the nation;" and had presently after added, "Better that one man should die, and that the whole nation perish not."[1] Still, let us refrain from an expression so frankly impious. There is no more revenge in history than in nature. Revolutions are no more just than the bursting volcano or the crushing avalanche. The year 1793 did not punish Richelieu, or Louis the Fourteenth, or the founders of a united France; it only proved that they were men of narrow views, if they did not perceive the vanity of their deeds, the frivolity of their statecraft, the uselessness of their profound policy, the stupid cruelty of their "reasons of State." The Preacher alone was wise, when in the day of his disillusion he declared that "all under the sun is vanity."

With Hanan, early in 68, perished the old Jewish priesthood, entailed upon a few great Sadducæan families, who had so hotly opposed the growth of Christianity. Deep was the impression, when men beheld, cast naked without the walls, a prey to dogs and jackals, those aristocrats held in so high honour, who were but lately seen clad in sumptuous priestly robes, presiding in pompous ceremonial, attended by venerating throngs of pilgrims that gathered at Jerusalem from all the world. In truth, a world was passing away. The democratic priesthood set up by the revolution was but for a day. The Christians thought at first to put in relief two or three persons by adorning

[1] John xi. 48, 50; xviii. 14.

their brow with the sacerdotal *petalon*. All this came to nothing. The priestly office was not, any more than the Temple that gave it dignity, destined to remain the chief thing in Judaism. The main thing was the enthusiast, the prophet, the zealot, the messenger of the Lord. The prophet had slain the royalty; the enthusiast, the heated sectary, slew the priesthood. Priesthood and royalty once slain, there remains the fanatic, who yet for two and a half years will wrestle against fate. When in his turn he too is crushed, there will remain the doctor, the rabbi, the interpreter of the Law. Priest and king will rise no more.

And the Temple no more than they. Those Zealots who, to the great scandal of priests friendly to the Romans, had made of the Holy Place a fortress and a hospital, were not so far as we might think at first from the feeling of Jesus: "Of what value are these stones?" The spirit is the only thing that counts: that which defends the spirit of Israel — the Revolution — has the right to defile the stones. Ever since Isaiah had said, "What care I for your sacrifices? They are an offence to me; an upright heart alone delights me," — ever since that day, the forms of worship have been an outgrown routine, which must at length cease to be.

From the time of Nehemiah, who is already a Pharisee,[1] we note the opposition between the priesthood and the nation, which is at bottom wholly democratic, admitting no other nobility than piety and observance of the Law. The true Aaron, in the opinion of the wise, is the good man.[2] The Asmonæans,

---

[1] Neh. xiii. 4-13.
[2] Bab. Talm. *Ioma*, 71 *b* (tale of Shemaiah and Abtalion).

at once priests and kings, inspire only aversion in the pious. Sadduceeism, every day more unpopular and more rancorous, is preserved only by the distinction which the people make between religion and its ministers.[1] "No king, no priest," — this is, at bottom, the Pharisee's ideal. Judaism is powerless to found a State; and hence it was forced into the condition in which we find it for eighteen centuries past, — to live a parasitic life in the commonwealth of others. Its destiny was, in like manner, to become a religion without temple and without priest. The temple necessitated the priest; its destruction proved the relief from a real difficulty. The zealots who, in 68, slew the pontiff and defiled the Temple in the defence of God's cause were not, then, out of line with the true tradition of Israel.

But it is clear that the ship, deprived of all steadying ballast, and abandoned to a frenzied crew, must drift to frightful wreck. After the slaughter of the Sadducees, terror reigned in Jerusalem without check or counterpoise.[2] Under its terrible oppression, no one dared openly to mourn, or to bury his dead. Compassion was a crime. The "suspects" of the better class, who perished by the assault of ruffians, are said to have amounted to twelve thousand. Here, no doubt, the reckoning of Josephus is suspicious. His story of the dominion of the Zealots is absurd: mere impious wretches do not expose themselves to death as those men did. As well account for the French Revolution

---

[1] Strabo xvi. 2: 37, 40. Strabo had his information from a liberal Jew, opposed to the priesthood and the temporal power. His phrase very well expresses the two opposed feelings entertained by a democratic Jew towards the Temple, — "loathing tyranny, but revering sanctity."

[2] For the impression made on the Romans by this fury of civil war, see Pliny, *H. Nat.* xii. 25 (54).

by the escape of a few thousand convicts from the galleys. Mere crime has never brought anything to pass. The truth is that popular movements, due to a vague sense of right and not to reason, defeat themselves by their own victory. The revolution at Jerusalem followed the rule of all such tumultuary movements: it spent its force in cutting off its own head. The best patriots, those who had contributed most to the success of the preceding year, — Gorion, Niger of Peræa, — were put to death. The entire class of the well-to-do perished.[1] The deepest impression was caused by the death of one Zacharias, son of Baruch (Barachias), the most esteemed citizen of Jerusalem, greatly loved by all good men. He was dragged before a revolutionary tribunal, and unanimously acquitted, but was struck down by fanatics "between the temple and the altar." He was not improbably a friend of the Christians; for we seem to find an allusion to him in the prophetic words Jesus is said to have spoken on the terrors of the Latter Day.[2]

The astounding events at Jerusalem made the profoundest impression upon the Christians. This peaceful community, deprived of its head, James, "the Lord's brother," continued to lead its ascetic life in the holy city, where the disciples of Jesus, clinging about the Temple, waited the great Second Coming. With them were the survivors of the family of Nazareth, — the sons of Cleopas, held in the greatest veneration, even by the Jews. Everything that happened must seem to them clearly to confirm the words of Jesus. What could these convulsions be, if not "the

---

[1] Jos. *Wars*, iv. 5: 3–7: 3.
[2] Matt. xxiii. 34–36: see, however, "Life of Jesus," p. 341, *n.*

beginning of sorrows"[1] which should precede the Messiah's birth? They were convinced that the triumphant coming of the Christ would be preceded by the appearance of numerous false prophets;[2] and these, as the heads of the Christian community would view it, must be the leaders of the Zealots.[3] The terrible words of Jesus, describing the horrors which would forewarn them of the Judgment, were applied to the existing condition. It may be that certain "new lights" arose within the Church itself, — men claiming to speak in the name of Jesus,[4] whom the elders warmly opposed, asserting that Jesus had foretold the coming of such misleaders, and warning the disciples against them. This was enough. The hierarchy, already well established, with the teachable spirit received from Jesus, put a stop to all these impostures, and the Church benefited by the marked ability it had shown in creating a real authority at the very heart of a popular movement. The rising episcopate (or rather, presbytery) checked the great disorders which the unguided conscience of a multitude never escapes. From this time forth we perceive that the controlling spirit of the Church in human affairs will be a moderate good sense, a conservative and practical instinct, a distrust of democratic dreams, — in striking contrast to the exalted strain of its supernaturalist assertions.

This sagacious policy in the leaders of the church at Jerusalem had its merits. Zealots and Christians had

---

[1] "Birth-pangs": Matt. xxiv. 8; Mark xiii. 8.

[2] Matt. xxiv. 4, 5.

[3] See Acts v. 36, 37; viii. 9, 10; xxi. 38; Jos. *Antiq.* xx. 5:1; 8:6; *Wars*, ii. 13:5; vii. 11.

[4] Matt. xxiv. 4, 5, 11, 23–26. The expression, "in the desert" (ver. 26), seems to refer to the Zealot deceivers.

the same enemies, — the "sons of Hanan," the Sadducees. The ardent faith of the Zealots could not fail to affect powerfully the equally exalted mood of the Jewish Christians. The enthusiasts, who drew crowds after them into the desert to show them the kingdom of God, were very much like John the Baptist, and a very little like Jesus. A few of the faithful, as it appears, joined their party, and were drawn along with them;[1] with most, however, the peaceful temper of Christianity carried the day. The heads of the Church checked these dangerous symptoms by injunctions for which they claimed to have the authority of Jesus: "Let yourselves not be deceived; for many will come in my name, saying, 'I am the Messiah,' and will deceive many. . . . Then, if any come and say, 'The Messiah is here,' or 'He is there,' do not believe it. For there will arise false messiahs and false prophets, who will work great wonders, so as to deceive, if possible, even the very elect. Remember that I have told you beforehand. If then they come and say, 'Come, see; he is in the desert,' do not go; or, 'Come, see; he is in a hiding-place,' do not believe it."

No doubt there were some apostasies, and even betrayals of brother by brother; and divisions of policy brought about coldness of heart.[2] But the greater number, while deeply feeling the critical state of Israel, lent no hand to anarchy, even under the guise of patriotism. The Christian manifesto of this solemn hour was a discourse ascribed to Jesus,[3] — a

---

[1] Matt. xxiv. 4, 5; Mark xiii. 5, 6. Simon, one of the apostles, is called a "zealot" in Luke vi. 15, and Acts i. 13; and "Canaanite" (*kanna*) in Matt. x. 4; Mark iii. 18.

[2] Matt. xxiv. 10, 12.

[3] Matt. xxiv.; Mark xiii.; modified, as usual, by Luke xix. 43, 44; xxi. 20–36. Comp. Assumpt. of Moses, ch. 8, 10.

sort of apocalypse, an enlargement, possibly, of words spoken by the Master, which pointed out the connection of the final catastrophe — now thought to be very near — with the political condition of the time. The entire passage was not written out till later, after the siege; but some words, reported as if from Jesus, refer to the very moment now under our eye: "When you see the abomination of desolation spoken of by the prophet Daniel,[1] standing in the holy place, — here let the reader understand" (a phrase familiar in such writings), — "then let those who are in Judæa flee to the mountains; let not him who is on the house-top come down to take anything from the house; let not him who is in the field come back to find his clothes. Alas for the women with child or who have nursing-infants in those days! Pray, too, that your flight may not be in the winter or on the sabbath; for then there will be such misery as there has not been from the beginning of the world till now, and will never be again."

Other visions of like purport were floating about, it would seem, under the name of Enoch, showing curious coincidences with those ascribed to Jesus. In one of them, the divine Wisdom, introduced as a prophetic

---

[1] Dan. ix. 27; xi. 31; xii. 11. Whatever the meaning in Hebrew, the Greek expression ($\beta\delta\epsilon\lambda\nu\gamma\mu\alpha$ $\tau\hat{\eta}s$ $\dot{\epsilon}\rho\eta\mu\dot{\omega}\sigma\epsilon\omega s$) certainly meant to the readers of the first century some profanation of the Temple (see Matt. xxiv. 15; Mark xiii. 14; 1 Macc. i. 54). The word "standing" would suggest a statue; but it is idle to suppose that Titus set up a statue within the precincts of the Temple. Besides, we have here to do with a profaning before the capture of the city by Titus, as appears both from the texts above cited, and from Josephus, *Wars*, iv. 6: 3, — the prophecies of which he speaks vaguely seem to be those of the "abomination." The passage shows, at all events, that the profanation by the Zealots was regarded as inseparable from the ruin of the city.

person, reproaches the people with its crimes, its murders of prophets, and its hardness of heart.[1] Fragments which we may suppose to have been taken from it allude to the murder of Zachariah, "son of Baruch."[2] There is hint, also, of a "culmination of horror" ($\tau\acute{\epsilon}\lambda\epsilon\iota o\nu$ $\sigma\kappa\acute{\alpha}\nu\delta\alpha\lambda o\nu$),[3] requiring that "for the elect's sake" those days should be shortened. This highest degree of horror to which man's depravity can attain seems to be the profaning of the Temple by the Zealots. Such atrocities prove that the coming of the "well-beloved" is near at hand, and that the vengeance of the just cannot be long delayed. The true Judæo-Christians still clung so strongly to the Temple that such a sacrilege must fill them with terror. Nothing like it had been seen since the days of Nebuchadnezzar.

All the family of Jesus felt that it was time to flee. The murder of James had already greatly weakened the attachment of the Christians at Jerusalem to Jewish orthodoxy; the rift between church and synagogue was widening every day. The hatred of the Jews for the pious sectaries, no longer restrained by Roman authority, led no doubt to many a deed of violence.[4] Besides, the life of those holy men who abode near the Temple, and offered their prayers in its courts, was greatly disturbed ever since the Temple had been changed to a barrack and stained by slaughter. Some went so far as to say that the proper name of a city

---

[1] Ep. of Barnabas, iv., xvi.; Luke xi. 49; "Life of Jesus," 20, 41, 43, n., 341.

[2] "Barachias," Matt. xxiii. 35. But there may be confusion with the son of Jehoiada. See "Life of Jesus," p. 341.

[3] Barnabas, iv.,—a passage not found in Enoch as now known; cf. Matt. xxiv. 22.

[4] Euseb. iii. 5: 2 (a poor authority).

so profaned was no longer Zion, but Sodom; and that the true Israelite was here held in bonds like his fathers in Egypt.[1]

The flight seems to have been resolved on early in the year 68.[2] To give more authority to this step, it was reported that a revelation to that effect had been given to the leaders, — according to some, through an angel.[3] All, it is likely, answered to the word of command, none of the brethren remaining in the city which a true instinct warned them was devoted to destruction.

There are indications that the flight of this peaceful flock was not effected without danger. The Jews, it appears, gave chase.[4] The terrorists, in fact, kept a sharp watch upon the roads, and slew as traitors all who tried to fly, except on payment of a heavy ransom.[5] A circumstance hinted to us in obscure words saved the fugitives: "The dragon poured forth after the woman [the Church] a flood of water to sweep her away and drown her; but the earth helped the woman, opened its mouth, and drank up the stream which the dragon poured forth after her; and the dragon was full of

---

[1] Rev. xi. 8: "the great city mystically called Sodom and Egypt."

[2] Matt. xxiv. 15-19; Mark xiii. 14-18 (ver. 7 shows that it was not at the beginning of the war). Luke (xxi. 20, 21) does not accord with these, and is surely of far less authority. He says that the order to flee was to be given when the city was first surrounded; but then it would have been too late (comp. xix. 43, 44). The Apocalypse (xii. 6, 13-17), written in 68 or 69, represents that the flight has already taken place: this is decisive (comp. Euseb. iii. 5; Epiph. xxix. 7; xxx. 2; *De mensuris*, etc., 15).

[3] Euseb. iii. 5; Epiph. *De mens*. 15. The expression of the latter in *Hær*. xxix. 7, may be understood of an order supposed to have been given from Jesus himself at the time, or may refer to Luke xxi. 20; but the other passage admits only the former sense, — "announced by an angel," etc.

[4] Rev. xii. 13, 15.   [5] Jos. *Wars*, iv. 7: 3.

wrath against the woman."[1] Here the dragon represents the spirit of Evil, sometimes as exhibited in the Roman power, sometimes in the violent party of Jerusalem. It is not likely that the mishap of the fugitives befell them from the Romans. Probably the Zealots attempted to drown the holy company in the Jordan, but they succeeded in fording the river where the water was shallow; or again, the troop sent to attack them may have missed its way, and so have lost trace of them.

The spot chosen by the leaders as the chief refuge of the escaping church was Pella,[2] a city of the Decapolis, near the left bank of the Jordan, finely situated on an eminence commanding the whole plain of the *Ghor* on one side, and on the other guarded by precipices with a torrent flowing at their foot.[3] A better choice could not have been made. Judæa, Idumæa, Peræa, and Galilee were in full insurrection; Samaria and the sea-coast were in great disturbance from the war; and thus Scythopolis and Pella were the two neutral towns easiest of approach from Jerusalem. Pella, from its position beyond Jordan, would offer greater quiet than Scythopolis,[4] which was a stronghold of the Romans. Pella was a free city, like all the towns of the Decapolis, but seems to have been given to Agrippa. To take refuge here was an open declaration of horror at the revolt. The importance

---

[1] Rev. xii. 13–15.
[2] Now *Fahl*, or *Tabakât Fahil* (Ritter, *Erdk.* xv. 786, 1003, 1025; Robinson, iii. 320; Van de Velde's maps; and comp. Euseb and Epiph. *loc. cit.* One of the victories that gained Palestine to the Moslems was at this place.
[3] Irby and Mangles (London, 1823), 304, 305; Robinson, *l. c.*
[4] Menke, *Bibelatlas*, No. 5.

of Pella dates from the Macedonian conquest. A colony of Alexander's veterans was established there, changing its former name into another which reminded the old soldiers of their fatherland.[1] It was taken by Alexander Jannæus; and the Greeks there, refusing to be circumcised, suffered greatly from Jewish fanaticism.[2] The pagan population had again struck root there; in the massacres of 66 Pella appears as a Syrian town, and was again sacked by Jews.[3] In this old anti-Jewish town the church of Jerusalem found a retreat during the horrors of the siege. Here it prospered, regarding this quiet abode as a sure place, a wilderness provided them by God, where they might peacefully await the hour of Jesus' coming, far from strifes of men.

The community lived from the stores it had laid aside. It was believed to be sustained by the care of God himself;[4] and many saw in this kindly lot, so different from that of the Jews, a miracle predicted by the prophets.[5] No doubt the Galilæan Christians, on their part, had passed to the eastward of the Jordan and the lake, into Batanæa and the Gaulonitis, and thus the dominions of Agrippa became an adoptive country for the Jewish Christians of Palestine. What gives unique importance to this Christian retreat is that the church brought with it the residue of the household of Jesus, who were held in the highest honour, and

---

[1] George Syncellus, p. 274. Apamæa was called Pella for the same reason (Strabo, xvi. 2: 10). Pella of the Decapolis had the distinguishing surname, "rich in water" (Pliny, v. 18).

[2] Jos. *Antiq.* xiii. 15: 4.

[3] *Ibid. Wars*, ii. 18: 1; iii. 3: 5.

[4] Rev. xii. 6, 14.

[5] Euseb. *Demonstr. evang.* vi. 18.

were designated by a special title, as "Kindred of the Master."[1] We soon find this trans-Jordanic Christian community continuing the Ebionite tradition, — that is, the tradition of the very word of Jesus;[2] and here the Synoptic Gospels have their birth.

---

[1] Δεσπόσυνοι: Euseb. i. 7: 14. [The word also means "Princes;" see Sophocles, Lexicon of later Greek.]

[2] Epiph. xxix. 7; xxx. 2.

CHAPTER XIII.

THE DEATH OF NERO. — A. D. 68.

VESPASIAN resumed his campaign at the first opening of spring in the year 68. His plan, as I have said before, was to crush Judaism step by step, advancing from the north and west toward the south and east; to force the flying to shut themselves up in Jerusalem, and here to slaughter the rebellious mass without mercy. He thus advanced as far as Emmaus,[1] seven leagues from Jerusalem, at the foot of the great ascent leading from the plain of Lydda to the holy city. He judged that it was not yet time to attack the city; meanwhile he ravaged Idumæa, then Samaria, and on the third of June fixed his headquarters at Jericho, whence he sent to slaughter the Jews of Peræa. Jerusalem was shut in on every side, surrounded by a circle of extermination. Vespasian then returned to Cæsarea, to get all his forces together. Here he received tidings which

---

[1] Emmaus or Ammaus, afterwards Nicopolis, at present the village Amwas, not far from the travelled road, about half-way between Jaffa and Jerusalem. There was, I think, another Emmaus, some five miles from Jerusalem, — the present village *Kulonié* (Luke xxiv. 13; Jos. *Wars*, vii. 6:6), whose name is probably derived from *Hammoça*, "the spring" (Josh. xviii. 26; Bab. Talm. *Succa*, 45a). See "The Apostles," 18, 19; but note Robinson, iii. 146; Guérin, *Palest.* i. 257, 293; Neubauer, *Geog. du Talm.* 100. The passage in Luke is absurd if applying to a place seven leagues away. *Kulonia* (or *Kulondia*) must be a Latin word, not the Κουλόν (LXX.) of Josh. xv. 60. Comp. Grätz, *Monatsschr.*, 1869, pp. 117–121.

stopped him short, and had the result of protracting for two years longer the resistance and revolution at Jerusalem.[1]

Nero died on the ninth of June. During the great struggles in Judæa just related he was living his artist life in Greece, and he did not return to Rome until the end of 67. He had never enjoyed so much in all his life. To gratify him, all the games had been crowded into a single year. All the cities sent him the prizes of their contests. Committees were continually waiting on him, to beg him to go and sing at every place. This big boy, insatiate of novelty (or else in mockery) beyond all parallel, was transported with delight. "The Greeks," said he, "are the only real listeners; the Greeks alone are worthy of me and my exertions." He loaded them with privileges; proclaimed the freedom of Greece at the Isthmian games; handsomely rewarded the oracles that prophesied to please him, and suppressed those he did not like; and, says Lucian, gave orders to strangle a singer who did not lower his voice so as to put his own in proper relief.[2] Helius, one of the worthless wretches whom he had left behind at Rome with full powers over the city and senate, urged him to return, as very serious political symptoms began to show themselves. Nero replied that his first duty was to his own reputation, for he must husband his resources against the time when he should no longer be emperor. His continual thought was, in fact, that if fortune should ever reduce him to a private condition, he might maintain himself by his art;[3] and when

---

[1] Jos. *Wars*, iv. 8–9:2.
[2] *Nero, seu de Isthmo*, 9.
[3] Suet. *Nero*, 40; Dion Cass. lxiii. 27.

any one remarked that he was fatiguing himself too much, he would say that the practice which was now only his relaxation as a prince might some day be the means of earning his daily bread. One of the things most flattering to the vanity of men of pleasure, who dabble a little in art or literature, is to imagine that if they were poor their talent would support them. Then, too, his voice was weak and dull; though he took the absurdest medical prescriptions of the time to preserve it; his singing-master never left him, and was constantly ordering the most childish precautions. One is ashamed to think that Greece was dishonoured by this ignoble masquerade. A few cities, however, preserved their self-respect. The wretched pretender did not dare to enter Athens, and was never invited there.[1]

Meanwhile the most alarming news kept coming in. He had now been almost a year away from Rome,[2] and gave orders to return. The return was like the journey.[3] In every city he received triumphal honours; the walls were torn down to let him enter. At Rome there was unexampled revelry. He rode upon the chariot in which Augustus had triumphed; beside him sat the musician Diodorus; on his head he wore the Olympic wreath; in his right hand he bore the Pythian laurel, while the other crowns were carried before him; on placards, to declare his victories, were written the names of those he had vanquished and the titles of the pieces he had played; then followed men trained in

---

[1] Suet. *Nero*, 20–25, 53–55; Dion Cass. lxiii. 8–18; Eus. *Chron.* 12; *Carm. Sibyll.* v. 136; xii. 90–92; Philostr. Apoll. iv. 39; v. 7, 8, 22, 23; Themistius, Or. 19; Lucian, *Nero*; Julien, *Cæs.* 310.

[2] Tillemont, *Hist. des Emp.* i. 320.

[3] Dion Cass. lxiii. 19–21.

the three kinds of applause he had invented, and the "Knights of Augustus;" and the archway of the Circus Maximus was overthrown to let him enter. On every side shouts were heard: "Cheers to the Olympian conqueror! To the Pythian conqueror! Augustus! Augustus! To the Nero-Hercules! to Nero-Apollo![1] The only all-round conqueror! the only one that ever was! Augustus! O sacred voice! happy he that hears!" The eighteen hundred and eight crowns he had won were displayed in the great Circus, fastened to the Egyptian obelisk which Augustus had set there as goal.[2]

At length there was a revolt of conscience in the nobler portion of the human race. The East, excepting Judæa, endured this shameful tyranny without a blush, and even found itself at ease under its burden; but in the West the sense of honour was still alive. It is one of the glories of Gaul that the overthrow of such a tyrant was her deed.[3] While the German soldiers, hating the Republic, and slaves to their maxim of fidelity, played — with Nero as with all the emperors — the part of good hirelings and body-guard,[4] a cry of

[1] Eckhel, vi. 275, 276; Suet. *Nero*, 25; Museum of the Vatican: bust No. 308.

[2] One would like to think that the circus and obelisk which Dion Cassius speaks of were the same that, four years before, had witnessed the horrid scenes of the Danaïds and Dirces and perhaps Peter's crucifixion. But the Circus Maximus — which, like that of the Vatican, had an obelisk from Heliopolis, now in the *Piazza del Popolo* — was better suited to Nero's exhibition. That of the Vatican was, it is likely, taken instead for the *piacula* of August, 64, because the other was ruined for the purpose by the fire.

[3] Suet. *Nero*, 40.

[4] Suet. *Caius*, 43, 58; *Galba*, 12; Tac. *Hist.* i. 31; iii. 69; Plut. *Galba*, 5, 6, 18. Comp. Henzen, *Annales*, etc., xxii. 13; and the inscriptions in Orelli, 2000, 3539; Fabretti, p. 687, Nos. 97, 98.

revolt was uttered by an Aquitanian, a descendant of ancient kings. The movement was truly Gallic;[1] without reckoning consequences, the Gallic legions plunged headlong into the revolution. The signal was given by Vindex about the fifteenth of March, 68. The news came speedily to Rome. The walls were soon scrawled with insulting inscriptions. "By his singing," said these ill jesters, "he has roused the cocks" (*gallos*)! At first, Nero only laughed at the jest; he was even well pleased with the chance of enriching himself by plunder of the Gauls. He continued to sing and amuse himself till Vindex posted placards in which he was described as a wretched artist. Then, from Naples, where he was, the play-actor wrote to the Senate demanding vengeance, and set out for Rome,—with the pretence, however, that his business was only about certain musical instruments, in particular a kind of hydraulic organ, about which he gravely consulted the Senate and the Knights.

The news that Galba had revolted on the third of April, and that Spain had sided with Gaul, which reached him while at dinner, struck him like a thunderbolt. He threw down the dinner-table, tore the letter, broke in a passion two costly carved vases from which he used to drink. In the absurd preparations he began to make, his first care was for his instruments and stage-equipment,[2] and for his women, whom he made to dress, like amazons, in skins, carrying axes, and with hair close cut. There were strange alternations of despondency and of woful jesting, which it is

---

[1] Tac. *Hist.* i. 51; iv. 17; Suet. *Nero*, 40, 43, 45; Dion Cass. lxiii. 22; Jos. *Wars*, pr. 2; iv. 8: 1.

[2] Suet. *Nero*, 44.

equally hard to take as sane or insane, since all of
Nero's acts hovered between the black malice of an
evil-hearted dunce and the dreary irony of a used-up
debauchee. He had no idea that was not childish.[1]
The world of affected art in which he lived had made
him a complete simpleton. At times he thought not of
resistance, but of going, unarmed, to weep before his
enemies, fancying he might move them; and already
he was composing the song of victory that should celebrate their reconciliation on the morrow. At other
times he wished to massacre the whole Senate, burn
Rome a second time, and during the conflagration turn
loose upon the city the wild beasts of the amphitheatre.
The Gauls were the chief objects of his rage: he talked
of slaughtering those who were in Rome, as favourers
of their countrymen, and ready to join them.[2] From
time to time he had the thought of changing the seat
of empire,[3] and retiring to Alexandria. He called to
mind that certain prophecies had promised him the
empire of the East, and in particular the kingdom of
Jerusalem. He dreamed that he might find a living in
his musical talent; and the chance of this, which would
be the best proof of his skill, gave him a secret joy.
Then he would console himself with literature: he remarked that his situation was peculiar; everything that
happened to him was without parallel; no prince had
in his lifetime lost so vast an empire. Even on the
days of his keenest anguish he changed nothing of his
customs; he would talk more of books than of the
doings of the Gauls; he would sing, make display of
wit, go to the theatre in disguise, or write privately to

---

[1] Suet. *Nero*, 43, 47; Dion Cass. lxiii. 27.
[2] Suet. *Nero*, 43.   [3] Aur. Vict. 14.

an actor whom he liked: "Hold back a man so busy as I? 't is a crime!"[1]

Discord in the Gallic camps, the death of Vindex, the weakness of Galba, might perhaps have delayed the deliverance of the world, but that the army at Rome at length declared itself. The prætorians revolted, and proclaimed Galba emperor on the eighth of June. Nero saw that all was lost. His perverse genius suggested to him nothing that was not grotesque. He would put on mourning, and thus arrayed would go forth to harangue the people, use all his scenic skill to move their pity, and thus obtain their pardon for the past, or, if nothing better, at least the government of Egypt. He wrote out his appeal, of which, says Suetonius, a draft was found after his death; but was warned that before he could reach the Forum he would be torn to pieces. He went to bed; then, waking at midnight, he found himself without guards: men were already plundering his chamber. He went out and knocked at several doors, but no one answered. He went back, wished to die, called for the gladiator Spiculus, a brilliant swordsman, one of the "stars" of the amphitheatre. Every one fell away. He went out again, roamed solitary about the streets, was going to throw himself into the Tiber, but returned upon his steps, the world seeming all void about him. His freedman Phaon then offered as a refuge his villa, situated between the *Salarian* and *Nomentan* ways, near the fourth milestone from the city.[2] Wretched and half-clad, wrapped in a shabby cloak, mounted on a

---

[1] Suet. *Nero*, 40, 42. [The last anecdote is not found in Suetonius.]

[2] It must have been a little beyond the Anio (*Teverone*) on the *via Patenaria*. Platner and Bunsen, *Beschreibung*, etc., i. 675; iii. 2, p. 455.

sorry beast, with his face covered so as not to be known, he went forth attended by three or four of his freedmen, among them Phaon, Sporus, and his secretary Epaphroditus. It was not yet daylight. As he went out by the Colline gate, passing near the prætorian camp, he overheard the cries of soldiers, who cursed him while proclaiming Galba. A dead body had been cast out on the highway, and his horse, starting suddenly, betrayed him. Still he succeeded in reaching Phaon's villa, crawling on his belly under some briers, or crouching behind the rushes.

His mocking temper, his street slang, did not fail him here. They wished to hide him in a shallow clay-pit, such as are common thereabout, and this gave him the opportunity for a grim joke: "What a fate it is, to go underground alive!" His discourse was like a running fire of classic quotations, interlarded with the stale buffooneries of a circus clown. At every point he had some bookish anecdote or some cold antithesis: "He who once walked proudly with a numerous train has with him now only three freedmen." At times the memory of his victims would come back to him, but led only to mere figures of speech, never to the moral emotion of remorse. The comedian outlived all else. The situation was to him only one more act in the play, which he had already rehearsed. Recalling the parts in which he had figured,—a parricide, or a prince reduced to be a beggar,—he remarked that he was now playing it through in his own person; and would sing the verse which a tragedian once put in the mouth of Œdipus: —

My doom of death is spoken by my father, mother, wife.[1]

[1] Dion Cass. lxiii. 28; Suet. *Nero*, 46.

Incapable of serious thought, he bade them dig a grave to the measure of his body, and bring bits of stone, wood, and water for his burial rites, — all the while sobbing, and saying, "What an artist is about to die!"

Meanwhile Phaon's messenger brought him a despatch, which Nero snatched from him and read, — that the Senate had declared him a public enemy, and condemned him to punishment "after the ancient custom." "What custom is that?" he asked. The reply was that the condemned person's bare head is made fast in a forked stick; he is then beaten to death with rods, and his body is dragged by a hook to be cast into the Tiber. He shivered, took two daggers which he had about him, felt their point, and put them back, saying "The fatal hour is not yet come." He then urged Sporus to begin the funeral wail, and tried again to kill himself, but could not. His awkwardness, his strange faculty of making every fibre of the soul ring false, the laughter as of both beast and devil, the clumsy vainglory which makes his whole life seem like the discordant cries of a grotesque witches' revel, reach the very sublime of the ridiculous. He could not succeed in killing himself. "May there not be some one here," he asked, "to set me the example?" He went back to his quotations, talked to himself in Greek, and made scraps of verse. All at once the sound was heard of a troop of horsemen, coming to seize him alive. And he recited from Homer, —

> The tramp of heavy horses is sounding in mine ears.[1]

Then Epaphroditus pushed against the dagger, and the point entered his throat. At this moment the centu-

---

[1] Iliad, x. 535.

rion came up, tried to stop the blood, and pretended that he had come to save him. "Too late!" gasped the dying wretch, his eyes standing out, and his flesh chilled with terror. "That is your fidelity!" were his last words in dying.[1] This was his master-stroke of comedy, — Nero, letting fall a melancholy plaint at the iniquity of his age, the vanishing of good faith and virtue! *Plaudite!* The play is over. This once, thou Nature of a thousand moods, thou hast found an actor worthy to play such a part!

He had it much at heart that his head should not be given up to insult, and that his entire body should be burned. His two nurses, and Acte, who still loved him, buried him secretly in a costly shroud of white, stitched with gold, with the luxury which they knew had been dear to him. His ashes were put in the tomb of the Domitii, a great mausoleum overlooking the hill of Gardens (the *Pincian*), in fine view from the Campus Martius, the site of the modern city.[2] From this site his phantom haunted the Middle Age like a vampire. To lay the ghosts which disturbed that quarter was built the church inscribed to the holy Virgin of the People (*Santa Maria del popolo*).

Thus, at the age of thirty-one, after a reign of thirteen years and eight months, died a sovereign, not the maddest or wickedest, but the most vain and ridiculous that chance ever lifted to the upper levels of

---

[1] Suet. *Nero*, 40–50; Dion Cass. lxiii. 22–29; Zonaras, xi. 13; Pliny, xxxvii. 2: 10.

[2] If Lactantius did not know this monument when he wrote *De mortibus persecutorum* (see chap. ii.), it follows that he had never been in Rome. Traces of the villa of Domitius are thought to have been found in the city wall at the end of the promenade of the Pincian (Platner and Bunsen, iii. 2: 569–571).

history. Nero is, first of all, a literary distortion. He was far from being devoid of all talent or all right feeling, — this unfortunate youth, drugged with base literature, drunk with declamatory nonsense, who forgot the empire in his music-lessons; who, when he learned the revolt of the Gauls, would not tear himself away from the spectacle he was witnessing, applauded the victorious athlete, and for several days thought only of his lyre and his voice.[1] In all this, the chief fault lay with the people, greedy of enjoyment, and demanding of its sovereign pleasure above all things; and with the false taste of the period, which reversed the standard of greatness, giving too high a prize of fame to the man of letters and the artist. The danger of literary education is that it inspires a measureless thirst for glory, without setting forth the stern lesson that shows the meaning of true glory. It was ordained that one by nature vainglorious and crafty, aspiring to the vast and boundless, unbalanced by sound judgment, should come to ghastly wreck. Even his better qualities, such as his aversion to war, were fatal to him, leaving to him only a taste for a kind of display that did not belong to him. Unless one were a Marcus Aurelius, one should not be too superior to the prejudices of his rank and condition. A prince has to do with arms and battles; his caste is that of the soldier. A great prince may and should be a patron of letters, but should not be himself a man of letters. Augustus and Louis XIV., leaders in a brilliant development of genius, are — next to cities of genius, like Athens and Florence — the finest spectacle in history; while Nero, Chilperic, and Louis of Bavaria are only

[1] Dion Cass. lxiii.26.

caricatures. In the case of Nero, the vastness of the imperial power and the brutality of Roman manners make the caricature look as if sketched in streaks of blood.

It is often said, to show the incurable corruption of the crowd, that Nero was in some respects popular. The truth is, there were two opposite drifts of opinion about him.[1] All that was grave and honourable detested him. The lower class were fond of him, — some simply, from the vague feeling that leads the poor plebeian to love a prince who has a showy outside;[2] others, because he intoxicated them with gala days. At such times he was to be seen mingling with the crowd, dining, or taking his repast at the theatre, in the heart of the mob.[3] And then, how he hated the Senate, the Roman nobility, whose temper was so harsh, so averse to the people! The high-livers who thronged about him were at least good-humoured and civil. The soldiers of the guard, too, always kept a liking for him. For a long time his tomb was to be found decked with fresh flowers, and images of him were laid on the Rostrum by secret hands.[4] The good fortune of Otho began through having been Nero's confidant and a follower of his ways. Vitellius, also, to find favour in Rome, affected openly to take Nero for his model, and to follow his rules of government. Thirty or forty years after, everybody wished he were still alive, and longed for his return.[5]

This popularity — at which we should not be too much

[1] Jos. *Ant.* xx. 8:3.   [2] Suet. *Nero*, 56.
[3] *Ibid.* 20, 22; Tac. *Hist.* i. 4, 5, 16, 78; ii. 95; Dion Cass. lxiii. 10.
[4] Suet. *Nero*, 57.
[5] Dion Chrys. Or. 21: 10: "All wish he were alive, and very many think he is."

surprised — had one singular result. A report spread abroad that the object of so much regret was not really dead. While he was yet alive, a notion had got started in his immediate circle that he would be dethroned at Rome, but then a new reign would begin for him in the East, almost a messianic reign.[1] There is always some difficulty in a people's believing that men who have long held the world's eye are actually gone. The death of Nero at Phaon's villa, in the presence of few witnesses, — only four, says Suetonius, — had not been exactly an event of public note. All that concerned his burial had passed among three women devoted to him. Hardly any one, except Icelus, had seen the dead body.[2] Nothing remained of him that could be recognized. It was easy to believe there was a substitute. Some said that the body had never been found; others, that the wound in his throat had been bandaged and healed.[3] Almost all held that, at the suggestion of the Parthian ambassador at Rome, he had taken refuge with the king of Parthia his ally, forever hostile to the Romans; or else with Tiridates, that king of Armenia whose journey to Rome in 66 had been attended by splendid festivals which struck the popular imagination.[4] There he was plotting the

---

[1] Suet. *Nero*, 40 ; Tac. *Ann.* xv. 36. The false Nero dreams only of Syria and Egypt (Tac. *Hist.* ii. 9).

[2] Plutarch, *Galba*, 7; Suet. *Nero*, 49.

[3] Tac. *Hist.* ii. 8 ; Sulp. Sev. ii. 29 ; Lact. *De mort. persec.* 2.

[4] Nero had certainly indulged the thought of flying to the Parthian king, Vologeses, and in fact that people were always friendly to him (Suet. 13, 30, 47, 57 ; Aur. Victor, *Nero*, 14; Epit. *Nero*, 8; *Carm. Sibyll.* v. 147). Tiridates had just visited the cities of Asia (Dion Cass. lxiii. 7: a text wrongly disputed). In any case, opinion was so definite, that all the false Neros appeared among the Parthians or were their agents (Zonaras, xi. 18 ; Tac. *Hist.* i. 2 ; Suet. *Nero*, 57).

ruin of the empire. He would soon return at the head of horsemen from the East, to torment those who had betrayed him.[1] His partisans lived in this hope. They were already restoring his images, and putting out edicts with his sign-manual.[2] The Christians, on the other hand, who looked on him as a monster, were struck with terror at hearing these rumours, which they believed in, being of the humbler class. These fancies continued for a long time, and, as it commonly happens in such cases, there were several pretenders to the name of Nero, — at least two : one who was killed at Cythnos, and whom we shall hear of again ; and one who appeared under Domitian, about 88.[3] We shall soon see the reaction of this opinion in the Church, and its effect upon the prophetic writings of the time.

Few people were left in their right senses after the strange spectacle they had witnessed. Human nature had touched the limits of possibility. A void was left in the mind, as after a stroke of fever; on all sides

---

[1] *Carm. Sibyll.* iv. 119, 137; v. 33, 34, 93, 100, 137, 142, 146, 215–223, 362, 385; viii. 70, 146, 152; xii. 93, 94; *Asc. of Isaiah*, iv. 2 ; Commodian, *Carm.* v. 820, 862, 925. Comp. Suet. 57 ; Lact. *De mort. persec.* 2 ; Zonaras, xi. 18.

[2] Tac. *Hist.* ii. 8.

[3] See Tac. *Hist.* i. 2; Suet. *Nero*, 57. Zonaras (xi. 18) speaks of another under Titus, but this seems a confusion of date: he may refer to the pretender of Domitian's time. Tacitus (*Hist.* ii. 8: "*ceterorum*") implies more than one after him of Cythnos; but the Parthian policy would hardly be guilty of the same fault twice, or of being duped by the same farce played by two impostors a few years apart. Dion Chrysostom, in the time of Trajan, asserts that many believed Nero to be still alive (Or. 21:10). The writer of the fourth Sibylline book (about 80) thinks that Nero is among the Parthians (ver. 119–124, 137–139) and will soon return ; ver. 137 (τότε) might incline us to put the pretended Nero under Titus (cf. 130–136), but the writer seems to speak of a future event. If written later, it would show the vanity of the prediction.

were spectres and visions of blood. It was told that as Nero passed the Colline gate to take refuge in Phaon's villa, lightning flashed before his eyes, the earth shook as if gaping open, and the souls of all he had slain thronged upon him.[1] There was, as it were, a thirst for vengeance in the air. We shall soon witness an interlude of the great celestial drama, in which the souls of the slaughtered victims, confined beneath the altar, cry with a loud voice, " How long, O Lord, dost thou not judge and avenge our blood on them that dwell upon the earth?"[2] And white robes are given them, that they may wait yet a little while.

[1] Suet. *Nero*, 48; Dion Cass. lxiii. 28.
[2] Rev. vi. 10.

CHAPTER XIV.

DISASTERS AND SIGNS.—A. D. 68.

BOTH Jews and Christians had at first greatly rejoiced when they heard of the revolt of Vindex. They supposed the empire would perish along with Cæsar's house; and that the insurgent generals, hating Rome, would think only of making themselves independent, each in his own province.[1] The insurrection of the Gauls was hailed in Judæa as meaning the same thing with that of the Jews themselves.[2] This was a complete mistake. No part of the empire, except Judæa, wished to see the breaking up of that vast confederation which gave peace and material prosperity to the world. All those countries about the Mediterranean, once enemies, were enchanted to dwell together in amity. Gaul itself, though less quiet than the rest, limited its revolutionary aspirations to the overthrow of evil emperors, the demand for reform, and the desire for a liberal empire. But we may readily conceive that those accustomed to the ephemeral royalties of the East might think it all over with an empire whose reigning house was just extinct, and believe that the several nations, subjugated within a century or two, would form separate States under the generals in command. For eighteen months, in fact, no one chief of

---

[1] Rev. xvii. 16. [2] Jos. *Wars,* pr. 2; vi. 6: 2.

the legions in revolt succeeded in keeping down his rivals permanently. There had never been such convulsions throughout the world, — Rome hardly roused from the nightmare of Nero's reign; in Jerusalem a whole people smitten with frenzy; the Christians still stunned by the frightful massacre of four years back; the very earth racked by the most furious tempests. All the world, in short, was dazed, as if the planet itself were shattered and about to perish. The shocking depth of corruption in which pagan society was sunk, the extravagances of Nero, his Golden House, his idiotic art, his colossal images, his portraits more than a hundred feet in height,[1] had literally made the world crazy. Then on all sides natural disasters broke forth,[2] and kept men's minds in a state of terror.

When we read the Apocalypse without knowing its date or holding its key, such a book seems to us a product of the most individual fancy or caprice. But when we set the vision in its place, in the interval between Nero and Vespasian, when the empire underwent the gravest crisis it had ever known, it is found to be a work marvellously adapted to the condition of the general mind just then.[3] We may say, too, the condition of the globe itself; for, as we shall soon see, the physical phenomena of the time made an element in the universal horror. Everybody was wild about miracles; never was the mind so taken up with prodigies and signs. The Divine Father seemed to have veiled his face. Loathsome spectres, monsters born of the slime, mysterious, seemed to float in the

---

[1] Pliny, xxxiv. 7: 8; xxxv. 7: 33; Dion Cass. lvi. 15.
[2] Juv. vi. 409-411.
[3] See, especially, Tac. *Hist.* i. 3, 18; *Ann.* xv. 47.

air. Every one thought himself at the eve of some unheard-of thing. Belief in signs and omens was universal; barely some few hundreds, better informed, saw the vanity of them.¹ Impostors, heirs more or less legitimate of old Babylonian chimeras, traded on the popular ignorance, and pretended to interpret the prodigies.² These wretches made themselves famous; they were always being driven away and then called back. Otho and Vitellius, especially, were wholly given to them. The highest statesmanship did not scorn to reckon with these childish dreams.³

One of the most important branches of Babylonish divination was the interpreting of monstrous births, considered as signs of coming events.⁴ This idea, more than any other, had taken hold upon the Roman mind. Progeny with several heads, in particular, were held to be evident forewarnings, each head, by the symbolism found in the Apocalypse, representing an emperor.⁵ So with real or pretended hybrids. In this regard, again, the misshapen visions and uncouth images of the Apocalypse reflect the popular tales that filled

---

¹ Pliny the Elder, the scientist of his day, is extremely credulous. The gravest historians, Suetonius, Dion Cassius (lxi. 16; lxv. 1, etc.), take omens to be of value. Tacitus (*Hist.* i. 18, 86) seems to see their vanity. Galba disdained them (see, however, Plutarch's *Galba*, 23), and Vespasian also at times laughed at them (Suet. *Vesp.* 23).

² Philostratus, *Life of Apollonius*, esp. v. 13.

³ See Val. Max. i. 3; Suet. *passim;* Tac. *Hist.* i. 3, 10, 18, 22, 38, 86; ii. 22, 62, 78; Dion Cass. lx. 35; lxi. 2, 16, 18; lxii. 1; lxiii. 16, 26, 29; lxiv. 1, 7, 10; lxv. 1, 8, 9, 11, 13; lxvi. 1, 9; Zonaras, vi. 5; xii. 16; Pliny, ii. 70, 72, 73 : 85, 103 : 106; Niceph. i. 17; Plut. *Galba*, 23; *Otho*, 4; Euseb. *Chron. ann.* 1973 Abr. 7, 9 Ner.; Philostr. *Apoll.* iv. 43; Jos. *Wars*, vi. 5 : 3, 4; Virg. *Georg.* i. 463; *Carm. Sibyll.* iii. 334, 337, 411; iv. 128, 172; Liv. xxx. 2.

⁴ *Journ. Asiat.*, Oct.-Dec. 1871, p. 449.

⁵ Philostr. *Apoll.* v. 13; Tac. *Ann.* xv. 47; *Hist.* i. 86.

men's minds. A hog with claws like a hawk was held to be a perfect image of Nero.[1] Nero himself had a curious eye for these monstrosities.[2]

Much thought was also given to meteors and signs in the sky. Meteoric stones made a prodigious impression. We know now that the fall of these bodies is periodical, at intervals of some thirty years. At such times there are nights when it seems literally to rain stars. Comets, eclipses, mock-suns, northern lights in which appear crowns, swords, and streaks of blood, fantastic forms of clouds in time of heat, with traces of battles or strange beasts, — drew eager attention, and seemed never to have been so vivid as in these tragic years. All the talk was of showers of blood, of wonderful thunderbolts, of rivers flowing up-stream, or of bloody torrents. A thousand things never noticed in ordinary times came to have a high importance in the feverish excitement of the public mind.[3] The odious charlatan Balbillus availed himself of the effect of these things on the emperor, to stir up his suspicions against the most illustrious, and get from him the most cruel orders.[4]

The disasters of the time, furthermore, were some justification for these insane fears. Blood was flowing in torrents on all sides. The death of Nero was in some ways a relief, but it opened a period of civil war. The conflict of the Gallic legions under Vindex and Virginius had been frightful. Galilee was a scene of unexampled desolation, and among the Parthians there

---

[1] Tac. *Ann.* xii. 64.   [2] Phlegon, *De rebus mirab.*, 20; Pliny, *loc. cit.*
[3] Tac. *Ann.* xv. 47; *Hist.* i. 18, 86 ; Dion Cass. lxiii. 26; Euseb. *Chron. ann.* 33; *Carm. Sibyll.* iv. 172; v. 154.
[4] Suet. *Nero*, 36, 56; Tac. *Ann.* xv. 47; Pliny, *Hist. nat.* ii. 25: 23 ; Dion Cass. lxi. 18.

was the murderous war of Corbulo. It was felt that something worse was coming: the fields of Bedriacum and Cremona were soon to smoke with human gore. Public executions made of the amphitheatres so many hells. The cruelty of military and civil manners had banished all pity from the world. The Christians shrank trembling to the depth of their retreats, and already, we may suppose, repeated to themselves words ascribed to Jesus[1]: "When you hear of wars and rumours of wars, be not troubled; all this must be, but the end is not yet. Nation will rise against nation, and kingdom against kingdom. There will be great earthquakes, terrors, famines, and pestilences on all sides, and great signs in the sky. These things are the beginning of sorrows."[2]

Famine was now added to massacre. In 68 supplies of grain from Alexandria fell short.[3] Early in 69 there was a disastrous inundation of the Tiber, with extreme misery.[4] A sudden inroad of the sea threw Lycia into mourning.[5] In 65 Rome was visited by a horrible pestilence; thirty thousand deaths were reported in the autumn.[6] The same year was a terrible conflagration at Lyons;[7] and Campania was swept by cyclones and tornadoes, whose ravages went as far as to the gates of Rome. The order of Nature seemed reversed; frightful tempests spread terror on every side.[8]

[1] Matt. xxiv. 6–8; Mark xiii. 7–9; Luke xxi. 9–11.
[2] On such calamities, particularly famine, considered as signs of the Messiah's coming, see Mishna, *Sota*, ix. 15; Bab. Talm. *Sanh.* 97 a; *Pesikta derabbi Kahna*, 51 b; *P. rabbathi*, i. xv.; the midrash *Othoth*, ii. 58–63.
[3] Suet. 45; Tac. xv. 43; *Carm. Sibyll.* iii. 475.
[4] Tac. *Hist.* i. 86; Suet. *Otho*, 8; Plut. *id.* 4.
[5] Dion Cass. lxiii. 26.   [6] Tac. *Ann.* xvi. 13; Suet. 39.
[7] Sen. *Epist.* 91.   [8] Tac. *Ann.* xv. 47; Sen. *Quæst. nat.* vi. 28.

But the most awful of all were earthquakes. The globe seemed to be undergoing a like convulsion to that of the moral world, as if the earth and man were stricken at once with fever.[1] In a popular commotion, anything that acts on the imagination of the crowd will be connected with the incidents of the moment: a natural phenomenon, a great crime, a multitude of things, accidental and disconnected, are bound and fused together in the great epic that makes man's story from generation to generation. Thus Christian history has embodied in itself all that at various times has moved the popular heart. Nero and a volcanic jet of sulphur-fumes (*Solfatara*) are quite as important here as a theological essay; we must make room for geological phenomena and the convulsions of the planet. And then, beyond all other natural events, earthquakes force man to bow himself before the Unknown. Where they are frequent, as near Naples, or in tropical America, there superstition is epidemic. And so we may say of those periods in which they rage most violently. Never were they more frequent than in the first century of our era. No time can be recalled when the crust of the old world had been so rudely shaken.[2]

Vesuvius was now preparing for the awful eruption of 79. In 63, on the fifth of February, Pompeii was almost buried by an earthquake; many of the inhabitants refused to return thither.[3] The volcanic centre of the Bay of Naples at this time was near Puteoli and Cumæ.

---

[1] Sen. *Quæst. nat.* vi. 1.

[2] Juv. vi. 411; *Carm. Sibyll.* iii. 341, 401, 449, 457, 459; iv. 128, 129. I have been favoured by the director of the observatory at Athens, who has compiled the statistics of earthquakes, with that portion of his record which relates to the period in view.

[3] Tac. *Ann.* xv. 22; Sen. *Quæst. nat.* vi. 1.

Vesuvius was still silent;[1] but the series of small craters making the region west of Naples, called the Phlegræan Fields, showed everywhere the trace of fire.[2] The Avernus, the marsh of Acheron (Lake Fusaro), Lake Agrano, Solfatara, with the little extinct volcanoes of Astroni, Camaldoli, Ischia, and Nisida, seem at this day something petty; the traveller receives an impression from them more pleasant than dreadful. But this was not the feeling of antiquity. These hot-pits, deep caverns, boiling springs, sulphurous vapours, hollow sounds, gaping cavities,[3] vomiting brimstone fumes and fiery vapour, were an inspiration to Virgil; they were also an essential feature in apocalyptic literature. The Jew who landed at Puteoli, for trade or intrigue in Rome,[4] saw this land steaming at every pore, incessantly shaken, and said to be the abode of giants and of torments.[5] The *Solfatara*, above all, seemed to him a pit of the abyss, a half-closed tunnel into hell. The continual escape of sulphurous vapour from its mouth — was it not a visible proof of a lake of fire underground, evidently destined (like the lake of Sodom and Gomorrah) for the punishment of the wicked?[6] The

---

[1] There had been eruptions in prehistoric times, but Vesuvius had long been quiet when it burst forth in 79 (Diod. Sic. iv. 21; Strabo, v. 4: 8; Dion Cass. lxvi. 21, 22; Vitruv. ii. 6: 2; Pliny, *Epist.* vi. 16). It was cultivated to the top, and only the plain showed a volcanic aspect (*Phlegræan*).

[2] Strabo, v. 4: 4–9.   [3] *Bocche d'inferno*, "hell-mouths."

[4] See "Saint Paul," chap. iv.; chap. i. above.

[5] Strabo, v. 4: 4, 5, 6, 9; vi. 3: 5; Diod. Sic. iv. 21. These titan-myths of the Greeks had been adopted by the Jews (see "Enoch," x. 12).

[6] Rev. xiv. 10; xix. 20; xx. 9; xxi. 8. This region was formerly much more volcanic in aspect than now; its plain was covered with brimstone-powder, and there appears to have been no vegetation (Strabo, v. 4: 6).

moral aspect of the region would no less astonish him. Baiæ was a bathing and watering place, a centre of luxurious pleasure, a place of fashionable country-houses, a favourite abode of frivolous society.[1] Cicero reproaches himself, in addressing sober people, for having his villa in the midst of this "kingdom" of brilliant and dissolute manners.[2] Propertius bids his beloved haste away from such a place; Petronius makes it the scene of Trimalcion's debaucheries; Seneca calls it a "hotel of vices."[3] Baiæ, Bauli, Cumæ, Misenum, were witnesses to every folly and crime. The pool of azure waves embraced in the shores of this delightful bay was the scene of those bloody sea-fights of Caligula and Claudius, where thousands of victims perished. What thoughts must fill the soul of a pious Jew, or a Christian fervently praying for the universal conflagration of the world, at sight of that nameless spectacle, those mad constructions amid the waves, those baths, which these puritan folk viewed with horror — like the abhorrence felt by monks of the thirteenth century for Frederick II., the restorer of these baths. The thought could be only this: "Fools and blind!" they would say; "their future abode is beneath this very spot; they dance over the hell that will soon swallow them up!"

Such an impression — which applies alike to Puteoli and to other similar places — is nowhere more striking than in the book of Enoch.[4] According to one of the

[1] Cic. *Pro Cœl.* 20.   [2] Cic. *Ad Att.* i. 16; xiv. 16.
[3] Sen. *Epist.* 51; cf. Mart. i. 63.
[4] Chap. lxvii. 4-13 (Dillmann). This passage has been supposed to have been written after the eruption of 79. But, apart from the doubt whether it refers to volcanoes in the West, we find very similar images in Diod. Sic. iv. 21, and Strabo, v. 4: 8, which were certainly written before 79.

writers of this strange apocalypse, the abode of fallen angels is a subterranean valley in the region of the West, near "the mountain of metals." This mountain is filled with floods of fire; a smoke as of brimstone pours forth; there flow from it boiling sulphur-springs (thermal waters), which serve for the healing of diseases, and near them the kings and great ones of the earth give themselves up to all manner of delights.[1] Fools and blind! every day they look upon the torment in store for them, and yet they do not pray to God! This valley of fire may be that of Gehenna, eastward from Jerusalem, connected by the "vale of fire" (*wadi en-nár*) with the sunken region of the Dead Sea; and in that case the hot springs are those of Callirrhoe, a pleasure resort of Herod, and the quite infernal country of Machærus, which is close by.[2] But, thanks to the elastic topography of seers, the baths may also be those of Baiæ and Cumæ; in the fiery valley we may recognise the *Solfatara* of Puteoli or the Phlegræan Fields;[3] in the "mountain of metals" we may

Diodorus, in particular, connects the Phlegræan Fields directly with Vesuvius, though they are more than twenty miles away. The allusion in "Enoch" may refer simply to volcanic phenomena near Cumæ and Baiæ. The phrase, "mountain of molten metal," thought to be descriptive of Vesuvius in action, applies well enough to Solfatara or Puteoli, or to Vesuvius before 79 (see Strabo, l. c.). The aspect of Vesuvius was certainly that of an extinct furnace (see Beulé, *Le drame du Vésuve*, 64). Besides, the Ethiopic text does not convey the idea of "molten" so clearly as has been supposed. At all events, the text does not say that streams of liquid fire "will one day pour forth" from the valley.

[1] Comp. Strabo, v. 4: 5: "The hot springs of Baiæ serve both for luxury and for healing."

[2] Jos. *Antiq.* xvii. 6: 5; *Wars*, i. 33: 5; ii. 21: 6; vii. 6: 3.

[3] As the *Solfatara* is only something more than 300 feet above the sea level, its crater may well be called a "valley," which expression would hardly apply to the crater of the *Somma*.

see Vesuvius before the eruption of 79.¹ We shall soon see how these strange regions inspired the writer of the Apocalypse, and how the "bottomless pit" was revealed to him ten years before, by an extraordinary coincidence, nature threw open the crater of Vesuvius. As to the people, it is no mere guess. It could not be without significance that the most tragic region in the world, the theatre of the impious orgies of Caligula, Claudius, and Nero, was at the same time the one region to display most conspicuously the phenomena which almost every one then thought to be typical of hell.²

Still, not Italy alone, but the entire eastern Mediterranean country, felt these earthquake-shocks. For two centuries Asia Minor was constantly disturbed by them.³ Cities had to be rebuilt, again and again. Some places, like Philadelphia, felt shocks almost daily.⁴ Buildings in Tralles were constantly crumbling down;⁵ and a way had to be contrived for banking the houses against one another.⁶ In the year 17 fourteen towns of the

---

¹ The title would not be justified by anything in the region about the Dead Sea. See, however, Neubauer, *Géogr. du Talmude*, p. 37, 40.

² Naturally, the apocalypses after 79 dwell still more upon these images. See *Carm. Sibyll.* iv. 130; and comp. "Esdras," iv. 6 *et seq.* (Ethiopic text).

³ "Nowhere in the world are there such continual earthquakes or so many overthrows of cities as in Asia" (Solinus, *Polyh.* 40). Comp. Texier, *Asia Minor, pass.;* Strabo, index, "terræ motus;" Philostr. *Apoll.* iv. 6. That is why there are comparatively so few monuments there earlier than the first century A. D.

⁴ Strabo, xii. 4:10; cf. 8 : 16, 17, 18.

⁵ Traces of these ruins may still be seen on the slopes of Tmolus and Messogis. Those mountains are most extraordinarily splintered, cloven, and cut into ravines, especially near Tralles (Aïdin).

⁶ For the first century B. C., see Jos. *Ant.* xv. 5:2; *Wars*, i. 19:3; Justin, xl. 2; Euseb. *Chron.* Aug. *Ann.* 19, 25, 39.

mountain region of Tmolus and Messogis were destroyed: this was the most dreadful calamity of the sort ever known till then.[1] In the years 23,[2] 33,[3] 37,[4] 46,[5] 51,[6] 53,[7] there were local disasters in Greece, Asia, and Italy. The island of Thera[8] suffered a period of volcanic action, and Antioch was frequently shaken.[9] Beginning with 59, almost every year is marked by some like disaster.[10] The valley of the Lycus, in particular, with the Christian towns Laodicæa and Colossæ, was overwhelmed in 60.[11] When we consider that right here was the centre of the millenarian ideas, the heart of the seven churches, the birthplace of the Apocalypse, we are convinced that there was a close connection between the revelation made at Patmos and the disturbances of the soil. Here, in short, is one of the few examples of a reciprocal influence between the geological history of the globe and the intellectual history of man. The Sibylline poems in like manner show the impression made by the convulsions in the valley of the Lycus.[12] These shocks in Asia Minor excited terror

---

[1] Tac. *Ann.* ii. 47; Plin. ii. 84 (86); Dion Cass. lvii. 17; Euseb. *Chron.* Tib. 4; Sen. *Quæst. nat.* vi. 1; Strabo, xii. 8: 16–18; xiii. 3:5; 4:8; Phlegon, *Mir.*, 13, 14; Solinus, 40; Syncellus, 319; *Corp. inscr. Gr.* 3450; Orelli, 687; Mommsen *Inscr. regni Neap.* 2486; Niceph. *H. E.* i. 17; *Carm. Sibyll.* iii. 341; v. 286. Comp., for B. C. 12, Dion Cass. liv. 30.

[2] Tac. *Ann.* iv. 13.
[3] Eus. *Ann.* 33.
[4] Suet. *Tib.* 74.
[5] Dion Cass. lx. 29 *et al.*
[6] Tac. *Ann.* xii. 43.
[7] *Ibid.* 58.

[8] Near Crete, now *Santorin*, "celebrated as a centre of great volcanic activity."

[9] Malala, x. *pass.*

[10] Euseb. *Chron.* 62, 65; Suet. *Nero*, 20; Philostr. *Apoll.* iv. 34; vi. 38, 41; Sen. *Q. N.* vi. 1; Pliny, *H. N.* ii. 83 (85).

[11] See "Saint Paul," chap. xiii.; p. 98 (*ante*); Euseb. and Orosius mistake the date: Tac. xiv. 27 settles the question.

[12] *Carm. Sibyll.* iii. 471; v. 286–291.

all about; they were talked of throughout the world;[1] and there were few, indeed, who did not look on them as signs of divine wrath.[2]

All this caused a sort of gloom in the air, strongly stimulating to the Christian imagination. In view of such dislocation of both the physical and the moral world, how should not the faithful cry out with deeper conviction than ever, *Maran-atha* ("The Lord cometh")? The earth seemed to them to be crumbling away. In fancy they already saw kings, men of power, and men of wealth in flight, saying to the mountains, "Fall upon us!" and to the hills, "Cover us!" The old prophets constantly appealed to natural disasters to announce the near coming of "the day of the Lord." A passage of Joel (chap. ii.), which was applied to messianic times,[3] announced as sure prognostics of that "great and dreadful day" signs in heaven and on earth, — prophets appearing on every side, rivers of blood, fire, smoke, rising like the stem of a palm-tree,[4] a darkened sun, a bloody moon. Jesus was thought, also, to have predicted "earthquakes, famines, pestilences in divers places" as the "beginning of birth-pangs,"[5] then, as immediate signs of his coming, eclipses, a darkened moon, stars falling from the sky, the air troubled, the sea roaring, populations fleeing in

---

[1] Juv. vi. 411.   [2] Comp. Dion Cass. lxviii. 25.
[3] Acts ii. 17–21.
[4] The word (*timroth*) rendered "pillars" of smoke in Joel ii. 30, means "palm-trees." So Pliny (*Epist.* vi. 16) compares the column of smoke from Vesuvius to a pine-tree [*non alia magis arbor quam pinus expresserit*].
[5] ἀρχὴ ὠδίνων: Matt. xxiv. 7, 8; Mark xiii. 8; Luke xxi. 1. Like all apocalyptic imagery, these ideas were taken from the old prophets. See Isa. xxxiv. 4; Ezek. xxxii. 7, 8; comp. *Carm. Sibyll.* iv. 172 *et seq.*

terror, not knowing on which side is death or safety.[1] Thus terror is a feature in every apocalypse, associated with the idea of persecution.[2] Evil, when just coming to an end, would redouble its fury, and make proof of fresh skill in its means for the destruction of saints.

[1] Matt. xxiv. 29; Mark xiii. 24, 25; Luke xxi. 25, 26. Comp. incidents in Luke to Seneca's account of the earthquake at Pompeii in' 63 (*Q. N.* vi. 1).

[2] Assumpt. of Moses, 8, 10; Apocal. of Baruch (Ceriani, i. 60, 80; v. 130).

CHAPTER XV.

THE APOSTLES IN ASIA. — A. D. 68, 69.

THE province most affected by these terrors was Asia Minor. The church at Colossæ had received its death-blow in the catastrophe of A. D. 60.[1] Hierapolis seems not to have suffered, though built among the most shapeless remains of a volcanic outburst; and it is possible that the faithful of Colossæ found refuge here. At this time Hierapolis appears, from all indications, to be a city by itself. Judaism was here openly professed. Inscriptions still extant among the marvellously preserved ruins of this singular place speak of the yearly doles to be made to corporations of workmen, at the time of "unleavened bread" and of the Pentecost.[2] Nowhere were acts of mercy, charitable institutions,[3] societies for mutual help among people of the same trade,[4] so important as here. Homes for orphans, shelters for infants, prove a developed philanthropy, such as was rarely to be found.[5] Philadelphia had points of similar interest. Here political divisions were drawn on the lines of difference in occupation. In

---

[1] See p. 98, *ante.*
[2] See *Rev. de l'instr. publ. en Belge,* May, 1868, p. 1.
[3] *Ibid.* p. 7.
[4] See "Saint Paul," chap. xiii.; Waddington, *Inscr.* 1687.
[5] Ἐργασία θρεμματική (Waddington); Wagener, 7, 8; *Corp. inscr. gr.* 3318; *Notices,* etc., xxviii. 2, p. 425.

almost all these rich cities of Asia Minor society was a peaceful democracy of labourers having nothing to do with politics. A slave might be honoured for his goodness, and virtue was held to belong especially to those who suffer. About the time of which I speak there was born in Hierapolis a child so poor that he was sold in the cradle, and was known by no other name than "New-bought,"[1] which, thanks to him, has become a very synonym of virtue. From his instructions was to come, one day, that admirable book, a manual for those strong souls who shrink from the supernaturalism of the gospel, and think it a betrayal of duty to ascribe to it any other charm than that of its own austere purity.

To Christian eyes Hierapolis had an honour greatly superior to that of having witnessed the birth of Epictetus; it had given hospitality to one of the few survivors of the first Christian generation, one of those who had seen Jesus, — the apostle Philip.[2] We may suppose that he came hither after the events which made Jerusalem unendurable for quiet people, and drove the Christians out of it.[3] Asia was the province where Jews were most at their ease, and they thronged into it. Intercourse between Hierapolis and Rome was easy and frequent; a trader is mentioned who made the journey seventy-two times.[4] Philip was a priestly person of the old school, like James. He had the repute of working miracles, and even of raising

[1] Epictetus ('Επί-κτητός), *i. e.*, "thrown into the bargain." — ED.

[2] Theodoret, *In Ps.* cxvi. 1; Niceph. ii. 39. On Philip "the deacon" and Philip "the apostle," see "The Apostles," chap. ix.; "Saint Paul," chap. xviii. (end).

[3] The Greek *menology* (Urbin, 1727, pt. 1) takes him thither after the death of John, but these are very late reckonings.

[4] *Inscr. Gr.* 3920.

from the dead. He had had four daughters, all prophetesses. One of them seems to have died before he came to Asia; two others grew old unmarried; the fourth married in her father's lifetime, prophesied like her sisters, and died at Ephesus.[1] These singular women became very distinguished in Asia.[2] Papias, who was bishop of Hierapolis about 130, had known them, but had not seen Philip himself. He heard from these aged and enthusiastically devout women wonderful accounts of their father's miracles. They also knew many things about other apostles or apostolic persons, particularly Joseph Barsabas, who, they said, drank a deadly poison without injury.[3]

Thus there was established in Asia, near John, a second centre of authority and apostolic tradition. John and Philip raised the country where they had chosen their abode almost to the level of Judea. These two "great lights of Asia,"[4] as they were called, were for several years the watchfires of the Church when deprived of its other leaders. Philip died and was buried at Hierapolis. His virgin daughters lived to a very advanced age, and were laid near him, the married one being buried at Ephesus; all their graves

---

[1] Acts (xxi. 9) and Proclus reckon four prophetesses; the latter relates that they were all buried at Ephesus. Polycrates, better informed, knows only three, two of them unmarried, and one a prophetess who was buried at Ephesus. Clement seems to speak of them all as married. The Greek menology brings two into Asia, and buries one at Ephesus.

[2] "The Apostles," chap. ix.; Papias (Euseb. iii. 39); Polycrates of Ephesus (*id.* iii. 31; v. 24); Clem. Alex. *Strom.* iii. 6; Proclus (Caius: Euseb. iii. 31); Euseb. iii. 30, 31, 37; v. 17; Jer. iv. 2: 181, 673, 785; Niceph. ii. 44; Menol. Gr. Sep. 4. When Irenæus rests the traditional date on the testimony of John and "other apostles," Philip may be intended. Note also the prominence given to Philip in the Fourth Gospel.

[3] Euseb. iii. 39.   [4] Euseb. iii. 31.

might be seen in the second century. Thus Hierapolis had its rival apostolic tombs, as well as Ephesus. The province seemed ennobled by these holy bodies, which men thought they should behold rising out of the earth at the coming of the Lord in glory to raise his chosen from the dead.

The crisis in Judæa, which in 68 scattered the apostles and apostolic men, may have brought back to Ephesus and the valley of the Mæander other important persons of the infant Church. In any case a large number of disciples, who had seen the apostles at Jerusalem, found themselves again in Asia, and seem to have led there that wandering life so dear to Jews.[1] Perhaps the mysterious persons called "John the Elder" and Aristion were of this number — though it seems to me more probable that they were a generation later. These hearers of the Twelve carried through Asia Minor the tradition of the church at Jerusalem, thus giving the preponderance here to Jewish Christianity. They were eagerly questioned about the sayings of the apostles and the actual words of Jesus. At a later time, those who had seen them were so proud of having drawn from this pure spring that they looked disdainfully upon the petty writings which professed to report those sayings.

The state of mind in which these churches lived — hidden in the heart of a province whose gentle climate and pure sky seem to invite to mysticism — had a very special effect on their beliefs. Nowhere else did the messianic ideas so fill men's thoughts. They aban-

---

[1] Papias in Euseb. iii. 39. The same thing follows from the constant appeal of Irenæus to "ancients" who had lived with the apostles, and whom he had heard of from his master Polycarp.

doned themselves to extravagant calculations.[1] The strangest parables were propagated, derived from the tradition of Philip and John. The gospel developed in this region had in it something mythical and singular.[2] It was commonly held that after the resurrection of the body (which was very near) there would be a "bodily" reign of Christ upon earth for a thousand years.[3] The delights of this earthly paradise were described in a wholly materialistic fashion: the bigness of the clusters of grapes and the abundance of wheat-ears in the Messianic reign were given in exact measure.[4] That ideal vein which gave so delicate a touch to the simplest words of Jesus is here almost wholly lost, and it may be noted that in the Synoptics the view of the sons of Zebedee as to the divine kingdom is wholly carnal.[5]

In Ephesus the greatness of John increased from day to day.[6] His commanding authority was recognized throughout the province, except perhaps at Hierapolis, where Philip lived: thus Hierapolis does not appear in the group of seven churches addressed in the Apocalypse. Those of Smyrna, Pergamos, Thyatira, Sardis, Philadelphia, and Laodicæa, had adopted him as their chief,

---

[1] The Jews in some parts of the East, devoted messianists, spend their time at this day in searching current events for signs of the Messiah, and in reckoning the date by means of wild *ghematrioth*. Thus a large number of impostors claim to be Messiah, especially in Yemen.

[2] Euseb. iii. 39.

[3] In all this Eusebius, irritated in his Greek rationalism by this unbridled millenarianism, sees only the personal errors of Papias.

[4] Papias in Iren. v. 33: 3, 4; Apoc. of Baruch (Ceriani), i. 80; v. 131. See "Life of Jesus," p. 41, *n*.

[5] Matt. xx. 20, 21; Mark x. 35–37.

[6] Epiphanius (*Hær.* 78:11) rejects as unfounded the legends which make Mary, the mother of Jesus, to have resided with him at Ephesus.

and listened with deference to his warning, counsel, or reproach. The apostle (or those who took upon them to speak in his name) generally assumed a tone of severity. His character was marked by great rudeness, extreme intolerance, with harsh and even coarse language against those whose opinion was opposed to his.[1] It was to him that Jesus addressed those words, "He that is not against us is on our side."[2] The anecdotes told afterwards, to put in relief his gentleness and softness of heart[3] seem to have been invented to be in accord with the tone of the epistles ascribed to him, of genuineness more than doubtful. Traits of an entirely opposite character, exhibiting much violence of temper, are more in keeping with the gospel accounts[4] or with the Apocalypse; and show that the passion which gave him the title "son of thunder" was only embittered by age. It may be, however, that the very opposite qualities ascribed to him need not for that reason be ruled out, as has been thought. Religious fanaticism often yields in the same person the extremes of harshness and gentleness: an inquisitor of the Middle Age, who burned his thousands of victims for the merest subtilties of doctrine, might at the same time be one of the gentlest and even humblest of men.

The animosity of John and his companions seems to have been especially deep and bitter against the little conventicles of the teacher whom they called "the new Balaam."[5] Such is the inherent injustice of

---

[1] Iren. iii. 3:4; Euseb. iii. 28:6; Rev. ii., iii.; 2 John, 10, 11; 3 John 9, 10.

[2] Mark ix. 40.

[3] Clem. Alex. *Quis dives*, 42; Euseb. iii. 23; Jer. *In Gal.* vi.

[4] Mark iii. 17; ix. 37, 38; Luke ix. 49, 54.

[5] See "Saint Paul," chap. xiii. In later time, the name "Balaam"

party-spirit, such was the passion which inflamed these hard Jewish souls that the disappearance of the "destroyer of the Law" was hailed by his adversaries with shouts of joy.[1] For many, the death of this troubler, this intruder, was a real relief. We have seen that Paul found himself at Ephesus surrounded by enemies.[2] His last words spoken at Miletus[3] are full of sad presentiment. Early in 69 we shall find hatred against him still obstinate and bitter. After this the controversy ceases, and silence veils his memory. At the time under view, no one seems to have spoken a word for him; and this is just what saved him afterwards. The silence, or (if we will) the feebleness of his adherents brought reconciliation. The boldest thoughts get accepted at length, provided they keep long silence, and make no reply to conservative attack.

With all believers, the dearest thought was of rage against the Roman empire, joy at the disasters that befell it, and hope to see it soon break in pieces. Their sympathy was with the Jewish insurrection, and they were persuaded that the Romans would not come out of it with success. It was long since Paul, and perhaps Peter, had taught submission to Roman rule, even ascribing to it something of a divine character. The principles of high-strung Jews about the refusal of tribute-money, the diabolic origin of all pagan power, the idolatry involved in civil actions done after Roman forms, had carried the day. This was the natural con-

was also given among the Jews to Jesus (Geiger, *Jud. Zeits.* vi. 31–37). It had become the type of a false prophet as to the pagans, and a deceiver of Israel.

[1] Primasius, Comment on the Epistles of Paul in the *Bibl. max. Patrum* (Lyons), x. 144.

[2] "Saint Paul," chap. xv. [3] Acts xx. 29, 30.

sequence of persecution: moderate views were no longer in place. Persecution, though not so ferocious as in 64, yet continued with a dull pressure.¹ The fall of Nero had nowhere else been felt as it was in Asia. In general opinion, the monster, healed by some satanic power, still kept somewhere hidden, and would presently reappear. We may conceive what effect such rumours must have among the Christians. Many of the faithful at Ephesus, including perhaps their Head, had escaped from the dreadful butcheries of Nero. What! will that horrible Beast return, then, swollen with luxury, folly, and vainglory? It must be so, those would think who still suspected that Nero was the Antichrist. He it is, that mystery of iniquity, that mortal foe of Jesus, who shall appear to slaughter and torture mankind, before the bright coming of the Latter Day!² Nero is that Satan in the flesh, who will complete the murder of the saints. Yet a little while, and the awful moment will have come! This thought was the more readily adopted by the Christians, since the death of Nero had been too mean an incident for an Antiochus: persecutors on such a scale commonly perish in a more striking way. The enemy of God, it was inferred, was reserved for some more tragic fate, which should be inflicted on him in view of all men and angels, gathered by the Messiah to the judgment.

This idea, from which the Apocalypse was born, took more definite shape from day to day. The Christian conscience had arrived at a pitch of ecstasy, when a thing took place in the islands off the Asiatic coast, which all at once gave body and form to what had hitherto been only fancy. A pretended Nero had just

---

¹ Rev. xii. 17; xvii. 14.   ² "Saint Paul," ch. ix.

appeared, and filled the provinces of Asia and Achaia with an eager sentiment of curiosity, hope, or terror.[1] He was, it would seem, a slave from Pontus; according to some, an Italian slave or freedman. In appearance he was much like the dead emperor, having his big eyes, his heavy head of hair, his hawk-like air, his fierce and theatrical aspect; practised, too, like him, with harp and song. This pretender gathered about him a nucleus of deserters and vagabonds, ventured to put to sea, hoping to reach Syria and Egypt, and was wrecked in a storm on the island of Cythnos, one of the Cyclades. This he made the centre of quite an active propaganda, increased his band by enlisting a few soldiers on their return from the East, made bloody executions, plundered some traders, and gave arms to slaves. There was great excitement among the common people, whose credulity made them a prey to the wildest rumours. From the month of December, 68, all the talk in Asia Minor and Greece was of him.[2] Apprehension and terror increased from day to day. The name whose evil celebrity had filled the world

[1] The story is told by Tacitus (*Hist.* ii. 8, 9). Dion Cassius also undertook to relate it, but Xiphilin has condensed his account in a brief summary. Zonaras, who also only abridges Dion, adds a few details. (In Zonaras we should read ἐν Κύθνῳ, not ἐν Κύδνῳ.)

[2] The false Nero perished under Otho, consequently between Jan. 15 and April 15, A. D. 69, probably near the earlier date. He was found at Cythnos by Sisenna, who was on his way from Syria to Rome to join the movement of the Pretorian guard who had proclaimed Otho. News went from Rome to Syria in ten days; Sisenna must have set out as soon as the proclamation had been made in Syria, and may have arrived in Cythnos about the sixth of February. Asprenas, who arrived after him, was still sailing under the orders of Galba, who was murdered on January 15. At latest, then, the false Nero was wrecked on Cythnos in January, 69. As his intrigues on the mainland had continued for some time, his insurrection must have begun towards the end of 68.

turned men's heads afresh, and made them think that all they had yet seen was as nothing compared to what they were about to see.

The excitement was further increased by events happening in Asia, or the Archipelago, which cannot be here set forth for lack of clear information. An ardent partisan of Nero, who besides his political passion had some repute as a conjurer, declared openly either for the pretender of Cythnos, or for Nero supposed to be in flight among the Parthians. He apparently compelled quiet people to acknowledge Nero; he restored his statues, and forced men to honour them; we might even be led to think that coin was struck with the legend, *Nero redux*. What we do know is that the Christians imagined it was the intention to make them worship Nero's image. Invincible scruples were roused in them by the coin, the "mark" (χάραγμα) or metallic ticket having the name of "the Beast," without which "they could neither buy nor sell."[1] Gold stamped with the sign of the great Head of idolatry burned their hand. Rather than yield to such acts of apostasy, some of the faithful seem to have exiled themselves from Ephesus: we may suppose that John was among them.[2] This incident, obscure to us, plays a great part in the Apocalypse, and perhaps was what first prompted the issuing of it. "Hark!" says the Seer, "this is the end of the long-suffering of the saints, who keep the command of God and the faith of Jesus."[3]

---

[1] Rev. xiii., xiv.; note especially, in xiv. 9–12, the writer's urgency, and the phrase, "patience of the saints" (ver. 12). Comp. xx. 4, where "they who had not worshipped the Beast" are put in the same rank with the martyrs under Nero.

[2] Rev. i. 9; xx. 4.   [3] Rev. xiv. 12.

Events in Rome and Italy justified this feverish outlook. Galba did not succeed in keeping his authority. Down to Nero, the legal title inherited from Julius and Augustus had stifled among the generals any thought of competing for the empire. But now that this title was extinct, any military chief might aspire to that inheritance. Vindex was dead; Verginius had loyally submitted; Nymphidius Sabinus, Macer, and Fonteius Capito had expiated their plots by death; still nothing had been settled. On the second of January, 69, the legions in Germany proclaimed Vitellius; on the tenth, Galba adopted Piso; on the fifteenth, Otho was proclaimed at Rome. For a few hours there were three emperors; but at night Galba was murdered. Faith in the empire was deeply shaken. It was not thought that Otho could reign alone. Hopes were openly expressed by partisans of the false Nero at Cythnos, and by those who dreamed from day to day that they might see the emperor they mourned returning from beyond the Euphrates. Then, at the end of January,[1] there went abroad among the Christians of Asia Minor a symbolic manifesto, claiming to be a revelation from Jesus himself. Did the writer know the death of Galba,[2] or did he only foresee it? This is the harder to decide, since (after the manner of apocalyptic books)

---

[1] This date may be open to one objection. The passages in Rev. xi. 2, and xx. 9, seem to assume the blockade of Jerusalem as already begun, which it was not till March of the following year. But these passages, in poetic style, are justified by the condition to which the revolt had been reduced by Vespasian's campaigns in 67 and 68 (see chap. xii.). Luke xxi. 20, 21, requires a similar explanation. It is clear that when the Apocalypse was written the Temple was still standing: the writer does not even fear lest it may be destroyed. Nor does Rev. xvii. 16 necessarily refer to the burning of the Capitol on December 19, 69.

[2] Rev. xvii. 10.

the writer at times avails himself of some recent event, which he thinks known only to himself, to give the more credit to his prophetic foresight: thus, for example, the composer of "Daniel" seems to have had some hint of the death of Antiochus; and Commodian may have had private knowledge of the defeat and death of Decius. In like manner the Seer of the Apocalypse seems to have had private information of the political events of his time. It is doubtful whether he knew Otho; he thinks that Nero will be restored directly upon the fall of Galba, whom he regards as already condemned, so that the return of the Beast is close at hand. His glowing imagination then displays to him a series of views of what will "shortly come to pass,"[1] and thus he unfolds chapter after chapter of a prophetic book, whose object is to enlighten the Christian conscience upon the events now passing, to reveal the true meaning of a political situation that disturbs the firmest minds, and, above all, to reassure them as to the destiny of their brethren already slain. We must call to mind that the credulous sectaries whose thought we are trying to retrace were a thousand leagues away from the ideas of the immortality of the soul borrowed from the Greek philosophy. The martyrdoms of recent years made a terrible crisis for a community which trembled like a child at the death of a saint, and questioned anxiously whether such a one should see the

---

[1] Rev. i. 1; xxii. 6. The Jews of the time were much inclined to form such conjectures as to the succession of emperors, and what will happen to each. These conjectures are founded on the frightful images of their dreams, eked out with texts of Scripture. A talent for interpreting these dark hints was highly prized. Thus Josephus claims to have known beforehand the accession of the Flavian family (*Wars*, iii. 8: 3).

kingdom of God.[1] They felt an unconquerable need to conceive of those who had died in the faith as in shelter, and already happy — though only in transitory bliss — amid the disasters which were to afflict the earth.[2] The brethren heard their cries for vengeance, felt their pious impatience, and called for the day when God would arise at length and avenge his own chosen ones.

The form of "apocalypse" chosen by the writer was not new in Israel. Ezekiel had introduced a considerable change in the old prophetic style, and he may be regarded as, in a sense, the creator of the class of literature known as apocalyptic. For burning appeal, sometimes accompanied by allegoric acts extremely simple, he had — doubtless under the influence of Assyrian art — substituted vision; that is, a complex symbolism, in which the abstract idea is represented by imaginary beings outside of all reality. Zechariah continued upon the same road; vision became the obligatory framework for all prophetic instruction. Finally, the writer of "Daniel," by the extraordinary fame he won, fixed definitely the rules for this order of composition. The Book of Enoch, the Assumption of Moses, certain Sibylline poems,[3] were the fruit of this powerful

---

[1] See "Saint Paul," chap. ix.   [2] Rev. xiv. 13.

[3] The specimens of apocalyptical literature, known or attested, may be approximately classed thus: 1. Daniel, about B. C. 164; 2. Sibylline poem (Jewish, iii. §§ 2, 4); 3. Book of Enoch; 4. Assumption of Moses; 5. Apocalypse of John; 6. Sibylline poem, iv., A. D. 80; 7. Apocalypse of Esdras, A. D. 97; 8. Apocalypse of Baruch; 9. Ascension of Isaiah; 10. Sibylline poems of the 2d century; 11. Apocalypse of Peter (canon of Muratori, 70, 71); 12. Apocalypse of one Judas, time of Sept. Severus (Eus. vi. 7); 13. Commodian, *Carmen;* about A. D. 250. To these we may add "Testament of the Twelve Patriarchs," and the "Shepherd" of Hermas. Others, "apocryphal apocalypses," published by Tischendorf (Leipzig, 1866), are more recent imitations.

stock. This framework of fancy was well suited to the prophetic genius of the Semites,[1] their habit of grouping events in some general scheme of history, and exhibiting their own thought in the guise of a divine necessity, with broad clear glimpses into the future. To every critical situation in the affairs of Israel there was thenceforth a book of visions to correspond. The persecution of Antiochus, the Roman conquest, the profane rule of Herod, — each had called out its ardent Seer. Inevitably, the reign of Nero and the siege of Jerusalem must have their apocalyptic message; just as afterwards the cruelties of Domitian, Hadrian, Septimius Severus, and Decius, and the invasions of the Goths (A. D. 250), called forth each its own.

The writer of this strange book, destined by a stranger fate to such wildly differing expositions, composed it in obscurity, freighted it with the whole weight of the Christian conscience, and sent it as an epistle to the seven chief churches of Asia, — Colossæ and Hierapolis, as we have seen, not being included. He required that it should be read, as was the custom with all apostolic letters, to the assembled brethren (i. 3). In this he perhaps had in mind the example of Paul, who had rather address his hearers by letter than in person.[2] Such missives were not rare, and their topic was always the looked-for coming of the Lord. Assumed revelations in the name of different apostles were current, predicting that the Last Day was at hand; so that Paul found himself compelled to warn his churches against the abuse that might be made of his name to

---

[1] See a letter from Abd-el-Kader, on the future of Islam: *Journal des Debats*, 14 July, 1860.
[2] 2 Cor. x. 10.

support such frauds.¹ The present book opens with an introduction to set forth its source and extreme importance: thus, —

Revelation (ἀποκάλυψις) of Jesus Christ, which God gave him to show his servants what will speedily come to pass, and which he sent by his own angel[2] to his servant John, who offers himself as an eye-witness, a pledge of the word of God and of the declaration of it made by Christ.[3] Happy is he that shall [publicly] read, and they who shall hear the words of this prophecy and heed them; *for the time is at hand.*

JOHN to the seven churches of Asia: Grace and peace be to you from Him who is, and was, and will be, and from the seven Spirits who stand before his throne,[4] and from Jesus Christ, the faithful witness, the first-born from among the dead, prince of the kings of the earth, who loves us and has washed us from sin in his own blood, who has made us kings and priests of God his Father, to whom be glory and power for ever. AMEN.

Behold, he comes upon the clouds, and every eye of those who pierced him[5] shall look upon him, and all tribes of the earth shall be in mourning ["beat their breasts"] at the sight of him. Yes, verily. "I am the *alpha* and the *omega*," saith the Lord God; "he that is, and was, and will be; the Almighty."

I, John, your brother and companion in persecution, in the kingdom and firm expectation of Christ, found myself in the island called Patmos, through (διά) the word of God and the testimony of Jesus Christ.[6] I was in a trance (ἐν πνεύματι)

---

[1] 2 Thess. ii. 2 ("nor by letter as from us").

[2] Or messenger: comp. xix. 9, 10; xii. 6.

[3] We might incline to render this: "Who has given testimony to the word of God and the preaching of Jesus, of which he was an eye-witness." But i. 19, 20, with **xx**. 4, show that these words are spoken of this present vision.

[4] Rev. viii. 2; Tob. xii. 15.   [5] See John xix. 37; Zech. xii. 10.

[6] The formula (i. 9) is obscure; cf. i. 2; vi. 9; xi. 7; xii. 11, 17; **xix**. 10; xx. 4.

on the Lord's Day, and I heard behind me a loud voice, like the sound of a trumpet, saying, "What thou shalt see write in a book, and send it to the seven churches at Ephesus, Smyrna, Pergamos, Thyatira, Sardis, Philadelphia, and Laodicæa." And I turned back to see the Voice that spoke to me; and when I had turned I saw seven candlesticks of gold, and in the midst of the candlesticks One like a son of man,[1] clad in a long robe[2] and girt about the breast with a belt of gold.[3] The hair of his head was glittering like a white fleece, or like snow; his eyes were like a flame of fire; his feet like fine brass in a blazing furnace; and his voice like the sound of many waters.[4] In his right hand he held seven stars, and from his mouth went forth a broad, sharp two-edged sword; and the sight of him was as of the sun in its strength. And when I saw him, I fell at his feet like a dead man; but he laid his hand on me, and said, "Do not fear. I am the first and the last, and am alive; I was dead, and behold I live forever [ages of ages]; and I hold the keys of death and of the grave [Hades]. Write, then, what thou hast seen, both that which is and that which will be after this, — the mystery of the seven stars in my right hand, and the seven candlesticks. The seven stars are the angels of the seven churches, and the seven candlesticks are the seven churches."

In the Jewish notions of the time, half gnostic or cabalistic, every person,[5] and even every ideal existence — as Death or Grief — has a guardian angel: there was an angel of Persia, of Greece, — as the "guards" (עירין) of Daniel and the "watchers" (ἐγρήγοροι) of Enoch;[6] an angel of the waters,[7] of fire,[8] of the winds,[9]

---

[1] The common title of the Messiah in apocalyptic books: Dan. vii. 13; Matt. viii. 20.

[2] Like the Jewish high-priest: Jos. Ant. iii. 7:4; xx. 1:1; Dan. x. 5.

[3] Comp. Jos. Ant. iii. 7:2 (πρὸς στέρνον).

[4] All this is imitated from Daniel x. 5, 6.   [5] Matt. xviii. 10.

[6] Dan. x. 13, 20; Deut. xxxii. 8. According to *Shir hasshirim* rabba, no people is punished but that its angel is punished first.

[7] Rev. xvi. 5.   [8] *Ibid.* xiv. 18.   [9] *Ibid.* vii. 1.

and of the Pit.¹ Naturally, then, each church had its celestial representative. To this " angel " (*ferouer* or *genius*²) of each community the Son of Man addresses his admonition, each in turn.

To the angel of the church in Ephesus: This is what He says who holds the seven stars in his right hand, and walks in the midst of the seven golden candlesticks: —

I know thy works and toil and patience; and that thou canst not endure the wicked. And thou hast tried those who call themselves apostles but are not [an allusion to Paul], and hast found them liars, and hast borne all things for my name, and hast not wearied. But I have it against thee that thou hast let go thy first love. Remember, then, from what thou hast fallen, and repent, and return to thy first works; or else I will come to thee quickly, and take thy candlestick out of its place, unless thou repent. But this is in thy favour, that thou hatest the works of the Nicolaïtans,³ which I also hate. Let him who has an ear hearken to what the Spirit says to the churches! To him that overcomes I will give to eat from the tree of life which is in the paradise of God.⁴

To the angel of the church in Smyrna: This is what He says who is first and last, who was dead and is alive:

I know thy works and suffering and poverty — yet thou art rich; and the evil words of those [the followers of Paul] who call themselves Jews while they are not, but are a synagogue of Satan.⁵ Be not afraid of what thou hast to suffer. Behold,

---

¹ Rev. ix. 11. So the angels of the winds (in Enoch xx.); of the sea (Bab. Talm., *Baba bathra*, 74 b); of rain (*id. Taanith*, 25 b); of hail (*id. Pesachim*, 118 a). See also *Apoc. of Adam*, in the *Journ. Asiat.*, Nov.-Dec., 1853; and especially an analysis of the *Divan* of the Mendaïtes in Migne's *Dict. des Apocr.* i. 283–285.

² So the "genius of indirect contributions:" *Comptes rendus de l'Acad.*, 1868, p. 109.

³ The partisans of Paul. See " Saint Paul," chaps. x., xiii.

⁴ Rev. ii. 1–7.

⁵ " Satan " here represents idolatry. The Pauline gatherings are here called idolatrous feasts, because "unclean" meats and those sacrificed to idols are eaten in them, as in pagan festivals.

the false accuser will cast many of you into prison, that you may have your ten days' trial.[1] But be faithful to death, and I will give thee a crown of life. Let him who has an ear hearken to what the Spirit says to the churches! He that overcomes will have nothing to suffer from the second death.[2]

To the angel of the church at Pergamos: This is what He says who holds the sharp two-edged sword: —

I know that where thou livest is the home of Satan.[3] But thou hast kept my name and hast not denied my faith, even when Antipas my faithful witness was slain among you, in the place where Satan dwells.[4] But I have something against thee; that there are with thee men who hold the doctrine of Balaam, who taught Balak to lay a snare for the sons of Israel, to eat meats sacrificed to idols, and to commit fornication.[5] So do those who profess the doctrine of the Nicolaitans. Repent, then; or I will come to thee speedily, and fight against thee with the sword of my mouth. Let him who has an ear hearken to what the Spirit says to the churches! To him that overcomes I will give of the hidden manna,[6] and I will bestow on him a white pebble,[7] on which will be written a new name, which no one will know excepting him who has received it.[8]

To the angel of the church at Thyatira: This is spoken by

---

[1] Dan. i. 14, 15.

[2] Rev. ii. 8–11. All men die once, but the wicked will die twice; for after the resurrection and judgment they will be thrust back into complete extinction.

[3] An allusion to the worship of Æsculapius at Pergamos. His serpent must have been taken by the Jews for a special symbol of Satan.

[4] The amphitheatre. See p. 160, *ante*.

[5] Num. xxiv., xxv. Another allusion to the partisans of Paul.

[6] Ex. xvi. 33; *Carm. Sibyll.*, proem, 87.

[7] The mark for acquittal at court. If the trial was by lot, names were written on white pebbles. Victors at the Olympic and other games received a ballot in like form, entitling them to sundry privileges; and similar ballots were used to indicate prizes in a lottery (Suet. *Caius*, 18; Dion Cass. lxvi. 25). The "new name" is that which the elect will bear in the heavenly kingdom.

[8] Rev. ii. 12–17.

the Son of God, whose eyes are as a flame of fire, and his feet as fine brass: —

I know thy works and thy love and thy faith and thy ministry of charity and patience, and that thy last works are more than those before. Yet I have this against thee, that thou leavest free that woman Jezebel,[1] calling herself a prophetess, who teaches and misleads my servants to commit fornication, and to eat meats sacrificed to idols. I have given her time to repent, and she will not repent.[2] Behold I will cast her upon a bed [of sickness], and those who have sinned with her I will punish with great suffering if they will not repent of their misdeeds; and her children I will put to death, and all the churches shall know that it is I who search the reins and the heart: I will repay to you every one according to his works. And to the others of you in Thyatira, who do not hold that doctrine, or know — to use their own words — "the deep things" of Satan,[3] I will not lay upon you any other burden.[4] But what you have, hold fast until I come. He who shall overcome and keep my works until the end, I will give him power over the nations; and he shall rule them with a rod of iron,[5] and like earthen vessels they shall be shivered in pieces, as I have received power of my Father; and I will give him the morning star. Let him who has an ear hearken to what the Spirit says to the churches!

To the angel of the church at Sardis: This is what He says who holds the seven spirits of God and the seven stars: —

I know thy works; thou hast a name that thou livest, and art dead. Be watchful, and strengthen the remaining things, which are ready to die; for I have not found thy work perfect before my God. Remember how thou hast received and heard

---

[1] This is some woman of influence at Thyatira, a disciple of Paul.

[2] See "Saint Paul," chap. vi.   [3] 1 Cor. ii. 10.

[4] The pagan converts might suppose, from his extreme severity as to unlawful meats, that he would force upon them all the burden of the Mosaic Law. He reassures them by saying they have only to observe the rule as laid down in Acts xv.

[5] Ps. ii. 9 (differently pointed), considered as applying to the Messiah. This passage is a favourite one with the Seer. Comp. xii. 5; xix. 15.

the word, and hold it fast, and repent. If thou watch not, I will come like a thief,[1] and thou wilt not know at what hour I shall come. Still, thou hast a few names in Sardis of those who have not defiled their garments; they shall walk with me in white apparel, for they are worthy. He that overcomes shall thus be clad in white raiment, and I will not blot his name from the book of life;[2] and I will confess him before my Father and his angels. Let him that has an ear hearken to what the Spirit says to the churches!

To the angel of the church in Philadelphia: Thus speaks the Holy One, the true, He who holds the key of David, who opens and no man can shut,[3] who shuts and none can open: —

I know thy works: behold, I have set before thee an open door [for the advancement of the gospel], which no man can shut; though weak, thou hast kept my word, and hast not denied my name. Behold, I will cause these men of the synagogue of Satan, who call themselves Jews and are not, but lie, — I will cause them to come and throw themselves at thy feet, that they may know thee to be dear to me. Because thou hast kept my command of patience, I too will preserve thee from the hour of bitter trial which must come upon all the world to prove those who live upon the earth. I come quickly; keep well what thou hast, that no one may take thy crown. Him that overcomes I will make a pillar in the temple of my God, and he shall no more go out, and I will write upon him (this pillar) the name of my God [Jehovah], and the name of the city of my God, the new Jerusalem, coming down out of heaven from my God, and my own new name.[4] Let him who has an ear hearken to what the Spirit says to the churches!

To the angel of the church of Laodicea: Thus speaks the AMEN,[5] the faithful and true witness, the first-born of the creation of God: —

---

[1] Matt. xxiv. 43; 1 Thess. v. 2.
[2] Dan. xii. 1; Enoch xxvii. 3.   [3] Isa. xxii. 22.
[4] Comp. Rev. xix. 12.
[5] Christ, in whom all is spoken and proved true (Isa. lxv. 16.)

I know thy works; thou art neither cold nor hot. Would that thou wert either cold or hot; but, since thou art lukewarm, and neither cold nor hot, I will spue thee out of my mouth. Thou sayest to thyself, "I am rich and full of abundance, and need nothing;"[1] and seest not that thou art wretched and miserable and poor and blind and naked. I counsel thee to buy of me gold tried in the fire,[2] that thou mayest be truly rich; and white raiment to wear, to hide the shame of thy nakedness; and ointment to anoint thine eyes, that thou mayest see clearly. Those whom I love I rebuke and chastise: be zealous, therefore, and repent. Behold, I stand at the door and knock! If any one will hear my voice, and open the door, I will come in to him, and will eat with him, and he with me. To him that overcomes I will grant to sit with me upon my throne; even as I too have overcome, and sit with my Father on his throne. Let him who has an ear hearken to what the Spirit says to the churches!

Now, who is this "John," who dares to make himself the interpreter of the celestial decrees, who speaks in such a tone of authority to the churches of Asia, who boasts of having endured the same persecutions with his readers?[3] It is either the apostle John, or another teacher of the same name, or some one who wishes to pass as the apostle. It is hardly to be admitted that in the year 69, in the apostle's lifetime or very soon after his death, any one assumed that name without his consent for counsels and reprimands so close-home. Nor among those bearing the same name would any one have dared to take that tone. "John the Elder," the only one suggested, if he ever existed, belonged (from all that appears) to a later generation.[4]

---

[1] Laodicea was a very wealthy city: Tac. *Ann.* xiv. 27.
[2] Isa. lv. 1.
[3] Rev. i. 9: the expression in ver. 2 is ambiguous.
[4] Papias in Euseb. iii. 39.

Doubts, I admit, beset all questions of genuineness of the so-called apostolic writings. We see how small scruple was felt at ascribing to apostles, or sainted persons, revelations for which authority was sought.[1] But I hold it as probable that the Apocalypse is really the work of the apostle John; or, at least, that it was acknowledged by him, and addressed to those churches by his sanction.[2] The deep impression made by Nero's massacres, the sense of the dangers which the writer has incurred, the horror of Rome, — all seem to suit the apostle, who, in my view of it, had been in Rome, and might say of those tragic events, "I, too, had my share in them."[3] He is choked and blinded with blood: he cannot see things as they are. The picture of the atrocities of that time besets him like a fixed idea. But serious objections here make the task of criticism very delicate. The fondness of the early Christian age for mystery and apocryphal writing has wrapped in thick darkness every question of New-Testament literary history. Happily, the soul speaks out in these nameless or misnamed books in tones which cannot deceive. It is out of our power to distinguish each man's part in a popular movement: the true creative genius is the spirit that animates all.

Whoever the writer of the Apocalypse may be, why did he choose the island of Patmos as the scene of his

---

[1] 2 Thess. ii. 2; Rev. xxii. 18, 19. Compare the cases of "Daniel" and "Enoch," observing that the assumed writer is at a distance of centuries; while the real and the pretended writer of the Apocalypse would be contemporary.

[2] See *Introduction* to this volume, pages 12-24, 28, 29.

[3] Compare the situation, in England (1706), of Élie Marion, who had taken part in the insurrection of the Camisards in the Cevennes under Louis XIV., whose testimony is mingled with ecstasies and visions.

vision? It is hard to say; there is no symbolic meaning in the name which we can detect. Patmos, or Patnos (*Patino*), is a little island some twelve miles long and very narrow.[1] In Greek antiquity it was flourishing and populous.[2] In the Roman period it retained all the importance which its size admitted, owing to its port, formed at the middle of the island by the isthmus which joins the northern and southern portions. In the coasting navigation of the time, Patmos was the first or the last stopping-place on the way between Rome and Ephesus. It is an error to speak of it as a reef or a desert. It was once, and may be again, one of the most important seaports of the Archipelago, being at the point where many lines meet. If Asia should revive, Patmos would be to that what Syra is to modern Greece, or what Delos or Rhenea was in antiquity, — a sort of way-station for marine traffic, and a centre of correspondence serviceable to travellers.

---

[1] See L. Ross, *Reisen* (1843), ii.; Tischendorf, *Reisen* (1846), ii. 258–265; *id. Terre Sainte* (tr., 1868), 278–284; V. Guérin, *Description*, etc., Paris (1856); Stanley, *Sermons in the East* (1863), 225; Julleville (*Rev. des cours litt.* March, 1867). It has now about 4,000 inhabitants. It is composed of three rocky masses, connected by narrow necks, the summits being somewhat under 1,000 feet high.

[2] Patmos is rarely mentioned by the ancient writers: Strabo, x. 5: 13; Pliny, iv. 23; Thucyd. iii. 33, according to the scholiast. But the inscriptions are instructive: *Corpus inscr. Gr.* 2261, 2262; Ross, fasc. ii. 189, 190; Guérin, 85, 86, besides two effaced. The ancient city was at the present port; its acropolis, part cyclopean and part hellenic, still exists. The principal legend of the Greek town regarded a temple built by Orestes to the Scythian Artemis (inscr 190, Ross): this was probably on the site of the monastery built by Christodoulos in the eleventh century. The island contains many ancient ruins, some from a very remote time (Guérin, 9–15, 85–93; Ross, 138). It appears to have formerly been better wooded and watered than now. The Greek population is estimated by Guérin to have been twelve or thirteen thousand. There were, besides, several villages, whose population he reckons at three or four thousand.

This was probably the ground of the choice which afterwards gave to Patmos such celebrity in Christian annals,—whether the apostle was compelled to withdraw thither to escape some local persecution at Ephesus;[1] or whether, returning from a visit to Rome,[2] he prepared the message, which he wished to send in advance into Asia, in one of the lodging-houses which must have lined the port;[3] or whether, taking (as it were) a step back, in order to strike a harder blow, and judging that Ephesus could not be well made the scene of the vision, he chose an island in the Archipelago, about a day's sail distant, connected with the city by

---

[1] Rev. i. 9 (comp. vi. 9; xx. 4: see p. 281, 282, *ante;* 322, 323, *post*). The idea of an exile, properly so-called (Tert. *Præscr.* 36), must be set aside. The islands which served as places of legal banishment were, as we know, Gyaros, Pandataria Pontia, and Planasia; Patmos is not among them. They were selected because they had neither harbour nor town; while Patmos has excellent anchorage (Guérin, 90–94), and had a considerable town. Gyaros, for example, is nothing like Patmos. The church tradition that John was exiled to Patmos under Domitian is an anachronism. There is, further, no question of solitude, the island being fairly populous.

[2] The entrance to the harbour of Patmos is easy to those coming from Rome, and hard to those from Ephesus. I tried it myself; and, after a day of effort, our boat had to abandon the attempt to run the channel.

[3] The "grotto" is an invention of the Middle Age. It is scarcely necessary to remark that the passage which speaks of Patmos (i. 9, 10) does not imply that the book was written there: the aorist, ἐγενόμην, would rather convey the contrary. Furthermore, the distrust as to the Apocalypse long felt in the Greek Church was such that Prochorus, in the fourth century, recounting in detail the stay of John at Patmos, says not a word of that book, and brings John thither only to write his gospel: see Guérin's analysis of the Patmos MS. (*l. c.* 27, 34, 39, 44), which seems most in conformity with the primitive text (compare eds. of M. Neander, following Luther's *Catechesis parva*, Basel, 1567, 526–663; Grynæus, *Monum. PP. orthod.* i. 85; Birch, *Auct. Cod. Apocr. N. T.*, 262–307, and the Latin translation in *Bibl. Max. Patr.* ii. 46). Before Saint Christodoulos, the island seems not to have been the object of special veneration.

daily navigation;[1] or whether he kept a remembrance of his last landing-place on his voyage, so full of deep emotion, when he returned from Rome in 64; or whether, finally, it was a mere accidental detention of a few days at that port. This could not, at all events, have been his first journey to Ephesus; for his relations with the churches of Asia imply that he must previously have lived in this region. The navigation of the Archipelago is full of risks, of which an ocean passage gives no idea; for in the great sea there are prevailing constant winds which you may take advantage of, even if they are contrary, while here it may be either dead calm or a stiff breeze when you are making a narrow channel; so that you are by no means master of your course, but must land where you can, not where you would.

Men of so warm temper as these harsh and fanatical descendants of the old Israelitish prophets took their imagination with them wherever they went; and this imagination was so strictly bound up within the circle of ancient Hebrew poetry that the nature about them was to them as if it were not. Patmos is like all the islands of that archipelago, — an azure sea, transparent air, bright sky, rocks with irregular peaks, barely covered at times with a down of verdure. The outlook is naked and barren; but the forms and colours of the cliffs, the bright blue of the sea with its lines of beautiful white birds, relieved against the ruddy tints of the rocks, are exquisite. These hundreds of isles and islets, of the most varied forms, which emerge like pyramids or float like shields upon the water, dancing

---

[1] It is at this day a six hours' sail from Scala Nova to Patmos, the means of passage being about the same as in ancient days.

as it were in an eternal round about the horizon, seem the fairy realm of sea-gods and ocean-nymphs, who lead their brilliant lives of love, youth, and melancholy in grottos of grayish green, on shores devoid of mystery, by turns gracious and terrible, of alternate brightness and gloom. Calypso, the Sirens, Triton and Nereid, the perilous fascination of the sea, its caress at once voluptuous and deceitful, — all those fine appeals to sense, which have their inimitable expression in the Odyssey, were as nothing to the sombre visionary. Two or three single points, — a certain haunting presence hinted in the words "there was no more sea" in the vision of a new creation;[1] the striking image of a fiery mountain cast upon the sea[2] turning a third part of its waves to blood (an image apparently taken from the volcanic island Thera, then in active eruption),[3] these alone give a touch of local colour.[4] Out of a little island, suited to be the background of some sylvan idyll of Daphnis and Chloe, or for scenes of shepherd life like those of Theocritus and Moschus, this writer has constructed a black volcano filled with ashes and flame. And yet, more than once, he must have felt upon these waves the calm silence of night, when is heard only the note of the kingfisher or the heavy puffing of the dolphin. For whole days Mount Mycale was in full view, yet he never once thought of the Greek victory over the Persians,[5] the finest ever won

---

[1] Rev. xxi. 1.   [2] *Ibid.* viii. 8.

[3] Sen. *Q. N.* ii. 26; vi. 21. Even when sleeping it has the look of an island half-burnt (Stanley, *Sermons*, p. 230, n. 8).

[4] Mount Kynops, in Patmos, shows some slight volcanic features (Guérin).

[5] The view of the mainland from Patmos is mostly intercepted by a chain of islands. But Mount Mycale, Miletus, and Priene are plainly seen.

after Marathon and Thermopylæ. At this central point of so many mighty works of Grecian genius, a few leagues from Samos, Cos, Miletus, and Ephesus, he thought of something else than the intellect of Pythagoras, Hippocrates, Thales, or Heraclitus; to him the glorious memories of Greece had no existence. The poem of Patmos should have been some Hero and Leander, or a pastoral of Longus, telling the sports of pretty children on the threshold of love. But the sombre enthusiast, thrown by chance upon this Ionian shore, could not escape his biblical traditions. Nature was to him the living chariot of Ezekiel, the monstrous cherub, the uncouth bull of Nineveh, a distorted zoölogy, setting the painter's or sculptor's art at defiance. The strange defect of vision in orientals, which distorts the images of things and causes all pictured representations that come from their hands to seem fantastic and devoid of life, was at its extreme in him. His inward malady discoloured everything. He saw with the eyes of Ezekiel or of the writer of Daniel; or rather, he saw only himself, his own passion, hope, or wrath. A vague and arid mythology, already cabbalist or gnostic, founded on the transforming of abstract ideas into divine *hypostases*, deprived him of an artist's truth or skill. No one was ever more estranged from surrounding influences; more completely blind and deaf to the outward world, for whose sights and harmonies he substituted the contradictory chimera of "a new heaven and a new earth."

CHAPTER XVI.

THE APOCALYPSE. — A. D. 69.

AFTER the message to the seven churches, the visionary panorama is unrolled. A door is opened into heaven; the Seer is caught up in spirit, and through this opening his eyesight pierces to the very depth of the celestial Court. The entire heaven of the Jewish Kabbala is revealed to him. Here stands one solitary throne, and on this throne, encircled by a rainbow, sits God himself, like a colossal ruby darting its rays of flame.[1] About the throne are twenty-four lower seats, on which are seated twenty-four old men, clad in white, with gold crowns upon their heads. These form a select Senate, representing humanity, and making the permanent court of the Eternal.[2] In front burn seven lamps, which are the seven spirits of God — the seven gifts of Divine wisdom.[3] About are four "beasts," or living creatures ($\zeta\hat{\omega}a$ "things of life") with features borrowed from the "cherubs" of Ezekiel[4] and the "seraphs" of Isaiah.[5] The first has the form of a lion, the second of a calf, the third the countenance of a man, the fourth the form of an eagle with wings outspread. These four

---

[1] All the features of this description are taken from Ezekiel i. and x. Comp. Dan. vii. 9, 10.

[2] The number 24 is taken from the classes of priests who served in the sanctuary. 1 Chron. xxv.; Isa. xxiv. 23; Ps. lxxxix. 8; Tanhuma, §§ *Shemini* and *Kedoshim*.

[3] Isa. xi. 2.   [4] Ezek. i.   [5] Isa. vi.

monsters symbolise in Ezekiel the attributes of Divinity, — "wisdom, power, knowledge, and creation." They have six wings, and are covered with eyes all over.[1] Angels — creatures inferior to the vast superhuman personifications just spoken of,[2] a sort of winged attendants — surround the throne in multitudes without number,[3] and from the throne proceed perpetual thunderings. On the level before the throne spreads a vast sheet of azure like a sea of crystal, — the firmament;[4] and a sort of divine liturgy goes on forever. For the four living creatures, organs of universal life, or Nature, never sleep, but sing night and day the anthem: "Holy, holy, holy is the Lord God Almighty, who was and is and shall be."[5] The twenty-four elders, representing Humanity, unite in the song, prostrating themselves and casting their crowns at the foot of the Creator's throne.

Christ has not yet appeared in this celestial court, and the Seer will now have us witness the pomp of his investiture.[6] On the right of Him who sits upon the throne is a book (in the form of a roll), written on both sides,[7] sealed with seven seals. It is the book of divine secrets, the great revelation. No one in heaven or on earth is found worthy to open it, or even to look upon it. Then John begins to weep: shall the Future, then, the Christian's only consolation, be closed to him? But he is encouraged by one of the elders; one is soon found who alone may open the book: and without difficulty we discover that it is Jesus. In the very centre of the vast heavenly assembly, at the foot of the

---

[1] Ezek. i. 18; x. 12. [2] Comp. Heb. i. 4–8, 14.
[3] Rev. v. 11; vii. 11; Dan. vii. 10; Ps. lxviii. 18.
[4] Ex. xxiv. 10; Ezek. i. 22–25. [5] Isa. vi. 3.
[6] Rev. chap. v. [7] Ezek. ii. 10.

throne, amid the living creatures and the elders, upon the crystal floor, appears a Lamb that has been slain. This was the favourite image under which Christian fancy loved to figure Jesus, — a slain lamb, made the passover offering, and always with God.[1] He has seven horns [2] and seven eyes, symbols of the seven spirits of God, whose fulness he has received, which through him will prevail over all the earth. The Lamb rises, advances to the throne, and takes the book. A thrill of profound emotion then fills the sky: the four living creatures and the twenty-four elders fall on their knees before the Lamb, holding in their hands harps and golden bowls ($\phi\iota\acute{\alpha}\lambda\alpha\varsigma$) full of incense, the prayers of the saints;[3] while they sing a new song: "Thou art worthy to take the book and open the seals; for thou hast been slain and with thy blood hast won to God a company of those chosen from every tribe, language, people, and race; and hast made them [4] a kingdom of priests, and they shall reign upon the earth." The myriads of angels join in this song, ascribing to the Lamb the seven great attributes, — power, riches, wisdom, strength, honour, glory, and blessing.[5] Every creature in heaven, on the earth, under the earth, or in the sea, joins in the heavenly rite, crying, "To Him who sits upon the throne and to the Lamb be blessing, honour, glory, and power for evermore." The four living creatures, representing Nature, with their deep voice respond, AMEN; the elders fall and worship.

Jesus is here introduced into the highest rank of the

[1] John i. 29, 36; 1 Pet. i. 19; Acts viii. 32; Jerem. xi. 19; Isa. liii. 7.
[2] Symbols of power in old Hebrew poetry: see Dan. vii. 20.
[3] Rev. viii. 3, 4; Ps. cxli. 2; Ezek. viii. 11; Tob. xii. 12; Luke i. 10.
[4] So the Sinaitic and Alexandrian; not "us," which is a later reading.
[5] See Rev. vii. 12.

celestial hierarchy. Not only the angels,[1] but the twenty-four elders and the living creatures, which are above the angels, bow down before him. He has ascended the steps of the throne, and has taken the book placed at the right hand of God, which no one could so much as look at. He is about to open the seven seals: the grand drama begins.[2]

It opens with a scene of splendour. By an historical conception singularly just, the writer represents the messianic movement as beginning at the time when Rome extends her dominion over Judæa.[3] As the first seal is opened, a white horse springs forward,—emblem of victory and triumph;[4] the rider carries in his hand a bow, his head is circled with a crown, and he goes forth, "conquering and to conquer." This is the Roman Empire, which, down to the time of the Seer, nothing has been able to withstand. But this triumphal prologue is of short duration: the forerunners of the Messiah's glorious appearing must be disasters as yet unheard-of; and the celestial tragedy unfolds with the most appalling images.[5] We are at what is called "the beginning of sorrows"[6] in the messianic story. From this time on, each seal that opens will bring upon mankind some dreadful woe.

At the opening of the second seal springs forth a red horse. To the rider the power is given to abolish

---

[1] Cf. p. 179, *ante*.   [2] Chap. vi.

[3] Comp. "Assumption of Moses" in Hilgenfeld: *N. T. extra can.* i. 113, 114.

[4] See Iliad, x. 437; Plut. *Camillus*, 7; Virg. *Æn.* iii. 538, with the comment of Servius.

[5] Comp. Zech. i. 7-17; vi. 1-8; Jer. xxi. 9; xxxii. 36; 4 Esdr. v. 6, 7; vi. 22, 23; ix. 3.

[6] Matt. xxiv. 8; Mark xiii. 9.

peace from the earth, and cause men to slaughter one another; and in his hand is placed a great sword. This is War. Since the uprising in Judæa, and above all since the revolt of Vindex, the world has been in truth only a field of blood, and the man of peace has not known whither he might flee.

At the opening of the third seal, a black horse bounds forth, with a rider holding a pair of scales. And from the midst of the living creatures a voice is heard prescribing the allowance to wretched mortals, and saying to the rider, " A measure of wheat for a penny [1] and three measures of barley for a penny; but touch neither oil nor wine." [2] This is Famine.[3] Not to speak of the great destitution under Claudius, there was extreme dearth in the year 68.[4]

At the opening of the fourth seal, springs forth a horse of pale yellow,[5] whose rider's name is Death. Hell (*Hades*) follows him; and power is given him to destroy a fourth part of the earth with sword, famine, pestilence, and the ravage of wild beasts.

These are the great scourges [6] which announce the near coming of the Messiah. In strict justice, the divine wrath should blaze out at once against the guilty world. And, in truth, at the opening of the fifth scene, the Seer beholds a touching spectacle. He sees beneath the altar the souls of those slaughtered for their faith, and for the testimony they have witnessed for Christ,

---

[1] A " measure " ($\chi o \tilde{\iota} \nu \xi$, 3 half-pints) was a day's ration; a " penny " (*denarius*, 20 cents) was a day's wages (Matt. xx. 2; Tac. *Ann.* i. 17).

[2] Suet. *Domit.* 7.   [3] Matt. xxiv. 7; Mark xiii. 7.

[4] See p. 263.

[5] Properly, the colour of honey (Il. xi. 631).

[6] Matt. xxiv. 6–8; Mark xiii. 8, 9; comp. Ezek. xiv. 21. In the gospels, pestilence seems to hold the second place, as in the Apocalypse.

— doubtless, the victims of Nero's persecution. These saintly souls cry to God,[1] and say to him, "How long, O God, holy and true, wilt thou not do justice, and exact the price of our blood of those who dwell on the earth?" But the time is not yet come; the number of martyrs which will cause the divine wrath to overflow is not yet made up. To each of the victims beneath the altar is given a white robe, as pledge of justification and coming triumph; and they are bidden to endure until their brethren and fellow-servants, who must be slain as well as they, have given testimony in their turn.

After this noble interact, we find ourselves no longer in the period of preliminary horrors, but amid the events of the Last Judgment. At the opening of the sixth seal,[2] the whole world is shaken by an earthquake.[3] The sky becomes black as a sack of haircloth; the moon takes the colour of blood; stars fall from heaven upon the earth like the fruit of a fig-tree shaken by the wind; the sky is withdrawn "as a scroll when it is rolled together;"[4] mountains and islands are cast from their places. Kings and great men, military chiefs, the rich and strong, slaves and free, hide themselves in caverns and among rocks, saying to the mountains and rocks, "Fall upon us, and

---

[1] Such imaginations are found also in pagan writers: compare with "souls of the slain" (Rev. vi. 9) "souls of those slaughtered by him" (Dion Cass. lxiii. 28).

[2] The entire description of the final catastrophe is made up of features taken from Isaiah ii. 10, 19; xxxiv. 4; l. 3; lxiii. 4; Ezek. xxxii. 7, 8; Joel iii. 4; Hosea x. 8; Nahum i. 6; Mal. iii. 2. The ancient prophets held that the Divine judgment, even when exerted on a separate nation, was attended by natural signs and prodigies: Joel i. 15; ii. 1-11. Comp. Matt. xxiv. 7, 29; Mark xiii. 8, 24; Luke xxi. 11, 25, 26; xxiii. 30.

[3] Matt. xxiv. 7; Mark xiii. 8; Luke xxi. 1. [4] Isa. xxxiv. 4.

hide us from the sight of him who sits on the throne, and from the wrath of the Lamb!"

Now the great execution is about to be accomplished.[1] The four angels of the winds[2] place themselves at the four corners of the earth; they have only to let loose the elements in their charge, when these, bursting forth with their own native fury, will overwhelm the world. To these four all power is given; they are already at their posts. But the fundamental idea of the composition is to show the great judgment incessantly deferred, just when it seemed ready instantly to take place. In the east appears an angel, bearing in his hand the seal of God, having, like all royal seals, graven on it the name of him to whom it belongs.[3] He calls to the four angels of the destroying winds to restrain for a time the forces at their disposal, until the elect who are still alive have been marked on the forehead with the stamp that will keep them safe from the scourge, as the blood of the paschal lamb sprinkled on the door-posts preserved the Israelites in Egypt.[4] The angel then marks with the divine seal one hundred and forty-four thousand persons belonging to the twelve tribes of Israel. This does not mean that the hundred and forty-four thousand elect are exclusively Jews.[5] "Israel" is here, doubtless, the true

---

[1] Rev. chap. vii.   [2] Comp. Zech. vi. 5; Enoch, xviii.

[3] ליהוה, *to Jehovah.* Comp. Isa. xliv. 5; Rev. xiv. 1. All Semitic seals give the owner's name preceded by ל (" to "). The custom was to mark, or brand, slaves with their master's name (see Herodotus, ii. 113: 2; Ezek. ix. 4).

[4] Ex. xii. 13.

[5] As we might suppose from the contrast of the "great multitude which no man could number" in ver. 9. But these are made up of martyrs (comp. ver. 9, 14), not of pagan converts. The one hundred and forty-four thousand elect appear in chap. xiv. as chosen for their virtue from the

spiritual Israel, Paul's "Israel of God,"[1] the chosen family, embracing all who have allied themselves with the race of Abraham, by faith in Jesus and practice of the essential rites. But there is one class of the faithful already brought into the abode of peace: those who have suffered death for Jesus. These the Seer figures as a countless multitude of men of every race, tribe, people, and tongue, standing before the throne[2] and before the Lamb, clothed in white, holding palm-leaves in their hands, singing the glory of God and the Lamb. One of the elders explains to him who these are. "They are men who come from great persecution,[3] and have washed their robes in the blood of the Lamb," — that is, the stain of martyr-blood. That is why they are before God's throne, and adore him night and day in his temple; and He who is seated on the throne will dwell with them forever.[4] They shall hunger no more, nor thirst any more, nor suffer any longer from burning heat. The Lamb will feed them, and will lead them to living springs, and God himself will wipe all tears from their eyes.[5]

---

whole earth (ver. 3). Also comp. v. 9. The distinction of Jewish and pagan Christians did not exist for this writer. Pagans who have not first accepted the Jewish rules are the disciples of Balaam, whom he rebukes in chaps. ii. and iii. To him every Christian belongs to Israel, and to the spiritual city, Jerusalem (xviii. 4; xx. 9; xxi. 2, 12. Comp. Matt. xix. 28; Jas. i. 1). The gentiles come simply, like good strangers, conquered and submissive, to pay their homage to God in Zion (xv. 3, 4).

[1] Gal. vi. 16.

[2] He does not name the Ineffable. Jews more or less inclined to the Cabbala speak of God under such expressions as "name," "throne," "heaven," etc.

[3] Θλίψεως μεγάλης, a common expression for the Neronian persecution. See notes on pp. 147 and 182.

[4] Lev. xxvi. 11; Isa. iv. 5, 6; Ezek. xxxvii. 27; Rev. xxi. 3.

[5] Isa. xxv. 8; xlix. 10.

The seventh seal opens.[1] Here we await the grand spectacle of the last scene of time.[2] But, in the vision as in fact, the final catastrophe still retreats; we think it already here, and it is naught. Instead of the closing scene which should follow the breaking of the seventh seal, "there is silence in heaven the space of about half an hour," showing that the first act of the mystery is finished, and another is about to begin.[3] After this sacramental silence the seven archangels who stand before the throne[4] (not spoken of till now) enter upon the scene. Seven trumpets are given them, each to announce its own event.[5] The sombre imagination of John is not yet satisfied; his wrath against the pagan world must find its fit penalties in the plagues of Egypt. Certain natural phenomena happening about the year 68, and deeply impressing the popular imagination, seemed to justify him in recalling those old horrors.

Before the sounding of the seven trumpets begins, there is a very striking scene in dumb show. An angel advances to the golden altar that is before the

---

[1] Rev. chap. viii.

[2] Like the suspense after opening the fifth and sixth seals, and at the sound of the seventh trumpet. See x. 7, and p. 312, *post*.

[3] We notice the same thing in the Song of Solomon, where the five acts are not a regular sequence, but with each its own action begins and ends. In general, Hebrew literature knows nothing of the unities of composition.

[4] Dan. x. 13; Tob. xii. 15; Luke i. 19; 1 Thess. iv. 16.

[5] The idea of a succession of trumpets announcing the end of all things is found in "the last trump" of 1 Cor. xv. 52, assuming that the others have preceded it. The expression "a *third* trumpet" in 4 Esdr. v. 4, is, however, an error (see Hilgenfeld). "The day of Jehovah" with the prophets is also announced by trumpets (Joel ii. 1, 15). The first hint of this image is given in the trumpets which proclaimed the Israelite festivals (4 Esdr. vi. 23).

throne, bearing in his hand a golden censer. Masses of incense (θυμιάματα πολλά) are heaped upon the coals of the altar, and a cloud of smoke rises before the Eternal One. Then the angel fills his censer with coals from the altar, and casts them upon the earth,[1] where, as they strike the ground, they produce noise of thunder, lightnings, voices, and earthquakes, — the incense, as we are told, being the prayers of the saints. The sighs of these holy persons rising silently before God, and calling for the downfall of the pagan empire, become burning coals, which rack and rend the guilty world, and utterly destroy it before it can suspect whence the destruction comes. Then the seven angels prepare to sound their trumpets.

As the first trumpet peals forth, hail mingled with fire and blood is cast upon the earth; and a third part[2] of the trees and all green grass are consumed with fire. In the years 63, 68, and 69, there were terrifying tempests, in which men saw something supernatural.[3]

At the sound of the second trumpet, a great mountain of fire is cast upon the sea; a third of the waters are changed to blood, a third of the fishes perish, and a third of the ships are destroyed. Here is an allusion to the volcanic island Thera,[4] which the Seer of Patmos had almost in plain view in the horizon, as it were a volcano plunged in the deep. In the middle of it[5] a new island had appeared in 46 or 47. In periods of eruption the surface of the surrounding sea seems on fire.[6]

---

[1] As in Ezek. x. 2.   [2] See Zech. xiii. 9.
[3] Tac. *Ann.* xv. 47; *Hist.* i. 3, 18; Comp. Ex. xii. 24; Isa. xxviii. 2.
[4] See pp. 269, 297. Comp. Ex. vii. 17; Jer. li. 25; Enoch, xvii. 13.
[5] An earthquake in 237 B. C. had engulfed a portion of the island, leaving the remainder in the form of a horseshoe. — Ed.
[6] Pliny ii. 87; iv. 12; Sen. *Q. N.* ii. 26; vi. 21; Dion Cass. lx. 29;

At the sound of the third trumpet, a great star falls from heaven, burning like a torch, upon a third part of the rivers and springs. Its name is Wormwood, and a third of the waters are turned to wormwood (that is, became poisonous and bitter [1]), and many men die because of it.[2] Here we seem to find an allusion to a meteoric stone, the fall of which was associated with some infection that may have affected the quality of water in some storage-basin. We must remember that the Seer looks at nature through the medium of the childish tales he has heard from the common people of Asia, the most credulous region in the world. Phlegon of Tralles, half a century later, may be said to have passed his life in compiling just such tales. In Tacitus we meet them on every page.

At the sound of the fourth trumpet, a third of the sun, of the moon, and of the stars are blotted out, and a third of the world's light is darkened.[3] This may refer to the terrifying eclipses of these years,[4] or to the frightful tempest of January 10, 69.[5] But all these terrors so far are as nothing. An eagle flies through the midst of the sky, uttering three cries of woe! and predicts calamities unspeakable to follow the trumpets that are yet to sound.

At the voice of the fifth trumpet, a star (that is, an angel [6]) falls from heaven, to whom is given the key of

---

Aur. Victor, *De Cæs.*, Claud. 14; Philostr., *Apoll.* iv. 34: 4; Orosius, vii. 6; Cedrenus, i. 197; Ross, *Reisen*, etc., i. 90. Comp. *Comptes rendus de l'Acad. des Sciences*, 19 Feb. 1866, 392 *et seq.*

[1] Ex. xv. 23-26.
[2] See Isa. xiv. 12; Dan. viii. 10; *Carm. Sibyll.* v. 157, 158.
[3] Ex. vi. 25; x. 21, 22; Joel iii. 4; Amos viii. 9.
[4] See p. 262, *ante.*
[5] Tac. *Hist.* i. 18; Plut. *Galba*, 23.
[6] See Enoch xviii. 13; xxi. 3; lxxxvi. 1; xc. 21.

the bottomless pit.[1] This he opens, and there comes forth smoke as of a great furnace;[2] the sun and the air are darkened. From this smoke locusts are produced, which cover the earth like troops of horsemen.[3] These locusts, led by their king, the angel of the Pit (called in Hebrew *Abaddon,* "destroyer," in Greek, *Apollyon*), torment men for five months — an entire summer. It is possible that there was an excessive visitation of locusts in some province about this time;[4] in any case, the imitation of the plagues of Egypt is manifest.[5] The bottomless pit is perhaps the *Solfatara* near Puteoli (which was called *Vulcan's Forum*),[6] or the old crater of *la Somma*,[7] conceived as openings-out from the infernal world. I have said[8] that the disturbances in the neighbourhood of Naples were just then very violent. The writer of the Apocalypse — who, I may assume, had been in Rome and hence at Puteoli — may well have been witness to such phenomena. He associates the clouds of locusts with the volcanic exhalations, — for, since their origin was wholly unknown, the popular mind was led to regard

---

[1] The abode, not of the dead (*Hades*), but of devils: see Luke viii. 31; Rev. xi. 7; xvii. 8; xx. 1, 3.

[2] Rev. ix. 2; cf. Gen. xix. 28.

[3] The strange description of these locusts, allowing for the exaggerations of oriental style, has nothing that may not apply to the common locust (see Niebuhr, *Descr. of Arabia*, p. 153; Joel ii. 4–9). At Naples these creatures are still called *cavaletti*, and would be very destructive but for the care taken to destroy their eggs. See Pliny, xi. 29; Livy, xxx. 2.

[4] Features like those in ix. 10 — tails with stings, like scorpions — might suggest an invasion of Parthian cavalry; but this is the topic of the sixth trumpet, and it is not the writer's way to bring different symbols of the same thing within the compass of the same cycle of seven.

[5] Ex. x. 12–15; Joel ii.; Wisd. xvi. 9.

[6] Strabo, v. 4 : 6.

[7] Beulé, *Le drame du Vésuve*, 62, 63.   [8] Pages 264–268.

them as a progeny of hell.[1] At this day a like phenomenon takes place at Solfatara. After a heavy rain, the pools of water which remain in hot places hatch out very rapidly vast numbers of locusts and frogs.[2] That what appeared to be spontaneous generation was regarded by the vulgar as an emanation from the mouth of the Pit itself, was the more natural, since the eruptions, being generally followed by abundant rains, covering the country with pools, must seem the direct cause of the clouds of insects that issue from these pools.

The sound of the sixth trumpet introduces another scourge: this is a Parthian invasion, which was everywhere thought to be impending.[3] A voice goes out from the four horns of the altar which is before God, commanding to let loose four angels held in chains along the Euphrates.[4] These four angels, — perhaps the Assyrians, Babylonians, Medes, and Persians,[5] — who were ready at the hour, day, month, and year, put themselves at the head of a fearful force of cavalry, of two hundred million men. The description of men and horses is purely fanciful. The horses, which kill by a sting in the tail, "like scorpions," probably signify the Parthian cavalry, who shoot their arrows backward when in flight. A third of the human race is exterminated. Those, however, who survive do not repent, but still worship demons, idols of gold and silver,

---

[1] "They are five months hidden," Pliny, *H. N.* ix. 30. This idea still exists. Œdman, *Samml. aus der Naturkunde*, ii. 147.

[2] M. S. de Luca. Locusts are very numerous in the crater of Solfatara.

[3] See above, p. 257; Tac. *Hist.* iv. 51; Jos. *Wars*, vi. 6: 2.

[4] Comp. Virgil, *Georg.* i. 509.

[5] Writers of apocalypses retain the old biblical geography, even when completely obsolete. See Commodian, *Instr.* ii. 1: 15; *Carmen*, ver. 884 and 900; Epiph. li. 34; Dan. vii. 6; Enoch lvi. 5-8.

which can neither see, hear, nor walk. They persist in their murderings, their sorceries, fornications, and robberies.

Here, again, we expect to hear the tones of the seventh trumpet; but, as before the seals were opened, the Seer appears to hesitate, or, rather, to take such a position as to keep the reader in suspense: at the critical moment he suddenly stops. The dread secret cannot even yet be told in full. A colossal angel, his head encircled by a rainbow, with one foot on the land and the other on the sea, whose voice is echoed in seven thunders (perhaps the thunders of the seven heavens [1]), speaks mysterious words, which a voice from heaven forbids John to write. The gigantic angel then lifts his hand to heaven, and swears by the Eternal that there shall be no more delay;[2] that at the sound of the seventh trumpet the mystery of God announced by the prophets — who (as Isaiah and Joel) have proclaimed the day of the Lord — shall be accomplished.

The apocalyptic drama, then, is about to close. But, to prolong his book, the writer assumes a new prophetic mission. Repeating a powerful image once employed by Ezekiel,[3] John receives from the mighty angel a book of fate, and devours it; and a voice says to him, "Thou must prophesy again before many peoples, nations, tongues, and kings." The scheme of the vision, which was about to close with the seventh trumpet, thus expands; the writer unfolds a second part, in which he may disclose his views on the destinies of kings and peoples of his time. The first six trumpets, like the opening of the first six seals, refer to facts

---

[1] Cf. Ps. xxix. 3–9; Dan. viii. 26; xii. 4, 9.
[2] Dan. xii. 7.   [3] Ezek. ii. 8–iii. 3; Jer. xv. 16.

which are already past;[1] that which follows belongs mostly to the future.

The Seer's gaze is now fixed upon Jerusalem.[2] By symbols sufficiently plain he gives us to understand that the city is to be surrendered to the gentiles;[3] and to foresee this early in the year 69 required no great prophetic effort. The porch and court of the gentiles will even be trampled under foot by the unholy;[4] but the imagination of so fervent a Jew cannot yet conceive of the Temple as destroyed. For the Temple is the only spot on earth where God can be truly worshipped: nay, worship in heaven itself is but the continuance of that established here; and John cannot so much as imagine a world without the Temple. This, then, will be preserved; and the faithful, sealed on the forehead with the mark of Jehovah, will continue to worship there. Thus it will be, as it were, a sacred space, the spiritual home of the entire Church. This will continue for forty-two months, or three years and a half; that is, half a "week of years" (*shemitta*).[5] This mystic cipher, borrowed from "Daniel,"[6] is several times repeated afterwards. This is the length of time the world has yet to live.

---

[1] It is true that the invasion to follow the sixth trumpet has not yet taken place; but the writer evidently regards it as a certain thing.

[2] Rev. xi.   [3] Comp. Ezek. xl.; Zech. ii.

[4] Luke xxi. 24; Dan. viii. 13.

[5] A *shemitta*, or period of seven years, is often taken as a unit of time, the Jubilee-period being composed of seven such units. See "Book of Jubilees" and the Samaritan chronicle published by Neubauer (*Journ. Asiat.* Dec. 1869).

[6] Daniel vii. 25, and elsewhere. Comp. Luke xxi. 24, and "days of their prophecy" (Rev. xi. 6) with "three years and six months" (Luke iv. 25); also, Jas. v. 17; Enoch x. 12; xci, xciii.; and the apocalyptic weeks of the Ismaelites, inherited from Persian formulæ.

During this time Jerusalem will be the scene of a great religious war, like the conflicts which have filled all its past history. God will give commission to his "two witnesses," who will prophesy for twelve hundred and sixty days — that is, three years and a half — clothed in sackcloth. They are compared to two olive-trees and two candlesticks standing before the Lord.[1] They will have the powers of Moses and Elijah, — to "shut heaven" and prevent the rain, to turn water into blood, or to strike the earth with whatever plague they will. If any shall attempt to do them harm, a fire will go from their mouth and destroy their enemies.[2] At the end of the days of their prophesying, the Beast ($\theta\eta\rho\iota\acute{o}\nu$) which comes up from the bottomless pit[3] — the Roman power, or rather Nero, reappearing as Antichrist — will slay them; and for three days and a half their bodies will lie unburied "in the open place of the great city symbolically called *Sodom* and *Egypt*,[4] where, also, their Lord was crucified," — that is, the rebellious city, which kills the prophets.[5] People of the world will rejoice with one another, and send gifts;[6] for these two prophets were intolerable to them through their austere exhortations and their appalling miracles. But, at the end of three days and a half, the breath of life comes back to them; they rise to their feet, and great terror comes upon all who see them.[7] Soon they ascend to heaven in a cloud, in full view of

---

[1] Zech. iv. [2] 2 Kings i. 10–12.

[3] Compare Rev. xvii. 8, with Dan. vii. 7. (The Alexandrian reading, $\dot{\alpha}\nu\alpha\beta\alpha\hat{\iota}\nu o\nu$, is explained by comparing the Sinaitic.)

[4] Isa. i. 10; iii. 9; Jer. xxiii. 14; Ezek. xvi. 48. Egypt, especially, is the country hostile to the chosen people, having reduced them to slavery.

[5] Matt. xxiii. 37. [6] Neh. viii. 10, 12; Esth. ix. 19, 22.

[7] Comp. Ezek. xxxvii. 10; 2 Kings xiii. 21.

their enemies; and at the same time comes a frightful earthquake, in which a tenth part of the city is destroyed, seven thousand men perish, and the remainder, terror-stricken, are converted, and give glory to the God of heaven.[1]

We have several times already been met by the idea that the last great day would be preceded by two witnesses, generally conceived to be Enoch and Elijah in person.[2] These two men, dear to God, were believed not to have died. Enoch was thought to have vainly foretold the Flood to the men of his time, who would not listen; he was the type of a Jew preaching penitence among the gentiles. Sometimes, also, the witnesses are compared to Moses,[3] whose death was in like manner obscure, and to Jeremiah.[4] The writer seems to conceive these "witnesses" as two men of high rank in the church at Jerusalem, apostles of great holiness, who will be killed, will rise again, and ascend into heaven like Elijah and Jesus. Possibly the Seer in the vision may look backward, and refer to the martyrdom of James the Greater and James the Less, — especially to that of "James the Lord's brother," which was

---

[1] Rev. xi. 11-13.

[2] See "Life of Jesus," 149, 151, 223; Ecclus. xliv. 16 ; xlviii. 10; Heb. xi. 5; Iren. iv. 16: 2; v. 5: 1; Tert. *De anima*, 50; Nicod. 25; Hippol. 21, 22, 104, 105; Jer. *Epist. ad Marcellam*, iv. 165, 166; Andrew of Crete and Aretas of Cæsarea in *Not. and extr.* xx. 2: 236; Mal. iii. 23; Matt. xvi. 14; xvii. 12; John i. 21; Justin, *Trypho*, 49; (as to Elijah) *Seder olam rabba*, 17; Mishna, *Sota*, ix. 15; *Shekalim*, ii. 5; *Baba metzia*, i. 8; ii. 8; iii. 4, 5; *Eduloth*, viii. 7; *Carm. Sibyll.* ii. 187; Commodian, *Carm.* v. 826, 827. All the mythology concerning Enoch and Elijah is collected in Malvenda's *Antichrist*, lib. ix. See also *Berichte* of the society of Leipzig, 1866, 213; *Sitzungsberichte* of the Academy of Munich, 1871, p. 462.

[3] Rev. xi. 6; Matt. xvii. 3 (account of the Transfiguration).

[4] See "Assumption of Moses;" "Life of Jesus," p. 223; Victorin: *Bibl. max. patrum*, iii. 418; Thilo, *Cod. apocr. N. T.*, 761, 762.

regarded by many in Jerusalem as a public calamity, a fatal event, and a sign of the time.[1] Possibly one of these preachers of repentance is John the Baptist, and the other is Jesus.[2] The belief that the end would not come until the Jews had been converted was general among the Christians; we find it also in Paul.[3]

Now that the rest of Israel has come to the true faith, the world is ready for the end. The seventh and last angel sounds his trumpet;[4] and at the sound, loud voices cry, "The hour is come when our Lord with his Christ shall reign upon the earth forever!" The twenty-four elders fall on their faces and adore, thanking God that he has established his reign, in spite of the impotent rage of the gentiles, and proclaiming the hour of reward to the saints, and of destruction to the spoilers of the earth. Then the doors of the heavenly temple are thrown open, and in its depths is seen the ark of the new Covenant, with lightnings, thunder, and earthquake.

All is now finished. The faithful have received the grand revelation which shall console them. The Judgment is at hand; it will take place within a sacred half-year, that is, three and a half years. But we have already found the writer, regardless of the unity of his work, holding in reserve the means of going on with it when it seems complete. The book, in truth, is only half done; a new series of visions is to unfold before us.

The first is one of the finest.[5] In the midst of heaven appears a Woman (the church of Israel), clothed

---

[1] See pp. 77, 78, *ante*. [2] Matt. xvii. 9-13.
[3] See "Saint Paul," chap. xvii.; Commodian, *Carmen*, v. 832, 930.
[4] Comp. 1 Cor. xv. 42. [5] Rev. chap. xii.

with the sun, having the moon under her feet, and about her head a crown of twelve stars (the twelve tribes of Israel). She cries out, as in the pangs of travail, about to bring forth the ideal Messiah.[1] Before her rises an enormous red Dragon with seven crowned heads and ten horns,[2] whose tail, sweeping the sky, drags down a third of the stars and casts them on the earth.[3] This is Satan, under the features of the most potent of his incarnations, the Roman Empire: the red colour figures the imperial purple; the seven crowned heads are, as the writer explains,[4] the seven Cæsars who have reigned up to this time, — Julius, Augustus, Tiberius, Caligula, Claudius, Nero, and Galba;[5] the ten horns are the ten proconsuls of the provinces.[6] The Dragon watches for the infant's birth, so as to devour him. The Woman gives birth to the child destined "to rule the nations with a rod of iron," — a characteristic trait of the Messiah.[7] The child (Jesus) is taken by God into heaven, and placed at His right hand upon the throne.[8] The Woman flees to the desert, where God has provided a shelter for twelve hundred and sixty days.

[1] Micah iv. 10.
[2] Bab. Talm. *Kiddushin*, 29 b.; Dan. vii. 6, 7; Rev. v. 6.
[3] Cf. Dan. viii. 10.   [4] Rev. xvii. 10.
[5] Josephus always reckons Julius as the first emperor, and Augustus, Tiberius, Caius (Caligula), as the second, third, and fourth (*Ant.* xviii. 2: 2; 6: 10). So 4 Esdras (xi. 12, 13, 17), Suetonius, Aur. Victor, Julian (*Cæs.* 308). St. Beatus, in the eighth century, knows no other reckoning: *sextus fuit Nero*, etc. (p. 498, Florez); he elsewhere (438) speaks differently, probably copying from writers who differed among themselves.
[6] See p. 337 (below), and Rev. xvi. 14; xvii. 12; xix. 19. The image is taken from Dan. vii. 7, 24. The writer thinks he sees the Roman Empire in Daniel's fourth beast, which is really that of the Greeks.
[7] Ps. ii. 9; Rev. ii. 27; xix. 15.
[8] The writer believes in the ascension of Jesus. That of the "two witnesses" (xi. 12) rests upon some legend known to him: see "The Apostles," chap. iii. (near the end).

Here is a plain reference either to the flight of the Church from Jerusalem, and the three-and-a-half years' peace it should enjoy within the walls of Pella till the end of the world; or else to the refuge of the Jewish Christians and the two apostles in Asia Minor. The image of the "desert" applies better to the former. Pella, beyond Jordan, was a peaceful district, near the Arabian desert, where the noise of war was hardly ever heard.

Then follows a great war in heaven. Until now, Satan, the Accuser,[1] the malicious critic of creation, has had his right of admission into the divine court, and availed himself of it — by the old custom which he has not lost since the time of Job[2] — to afflict pious men, Christians especially, and bring upon them frightful sufferings, as in the persecutions of Rome and Ephesus. He must now lose this privilege. The archangel Michael, heavenly protector of Israel, with his angels,[3] gives him battle. Satan is conquered, driven out of heaven, and cast down to earth with his accomplices; and a song of triumph breaks forth when the celestial hosts see, hurled from on high, the calumniator, him who maligns all good, who never, by day or night, ceased to accuse and vilify their brethren dwelling on the earth.[4] The Church above and that below join hands in the defeat of Satan, which is due to the blood of the Lamb and to the courage of the martyrs who have endured torment unto death. But woe to the

---

[1] The writer employs here (xii. 10) the rabbinic form κατήγωρ (*katigor*) for the Greek κατήγορος.

[2] Job, prologue; 1 Chron. xxi. 1; comp. *zabulus* (*diabolus*) in the *Assumption of Moses*.

[3] Dan. x. 13, 21; xii. 1; Jude 9.

[4] Gen. iii. 1; Job i.-ii.; Zech. iii. 1.

guilty world! The Dragon has gone down into it, and anything may be feared from his despair, for he knows that his time is short.

The first object of the Dragon's rage when cast down to the earth is the Woman (the church of Israel), who has given birth to the divine Child whom God has set at his own right hand. But she is shielded by protection from above, and two wings are given her, wings of a great eagle, by means of which she flies to the desert-retreat provided for her, — that is, Pella. Here she is nourished for three years and a half, unseen by the Dragon, whose fury is at its height. He pours forth from his mouth a flood of water to drown her, and carry her away; but the earth comes to her help, opens, and drinks in the flood, — an allusion to some unknown circumstance of the flight to Pella.[1] The Dragon, finding himself powerless against the Woman (the mother-church of Israel), turns his rage against "the remnant of her race," — that is, the churches of "the Dispersion," which keep the commands of God,[2] and are faithful witnesses of Jesus. This is evidently an allusion to the later persecutions, and especially to that under Nero.

Then[3] the prophet beholds, coming up from the sea, a Beast,[4] in many points like the Dragon. It has ten horns, seven heads, crowns upon the ten horns, and on each of the heads a name of blasphemy. Its general appearance is that of a leopard; but its feet are those of a bear and its mouth that of a lion: its strength,

---

[1] See above, pp. 240, 241; and comp. Jos. *Wars*, iv. 7: 5, 6.

[2] As contrasted with the Pauline churches, which, said the Judæo-Christians, refused the commandments of Noah and the compact of Jerusalem.

[3] Chap. xiii. [4] $\theta\eta\rho\iota\sigma\nu$: cf. Dan. vii. 3, 8; xi. 36.

throne, and power are given to it by the Dragon (Satan). One of the heads has received a deadly wound, but this has been healed. The whole earth falls down in amazement at this mighty creature, and all men set themselves to worship the Dragon that has given power to the Beast. They worship the Beast also, saying, "Who is like the Beast, or is able to war against him?" And there is given him a mouth uttering great boasts and blasphemies, and the term of his power is set as forty-two months — three years and a half. Then the Beast begins to utter blasphemies against God, his name, his tabernacle, and those who dwell in heaven. And it is given him to make war upon the saints and conquer them,[1] and power is given him over every tribe, people, language, and race; and all men bow down to him, excepting those whose names are written from the foundation of the world in the book of life of the Lamb that was slain. "If any man have an ear, let him hear! If any one leads into captivity, he shall go into captivity. If any shall kill with the sword, he shall perish by the sword.[2] Here is the secret of the faith and patience of the saints."

The symbol is very plain. Already in the Sibylline verses of the second century before Christ, the Roman power is called "the power of many heads."[3] Allegories founded upon many-headed beasts were then much in fashion; and in interpreting such emblems the fundamental principle is that each head signifies a sovereign.[4] The monster of the Apocalypse is, besides, made up by

[1] Dan. vii. 21 (in the Sinaitic MS.).
[2] Jer. xv. 2; Matt. xxvi. 52.
[3] πολύκρανος: *Carm. Sibyll.* iii. 176.
[4] Tac. *Ann.* xii. 64; xv. 47; Philostr. *Apoll.* v. 13; see p. 261, *ante*. Comp. Dan. vii.; 4 Esdr. xi., xiii.

joining together the attributes of the four empires in Daniel;[1] and this alone would show that we have here to do with a new empire, which absorbs into itself the older empires. The Beast which comes forth from the sea is, then, the Roman Empire, which to the people of Palestine must seem to come "from the western sea."[2] This Empire is but one form of Satan (the Dragon), or rather, is Satan himself, with all his attributes. It holds its power from Satan, and uses all its energies in Satan's service, — that is, to maintain idolatry, which in the writer's view is simply the worship of devils. The ten crowned horns are the ten imperial provinces, — Italy, Achaia, Asia, Syria, Egypt, Africa, Spain, Gaul, Britain, and Germany, — whose proconsuls are real [though temporary] kings.[3] The seven heads are the successive Emperors from Julius Cæsar to Galba; the "name of blasphemy" written on each head is Σεβαστός ["worshipful"] or *Augustus*, which to strict Jews appeared an insult to God. The whole earth is given over by Satan to this Empire, in recompense for the worship procured for Satan by the Empire. The grandeur and pride of Rome, the *imperium* (or military rule) which it creates, its divinity as an object of special and public homage,[4] are a perpetual blasphemy against God, who is the sole real lord of the earth. Thus the Empire is naturally a foe to the Jews and to Jerusalem. It makes a fierce war against the holy people (the writer appears on the whole to favour the insurrection), and will conquer them; but its power will last

---

[1] Dan. vii.
[2] *Carm. Sibyll. l. c.* (ἀφ' ἑσπερίου τε θαλάσσης).
[3] As made plain in Rev. xvii. 12; comp. Dan. vii. 24.
[4] Suet. *Aug.* 52.

no more than three years and a half. The head "wounded to death," whose wound is, however, healed, is Nero, lately overthrown but miraculously preserved from death,[1] and believed to have taken refuge with the Parthians. The adoration of the Beast is the worship of "Rome and Augustus,"[2] so extended throughout the province of Asia, and making the basis of the popular religion.[3]

The symbol that follows is far from being equally clear to us. Another beast comes out from the earth, having two horns like those of a lamb, but speaking like a dragon (Satan). It wields all the power of the former beast in its presence and under its eye, serving as its delegate, and exerting all its authority to compel the inhabitants of the earth to worship "the first beast, whose deadly wound was healed,"[4] — a confusion between the beast itself and the wounded head. This second beast performs great miracles, even to "making fire come down from heaven to earth in the sight of men;" and deceives the world by the wonders it performs in the name and for the service of the former beast, which was wounded by a sword and yet lives. And it has power to infuse the breath of life into the image of the former, so that this image speaks,[5] and to cause all who refuse its worship to be put to death. And it compels all — small and great, rich and poor, slave or free — to carry a mark on their right hand or on their forehead; and ordains that no one can buy or sell unless he

---

[1] Sulp. Sev. *Hist.* ii. 29.

[2] The title of its priesthood was *Flamen Romæ divorum et Augusti.* — ED.

[3] See "Saint Paul," chap. ii.; Waddington, *Inscr.*, iii. No. 885.

[4] Rev. xiii. 12.

[5] On the speaking statues of the Romans, see Val. Max. i. 8: 3–5; also, *Comptes rendus*, etc., 1872, p. 285.

carries the mark (χάραγμα) of the beast, or its name, or the number of its name, — that is, the number made by adding the numerical values of the letters that compose the name. "Here is wisdom!" cries the writer. "Let him that has understanding calculate the number of the beast, for it is the number of a man (that is, of a man's proper name); and its number is six hundred and sixty-six."

In fact, if we add together the letters of Nero's name as written in Hebrew, — קסר נרון,[1] Νέρων Καῖσαρ, — with their numerical values, we obtain the number 666.[2] The Asiatic Christians no doubt designated the monster by the term *Neron Kesar*; his Asiatic coins bearing the inscription ΝΕΡΩΝ ΚΑΙΣΑΡ.[3] Calculations like these

---

[1] The word הסר is found thus written (without quiescents) in Palmyrene inscriptions of the third century (Vogüé, *Syrie centr. inscr. sémit:* comp. the Syriac form in the *Peshito*, and Buxtorf, *Lex. chald.* 2081, 2082; Ewald, *Die johann. Schriften*, ii. 263, n. The Nabathæan inscription of Hebran (A. D. 47) has קיסר (Vogüé, *id.* 100. He wrongly reads צ for ס, not observing the difference as written in Nabathæan: cf. pp. 113, 114). See *Journ. Asiat.* June, 1868, p. 538; April, May, 1873, p. 316, *n.* 1; *Zeitsch. der d. m. G.* 1871, p. 431. To distinguish the two letters, notice the *certain* צ of the inscriptions of Bosra and Salkhat (Vogüé, pl. xiv. 4, 6), observing that, as a purely Semitic letter, it rarely occurs in Syriac in the transcription of Greek and Latin names. In Palmyrene (Vogüé, pp. 18, 20, 21, 25), in Talmudic (Buxtorf), the σ in στρατηγός, etc., is rendered by ס. The Arabic spelling belongs to a time when the *tsaddi* had lost its special native force. The omission of י (*yod*) may seem singular in the first century. It is probably suppressed designedly, that the cipher may be symmetrical, — 666. With the י (= 10) it would have been 676, which would be less striking. In talmudic writings, *Cesarœa* is sometimes written קיסרי (Midrash, *Esther*, 1).

[2] Thus: נ, 50; ר, 200; ו, 6; ן, 50; ק, 100; ס, 60; ר, 200, — the sum of which is 666. The reading 616, mentioned by Irenæus, v. 30: 1, is made by omitting the final ן (50), reducing the name to the Latin form, *Nero*.

[3] Mionnet, iii. 93; Suppl. vi. 128 *a*. Mr. Waddington tells me that this legend is common on Asiatic coins (comp. Krafft's *inscr. of Topog. Jerus.* no. 31. (*Corpus*, etc., Syria, 135.)

were familiar to the Jews, and made a cabalistic puzzle, called *ghematria* (γεωμετρία).[1] It was, further, not unknown to the Asiatic Greeks,[2] and the Gnostics of the second century delighted in it.[3]

Thus the emperor signified by the head mortally hurt, but not killed, — as the writer himself signifies, — is Nero,[4] who was widely supposed by the people of Asia to be still alive. Of this there can be no doubt. But what is the second beast, that agent of Nero, — having the ways of a pious Jew and the language of Satan;[5] Nero's double, working in his interest, performing wonders, going so far as to make his statue speak, persecuting the faithful Jews who will not render to Nero the same honours with the pagans, or wear the mark that denotes them as members of his party; rendering their life intolerable, and forbidding to them those most essential acts, purchase and sale? Some points might apply to a Jewish functionary (like Tiberius Alexander), devoted to the Romans, and regarded as an apostate by his countrymen. The mere fact of paying tribute to the Empire might be called "worship of the Beast," since tribute had in Jewish eyes the aspect of a religious offering, implying homage to the person of the sovereign.[6] The sign or "mark" of

[1] Comp. *Assump. of Moses*, 9; *Carm. Sibyll.* i. 141, 326; v. 28 (referring to Nero); viii. 148–150; and the number 153 in John xxi. 11 (?). As to the use of the *ghematrioth*, at the talmudic period, see *Litteraturblatt des Orients*, 1849, 671, 672, 762–764; 1850, 116, 117.

[2] Inscriptions at Pergamus, ἰσόψηφοι [in which the numerical value of the letters in two different lines or words is equal], *Corp.* etc., 3544, 3545, 3546; cf. 5113, 5119; Boissonade, *Anecd. Gr.* ii. 459–461.

[3] Iren. i. 14, 15, *passim*.

[4] In the "Cæsars" of Julian, Caligula and Domitian are also represented by two beasts (pp. 310, 311).

[5] Matt. vii. 15. ["false prophets in sheep's clothing"].

[6] Melito, *De veritate*, xli.; he commented upon portions of the Apocalypse.

the Beast (Νέρων Καῖσαρ), which one was required to wear to secure civil rights, may have been a ticket of Roman citizenship, without which life in some countries was full of hardship, but which by a Jewish fanatic was held to be the crime of complicity in the work of Satan; or it may have been coin with Nero's image, which was held by Jews in revolt to be abominable, on account of the blasphemous images and inscriptions on it, so that they made haste, as soon as they were free in Jerusalem, to substitute an orthodox coinage of their own. The Roman partisan, we are supposing, might seem guilty of a horrid crime in upholding money of Nero's coinage as current by compulsion in trades.[1] Such coinage would fill the market; and those who from religious scruple refused to deal with it were practically outlawed.

The proconsul of Asia at this time was Fonteius Agrippa,[2] a grave magistrate, whom we cannot once think of as a means of relieving our perplexity. A high-priest of Asia, zealous for the worship of Rome and Augustus,[3] and employing his delegated civil power to distress the Jews and Christians, would meet some of the conditions of the problem. But the features shown us in the second beast, as a deceiver and wonder-worker, do not suit such a character. They rather make us think of a false prophet, a magician, Simon Magus, for example,[4] — an imitator of Christ

---

[1] It was remarked as a singular thing (Zonaras, *Ann.* xi. 16) that Vitellius permitted the circulation of Nero's, and even of Galba's and Otho's coinage.

[2] Waddington, *Fasti of the Province of Asia*, 140, 141.

[3] Waddington, *Inscr.* (Le Bas), iii. 885.

[4] Simon, according to the legend, went to Rome in the reign of Nero, to display before him his magic skill. An incident that happened in the

(whence the lamb's horns of ver. 11); then, in the legend, the flatterer, parasite, and professional juggler of Nero;[1] or Balbillus of Ephesus;[2] or the "Man of Sin" (Antichrist) obscurely spoken of by Paul.[3] It is probable that the person had in view by the writer of the Apocalypse is some impostor of Ephesus, a partisan of Nero, or, it may be, the pretended Nero himself, or an agent of his. In fact, the same man is afterwards called "the false prophet,"[4] in the sense that he proclaims a false god, — as Aaron is the "prophet" of Moses in Ex. vii. 1, — that is, Nero. We must keep in view the importance attached at this time to magi, Chaldæans, "mathematicians" (or magicians), — a form of nuisance particularly at home in Ephesus. We must recall, too, the fact that Nero dreamed once of a "kingdom at Jerusalem;" that he was in close league with the astrologers of his time;[5] and that,

amphitheatre in Nero's presence (Suet. *Nero*, 12; Dion Chrys. *Or.* xxi. 9; Juvenal, iii. 78–80) strongly suggest the tragic end of Simon's career. The prodigies attributed to "the false prophet" of the Apocalypse have some likeness to those ascribed to Simon in the Christian romance (Pseudo-Clem. *Hom.* ii. 34; iv. 4; *Recogn.* ii. 9; iii. 47, 57; Const. Apost. vi. 9; *Acta Petri*, etc., 32, 35, 52, 70–77; Pseudo-Hegesippus, iii. 2; Epiph. xxi. 5; Maximus, in *Bibl. max. Patr.* vi. 36; Arnobius, *Adv. gentes*, ii. 12). This is one reason which might lead us to suspect in the false prophet a symbolic representation of Saint Paul. (Comp. pp. 59, 60, *ante*.)

[1] Greg. of Tours, i. 24. The false Icarus was a domestic of Nero's (Dion. Chrysost.).

[2] Suet. *Nero*, 36; Dion Cass. lxvi. 9; Arnob. *Adv. gentes*, i. p. 15, ed. Rigault (*Bœbulus = Balbillus?*). For the games founded in his honour (βαλβίλλεια), comp. *Corp. inscr. Gr.* 2810, 3208, 3675, 5804, 5913. The expression "before him" (ἐνώπιον, Rev. xiii. 12, 14; xix. 20) does not necessarily mean in bodily presence: a prophet who speaks for another is represented as acting or speaking *before him* (לפניו); cf. *Acta Petri et Pauli*, 75.

[3] 2 Thess. ii. 3, 4.

[4] Rev. xvi. 13; xix. 20; xx. 10; cf. Matt. xxiv. 24.

[5] Suet. *Nero*, 34, 36, 40; Pliny, *H. N.*, xxx. 2.

almost alone of the emperors [before Diocletian], he was adored in his lifetime as a deity,[1] — a sign of Antichrist.[2] During his visit to Greece, in particular, the adulation paid him by Achaia and Asia surpassed all that we could imagine. And, further, we must not forget the gravity, in Asia and the Greek islands, of the uprising under the pretended Nero.[3] The circumstance that the second beast comes from the land, not like the first from the sea, shows that the event spoken of happened in Asia or Judæa, not in Rome. All this, however, is not enough to lift the darkness covering this vision. Without doubt it had, in the writer's mind, the same distinct basis in fact as the others; but, referring as it does to some provincial incident unknown to historians, and important only in the personal feeling of the Seer, it remains an unanswered riddle.

Amid these floods of wrath now appears an islet of verdure.[4] In the most frightful conflicts of the last days, there is one place of refuge and comfort: it is the Church, the little household of Jesus. The prophet sees, reposing upon Mount Zion, the hundred and forty-four thousand ransomed of the whole earth, bearing the name of God upon their foreheads. The Lamb rests peacefully in the midst of them. Celestial harmonies fall from harps upon the gathering; the singers sing a new song, which none other may repeat except the hundred and forty-four thousand. The test of these

---

[1] Tac. *Ann.* xv. 74.   [2] 2 Thess. ii. 3, 4.

[3] See the expressions of Tacitus (*Hist.* ii. 8, 9): "wide-spread terror," "false alarm in Achaia and Asia," etc.; also, Zonaras (in Dion.): "terrified almost all Greece" (*Ann.* xi. 15). Asia Minor continued to produce these impostors (Zonaras, xi. 18); and we feel that here is the home of Neronianism.

[4] Rev. chap. xiv.

blessed ones is strict chastity: all are virgin without stain; their lips have never spoken a lie;[1] thus they follow the Lamb wherever he goes, as first-fruits of the earth and nucleus of the future realm.

After turning aside thus swiftly to a haven of peace and innocence, the writer reverts to his dreadful visions. Three angels pass swiftly through the sky. The first flies to the zenith bearing the eternal gospel. He proclaims before all nations the new doctrine, and announces the Judgment day. The second celebrates by anticipation the destruction of Rome: "She is fallen, is fallen, Babylon the mighty city,[2] which has made all nations drunk with the wine of her fornication."[3] The third angel forbids the worship of the Beast, or of his image made by the false prophet: "Those who worship the Beast or his image, or who bear the mark of the Beast on their forehead or their hand, shall drink wine of the wrath of God, undiluted wine mingled in the cup of his anger,[4] and shall be tortured with fire and brimstone before the angels and the Lamb. And the smoke of their torment rises through ages of ages, and they have no respite day or night,[5] — they who worship the Beast or his image, and who take upon them the mark of his name. Here is the patience of the saints, who keep the commandments of God[6] and the faith of Jesus." To re-

---

[1] Zeph. iii. 13.

[2] On the prophetic or symbolic use of this name, see p. 115.

[3] Isa. xxi. 9; Jer. li. 7; Dan. iv. 27. The word here signifies incitement to idolatry, which, according to the Seer, is the great crime of the Roman Empire. In the language of prophecy, impurity is inseparable from idolatry.

[4] Psa. lxxv. 9; *Carm. Sibyll.* proem, 76–78.   [5] Isa. xxiv. 9, 10.

[6] The strict Judæo-Christians, who observe the Law, or at least those converts who keep the commandments of Noah.

assure their faith upon a question that sometimes troubles them, as to the doom of their brethren who die from day to day,[1] a voice directs the prophet to write, "Blessed henceforth are the dead who die in the Lord. Yea, saith the Spirit, they will rest from their labours, for their works follow them."[2]

The images of the Great Judgment crowd upon the heated imagination of the Seer. A white cloud appears in the sky, and on the cloud is seated, as it were, a Son of Man (an angel like the Messiah),[3] his head crowned with gold, and in his hand a sharp sickle.[4] The harvest of the earth is ripe. The Son of Man puts in his sickle, and the harvest of the earth is reaped. Another angel goes on to the vintage;[5] he casts the whole into the great vat of the wrath of God.[6] The vat is trampled with feet outside the city;[7] and the blood which gushes from it rises to the height of the horses' bridle-reins, over an extent of sixteen hundred furlongs.

After these various episodes a celestial ceremony, like the two mysteries of the opening of the seals and sounding of the trumpets, takes place in view of the Seer.[8] Seven angels are empowered to strike the earth with the seven last plagues, through which the wrath of God will be spent. But first we are reassured as to

---

[1] See "Saint Paul," chaps. ix., xiv.; 1 Thess. iv. 14, 16; 1 Cor. xv. 18; comp. Phil. i. 23; John v. 24; Luke xxiii. 43.

[2] *Pirké Aboth*, vi. 9.

[3] Dan. vii. 13; Matt. xxiv. 30; Luke xxi. 27; Rev. i. 13.

[4] Joel iii. 13; Jer. li. 33.

[5] Joel iii. 13; Isa. xvii. 5; lxiii. 1-6.

[6] Isa. lxiii. 3; Micah iv. 13; Hab. iii. 12.

[7] Alluding probably to the valley of Jehoshaphat (Joel iii. 2, 11-14). The name was already beginning to be identified with the vale of Kedron.

[8] Rev. chap. xv.

the destiny of the elect. Upon a vast sea of crystal mingled with fire we see the conquerors of the Beast — that is, those who have refused to worship his image or to bear the mark of his name — holding in their hands the harps of God, singing the song of Moses (that after the passage of the Red Sea) and of the Lamb. The door of the heavenly tabernacle is open, and there issue the seven angels clad in white linen, and girt about the breast with golden girdles, — the costume of Jewish priests.[1] One of the four "living creatures" gives them seven golden bowls, full to the brim with the wrath of God.[2] The temple is then filled with the "smoke from the glory of God," and none can enter till the end of the scene of the seven bowls.[3]

The first angel[4] pours his bowl upon the earth, and "there falls a noisome and grievous sore" upon all those who bear the image of the Beast, or worship his image.

The second angel pours his bowl into the sea; and the sea is changed into blood, and all living creatures in it perish.

The third angel pours his bowl upon the rivers and springs, and they are turned into blood. The angel of the waters complains not of the loss of his own element, but says, "Thou art just, O Lord, that art and wast and shalt be, in that thou hast judged thus. They have shed the blood of saints and prophets, and thou hast given them blood to drink. This they have deserved." And a voice is heard from the altar, saying,

---

[1] Ex. xxviii. 39, 40; Lev. vii. 3.
[2] Ezek. xxii. 31; Zeph. iii. 8; Ps. lxxxix. 6; Ezek. x. 7.
[3] Ex. xl. 34; 1 Kings viii. 10, 11; Isa. vi. 4; esp. Ecclus. xxxix. 28–31. There is much likeness to the plagues of Egypt (Ex. vii.-x.).
[4] Rev. chap. xvi.

"Yes, Lord God Almighty, thy judgments are true and just." [1]

The fourth angel pours his bowl upon the sun; and the sun burns men like fire. But they, far from repenting, blaspheme God, who has the power to strike them with such plagues.

The fifth angel pours his bowl upon the throne of the Beast (the city of Rome); and all the kingdom of the Beast (the Roman Empire) is plunged in darkness. Men gnaw their tongues for pain;[2] but instead of repenting, they mock at the God of heaven.

The sixth angel pours his bowl upon the river Euphrates, which immediately dries up, so as to prepare the way for the coming of the kings of the East.[3] Then from the mouth of the Dragon (Satan), from the mouth of the Beast (Nero), and from the mouth of the False Prophet (?) come forth three foul spirits like frogs (a sign of sorcery and magic),[4] spirits of demons who work miracles. These three spirits go in search of the kings of all the earth, and bring them together for the battle of the great day of God. "Behold," says Jesus, "I come as a thief. Blessed is he that watches and keeps his garments, lest he go about naked and his shame be seen."[5] They gather, accordingly, in a place whose Hebrew name is Armageddon. The general thought of all this is plain. The Seer, as we have seen, adopts the opinion universally held in Asia, that Nero, after escaping from Phaon's villa, had taken refuge with the Parthians, and would return from among them to

---

[1] Comp. "Wisdom" xi. 15, 16; xvi. 1, 9; xvii. 2, 3.
[2] Wisd. xvii. 2, 3.
[3] Comp. Isa. xi. 15, 16; *Carm. Sibyll.* iv. 137-139.
[4] Artemidorus, *Onirocrit.* ii. 15.
[5] Rev. xvi. 15; comp. Matt. xxiv. 42; Luke xii. 37-39.

crush his enemies. It was believed, with some show of reason,[1] that the Parthian princes (Arsacidæ), friends of Nero during his reign, sustained him still; in fact, their court was the refuge of false Neros for more than twenty years.[2] All this appears to the writer of the Apocalypse an infernal plan,[3] conceived between Satan, Nero, and some person figured by the second beast. These creatures of Hell are busied somewhere in the East with forming a league, whose army will soon pass the Euphrates, and crush the Roman Empire. What especial enigma there may be in the name Armageddon is to us undecipherable.[4]

The seventh angel pours out his bowl upon the air, and a cry comes from the altar, "It is done!" There are lightnings, voices, thunders, and an earthquake, "such as was not, since men were upon the earth, so mighty an earthquake and so great." In consequence of it, the great city (Jerusalem)[5] is broken in three parts; the cities of the nations fall; and the great Babylon (Rome) comes into God's remembrance, and is now to be compelled to drink "the cup of the wine of the fierceness of his wrath." The islands disappear, the mountains are no longer seen; hailstones of a hundred-weight[6] fall upon men, so that they "curse God

---

[1] Suet. *Nero*, 57.

[2] Tac. *Hist.* i. 2; Suet. *Nero*, 57; Zonaras, xi. 18.

[3] Comp. 1 Kings xxii. 20–23.

[4] No doubt an allusion to "Hadad-rimmon," and "Megiddo" in Zech. xii. 11. Some special place is probably had in mind, we cannot tell what. The explanation הרומה הגדולה (*ha-roma-gedôl* "the great Rome") is unlikely. Almost all the historic battles in Palestine were fought near Megiddo (Judges v. 19; 2 Kings xxiii. 29; Zech. *l. c.*).

[5] Comp. Rev. xi. 8; also the contrast with "cities of the nations." Besides, Rome would hardly be indicated in the same verse by two different names.

[6] A talent-weight is 110 pounds. — ED.

because of the plague of the hail, for the plague thereof was exceeding great." [1]

The series of preludes is now finished, and it only remains to unveil the Divine Judgment. The Seer introduces us first to the condemnation of the guiltiest of all, the city of Rome.[2] One of the seven angels who have poured the bowls of wrath upon the earth approaches John and says, "Come, and I will show you the judgment of the great Enchantress who sits upon many waters,[3] with whom the kings of the earth have done iniquity,[4] and who has made the world drunk with the wine of her adulteries." Then John sees a Woman seated upon a monster like at every point to that which came out of the sea, whose entire figure represented the Roman Empire, and one of its heads the emperor Nero. The monster is scarlet, covered with names of blasphemy, having seven heads and ten horns. The Woman wears the garb of her profession as courtesan; she is clad in purple and scarlet, glittering with wrought gold ($\chi\rho\upsilon\sigma\acute{\iota}\wp$), precious stones, and pearls; and bears in her hand a golden drinking-cup, full of the abominations and impurities of her prostitution. On her forehead is written a name of mystery: "Babylon the Great, mother of harlots and of the abominations of the earth."

And I saw the woman drunken with the blood of the saints, and with the blood of the martyrs of Jesus. And I wondered with great wonder. And the angel said to me, "Why do you wonder? I will tell you the meaning of the woman and of

---

[1] Rev. xvi. 17–21. [2] Rev. chap. xvii.

[3] Originally said of Babylon (Jer. li. 13), but afterwards applied metaphorically to Rome.

[4] The Herods, Tiridates king of Armenia, and others, eager to visit Rome, give banquets there, and make their court to her.

the beast that carries her. The beast which you have seen was, and is no more; and it must come up again from the Pit,[1] then go into perdition; and the inhabitants of the earth whose names are not written in the book of life from the beginning of the world will be full of consternation in seeing the beast reappear, which had been and was no more. Here it needs a mind that has understanding. The seven heads are the seven hills on which the woman dwells. They represent also seven kings; five of these are fallen, and one now reigns; the other is not yet come, and when he comes he will continue but a little time.[2] The beast which was and is no more is the eighth king, and at the same time one of the seven, and goes straight to destruction. And the ten horns which you have seen are ten kings, who have not yet received a kingdom, but receive for one hour authority as of kings, sharing it with the Beast. These all have one purpose, and yield up their power and authority to the Beast. They will make war upon the Lamb, and the Lamb will conquer them; for he is Lord of lords and King of kings; and those who are called and chosen with him, his faithful ones, will conquer likewise." And he added, "The waters which you have seen, on which the Harlot sits, are the peoples and nations and races and tongues. And the ten horns which you have seen, and [3] the Beast itself, will hate the Harlot, and make her naked and desolate, and will devour her flesh, and burn her with fire.[4] For God has put it in their hearts to fulfil his purpose, and to combine together, and to give their royal power to the Beast, until the will of God shall be accomplished. And the Woman whom you have seen is the great City which has royal power over the kings of the earth."

This is quite clear. The Harlot is Rome, which has

[1] Comp. xi. 7: $ἄβυσσος$, "the abyss," the abode of devils, not of the dead.

[2] Comp. *Assumption of Moses*, 7: see Hilgenfeld, *Nov. Test. extra canonem*, i. 113, 114.

[3] The reading of the Alexandrian and Sinaïtic, etc., instead of "on."

[4] Signifying plunder and conflagration.

corrupted the earth,[1] has employed its power to extend and strengthen idolatry,[2] has persecuted the saints, has shed in streams the blood of martyrs. The Beast is Nero, who has been thought dead, but will return, though his second reign will be short and his ruin complete. The seven heads have a twofold meaning: they are the seven hills on which Rome is seated; but, and above all, they are the seven emperors down to and including Galba.[3] The first five are dead; Galba reigns for the time, but he is old and weak, and his power will soon pass away. The sixth, Nero, who is at the same time the Beast itself and one of the seven kings,[4] is not really dead; he will reign again, but for a short time, — not more than three years and a half, thinks the writer; thus he will be the eighth, then will perish. The ten horns are the proconsuls and imperial legates, who are not real kings,[5] but receive their power from the emperor for a limited time ($\mu\iota\alpha\nu$ $\omega\rho\alpha\nu$), govern after the same policy, which comes to them from Rome, and are wholly subject to the empire, from which they hold their power. These partial kings bear equal malice with Nero himself against the Christians.[6] Since they represent provincial interests, they will humble Rome, and take from her the right to dispose of the empire, which she has held till now;[7] they will abuse her, set fire to her, and share her ruins

[1] See *Carm. Sibyll.* iii. 182, 356; v. 161 *et seq.*

[2] Comp. the two *hagadas* on the origin of Rome: Jerus. Talm., *Aboda zara*, 1, 3; Sifré, sect. *Ekeb*, 52; Bab. Talm., *Shabbath*, 56, *b;* Midrash, *Shir hasshirim*, i. 6.

[3] See pp. 317, 321.

[4] Rev. xvii. 11.

[5] See the use of *dux* in the Midrash rabba, *Eka*, 1, 5.

[6] See Commodian, v. 864.

[7] Tac. *Hist.* i. 4.

among themselves.¹ Meanwhile, God does not yet desire the dismembering of the empire. He puts it into the minds of the provincial military chiefs, and of all those who in turn control the destiny of the empire, — Vindex, Verginius, Nymphidius Sabinus, Galba, Macer, Capito, Otho, Vitellius, Mucian, Vespasian, — to agree in the policy of restoring the Empire; and, instead of making themselves independent of it (which to a Jewish writer seemed the more natural thing), to do homage for their royalty to the Beast.²

We see how deeply this manifesto from the head of the churches in Asia enters into the spirit of a situation which, to fancies so impressible as those of the Jews, must needs be strange. Nero, in fact, by his exceptional guilt and madness, had thrown men's reason off its balance. The Empire, at his death, was like an estate without heirs. After the murder of Caligula there was still a republican party left, and, besides, the adoptive family of Augustus retained its full prestige; while, after the death of Nero, there was almost no republican party whatever, and the Augustan family was extinct. The Empire was in the hands of eight or ten generals, who held high commands. The writer of the Apocalypse, knowing nothing of the Roman State, wonders that the ten chiefs, who seem to him kings, do not declare themselves independent, — that they agree in one policy;³ and attributes this to a special act of

---

[1] The project of starving the capital was entertained, says Josephus (*Wars*, iv. 10: 5), in the party of Mucian.

[2] In xvii. 13 ("give their power to the Beast"), the writer seems to imagine that the generals of the different provinces will combine for the restoration of Nero. The reigns of Otho and Vitellius were, in fact, reactions in Nero's favour.

[3] Ποιῆσαι μίαν γνώμην: Rev. xvii. 13, 17.

the divine will. Evidently the Jews of the East —
who had been for two years oppressed by the Roman
power, and now felt their burden lighter since Nero's
death, because Mucian and Vespasian were occupied
with general affairs of State — believed that the Empire
was about to dissolve, and were in triumph for a while.
This was not so superficial a view as it might seem.
Tacitus, in sketching the events of the year just before
the Apocalypse was written,[1] calls it "very nearly the
last year of the republic."[2] It was a great surprise to
the Jews when they saw the "ten kings" return to
the Beast (the unity of the Empire) and lay their kingdoms at his feet. They had hoped that the independence of the "ten kings" would result in the ruin of
Rome. Hostile as they were themselves to a great central organisation of the State, they supposed that the
proconsuls and legates must hate Rome also. Judging
them by themselves, they supposed that these powerful chiefs would act like Satraps, or else like Hyrca-
nus or Jannæus,[3] — kings who destroyed their enemies.
Like jealous provincials, they at least gloated over the
great humiliation endured by the queen-city of the
earth, when the right of creating sovereigns passed
over to the provinces; when Rome received within
her walls masters whom she had not the first voice in
proclaiming.

How far, then, was the Apocalypse connected with
that strange episode of the false Nero, which stirred
all hearts in Asia and the Grecian isles[4] at the very
moment when the Seer of Patmos wrote? Such a

---

[1] Tac. *Hist.* i. 11.   [2] Comp. Jos. *Wars*, iv. 11: 5.
[3] See "History of the People of Israel," iv. 239, 240; v. 96–115. — ED.
[4] See pages 280, 281, *ante.*

coincidence is surely most remarkable. Cythnos and Patmos are only a hundred and twenty miles apart, and news travels fast in the Archipelago. The days when the Christian prophet wrote were those when the impostor was most talked about, enthusiastically hailed by some, and watched with terror by others. I have shown that he announced himself at Cythnos in January of 69, or perhaps in December of 68. The centurion Sisenna, who touched at Cythnos early in February, on his way from the East, whence he brought pledges of agreement from the army in Syria to the Pretorians at Rome, had some difficulty in escaping him. A few days later, Calpurnius Asprenas, who had received from Galba the government of Galatia and Pamphylia, arrived at Cythnos, accompanied by two galleys of the fleet of Misenum. Emissaries of the Pretender tried upon the captains of these galleys the magic effect of Nero's name; and the scamp, affecting an air of sadness, appealed to the fidelity of those who had once been "his soldiers." He entreated them to convey him, at least, to Syria or Egypt, on which he rested his hopes. The captains, whether by cunning or from hesitation, asked for time. Asprenas heard all, seized the impostor by surprise, and put him to death. His body was carried to Asia, then to Rome, so as to confute those of his partisans who might raise doubts of his death.[1] Might it be that this poor wretch was alluded to in the words, "the Beast which you see was, and is no more; he will come forth from the Pit, and run swiftly to his end; the other king is not yet come, and when he shall come he will not continue long"?[2]

---

[1] Tac. *Hist.* ii. 8, 9.
[2] Rev. xvii. 8, 10, 11. Compare the expressions of ver. 8 with those

It is possible. The monster rising from the Pit would be a lively image of the ephemeral power which the sagacious historian discerned, not far from Patmos, appearing upon the sea-horizon. We cannot speak confidently of this: the general opinion that Nero was in hiding among the Parthians is enough to explain everything. But this opinion did not prevent belief in the false Nero of Cythnos; since it might be supposed that his appearing was really the return of the "monster," coincident with the crossing of the Euphrates by his Eastern allies.[1] In any case, it seems to me impossible that these passages should have been written after the false Nero was put to death by Asprenas. The sight of the impostor's body, conveyed from town to town, and the view of his features pallid in death, would have confuted too plainly the apprehensions of the Beast's return, which has such a hold upon the writer's mind.[2] I fully admit, then, that John at Patmos had knowledge of the events at Cythnos,[3] and that the effect produced on him by these strange rumours was the chief occasion of the letter he wrote to the churches of Asia, to notify them of the great tidings that Nero was risen from the dead.

Interpreting political events in the interest of his own hate, the writer — a Jewish fanatic — has pre-

of Tacitus in the passage just referred to, and in the note on p. 327 (above).

[1] In the two passages relating to the Parthian invasion, — the sixth trumpet and the sixth bowl, — it is not said that Nero was with his allies, but only that the invasion was made in concert with him.

[2] This disproves the opinion of those who think to find in the Apocalypse allusions to the final struggles of Otho and Vitellius.

[3] The words "was not yet come" (ver. 10) would well fit the time when the impostor, though much talked of, had not yet committed himself by any public acts.

dicted that the provincial commandants, whom he supposes to be full of rancour against Rome, while to a certain extent in league with Nero, will ravage and burn the city; and then, assuming this to be already accomplished, he chants the ruin of his foe.[1] For this, he has only to copy the declamations of the old prophets against Babylon or Tyre.[2] Israel has staked out, so to speak, the literature of malediction. To all the great secular States, such words as these have been spoken: "Happy he that shall repay to thee the evil thou hast done!" A shining angel comes down from heaven, and cries in awful tones, "Fallen, fallen, is Babylon the great, and is now but the habitation of devils,[3] an abode of unclean spirits, a refuge of filthy birds; because all the earth has drunk of the wine of her fornication, and the kings of the earth have defiled themselves with her, and the merchants of the earth have enriched themselves by her wealth!" Another voice from heaven is heard: —

Go out of her, you who are my people, lest you make yourselves guilty of her crimes, and be stricken by the plagues that shall afflict her! Her abominations have come before the face of heaven, and God has taken note of her iniquities. Return upon her what she has done to others, repay her double for her evil deeds; pour out to her twice over the cup which she has poured out upon others! All that she has had of glory and prosperity, so much shall be given her of torment and affliction. "I sit as a Queen," she says; "I am no widow, and I shall never know what it is to mourn." That is why her punishment shall come all in one day, — death, desolation,

[1] Rev. chap. xviii.
[2] As examples, Isa. xiii., xxiii., xxiv., xxxiv., xlvii., xlviii., lii.; Jer. xvi., xxv., li.; Ezek. xxvi., xxvii.
[3] That is, the strange wild animals living in the ruins, which were taken to be evil demons. Isa. xiii. 21; xxxiv. 14.

famine, and fire; for mighty is the God who judges her. And the kings of the earth shall be seen weeping over her, they who have shared her uncleanness and debaucheries.[1] At the sight of the smoke of her conflagration, the companions of her luxury shall cry out, "Woe, woe!" and hold themselves afar off in terror. "What! the great, the mighty Babylon! In one hour her judgment is come upon her!" And the merchants of the earth will lament, for no one any longer buys their merchandise. Ornaments of gold and silver, precious stones, pearls, fine linen, purple, silk, scarlet, cypress-wood, ivory, brass, steel, marble, cinnamon, balsam, perfumes, aromatic oils, incense, wine, oil, fine flour, wheat, cattle, sheep, horses, chariots, bodies[2] and souls of men, — the traders in all these things, who had gained wealth from her, keep far away in dread of her torments. "Woe, woe!" will they say. "Alas! that is the great city which was clothed in scarlet, purple, and fine linen; which was adorned with gold, precious stones, and pearls! In one hour so great wealth is come to naught!" And the sailors who once came to her, and all who traffic by the sea, stand afar off at the sight of the smoke of her burning, cast dust upon their heads, and break into cries, weeping, and lamentation: "Woe, woe!" they say; "The great city, which enriched with her treasures all who had ships upon the sea, behold! in one hour she has been turned into a desert!" Rejoice at her ruin, O heaven! Rejoice, saints, apostles, and prophets! For God has judged your cause, and has given you vengeance upon her.[3]

Then an angel of mighty strength takes a stone great as a millstone, and casts it into the sea, saying, —

---

[1] An allusion to the Herods, whose flatteries of the Romans were deeply wounding to the Jews, especially after the revolt of 66.

[2] Slaves at sale were counted as "bodies" ($\sigma\omega\mu\alpha\tau\alpha$); see Inscr. at Delphi (*Journ. asiat.* June, 1868, 530, 531); Demosth. *In Everg.*, etc., 11; Tob. x. 10; 2 Macc. viii. 11; Gen. xxxvi. 6 (Gr. vers.); comp. Gen. xii. 5; Ezek. xxvii. 13; Jos. *Life*, 75; Wescher, in *Ann. de l'assoc. des études grecques*, 1872, 88.

[3] Rev. xviii. 4-20.

Thus with violence shall Babylon, that great city, be thrown down, and no more trace of her shall be found. And the sound of the harp and of musicians, the sound of the flute and trumpet shall be heard no more within her walls; no craftsman of any craft shall be found in her; and the sound of a millstone shall no more be heard in her; the light of a candle shall shine in her no more; the voice of the bridegroom and the bride[1] shall no more be heard. For her merchants were the great ones of the earth,[2] and by her sorceries all nations were deceived. And in her was found the blood of prophets and saints, and of all who have been slain upon the earth.[3]

The ruin of this chief enemy of the people of God is the occasion of great rejoicing in heaven.[4] A voice as of a countless multitude is heard, saying, "Hallelujah! Salvation, glory, and power to our God! For his judgments are just, and He has judged the great Harlot who has corrupted the earth by her adulteries; and He has avenged the blood of his servants shed by her." Another chorus responds: "Hallelujah! the smoke of her burning rises up forever and ever." Then the twenty-four elders and the four living creatures prostrate themselves and do homage to God, who sits upon the throne, saying, "Amen! hallelujah!" A voice then comes from the throne, singing the inaugural Psalm of the new kingdom: "Praise our God, all ye who are his servants and who fear him, both small and great."[5] A voice like that of a multitude, or the voice of many waters, or the noise of loud thunder, responds:

---

[1] Responsive chants, as in the Song of Solomon, used for popular song in general.

[2] Not specially applicable to Rome, but taken from the invectives of ancient prophets against Tyre.

[3] Rev. xviii. 21-24.   [4] *Ibid.* chap. xix.

[5] Ps. cxv. 13; cxxxiv. 1.

"Hallelujah! now reigns the Lord God Almighty! Let us rejoice and give ourselves up to joy, and render to him glory; for this is the marriage-hour of the Lamb,[1] and his Bride (the Church) has made herself ready: a robe of fine linen is given for her apparel, clean and white." The fine linen, the writer adds, is the righteousness of the saints.

Delivered now from the presence of the great Adulteress (Rome), the earth is ripe for the celestial marriage, the Messiah's reign. An angel says to the Seer, "Write, happy are they who are bidden to the marriage-supper of the Lamb!" Then heaven opens and Christ — who is here for the first time called by his mystic name, the Word of God — appears as a conqueror,[2] mounted on a white horse. He comes to trample the wine-press of the wrath of God, to inaugurate for the pagans the rule of the iron sceptre. His eyes flash fire; his robe is stained with blood; he wears upon his head several crowns, with an inscription in mysterious characters.[3] From his mouth proceeds a sharp sword, to smite the gentiles; and on his thigh is written his title, *King of kings*, *Lord of lords*. All the heavenly host follow him, riding on white horses, and clad in fine linen. We may now look for a peaceful triumph, but the time for that is not yet. Though Rome is destroyed, yet the Roman world, represented by Nero, the Antichrist, is not annihilated. An angel standing in the sun calls with a loud voice to all the birds flying in the vault of heaven, "Come, gather to

---

[1] Matt. xxii. 2-14; xxv. 1-13.

[2] All these images are taken from Isa. lxiii. 1-3; Ps. ii. 9; comp. Rev. i. 16; vi. 2; xiv. 19.

[3] The true reading in ver. 12 seems to be "names" (ὀνόματα): Tisch. and *Cod. Sinait.*

the great feast of God; come, eat the flesh of kings, of captains, of mighty men, of horses and their riders, of freemen and slaves, both small and great![1] Then the prophet sees the Beast (Nero) and the kings of the earth (generals of provinces, almost independent) with their armies, gathered to make war upon him who rides the white horse, and his forces; and the Beast is seized, and with it the False Prophet,[2] who wrought miracles before it; and both are cast alive into an ever-burning lake of fire and brimstone.[3] Their armies are wholly destroyed by the sword which proceeds from the mouth of the rider of the white horse, and the birds glut themselves with their flesh.

The Roman armies, the great instruments of Satan's power, are now subdued; Nero the Antichrist, their last chief, is imprisoned in hell; but the Dragon, the old serpent, Satan, still lives. We have seen how he was cast from heaven upon the earth;[4] the earth must now be delivered from his presence.[5] An angel comes down from heaven, holding the key of the Pit, and having a great chain in his hand. He seizes the Dragon, binds him for a thousand years, thrusts him into the Pit,[6] locks with the key the entrance of the Pit, and seals it with a seal.[7] The Devil will remain in chains for a thousand years. Moral evil and physical (which is its consequence) will be suspended, but not destroyed. Satan can no longer deceive the nations, but he is not annihilated for all eternity.

A judgment-seat is set, to declare who are those that

---

[1] Comp. Ezek. xxxix. 17-20.
[2] See pp. 322-327.
[3] See pp. 267, 268.
[4] Rev. xii. 7, 8.
[5] Chap. xx.
[6] Jude 6.
[7] Comp. Bab. Talm. *Gittin*, 68 a.

shall share the reign of a thousand years.¹ This is reserved exclusively for martyrs. The first place in it belongs to the souls of those who were beheaded for bearing witness to Jesus and to the word of God (the martyrs of Nero's persecution); then come those who have refused to worship the Beast or his image, and have not received his mark on their foreheads, or in their hands (the confessors of Ephesus, of whom the Seer is one: comp. i. 9). The elect of this first kingdom revive and reign with Christ a thousand years upon the earth. Not that the rest of mankind has disappeared, or even that the whole world has become Christian. The *millennium* is at the centre of the earth, like a little paradise. Rome exists no more; Jerusalem has taken its place as the capital of the world; the faithful here make a kingdom of priests;² they serve God and Christ; there is no longer any great pagan empire, or civil power hostile to the Church; the nations come to Jerusalem to render homage to the Messiah, who controls them by terror. During these thousand years the dead, who have no part in the first resurrection, are not alive: they wait. Those, then, who share in the first kingdom have a special privilege: over and above eternity without end, they have the thousand years on earth with Jesus. No death will ever touch them more.

When the thousand years shall be fulfilled, Satan will be set free from his prison for a time, and evil will begin again to prevail upon the earth. Satan, unchained, will again deceive the nations, driving them from one end of the earth to the other in frightful wars. Gog and Magog (mythic personifications of bar-

---

¹ Dan. vii. 9, 22, 27. ² Isa. lxi. 6.

barian assaults)¹ will lead to the conflict armies more numerous than the sands of the sea. The Church will be, as it were, drowned in this deluge. The barbarians will besiege the camp of the saints, the beloved city,— that is, Jerusalem, still of earth, but altogether holy, where the faithful friends of Jesus are; but fire will fall from heaven upon them and consume them. Then Satan, who had seduced them, will be cast into the lake of burning brimstone, where already are the Beast (Nero) and the False Prophet, and where all these accursed ones will henceforth be tormented day and night for ages upon ages.

The work of the creation is now finished; it remains only to proceed to the final Judgment.² A throne appears, shining white, and upon it the Supreme Judge. At sight of him, heaven and earth flee away: there is no longer space for them. The dead, great and small, come to life. Death and the Grave (*Sheol*) render up their prey; the sea, too, yields back the drowned, who were swallowed up therein, and did not go down regularly into *Sheol* (Hades).³ All appear before the throne. The great books are brought, in which is kept a strict

---

[1] The myth comes from Ezek. xxxviii., xxxix. Among certain tribes speaking Ossetic [an Iranian dialect of the Caucasus], *Gogh* (mountain) and *Mugogh* (great mountain) denote two chief ranges of the Caucasus; and these names came to be applied to the Scythian populations near the Black and Caspian seas. In Ezekiel they personify Scythian, or, in general, any barbaric invasion (comp. *Koran*, xviii. 94, 95; xxi. 96). The messianic application of this geographical myth begins to appear in the Sibylline verses (iii. 319, 512); still more plainly in the Targum of Pseudo-Jonathan, or Jerus. Targ., Levit. xxvi. 44; Num. xi. 27; comp. Bab. Talm. *Sanh.* 94 a, 97 b; *Aboda zara*, 1 b. See *Zeitsch. der d. m. G.* 1867, 575.

[2] See Dan. vii. 9.

[3] Comp. Achilles Tatius, v. 116, 117 (ed. Jacobs), and the curious mosaic of Torcello.

account of the actions of every man.[1] Another book, too, is opened,— the "book of life," in which are written the names of those predestinate to bliss. Then all are judged according to their works. Those whose names are not found written in the book of life are cast down into the lake of fire; and into this Death and Hell (*Sheol*) are also cast.[2]

Now that Evil is destroyed without recovery, the reign of absolute Good is about to begin.[3] The old earth and the old heaven have passed away; a new earth and a new heaven succeed to them,[4] and there is no more sea.[5] Still, this new earth and sky are only a renewing of the present earth and sky; and, just as Jerusalem was the pearl and jewel of the former earth, just so Jerusalem will be again the radiant centre of the new. The apostle sees this new Jerusalem coming down from heaven, from the presence of God, arrayed like a bride adorned for her husband. A loud voice is heard, coming from the throne: "Behold the tabernacle wherein God will dwell with men; and they will henceforth be his people, and he will be always present in the midst of them.[6] And he will wipe every tear from their eyes, and there shall be no more death, nor sorrow, or crying, or pain;[7] for the former things are passed away." Jehovah himself speaks, to declare the

---

[1] Mal. iii. 16; Dan. vii. 10; Bab. Talm. *Rosh hash-shana*, 16 *b*.
[2] Comp. Dan. vii. 11; Luke xvi. 23; 1 Cor. xv. 26.
[3] Rev. chap. xxi.
[4] Comp. Isa. lxv. 17; lxvi. 22; 2 Pet. iii. 13.
[5] The sea [in this writer's view] blots out and sterilises a portion of the earth, and so is a relic of the primal chaos, or a penalty inflicted by God, engulfing guilty lands. It is bottomless ($\mathring{a}\beta v\sigma\sigma os$); now the abyss is the domain of Satan (comp. xi. 7; xiii. 1). In Paradise (Gen. ii.) there was no sea: comp. Job vii. 12.
[6] Ezek. xxxvii. 27; 2 Cor. vi. 16.   [7] Isa. xxv. 8; lxv. 19.

law of this eternal world: "It is done; behold I make all things new.[1] I am the *Alpha* and the *Omega*, the first and the last. Him who thirsts, I will cause to drink of the fountain of life freely.[2] He that overcomes shall inherit all these things, and I will be his God, and he will be my son.[3] The fearful, the unbelieving, the abominable, — murderers, fornicators, sorcerers, idolaters, liars, — their part shall be in the lake of fire and brimstone."

Then an angel draws near the Seer, and says, "Come, I will show you the Bride of the Lamb." And he bears him in spirit to a high mountain, from which he shows him in detail the new Jerusalem,[4] filled and clothed with the Divine glory. Its splendour is that of a crystal of jasper. In form it is a perfect square,[5] with sides of three thousand furlongs, set to the four winds of heaven (the cardinal points), and surrounded by a wall one hundred and forty-four cubits high, pierced with twelve gateways. At each gate an angel stands as guard, and above it is written the name of one of the twelve tribes of Israel. The foundation of the wall consists of twelve layers of stones, and on each shines the name of one of the apostles of the Lamb,[6] each suc-

---

[1] Isa. xliii. 19; Jer. xxxi. 22; 2 Cor. v. 17.

[2] Isa. lv. 1.   [3] 2 Sam. vii. 14.

[4] All that follows is taken from Ezekiel xl., xlvii., xlviii.; compare Herodotus, i. 178 [the description of Babylon].

[5] The word "height" (ver. 16) must be either a freak of fancy or a careless revision. But comp. Bab. Talm. *Baba bathra,* 75 *b.*

[6] The vague Jewish fancy shows here. The writer is drawn on by his symbols to a picture unsatisfying to the mind. The "twelve foundations" are commonly understood as so many sections of the basement wall, running from one gate to another. I think it better to put them one above another as so many layers, each set a little back from that under it, below the wall proper, as almost necessarily implied in vers. 18–20. Compare the walls of the *haram* at Jerusalem, as shown by the English excava-

cessive layer being adorned with precious stones,[1] — jasper, sapphire, chalcedony, emerald, sardonyx, cornelian, chrysolite, beryl (aquamarine), topaz, chrysoprase, jacinth, and amethyst. The wall itself is of jasper; the city pavement, of pure gold, bright "like transparent glass;" each gate is composed of a single great pearl.[2] There is no temple in the city; for God himself and the Lamb are its sanctuary. The throne, which the prophet at the opening of his revelation saw in heaven, is now in the midst of the city, — that is, at the centre of a humanity regenerate and harmoniously reconstructed. On this throne are seated God and the Lamb. From the foot of the throne flows the river of Life,[3] bright and clear as crystal, crossing the principal street. On its border grows the tree of life,[4] which bears twelve kinds of fruits, one in every month, which fruits seem to be reserved for Israel, — the leaves having a medicinal virtue for the healing of the nations. The city has no need of sun or moon to light it;[5] for the glory of God makes it bright, and the Lamb is its illumination. The nations will walk by its light;[6] the kings of the earth will pay it the homage of their own glory; and the gates will be shut neither day nor night, so great will be the throng of those who will come to bring their tribute. Nothing unclean or foul will enter there;[7] those only will find place in it whose

---

tions: *Palestine exploration fund*, No. 4; also, *Mém. de l'Acad. des inscr.* xxvi. pl. 2, 5; and *Les derniers jours de Jérus.*, 246. Observe, too, the use of the same word ($θεμέλιος$) in Jos. *Antiq.* vii. 14: 10; viii. 2: 9; xv. 11: 3; *Wars*, v. 5: 2, as designating the substructure of the Temple.

[1] Ex. xxvii. 17-20; xxxix. 10-14.
[2] Isa. liv. 11, 12.
[3] Rev. chap. xxii.
[4] Gen. ii. 10-14.
[5] Dan. vii. 27.
[6] Isa. lx. 3, 5-7, 19, 20.
[7] Isa. lii. 1.

names are written in the Lamb's book of life. There will be no more religious division or curse;[1] the pure worship of God and the Lamb will bind all the world together. At every hour the servants of God will enjoy the Divine vision, and his name will be written on their foreheads. This blessed reign will last forever and forever.

[1] Zech. xiv. 11.

CHAPTER XVII.

LATER FORTUNES OF THE BOOK. — A. D. 69.

THE work ends with an epilogue, which opens thus: —

I, John, heard and saw all these things. And when I had heard and seen them, I fell down before the feet of the angel who showed them to me, to worship him. But he said, "Do not do that. I am your fellow-servant; we have all one master, — I, and you, and your brothers the prophets, and all those who keep the words of this book.[1] Worship God." Then he said to me, "Do not seal" — that is, do not keep back — "the words of the prophecy of this book, for the time is near. Let the unjust act unjustly still, and he that is filthy let him still defile himself; and let the just man continue to do justice, and the holy let him still be holy!"

A voice far off, the voice of Jesus himself, is heard, responding to this assurance, and confirming it: —

Behold, I come quickly, and bring with me the reward which I will bestow on every man according to his works.[2] I am the *Alpha* and *Omega*, the first and last, the beginning and the end. Happy are they who make clean their garments![3] They will have right to the tree of life, and will enter by the gates into the city. But without are dogs [pagans], sorcerers, the impure in life, murderers, idolaters, and all who love or commit falsehood. I, Jesus, have sent my messenger to testify these things to you in the churches. Happy are they who

---

[1] A caution against those who, like the Essenes, exaggerate angel-worship.
[2] Isa. xl. 10.
[3] The reading here adopted by the author.

keep the words of the prophecy of this book! I am the stem and offshoot of David, the bright star of the morning.[1]

Here the voices from heaven and from earth intermingle, and come in softer strain to a cadence in perfect harmony : —

"Come!" say the Spirit and the Bride.[2] And let him who hears the call say also, "Come!" Let every one that thirsts come! Let him who will take the water of life freely.

I myself [says the Revealer] testify to every one who hears the words of the prophecy contained in this book, that if any shall add anything to them, God will lay on him all the plagues that are written here. And if any shall take away from the words of the book of this prophecy, God will take from him his share of the tree of life and of the holy city, of which it is written in this book.[3]

He who testifies of these things repeats, "Yes, I come quickly." Even so, come, Lord Jesus.

The grace of the Lord Jesus Christ be with all.

There can be no doubt that this Book of Visions made a very deep impression on the churches of Asia, communicated as it was under the most venerated name of the Christian world. A multitude of details, now grown obscure, were clear to the mind of that time. These bold predictions of a coming convulsion had nothing to cause surprise. Discourses just as formal, ascribed to Jesus,[4] were in daily circulation, and were accepted in good faith. Besides, throughout a year, public events might seem marvellously to confirm the book. Toward the first of February, the death of Galba and accession of Otho were reported in

---

[1] Isa. xi. 1.
[2] The spirit of prophecy in the Church, and the Church herself.
[3] Deut. iv. 2. [4] Matt. xxiv.

Asia. Every succeeding day brought some evident sign of the decay of imperial power. All the provinces well knew that Otho was powerless; that Vitellius held his title against Rome and the Senate; that two bloody battles had been fought at Bedriacum;[1] that Otho was defeated in his turn, and Vespasian was victorious; that a fight had taken place in the Roman streets, during which the Capitol was set on fire; and that from this conflagration many inferred that the destinies of Rome were drawing to an end. All this would appear wonderfully to confirm the gloomy predictions of the prophet. Believers in them only began to be undeceived when Jerusalem was taken, the Temple destroyed, and the Flavian dynasty set firmly on the throne. But religious faith never accepts the refutation of its hopes. Then, too, the book was obscure, and much of it might be variously explained. And thus, within a few years of its publication, a meaning was sought for several portions quite different from what the writer had put into them. He had foretold that the Roman empire would not be re-established, and that the Temple at Jerusalem would not be destroyed. Some way of escape must be found from these two misreadings of the event. The reappearance of Nero was not so quickly despaired of; even under Trajan, thirty years later, some of the common people still thought he would return.[2] The "number of the Beast" long survived; and a variant was current in western lands to adjust the figure to Latin ways of thinking. Some copies gave 616 instead of 666,[3] corresponding to

---

[1] In Italy. In the first, Otho was defeated by Vitellius; in the second, Vitellius by Vespasian. — ED.

[2] Dion Chrys. *Orat.* xxi. 10.   [3] Iren. v. 30: 1.

the Latin form *Nero* instead of *Neron* — the Hebrew *nun* standing for 50.

During the first three centuries the general sense of the book was retained, at least among some few of the initiated. The writer of the Sibylline poem dating not far from the year 80 had heard of the vision of Patmos, if he had not read it. He lived amidst an order of ideas very similar. He knows the meaning of the sixth "bowl." To him Nero is the Anti-Messiah; the monster has taken refuge beyond the Euphrates, and will come back with thousands of armed men.[1] The writer of the "Apocalypse of Esdras," of date from 96 to 98, is well known to have imitated John's Apocalypse,[2] and to have employed his symbolic method, his notations, and his style. The same may be said of the "Ascension of Isaiah," a work of the second century, in which Nero, an incarnation of Belial, plays a part which shows that the writer knew "the number of the Beast."[3] The writers of Sibylline verses dating at the time of the Antonines (about 160) see just as clearly the enigmas of the apostolic manifesto, and accept its dreams of the future, even those which, like the return of Nero, events had fully disproved.[4] Justin and Melito seem to have almost completely understood the book. The same may be said of Commodian (about 250), who mingles foreign elements in his exposition, but never an instant doubts that Nero the Antichrist is to return from Hell to maintain a final conflict with

---

[1] *Carm. Sibyll.* iv. 117, 137–139.

[2] Thus, compare 4 Esdr. iv. 35 *et seq.* with Rev. vi. 9–11; vii. 32 with Rev. xx. 13; x. 50 *et seq.* with Rev. xxi. 2–4. See also xv. 5.

[3] *Ascen. of Isaiah*, iv. 2 *et seq.*

[4] *Carm. Sibyll.* v. 28, 93, 105, 142 *et seq.*, 363; viii. 151, 169 *et seq.* See above, p. 257, n. 1; and comp. iii. 397.

Christianity,[1] and conceives the destruction of Rome-Babylon just as it was conceived two centuries before.[2] Finally, Victorinus of Pettau[3] comments very justly on the Apocalypse, understanding fully that Antichrist is Nero risen from the dead.[4] The number of the Beast was probably lost sight of before the end of the second century. Irenæus (about 190) is grossly mistaken about this, as well as some other points of greater importance; and opens the series of chimerical comments and arbitrary symbolism,[5] making the strongest reason for distrusting his relations with those who had seen the apostle John.[6] Several subtile points, such as the meaning of the False Prophet, and of Armageddon, were early lost.

When the Empire and the Church were reconciled, under Constantine, the position of the Apocalypse was gravely compromised. The Greek and Latin theologians, who no longer separated the destinies of Christianity from those of the Empire, could not accept as inspired a seditious book, whose mainspring was hatred of Rome and the prediction of its downfall. Almost all the enlightened portion of the Eastern Church, having received a Grecian culture, declared the book apocryphal.[7] The book had come to be so firmly fixed

---

[1] *Instr.* acrost. 41, 42: 36; *Carm.* 816, 831, 845, 862, 878, 903 *et seq.*; Pitra, *Spic. Sol.* i. (see emendations of Ebert in *Abhandl. der phil. hist. classe der sächs. Gesells. der Wiss.* v. 325).

[2] Commod. *Carm.* ver. 907 *et seq.*

[3] In Pannonia, d. A. D. 303. — ED.

[4] *Bib. max. patr.* i. 580.

[5] Iren. v. 30: 3.

[6] Commodian, in his *Instructiones*, also calls the Antichrist *Latinus*. Hippolytus (*De Antichristo*, 50, 52), is quite out of the way.

[7] See "Life of Jesus," p. 290, n. 3; also, pp. 295, 296, above. Dionysius of Alexandria, in the third century, — swayed, doubtless, by his

in the Greek and Latin Testament — the Syrian and Armenian did not contain it — that it could not be displaced; and, to clear it of the objections it raised, recourse was had to strange feats of exegesis. The evidence, however, was overwhelming. The Latins, less hostile to millenarianism, still identified Antichrist with Nero.[1] Until the time of Charlemagne, there was a sort of tradition as to this. Saint Beatus of Liebana, who wrote on the Apocalypse in 786, asserts (with more than one inconsequence) that the "Beast" of chapters xiii. and xvii., who is to reappear at the head of ten kings to annihilate the city of Rome, is Nero the Antichrist. At one moment, even, he barely misses a point which, in our century, has conducted critics to the true reckoning of the emperors, and the right fixing of the date.[2]

It is not until about the twelfth century, when the Middle Age is astray in the paths of scholastic rationalism, with little care for the tradition of the Fathers, that the meaning of John's vision is completely dis-

---

literary training, — speaks of the Apocalypse in a hesitating tone, confessing that he does not at all understand it (see Epiph. li. 32, 33; Euseb. vii. 25). Chrysostom has no homilies on the book.

[1] Victorinus of Pettau (*Bibl.* etc., iii. 418), Lactantius (*Inst.* vii. 14–20; *De mort. persec.* 2), Sulp. Sev. (*Hist. sacra*, ii. 28, 29; *Dial.* ii. 14). By these writers the early theory of Antichrist is altered as in the *Carmen* of Commodian. Comp. Aug. *De civ. Dei*, xx. 19; Jerome, *in Dan.* xi. 36; *in Isaiam*, xvii. 12; Chrys. *in 2 Thess.* ii. (*Opp.* xi. 529, 530). Read Malvenda, *De Antichristo*, lib. vi. *De vitiis Antichr.*; it is a veritable portrait of Nero.

[2] The text of Saint Beatus, as edited by Florez (Madrid, 1770), can hardly be found. Didot has collated the most important portions of his commentary with the sole copy of Florez in Paris, in the hands of M. l'abbé Nolte, and with two important manuscripts, one of which belongs to him. *Des apocalypses figurées manuscrites et xylographiques* (Paris, 1870), pp. 3, 16, 17, 24, 25, 76, 77; ed. Florez, 438, 498.

torted, yet not wholly lost.[1] Joachim of Floris may be regarded as the first who boldly carried the Apocalypse into the limitless field of fancy, and sought to find the secret of the entire future of mankind in the strange figures of a book written for a special end, whose horizon does not extend beyond three and a half years.

The wildly fanciful commentaries that have resulted from this false notion have cast unmerited discredit on the book itself. Thanks to a sounder exegesis, the Apocalypse has in our own day regained the high position which belongs to it in sacred Scripture. It is, in a sense, the seal of prophecy, the last word of Israel. Read in the ancient prophets[2] the description of "the day of Jehovah," — that is, of that grand Assize which the supreme Judge of human things holds from time to time to restore the moral balance so constantly disturbed by men, — and you will find the germ of the Vision of Patmos. Every revolution, every historical crisis, was to the imagination of the Jew — who persisted in dispensing with the immortality of the soul, and in demanding the establishment of a reign of justice upon the earth — a providential event, the prelude to a far more solemn and definitive judgment. At every such event a prophet arose, crying, "Sound, sound the trumpet in Zion! for the day of Jehovah comes, — it is at hand."[3] The Apocalypse is the sequel and the crown of that strange literature which is the peculiar glory of Israel. Its writer is the last of the great prophets, inferior to those who came before only so far as he is their copyist; he has the same soul

---

[1] *Hist. litt. de la France*, xxv. 258.
[2] In Joel, for example, chap. ii.
[3] Joel ii. 1.

with them, the same inspiration. The Apocalypse offers the almost unique exhibition of an inspired imitator, a plagiarist of genius. Excepting two or three inventions of marvellous beauty, which are the writer's own, — in particular, the episode of the martyr-souls beneath the altar,[1] a passage purely divine, which will forever abide for the consolation of a heart that suffers for its faith or virtue, — the composition as a whole is made up of passages borrowed from preceding prophetic and apocalyptic writings; especially from Ezekiel, the book of Daniel, and the two Isaiahs. The Christian Seer is the true disciple of these great men; he knows their writings by heart, and draws from them their final consequences. He is a brother of that marvellous poet of the time of the Captivity, the second Isaiah, — lacking only his serenity and harmony, — whose luminous soul seems to have absorbed, six centuries in advance, all the dews and perfumes of the larger faith that was to come.

Like most peoples who have a brilliant literature in the past, Israel lived on images consecrated by the old and admirable writers of the Hebrew scripture. Little was now composed, excepting from fragments of the ancient texts. Christian poetry, especially, knew no other way of literary production: take, for example, the canticles in the first two chapters of Luke. But, when the passion is genuine, even the most artificial form is full of beauty. Lamennais' "Words of a Believer" are to the Apocalypse what this is to the ancient prophets; yet they make a book of real power, which one can never read over without deep emotion.

As in the style, so in the dogmas of this time we find

[1] Rev. vii. 9–11.

something artificial; but they respond to a genuine conviction. The method of the theological mind was to transfer boldly, and apply to the Messianic reign of Jesus whatever in the ancient writers seemed capable of a relation however vague to an ideal however obscure. As the interpretation thus given was to the last degree commonplace, the strange results that followed often involved serious misunderstandings. This appears conspicuously in those passages of the Apocalypse which concern Gog and Magog as soon as they are compared with the corresponding passages in Ezekiel. Here Gog, king of Magog, will come after many days ("in the sequel of days"[1]), when the people of Israel have returned from the Captivity and are established in Palestine, and make an exterminating war upon them. As early as when the Hebrew scripture was rendered into Greek, and the Book of Daniel was composed, the phrase which in classic Hebrew signifies merely an indefinite future had come to mean "at the end of time," and was used only of the coming of the Messiah.[2] The writer of the Apocalypse is thus led to refer those passages of Ezekiel[3] to the Messianic times, and to consider Gog and Magog as representing the barbarian and pagan world, which will survive the fall of Rome, and subsist along with the thousand years' reign of Christ and his saints.

This fashion of creating by way of outside pressure (so to speak), — this method of putting together phrases picked up here and there by dint of a forced exegesis,

---

[1] באחרית הימים: Ezek. xxxviii. 8.

[2] See Gesenius, *Thesaurus* (Heb. Chald.), under אחרית. It was commonly so applied to the Messianic times by the Jews of the Middle Age (*Bereschith rabba*, 88).

[3] Chaps. xxxviii. and xxxix.

and building up a new theology by a certain sport of self-will, — we find in the attempt to solve, by means of the Apocalypse, the mystery of the last days. The theory of the Apocalypse, thus regarded, is essentially different from anything we find in Paul, or in what the Synoptics report to us from the lips of Jesus. Paul seems, at times,[1] to believe in a temporary reign of Christ, which will take place before the Last Day; but he never expresses himself with the precision we find here. In the view of the Apocalypse, the coming reign of Christ is near at hand; it will follow close upon the downfall of the Roman Empire. The martyrs alone will come to life for this first resurrection; the other dead will rise not yet. Such distorted views follow from the slow and incoherent way in which Israel formed its conceptions of the other life. We may say that the Jews were never led to the doctrine of a future life, except by the need of such a doctrine to reconcile them to the fact of martyrdom. In Second Maccabees, the seven young martyrs and their mother are strong through the faith that they will rise again, while Antiochus will never rise.[2] The first clear affirmations of an eternal life[3] in Jewish literature are made in reference to these legendary heroes of the national faith: we find, in particular, this fine expression, "They who die for God's sake live in God."[4] We see, too, the dawning of a belief in some special destiny for them beyond the grave; that "they *now* stand near the throne of God, and live a blessed life,"[5] not awaiting

---

[1] As in 1 Cor. xv. 24–28.
[2] 2 Macc. vii. 9, 11, 14, 23, 36; vi. 26.
[3] *Ibid.* vii. 36; Wisd. ii.–v.; esp. iii. 2–5; *De rat. imp.* 9, 16, 18, 20.
[4] *De rat. imp.* 16.   [5] *Ibid.* 18.

resurrection. Tacitus, on his part, remarks that the Jews impute immortality only to those who have died in battle or in torment.[1]

The reign of Christ with his martyrs will doubtless come to pass on the earth, at Jerusalem, amidst the unconverted nations, which hold the saints in veneration. This reign will last for only a thousand years, and is distinct from that which will follow the final Judgment. This conception of the Messianic reign as anterior to that event is found in the apocalypse of Esdras (about 97). After the thousand years, there will be a new reign of Satan, in which the barbarous tribes, still unconverted, will make horrible wars upon one another, and will be on the point of crushing the Church itself; but God will destroy them, and then will come "the second resurrection," — this time general, — and the final Judgment, which will be followed by the end of all things. This is the doctrine called "Millenarian," which was widely diffused in the first three centuries.[2] It never succeeded in becoming dominant in the Church, but has constantly reappeared at critical periods, resting on texts far older and more precise than can be claimed for some other doctrines everywhere accepted. It was the result of a too literal interpretation, controlled by the twofold need of finding those phrases true which describe the kingdom of God as destined to last forever; and, at the same time, holding to those which denote a Messianic reign of indefinite duration, by saying that it will last "a thousand years." Following a rule of explanation called *harmonistic*, the

---

[1] Tac. *Hist.* v. 5.
[2] Cerinthus in Euseb. iii. 28; Papias, id. iii. 39; Justin, *Trypho*, 80, 81; Iren. in Euseb. iii. 39; Tert. *Contra Marc.* iii. 24; Lact. *Inst.* vii. 20.

millenarians mechanically pieced together, end to end, data which could not possibly be made to agree. They were guided in their choice of the numeral "thousand," by combining passages in the Psalms which seem to say that a day with God is equal to a thousand years.[1] Among the Jews is also found the notion that the reign of the Messiah will not be an eternity of blessedness, but an era of felicity *preceding* the end of the world. Many rabbis, like the writer of the Apocalypse, extend the duration of this reign to a thousand years.[2] The writer of the epistle ascribed to Barnabas asserts that, as the Creation occupied six days, so the destiny of the world will be fulfilled in six thousand years (one day with God being equal to a thousand years); and that then, as God rested the seventh day, so, too, "when his Son shall come and abolish the time of iniquity, and shall judge the ungodly, and shall change the sun and moon and all the stars, he will rest again the seventh day," — that is, he will reign a thousand years; since the reign of the Messiah is always compared to a Sabbath, which by its repose will put an end to the incessant turmoil found in the evolution of all things. So Commodian and Hippolytus fix the duration of the world at six thousand years. The idea of endless life to the individual is so foreign from Jewish thought that the era of future retribution is expressed by a number of years always limited, though doubtless of great extent.

The Persian aspect of these dreams is obvious at

---

[1] Ps. xc. 4, comp. with lxxxiv. 11. Comp. Epist. of Barnabas, xv.; 2 Pet. iii. 8; Justin, *Tryph.*, 81; Iren. v. 23: 2.

[2] *Pesikta rabbathi*, § 1; *Jalkut* on the Psalms, 806; Ammonius in Mai, *Script. vet. nova coll.* i. 2, p. 207. According to the Apocalypse of Esdras, vii. 26, 27, the Messiah's reign will last 400 years.

a glance.¹ Millenarianism, and, if we may so call it, Apocalyptism, flourished in Irania from a very ancient date.² At the bottom of the Zoroastrian ideas is a tendency to put in figures the ages of the world, reckoning the periods of universal life by *hazars*, — that is, thousands of years, — and imagining a reign of salvation, which will crown at last the trials of humanity.³ These ideas combined with assertions regarding the future which abound in the old Hebrew prophets, became the soul of Jewish theology in the centuries before our era. Apocalyptic writings, especially, are full of them. The revelations passing under the names of Daniel, Enoch, and Moses, are almost Persian in style, doctrine, and imagery. Does this imply that the writers of these strange books had read the Zendic writings as these existed in their time? Not at all. The transmission of such ideas was indirect, resulting from the hue caught by Jewish fancy from the colouring of Iranian thought. So with the Apocalypse of John. The writer of that book had no direct relations with Persia, more than any other Christian. The exotic matters which he carried into his book were already embodied in the traditional *midrashim* ;⁴ and this Seer imbibed them from the atmosphere in which he lived. In fact, all the features which appear on the apoca-

---

[1] Similar ideas are found among the Etruscans, and no doubt made the groundwork of the old Sibylline books, so that a natural connection is found between the Italic Sibylline verse and the Jewish apocalyptic ideas (as in the fourth Eclogue of Virgil).

[2] See the *Ardai Viraf-Nameh*, a sort of apocalypse, which is not, as has been supposed, an imitation of the "Ascension of Isaiah." Comp. *Sitzungsberichte* of the Academy of Munich, 1870, i. 3.

[3] *Zeitschr. der d. m. G.* 1867, 571, 572; Theopompus in the treatise *De Iside et Osir.*, 47.

[4] *Zeitschrift*, as above pp. 552, 553.

lyptic stage are to be found in the Parsee theory of the latter days—from Hoshedar and Hoshedar-mah, the two prophets who preceded Sosiosh [the Zoroastrian Messiah], down to the plagues which will afflict the world at the eve of the Great Day, and the wars of the kings together, which will be the symptoms of the final conflict.[1] The seven heavens, also the seven angels, seven spirits of God, recurring incessantly in the visions of Patmos, carry us fully over to Parsism, and even beyond. The hieratic and astrological sense of the number seven seems, indeed, to have originated in the Babylonian doctrine of the seven planets[2] regulating the destiny of men and empires. Similarities still more striking may be found in the mystery of the seven seals.[3] Just as in the Assyrian mythology each of the seven tables of destiny[4] was dedicated to one of the planets, so the seven seals are curiously related to the seven planets, the days of the week, and the colours which Babylonian science connected with the planets. Thus, the white horse seems to represent the Moon; the red, Mars; the black (dark-blue), Mercury; the pale (or yellow), Jupiter.[5]

The defects of this method are obvious, and it would be vain to try to hide them. Colours hard and fixed,

---

[1] *De Iside*, etc., *l. c.*; Spiegel, *Parsigrammatik*, 194; *Zeitsch.*, etc., 1867, 573, 575–577.

[2] These, in the view of astrology, are all the heavenly bodies which change their position among the fixed stars; that is, the sun, the moon, and the five visible planets.

[3] Rev. i. 16; xii. 1.

[4] Nonnus, xli. 340, 341; xii. 31, 32; comp. J. Brandis: *Die Bedeutung der sieben Thore Thebens* (Berlin, 1867), 267, 268.

[5] On the various colours as related to the planets, see Chwolsohn, *Die Ssabier*, iii. 658, 671, 676, 677. Comp. the supplementary Turkish MS. in the *Bibliothèque Nationale*, 242.

a complete lack of flexibility, the sacrifice of harmony to symbolism,—something raw, dry, and lifeless put the Apocalypse in direct contrast with Greek art, whose type is the living beauty of the human form. A certain materialism deadens the writer's most ideal conceptions. He heaps on gold; he has the extravagant oriental taste for precious stones. His heavenly Jerusalem is clumsy, childish, impossible, violating all good rules of architecture, which are the rules of good sense. He makes it brilliant to the eye, but has no thought of having it wrought by the artist-hand of a Phidias. To him, in like manner, God is a "vision of emerald," a sort of prodigious diamond, glittering in a thousand flashes, upon a throne.[1] Surely, the Olympian Zeus was a far nobler image. The bad taste which has often debased Christian art to mere gaudiness of decoration has its germ in the Apocalypse. A Jesuit chapel, adorned with gilding and *lapis-lazuli*, is far finer than the Parthenon, as soon as we admit the idea that God is honoured by the consecrated use of rich materials.

A more painful feature is the sullen hatred of the pagan world, common to the Apocalypse and all apocalyptic writings, in particular the book of Enoch. We are shocked by the harshness, the passionate and unjust attacks upon Roman society, which in a measure justify those who, like Tacitus, sum up the new religion in the phrase, "hatred of mankind."[2] The virtuous poor are always under some temptation to regard the world, of which they know little, as wickeder than it really is. The crimes of rich men and courtiers are magnified in their eyes. Jews of the prophetic and apocalyptic

[1] Rev. iv. 3. [2] Tac. *Ann.* xv. 44.

school carried to violent excess that virtuous rage against civilized luxury, which the Vandals displayed four hundred years later. We find among them a remnant of the old nomadic temper, whose ideal is patriarchal life, deep aversion to great cities, which it regards as centres of corruption, heated jealousy against powerful States established on a military foundation, which is either beyond its attainment or hateful in its sight.

These qualities have made the Apocalypse, in many regards, a dangerous book. Above all others, it is the intense expression of Jewish pride. In its writer's view, the distinction of Jew and gentile will be carried over into the kingdom of God. While the twelve tribes eat the fruits of the tree of life, the gentiles must content themselves with a medicinal decoction of its leaves.[1] The writer regards the gentiles — even believers in Jesus, even martyrs for Jesus — as adopted sons, as strangers introduced into the family of Israel, as plebeians permitted as a favour to claim a place near the aristocracy.[2] His Messiah is essentially the Jewish Messiah; Jesus is, as his highest distinction, a son of David,[3] a product of the Israelitish church, a member of the holy family which God has chosen. The church of Israel has really wrought the work of salvation by this elected one of its own children.[4] Any practice that may possibly bring about a connection between the pure race and the pagans — such as eating the usual food or celebrating marriage under the usual conditions — seems to him an abomination. Pagans in

---

[1] Rev. xxii. 2; "for the healing of the nations" is a touch of irony.
[2] *Ibid.* vii. 9; xiv. 3.   [3] *Ibid.* v. 5.
[4] *Ibid.* ii. 9; iii. 9; xi. 19; xix. 1–3; comp. xii., xiii., xxi. 42.

the mass are in his eyes wretched creatures, stained with every crime, to be controlled only by terror. The real world is the realm of devils. Disciples of Paul are disciples of Balaam and Jezebel. Paul himself has no place among "the twelve apostles of the Lamb," who are the only foundation of the true Church; and the church at Ephesus, Paul's own creation, is praised "for having tried those who call themselves apostles and are not, and having found them to be only liars."

All this is very far from the gospel of Jesus. The writer is too passionate. He sees everything, as it were, through bloodshot eyes, or in the glare of a conflagration. The most dreadful thing in Paris, on the twenty-fifth of May, 1871, was not the flames; it was the general colour cast upon the city when seen from an elevated point, — a yellowish false tone, a sort of ghastly pallor. That is the light that rests on the visions of the Apocalypse, — the least possible like the clear sunlight of Galilee. From this time forth we see that the apocalyptic style will not be, any more than the style of the epistles, the literary form that will convert the world. This will rather be those brief collections of precepts and parables, scorned by seekers of exact tradition, — it will be those notes and hints in which the most ignorant and the least informed store by for their own use what they know of the words and acts of Jesus,[1] — that make for each coming generation its gospel and its charm. The simple outline of the anecdotic life of Jesus was clearly worth far more for the delight of the world, than the symbolic piling-up of visions, or the touching admonitions of apostolic letters. So true it is that, in the mysterious process of Christian

---

[1] See Papias in Eusebius (iii. 39).

growth, Jesus, and he alone, has always held the great, triumphant, decisive part. Every Christian book or institution has value in proportion to what it holds of him. The Synoptic Gospels, in which he is all,—which we may say were in a sense written by himself,—will be above all else the Christian, the enduring, book.[1]

Still, the place held by the Apocalypse in the Christian canon is one to which it is well entitled. A book of threats and terror, it gave body and form to the sombre antithesis set up over against Jesus by the Christian conscience when profoundly and passionately stirred. If the Gospel is the book of Jesus, the Apocalypse is the book of Nero. It is due to this that Nero has in Christian history a certain importance as a second founder. His hateful face has been inseparable from that of Jesus. Growing vaster from age to age, the monster born of the nightmare of the year 64 became the terror of the Christian conscience, the baleful spectre haunting the darkness of the world.[2] A folio of five hundred and fifty pages was composed[3] on his birth, education, vices, and wealth,—on his jewels, perfumes, and women,—on his doctrines, miracles, and banquets.

The Antichrist is no longer a terror to us, and Malvenda's book is read by few. We know that the end of the world is not so near as the enlightened of the first century supposed, and that the end, when it

---

[1] The composition of the Gospels will be the special topic of the succeeding volume.

[2] Even to-day, in Armenian, the name of Antichrist is *Neren* (see the great dictionary of the Armenian Academy of St. Lazare at the word *Neren*).

[3] Th. Malvenda, *De Antichristo, libri undecim:* Rome, 1604.

comes, will not be a sudden catastrophe. It will come to pass by increasing cold, when in the course of a thousand centuries our system can no longer make good its losses; when the earth has exhausted the treasures of the sun's heat stored by in its depths, as the provision for its journey. Before the planetary capital is thus spent, will mankind have attained perfect science — which is nothing else than power to master the forces of the world? or else, will the earth — one more abortive experiment among so many million others — be frozen before the problem how to overcome death has been solved? We know not. But, with the Seer of Patmos, we discern the ideal beyond these shifting alternations, and we assert that that ideal will at length be realised. Through the mist of an embryonic universe we perceive the laws of progress and life. We witness the unceasing expansion of human thought; and we anticipate a condition when all shall be enfolded in one Absolute Existence (God) as numberless buds are contained in the tree, or as myriads of cells are included in a single organism. Then the life of all will be complete. Then each individual being that has lived will live again in God, will see and rejoice with Him, with Him will sing an eternal song of praise. Under whatever form each of us may conceive this future advent of the Absolute, the Apocalypse cannot fail to give us pleasure. It sets forth in symbol the fundamental thought that GOD IS, but, above all, that He WILL BE. The drawing is heavy, the outline inadequate and mean; it is but the hand of a child that traces with a rude pencil, or shapes, with a tool he does not know how to handle, the design of a city he has never seen. His childish picture of the City of

God, a big plaything of gold and pearls, nevertheless continues with us a part of the substance of our dreams. Paul spoke a truer word, no doubt, when he summed up the final destiny of creation in the phrase, "that God may be all in all."[1] But for a long time to come, humanity will crave a God "whose tabernacle is with men,"[2] who has compassion on their trials, keeps a reckoning of their conflicts, and at length "shall wipe away all tears from their eyes."

---

[1] Πάντα ἐν πᾶσιν: 1 Cor. xv. 28.
[2] Καὶ σκηνώσει μετ' αὐτῶν: Rev. xxi. 3.

CHAPTER XVIII.

ACCESSION OF THE FLAVII. — A. D. 69, 70.

THE aspect of the world, as I have already said, answered but too well to the visions of the Seer of Patmos. The rule of military adventurers was bearing its fruit. The camps were full of politics; the Empire was for sale to the highest bidder. In Nero's day, there were assemblies where one might see together seven future emperors and the father of an eighth.[1] Verginius, the true republican, who wished the sovereignty to be with Senate and people, was a mere dreamer.[2] Galba, an honest old general, who refused to be a party to the military revel, soon perished. The soldiers had for a moment the idea of killing all the senators, to simplify the task of government.[3] The unity of Rome seemed to be on the point of breaking up. The Christians were not the only ones to whom so tragic a situation suggested prophecies of evil. Report said that a child was born at Syracuse with three heads; and in this was seen a symbol of the three emperors who rose to power within a year, and for a few hours reigned all three together.

A few days after the prophet of Asia completed his

---

[1] Galba, Otho, Vitellius, Vespasian, Titus, Domitian, Nerva, and the father of Trajan.

[2] Dion Cass. lxiii. 25.

[3] Tac. *Hist.* i. 80; Suet. *Otho*, 8; Dion Cass. lxiv. 9.

strange work, Galba was killed, and Otho was proclaimed (Jan. 15, 69). This was like Nero come again to life: while Galba — grave, frugal, and austere — was at all points the opposite of his predecessor.[1] If he had succeeded in securing his adoption of Piso, he would have been a sort of Nerva, and the series of emperor-philosophers would have begun thirty years before it did; but the detestable school of Nero carried the day. Otho was like that monster; the soldiers, and all who had loved Nero, found their idol in him. They had seen him beside the dead emperor, playing the part of first court favourite, rivalling him in his affectation of sumptuous feasts, his vices, and his mad prodigality. The lower people gave him the name of Nero from the first, and he seems to have assumed it in some of his letters. At all events, he permitted the erection of statues to the Beast; he put back the favourites of Nero in high places, and loudly announced that he should continue the practices of that former reign. The first act he signed was for the completion of the Golden House.[2]

Worst of all, the political degradation now reached gave no security. The worthless Vitellius had been proclaimed in Germany a few days before Otho (Jan. 2, 69), and did not withdraw his claim. A horrible civil war, such as there had not been since that between Augustus and Antony, seemed inevitable. The popular imagination was inflamed; frightful prognostics were seen;[3] crimes committed by the soldiery spread terror

---

[1] Suet. *Galba*, 12–15.

[2] Tac. *Hist.* i. 13, 78; Suet. *Otho*, 7; Dion Cass. lxxiv. 8; Plutarch, *Galba*, 19; *Otho*, 3.

[3] Tac. *Hist.* i. 86, 90; Suet. *Otho*, 7, 8, 11; Dion Cass. lxiv. 7, 10; Plut. *Galba*, 23; *Otho*, 4.

everywhere. Never had such a year been known; the world reeked with blood. The first battle of Bedriacum, which left the empire to Vitellius alone, cost the lives of 80,000 men.[1] Disbanded legionaries pillaged the country, and fought among themselves.[2] The populace mingled in the quarrel; it seemed the overthrow of society itself. At the same time astrologers and all manner of charlatans swarmed, taking complete possession of the city.[3] Reason seemed drowned in a deluge of crime and madness, defying all control. Certain words of Jesus,[4] repeated in secret among the Christians, kept them in a sort of constant fever. Above all, the fate of Jerusalem was an object with them of extreme anxiety and concern.

The East, indeed, was no less troubled than the West. Ever since June of the preceding year, as we have seen, the military operations of the Romans against Jerusalem were suspended; yet anarchy and fanaticism were no less furious among the Jews. The violence of John of Gischala and the Zealots was at its height.[5] The authority of John rested chiefly on a body of Galilæans, who committed every conceivable excess. At last the population of the city rose, and forced John, with his assassins, to take refuge in the Temple; but the dread of him was such that a rival leader was set up for defence against him. Simon, son of Gioras, a native of Gerasa, who had distinguished himself since the beginning of the war, filled Idumæa with his robberies. He had already had to contend

[1] Dion Cass. lxiv. 10.
[2] Tac. *Hist.* ii. 66-68; comp. *Agric.* 7.
[3] Dion Cass. lxv. 1; Tac. *Hist.* ii. 62; Suet. *Vitell.* 14; Zonaras, vi. 5.
[4] Matt. xxiv. 6, 7: "Ye shall hear of wars and rumours of wars," etc.
[5] Josephus, *Wars*, vii. 8: 1.

against the Zealots, and twice he had threatened the gates of Jerusalem. He was now about to make a third attempt, when the people summoned him, in the hope of protecting themselves against a violent return of John. This new master entered the city in March, 69, John remaining in possession of the Temple. The two leaders rivalled each other in ferocity. The Jew is a cruel master. Of the same blood with the Carthaginians, he would show himself, at a crisis, to be of the same nature. This people has always had a noble minority: there is its glory. But never, in any human society, has there been seen such jealousy, such thirst for mutual extermination. At a certain stage of fury the Jew is capable of anything, even against his own religion. The history of Israel shows us a people of men maddened against one another.[1] Say what good or what evil you will of this race, it is all true. For, I repeat, while a good Jew may be the best of men, a bad Jew is certainly the worst; and this is especially true of Jews in the East. This may explain the possibility of a fact which might seem incredible,—that the gospel idyll and the horrors recounted by Josephus were realities on the same land, in the same people, at nearly the same time.

Vespasian all this while remained inactive at Cæsarea. His son Titus had succeeded in involving him in a tangle of intrigues, skilfully contrived. Under Galba, Titus had hoped to find himself adopted by the aged emperor. After Galba's death, he saw that he could arrive at supreme power only as his father's successor. With consummate political adroitness, he succeeded in turning all chances in favour of a sober-minded, upright

---

[1] See, for example, Josephus, *Wars*, vii. 11; *Life*, 76.

general, without brilliant parts, without personal ambition, who did almost nothing for his own private advantage. All the East gave help. Mucian and the Syrian legions chafed with impatience to see the Western legions alone disposing of imperial power, and aspired to make an emperor in their turn. Mucian, a sort of sceptic, more desirous to dispense power than to wield it, did not wish the purple for himself. Spite of his advanced age, his plain birth, his second-rate intelligence, Vespasian thus found himself the coming man. Titus, at the age of twenty-eight, by his talent, activity, and address, put into relief whatever modest ability his father had. After Otho's death, the Eastern legions took the oath to Vitellius very grudgingly. They were disgusted by the insolence of the troops from Germany. They had been made to believe that Vitellius meant to send his favourite legions into Syria, and transfer those of Syria to the Rhine, — loved as they were in their own province, and attached to it by many ties.

And then Nero, though dead, still held a controlling power in the course of events. The fable of his resurrection had some real truth of fact: his party yet survived him. After Otho, Vitellius, to the delight of the lower orders, posed as an open admirer, an imitator, an avenger of Nero. He urged that, in his judgment, Nero had given a model of good government to the Republic. He paid him the honour of a splendid funeral, ordered his musical compositions to be performed, and when the first note was heard, rose enthusiastically from his seat to give the signal for applause.[1]

---

[1] Tac. *Hist.* ii. 71, 95; Suet. *Vitell.* 11; Dion Cass. lxv. 4, 7. If we could allow later touches in the Apocalypse, we might suppose that verses

Men of sense and character, tired of these wretched parodies of an abhorred reign, desired a strong reaction against Nero, his favourites, and his style of building. They demanded, first of all, reversal of sentence against the noble victims of that tyranny. It was known that the Flavian house would scrupulously perform this duty. Finally, the native Syrian princes declared strongly for a chief in whom they saw a defender against the fanaticism of the revolted Jews. Agrippa and his sister Berenice were heart and soul with the two Roman generals. Berenice, though forty years of age, gained an influence over Titus by blandishments against which a young man could not well be on guard who was at once ambitious, active, a stranger to the world, and wholly occupied with his own advancement; while the elderly Vespasian was completely won by her flatteries and her gifts. These two rude captains, till now poor, plain men, were not proof against the aristocratic charm of a woman admirably beautiful (if we may judge from busts in Naples and in Florence [1]), or the outside glitter of a world they knew nothing of. The passion which Titus conceived for Berenice did no harm to his interests; everything shows, on the contrary, that this woman, trained in oriental intrigue, was one of his most useful agents. Through her influence the petty kings of Emesa, Sophene, and Commagene — all of them kindred or allies of the Herods, and more or less converted to the Jewish faith [2] — were

---

12 and 13 of chapter xvii. — that "they shall give their power to the Beast," etc. — refer to these efforts to revive the memory of Nero. I have made many attempts to find Otho in the Second Beast or False Prophet. The verses xiii. 12, 16, 17 would well conform to such a theory; but verses 13-15 [the acts of sorcery or magic] stand in the way.

[1] That numbered 312 in the *Uffizi*.   [2] Jos. *Antiq.* xix, 9: 1.

gained over to the plot.¹ The apostate Jew, Tiberius Alexander, prefect of Egypt, was fully committed to it;² and even the Parthians professed themselves ready to support it.³

The most surprising thing is that the moderate Jews, like Josephus, also came into it, and insisted on ascribing to the Roman commander their own special views. We have seen that the Jewish group about Nero had succceded in persuading him that, if dethroned at Rome, he would find a new kingdom in Jerusalem, which would make him the greatest sovereign on earth.⁴ Josephus asserts that, from the moment when he was made prisoner by the Romans in 67, he foretold to Vespasian the future awaiting him,⁵ as proved by certain texts of the Jewish scriptures. By reiteration of their prophecies the Jews had made many, even of those not belonging to their sect, believe that the East would gain the day; and that the master of the world would soon come from Judæa.⁶ Virgil had soothed the vague sadness of his pensive fancy by applying to his own time a "Cumæan song," seeming to have some relation to the second Isaiah.⁷ Magi, Chaldæans, and astrologers also availed themselves of the belief of a "star in the East," heralding a king of the Jews, and Christians gave serious heed to these

---

[1] Tac. *Hist.* ii. 2, 81; Suet. *Titus*, 7; Josephus, *Wars*, xii. 7: 1–3.

[2] *Mém. of the Acad. of Inscr.* xxvi. 294 *et seq.*; "The Apostles," chap. xiv.; "Saint Paul," chap. v.

[3] Tac. *Hist.* ii. 82; iv. 51.

[4] Suet. *Nero*, 40.

[5] Jos. *Wars*, iii. 8: 3, 9; iv. 10: 7; Suet. *Vesp.* 5; Dion Cass. lxvi. 1; Appian in Zonaras, xi. 15 (note the comment); comp. Tac. *Hist.* i. 10; ii. 1, 73, 74, 78; Suet. *Vesp.* 5; Jos. *Wars*, iii. 8: 3.

[6] Jos. *Wars*, vi. 5: 4; Suet. *Vesp.* 4; Tac. *Hist.* v. 13.

[7] Virgil, *Ecl.* iv.; Suet. *Aug.* 94; Servius on *Æn.* vi. 799.

fancies.[1] The prophecy had a double meaning, like all oracles.[2] It might appear sufficiently verified if the chief of the Syrian legions, posted a few leagues from Jerusalem, should attain the empire in Syria, by aid of a movement there begun.[3] Vespasian and Titus, in the midst of Jews, listened readily to such words, and took pleasure in them. While displaying their military talent against the fanatics at Jerusalem, they had a strong attraction toward Judaism, studied it, and paid deference to the Jewish books.[4] Josephus had found his way into their companionship, especially that of Titus, through his soft, easy, and insinuating temper.[5] He boasted before them of his Law, told them the old Scripture stories, which he often set forth in Greek style, and spoke mysteriously of the prophecies. Other Jews entered into the same views,[6] and induced Vespasian to accept a sort of messianic character. To this were added miracles, and works of healing were reported, much like those told by the evangelists, brought to pass by this novel Messiah.[7]

The pagan priests of Phœnicia would not be behindhand in this rivalry of adulation. The oracles of

---

[1] Matt. ii. 1, 2; comp. Num. xxiv. 17.

[2] Comp. Jos. *l. c.* and *Wars*, iii. 8: 3; also Tacitus. Josephus seems chiefly to have had in view Dan. ix. 25-27. What proves that he made no serious account of the prediction is that we find it only in his "Wars," written under Vespasian, while he omits it in the "Life," written in 94, when his two patrons were dead, and the fall of Domitian could be easily foreseen.

[3] Jos. *Wars*, vi. 5: 4.

[4] Jos. *Life*, 65, 75.

[5] Jos. *Wars*, iii. 8: 8, 9; *Life*, 75.

[6] Bab. Talm. *Gittin*, 56 *a, b*; *Aboth derabbi Nathan*, iv., at the end (comp. Midrash *Eka*, i. 5), a tale of Johanan ben Zakia, quite parallel with that of Josephus, and perhaps an echo of it.

[7] Tac. *Hist.* iv. 81, 82; Suet. *Vesp.* 7; Dion Cass. lxvi. 8.

Paphos and of Carmel[1] claimed to have announced beforehand the fortunes of the Flavii. The results of all this were presently seen. Coming to power by the support of Syria, the Flavian emperors were far more open to Syrian ideas than the disdainful Cæsars had ever been. Christianity, as we shall see, found its way to the very heart of this imperial house, reckoned its adepts there, and by its help entered upon a wholly new period in its destinies.

Toward the end of springtime in 69, Vespasian seemed disposed to abandon the military inactivity in which he was held by his political schemes. On the 29th of April he marched forward, and soon appeared before Jerusalem. Meanwhile Cerealis, one of his lieutenants, set fire to Hebron, and all Judæa submitted to the Romans except Jerusalem and the three fortresses of Masada, Herodium, and Machærus, which were held by the Assassins. These four must be subdued by obstinate siege. Vespasian and Titus hesitated to make the attempt in the present precarious situation, when a new civil war was impending in which they might need all their strength. Thus for a whole year longer continued a state of revolution, which for three years had already held Jerusalem in the most extraordinary state of crisis anywhere recorded in history.[2]

On the first of July, Tiberius Alexander proclaimed Vespasian at Alexandria, and caused the oath to him to be taken. On the third, the army of Judæa saluted him emperor at Cæsarea. Mucian, at Antioch, caused him to be recognised by the legions of Syria; and by

---

[1] Tac. *Hist.* ii. 2-4, 78; Suet. *Vesp.* 5; *Tit.* 5; comp. Scylax, 104; Jamblichus, *De Pythag. vita*, 14, 15.

[2] Tac. *Hist.* v. 10.

the fifteenth all the East was obedient to him. A congress was held at Beyrout, where it was decided that Mucian should march upon Italy, while Titus should conduct the war against the Jews; and that Vespasian should wait the issue of events at Alexandria. After a bloody civil war — the third within eighteen months — power remained firmly established with the Flavian house. A citizen-dynasty, diligent in business, moderate of temper, without the energy of the Cæsars, but clear of their extravagances, took the place of the heirs of the title created by Augustus. Those spendthrifts and madmen had so abused their privilege as spoiled children that Rome gladly welcomed the accession of a good honest man, of undistinguished rank, who had laboriously made his way by his own merit, — in spite of his little awkwardnesses, his vulgar looks, and his want of manners. For ten years, as it proved, the new dynasty conducted affairs with sense and judgment. It kept the Empire whole, and completely belied the predictions of both Jew and Christian, who were now looking in their dreams to see the empire broken up and Rome destroyed. The burning of the Capitol on the 19th of December, the dreadful massacre in Rome the next day,[1] might for the moment make them think that the Great Day had come. But the undisputed possession held by Vespasian, after the 20th, taught them that they must resign themselves to live yet longer, and forced them to make shift to put off their hopes to a remoter future.[2]

---

[1] Tac. *Hist.* iii. 83; Dion Cass. lxv. 19; Jos. *Wars*, iv. 11 : 4.

[2] Josephus admits that the fate of the Empire had seemed desperate, and that the secure seat of Vespasian saved the Roman State against all hope (*Wars*, iv. 11 : 5).

The prudent Vespasian, far less disturbed than those who fought to conquer the empire for him, passed the time in Alexandria with Tiberius Alexander, and did not return to Rome till towards July, a little before the fall of Jerusalem. Titus, instead of pushing the war in Judæa, had followed his father into Egypt, where he remained with him till near the first of March.

The conflicts in Jerusalem, meanwhile, became only the more obstinate and bitter. The actions of fanatics are far from excluding mutual hate, jealousy, and distrust from among those who take part in them. Men of strong convictions and strong passions, when leagued together, watch one another with suspicion, and find their strength in it; for mutual suspicion creates mutual dread, binds them as by an iron band, prevents desertion, and braces them against moments of weakness. Artificial politics, on the other hand, without conviction, may go on with the appearance of harmony and the forms of good-will. Interest creates the party or clique. Principles create division, and kindle men to decimate, expel, or kill their opponents. Those who judge of human affairs from the shopkeeper's point of view think it is all over with a revolution when the revolutionists begin (as the saying is) to devour one another. But, on the contrary, this is a proof that the revolution is in the full tide of energy, that its heat has no respect of persons. This was never more plainly seen than during that frightful tragedy of Jerusalem. The actors in it seemed to have made a death-pledge amongst themselves. As in those infernal rounds where (as the Middle Age believed) Satan was seen forming the chain to drag into a dreadful gulf files of men dancing and holding each other by the hand, so a revolution suffers no one to escape from the mad dance which it excites. Terror drives the actors on. In turn exciting and excited, they reel towards the abyss. No one can draw back, for behind each man is a hidden sword which, at the moment when he would stop, forces him to advance.

Simon, son of Gioras, was commandant in the city, while John of Gischala, with his assassins, was master of the Temple. The power of Simon seems to have been the more regular: we have coins of his, but apparently none from John. Simon, too, was recognised by the Romans as the real chief, and alone was executed by them.[1] A third party was formed under the lead of Eleazar, son of Simon, of priestly race, who drew off a party of Zealots from John, and established himself in the inner court of the Temple, where he lived on the consecrated provisions he found, and on those which were constantly brought in as first-fruits to the priests. These three parties[2] made continual war on one another. Their march was over heaps of corpses, for the dead were no longer buried. A vast store of wheat had been laid by, and this might have prolonged the struggle for years; but John and Simon burned it, each that he might starve out the other.[3] The condition of the city was frightful. Peace-loving people besought that order might be restored by the Romans; but all ways of escape were blocked by the terrorists, and no man could fly. Meanwhile, it was strange to

---

[1] Dion Cass. lxvi. 7. For the above points, see p. 224, note 1 (above), and Madden, 166, 167. Tacitus (*Hist.* v. 12) puts the two on the same footing.

[2] Tac. *Hist.* v. 12.

[3] Jos. *Wars*, v. 1:4; Tac. *Hist.* v. 12; Midrash rabba on Eccles. vii. 11; Bab. Talm. *Gittin*, 56 a; Midr. Rabba on *Eka*, i. 5.

see how they still came to the Temple from the ends of the earth. John and Eleazer welcomed the proselytes, and profited by their gifts. The pious pilgrims were often killed by bolts and stones from John's engines, in the midst of their sacrificial rites, with the priests who recited the service for them. The revolutionists were actively busied beyond the Euphrates to secure aid, whether from the Jews dwelling there, or from the king of Parthia. They had imagined that all the Jews of the East would take up arms. The civil wars in Italy inspired them with wild hopes: they fancied that the Empire was just about to break in pieces. In vain did Jesus, son of Hanan, roam through the city calling on the four winds of heaven to destroy it. Up to the eve of their extermination, the fanatics proclaimed Jerusalem as the capital of the world; exactly as we have in our day seen Paris, besieged and famished, still maintaining that the world was in her, toiled for her, suffered with her.

And, what is strangest of all, they were not wholly wrong. Those madmen at Jerusalem, who insisted that the holy city was eternal when it was already in flames, were far nearer the truth than those who saw none but assassins among them. They were mistaken as to the military situation then, but not as to the religious result thereafter. These disastrous days, in fact, clearly mark the point of time when Jerusalem became the spiritual centre of the world. The Apocalypse, that told in words of fire the love which she kindled, has taken a place among the inspired writings of the world, and has enshrined in them the image of "the beloved city." How hard it is to say beforehand who will be hereafter held as saint or scoundrel, as madman or as sage! A sudden change in the log-book shows that the ship is falling behind and not advancing, that she is struggling against head-winds, not borne on by a favouring breeze. When revolutions, with thunderings and earthquakes, are before our eyes, let us rank ourselves among the blessed ones who are ever singing, "Praise the Lord!" or, with the four Living Creatures, spirits of the Universe, who, after each act of the celestial tragedy, respond AMEN!

CHAPTER XIX.

THE FALL OF JERUSALEM. — A. D. 70.

AT length the iron circle closed about the doomed city, never to relax. As soon as the season allowed, Titus set out from Alexandria, reached Cæsarea, and thence advanced upon Jerusalem at the head of a formidable army. He took with him four legions, — the fifth, *Macedonica*, the tenth, *Fretensis*, the twelfth, *Fulminata*, and the fifteenth, *Apollinaris*, — besides many auxiliaries furnished by his Syrian allies, and troops of Arabs who came to pillage;[1] and he was accompanied by all the Jews, who had joined him, — Agrippa,[2] Tiberius Alexander, now prefect of the prætorium,[3] and Josephus the future historian. Berenice, no doubt, stayed behind at Cæsarea. The soldierly conduct of the commander matched well the strength of the army. Titus was a man of military talent, above all an excellent officer of high merit, a man of strong good sense, a deep politician, and of fairly humane temper, considering the cruelty of the time. Vespasian had enjoined on him great severity, angered as he was at the gratification the

---

[1] Tac. *Hist.* v. 1; comp. the curious Midrash on *Eka*, i. 5 (Derenbourg, 291).

[2] Tacitus records Agrippa as present at the siege; Josephus strangely gives him no part in any incident. Agrippa's letter (Jos. *Life*, 65) seems to assume his presence at these events; but possibly he requested the historian to blot out anything that might make him hateful to his co-religionists.

[3] See *Mém de l'Acad. des Inscr.* xxvi. 1, 299, 300.

Jews took in the outbreak of civil wars, and at the efforts they made to bring on a Parthian invasion.[1] Gentleness, as he regarded it, was always taken to be a mark of weakness among these haughty races, convinced that they fought for God with God on their side.

The Roman army reached Gabaath Saul,[2] some five miles from Jerusalem, early in April. It was a little before the Passover, and a vast number of Jews from all countries were gathered in the city.[3] Josephus puts the number of those who perished in the siege at 1,100,000.[4] All the nation seemed to have met there by appointment for extermination. About the tenth, Titus fixed his camp at the corner of the tower Psephina (*Kasr-Jaloud*). Some petty advantages gained by a surprise, and a severe wound received by Titus, gave the Jews excessive confidence in their strength, and taught the Romans how carefully they should keep guard in this war with maniacs.

The city might be reckoned one of the strongest in the world.[5] The walls were a perfect type of that structure in enormous blocks of stone which has always prevailed in Syria.[6] Within, the Temple-enclosure,

---

[1] Jos. *Wars*, vi. 6: 2.

[2] *Tuleil el Foul* (?), Robinson, i. 577 *et seq.*

[3] A circumstance like that told of Lydda (Jos. *Wars*, ii. 19: 1) shows how prodigious were the gatherings at these feasts: cf. ii. 14: 3.

[4] Jos. *Wars*, vi. 9: 3; comp. v. 13: 7. The number is greatly exaggerated. Tacitus speaks of the besieged as 600,000 (*Hist.* v. 13; Oros. vii. 9; Malala, p. 260). The circuit of the walls, further reduced by the capture of the northern quarter, would not have held so many. The water-supply is poor, and must have given out: see "Life of Jesus," 357.

[5] Its site was the same as at present, excepting toward the south. Comp. Saulcy, *Dern. jours de Jérusalem*, plans, p. 218 *et seq.*

[6] Jos. *Wars*, v. 4: 2, 4; vi. 9: 1; vii. 1: 1; Tac. *Hist.* v. 11.

with those of the upper town, and Acra, made separate walls of defence, like so many distinct fortresses.[1] The number of defenders was very great, and as yet there was abundance of provisions, though lessened by the fires. The parties continued to fight within the city, but acted together in the defence. After the Feast of Passover, the faction of Eleazar almost disappeared, blending with that of John.[2] Titus conducted the attack with consummate skill; the Romans had never shown such capacity for siege-works as now.[3] By the end of April, the legion had broken through the outer defences on the north, and held that portion of the city.[4] The second wall, that of Acra, was forced five days later, and half the city was thus in the hands of the Romans. On the 12th of May they assaulted the tower of Antonia. Titus was surrounded by Jews, who (excepting, perhaps, Tiberius Alexander) were desirous of saving the city and Temple; and was, besides, more than he would admit, controlled by his affection for Berenice, who seems to have been a pious Jewess, devotedly attached to her nation.[5] Under these influences he is said to have attempted means of reconciliation, and offered favourable conditions of surrender,[6]

---

[1] Tac. *Hist.* v. 8, 11; Dion Cass. lxvi. 4; Jos. *Wars*, v. 4, 5.

[2] Jos. *Wars*, v. 3: 1; Tac. *Hist.* v. 12.

[3] Tac. *Hist.* v. 13.

[4] For the topography see authorities cited in *n*. 1, p. 203, above.

[5] Jos. *Wars*, ii. 15: 1; 16: 1, 3. The Herodian princesses are represented by Josephus and in the Talmud as devotees, given to making vows, and much attached to the Temple (Derenb. 253, 290, notes). Agrippa seems also to have been a very strict Jew: Bab. Talm. *Succa*, 27 *a*; *Pesachim*, 107 *b*.

[6] This is open to some doubt; for, as we shall see, Josephus systematically praises the clemency of the Flavii, insisting that their severities were wholly due to Jewish obstinacy (*Wars*, v. 9; vi. 2, 6; cf. 3: 5).

but in vain. The besieged replied to his propositions only by jeers and insults.

The siege thereupon took a character of atrocious cruelty. The Romans made ostentatious display of preparations for inflicting awful vengeance; but the daring of the Jews only increased. On the 27th and 29th of May they burned the military engines of the Romans, and attacked them in their camp. The besiegers began to be discouraged. Some of them were persuaded that the Jews told the truth, — that Jeru-

---

Sulpicius Severus (ii. 30), who here as elsewhere (see note on p. 392 below) seems to copy from portions of Tacitus now lost, says quite the contrary: "because no opportunity of peace or surrender was offered." Certainly, a full intention on the part of Titus to destroy Jerusalem is more in accordance with the general policy of the Empire and the interest of his own family; and he clearly shows the motive of inaugurating the new dynasty by a striking exploit and a triumphal return to Rome. Jerusalem would thus, in a sense, pay the costs of the dynastic revolution. Still, we may not overlook the influence of Agrippa, Berenice, and even of lesser persons, like Josephus: these may well have urged upon him the value of the gratitude which moderate Jews in Rome, Alexandria, and Syria would feel toward the protector of the Temple. Here, as in the matter of counsel and war, Tacitus may ascribe to Titus an ideal of Roman sternness, such as had grown familiar since the day of Trajan. Dion Cassius (lxvi. 4, 5) agrees fully with Josephus; but his testimony, while it may be only a copy of what was reported by the Jewish historian, only proves that, beside the reading of Tacitus, there was another version of the facts tending to show the clemency of Titus. The talmudic tradition seems to hint a knowledge of negotiations with a view to prevent the utter ruin of the city (*Aboth derabbi Nathan*, iv., vi.). It is noteworthy that in 70 Josephus was liberally rewarded for having served as an agent in efforts for conciliation (*Life*, 76). Perhaps Titus allowed such efforts to be continued, though knowing they would not succeed, and reserving his own liberty of action. In the accounts of Josephus a large allowance has to be made for exaggeration, his wish to give himself consequence, and his pretension of having rendered valuable service to his nation. Some of his co-religionists charged him with treason. Was it not an excellent answer to such charges, to exhibit himself as using his favour with Titus to avert from his country all the calamity he could? (See *Life*, 75.)

salem was in fact impregnable; and some deserted. Titus gave up the hope of taking it by storm, and put it under strict blockade. A wall of contravallation was rapidly thrown up, early in June,[1] supported toward Peræa by a line of forts crowning the heights of Olivet, and completely cut off the city from the country outside.[2] Till then, vegetables and the like had been brought in from the neighbourhood; but now the famine became dreadful.[3] The fanatics, who had all they needed, cared little: though we need not credit the wanton atrocities ascribed to them by Josephus, there were strict searchings with torture, to discover hidden stores of grain. Any air of vigour in one's face was a sign that he was guilty of concealing food, and morsels of bread were snatched from the very mouths of those who ate them. Hideous diseases sprang up among these masses heaped together, weak and fever-stricken. Dreadful tales were put in circulation, which doubled the common terror.

From this time on Jerusalem was filled by famine, rage, despair, and madness. It was a cage of ferocious maniacs, a city of howling cannibals, a hell. Titus on his part displayed enormous cruelties. Five hundred wretches every day were crucified in plain sight of the city, with hateful aggravations of torment. There was not wood enough to make the crosses, or room enough to plant them.

[1] See Saulcy, p. 309, with the plan, p. 222.
[2] Alluded to in Luke xix. 43: "thine enemies shall cast a trench about thee," etc.
[3] The memory of this famine is vivid in the talmudic tradition: Bab. Talm. *Gittin*, 56 a, b; *Abboth derabbi Nathan*, vi.; Midr. on *Koh*, vii. 11; on *Eka*, i. 5. Comp. Josephus, *Wars*, vi. 3: 3; Sulpicius Severus, ii. 30 (probably after Tacitus).

In this excess of misery the faith and fanaticism of the Jews burned with more heat than ever. The Temple was supposed to be indestructible.[1] Most were persuaded that, since the city was under the special protection of the Eternal, it could not possibly be taken.[2] Prophets went about among the people promising speedy relief. There was such confidence in this that many who might have saved themselves remained to witness the miracle of Jehovah. The frenzied leaders, however, had complete mastery. All who were suspected of advising surrender were put to death. Thus the high-priest Matthias, who had brought into the city that brigand Simon, son of Gioras, perished by his order, his three sons being first put to death before his eyes. Many men of note suffered the same fate. The smallest gathering was forbidden; merely to weep together, to gather in company, was a crime. Josephus tried in vain to signal information into the town from the Roman camp; he was suspected on both sides.[3] The situation had come to be such that reason and moderation had no chance to make themselves heard.

Titus, meanwhile, was growing weary of these delays. His mind was full only of Rome, its splendours, and its pleasures.[4] A city taken by famine seemed too ignoble an exploit to shine at the inauguration of a dynasty. He accordingly built four new embankments (*aggeres*) for an attack by main force. The orchards and ornamental trees within a distance of four leagues from Jerusalem were cut down. In twenty-one days all was ready. On the first of July the Jews repeated the attempt which they had once made successfully:

---

[1] Enoch, cxiii. 7.
[2] Jos. *Wars*, vi. 2: 1; 5: 2.
[3] Comp. *Aboth derabbi Nathan*, iv.
[4] Tac. *Hist.* v. 11.

they went out to set fire to the timbers, but this time completely failed. From that day forth the city's fate was sealed. On the second the Romans began to batter and undermine the tower Antonia. On the fifth Titus was master of it, and had it almost wholly demolished, so as to open a broad passage to his cavalry and engines to the point at which all his efforts aimed, and where the final struggle must be met.

The Temple, by its peculiar style of construction, was (as I have said) the most formidable of citadels.[1] The Jews intrenched there with John of Gischala prepared for battle. The priests themselves were under arms. On the seventeenth the daily sacrifice ceased for want of officiating ministers. This made a great impression upon the people,[2] and was known outside the town. The suspension of sacrifice was as grave an event to the Jews as a stop in the order of the universe. Josephus took occasion of it to try once more to break down the obstinacy of John. From the battlements of the tower Antonia, which was at only some sixty yards' distance from the Temple, he called out in Hebrew, by command of Titus (if in this the historian is to be believed), that John might withdraw with such number of his men as he wished; that Titus would take on himself the continuing of the legal offerings by Jews; that John might even select the men to offer them. But John refused to listen. Those not blinded by fanaticism now fled to the protection of the Romans. As many as remained deliberately chose death.

On the twelfth of July Titus began his advance

---

[1] Tac. *Hist.* v. 12.
[2] It was the occasion of a fast on the 17th of the 10th month: Mishna, *Taanith*, iv. 6.

against the Temple.¹ The resistance was most obstinate. On the twenty-eighth the Romans held the entire north gallery, from the tower of Antonia to the vale of Kedron. Then the attack on the Temple itself began. On the second of August the most powerful engines were set to batter the solidly built walls of the porches (*exedræ*)² that enclosed the inner courts. The effect was hardly noticeable; but on the eighth the Romans set fire to the wooden doors. The Jews were thrown into unspeakable confusion. They had never thought of such a thing as possible; and, at the sight of the crackling flames, they hurled upon the Romans a torrent of imprecations.

The next day Titus gave orders to extinguish the flames, and held a council of war, which was attended by Tiberius Alexander, Cerealis, and his chief officers,³ to discuss the burning of the Temple. Several among them held that, as long as this should stand, the Jews would never be at peace. The opinion of Titus himself it is hard to know, for the two accounts contradict each other. Josephus reports that he desired to spare so admirable a structure, whose preservation would be a glory to his reign and a proof of Roman moderation; while Tacitus says that he urged the necessity of destroying an edifice hallowed by two superstitions equally deadly, — the Jewish and the Christian;⁴ adding that

[1] For the topography, see Vogüé, pp. 60, 61, pls. xv., xvi.

[2] These were arcades, or cloisters, built about the entire circuit, open to the inner courts, and protected by walls of great thickness without. — ED.

[3] See Léon Renier, in the *Mém. de l'Acad. des Inscr.* xxvi. 269 *et seq.*

[4] Bernays (*Chron. des Sulp. Severus*, Berlin, 1861, p. 48) has shown that the passage of Severus (ii. 30: 6, 7) is taken almost word for word from the lost portion of the *Histories* of Tacitus, who himself drew his information from a book entitled *De Judæis*, written by Antonius Julia-

"these two, though hostile to each other, are from the same source: the Christians come from the Jews; pluck up the root, and the branch will presently wither."

It is hard to decide between two accounts so absolutely contradictory. On the one hand, the view which Josephus ascribes to Titus may well be regarded as an invention of his own, eager as he was to prove the sympathy of his patron for Judaism, to clear him in Jewish eyes from the guilt of having destroyed the Temple, and to satisfy the strong desire of Titus to pass as a man of moderation.[1] On the other hand, we cannot deny that the words which Tacitus puts in the mouth of the conqueror, both as to style and in the order of thought, exactly reflect the view of the historian himself. We have a right to suspect that — full as he was of the contempt of both Jew and Christian which marks the period of Trajan and the Antonines — he has made Titus speak like a Roman aristocrat of his own day; while, in fact, the citizen-prince had a far more kindly feeling toward oriental superstitions than the haughty nobility which succeeded the Flavian house.[2] He had lived for three years among the Jews, who had boasted to him of their Temple as the wonder of the world; he was won by the flattering attentions of Josephus (who owed all his fortune to Titus's special

---

nus, an officer in the council of war (Minuc. Felix, *Octav.* 33; Tillemont, *Hist. des Emp.* i. 588). Orosius, like Sulp. Severus, had in his hands the full text of the "Histories;" but he leaves it uncertain, saying only, "He long deliberated;" but ends by attributing the act to Titus, — "he burned and destroyed" (*diruit*, vii. 9).

[1] Note that the "Jewish War" (as Josephus himself asserts) was submitted to the judgment of Titus, and the approval of Agrippa; that, in a word, it was composed, as far as possible, to flatter the self-love of Titus, and to serve the Flavian interest (Jos. *Life*, 63; *c. Apion*, i. 9).

[2] Suet. *Titus*, 5; Philostr. *Apoll.* vi. 29; p. 408 (below).

favour[1]), of Agrippa, and still more of Berenice; and he may well have wished to preserve a sanctuary whose worship, as many of those nearest him asserted, tended wholly to peace. It is quite possible, then, that (as Josephus relates) orders were given to extinguish the flames, and that measures were taken against a general conflagration, in view of the frightful tumult sure to follow. In the character of Titus, along with a vein of genuine kind-heartedness, there was a good deal that was theatrical, and something of hypocrisy. Most likely he did not order the burning, as Tacitus asserts; he did not forbid it, as Josephus represents; but he tacitly allowed it, holding himself in reserve for any explanation it might suit him to allow, to satisfy the various phases of popular opinion. However that may be, a general assault was ordered against the edifice, now stripped of its doors. To a trained soldiery, what remained to be done was only a single effort, which might be bloody, but could be no longer doubtful.

The Jews were beforehand in the fight. On the morning of the tenth[2] they opened a furious though unsuccessful conflict. Titus withdrew into the tower Antonia to rest and prepare for assault on the morrow, leaving a detachment to prevent the fire from rekindling. Then, as Josephus relates it, befell the incident which brought on the ruin of the sacred structure. The Jews threw themselves madly upon the troop which was watching near the fire; the Romans, in a fury of rage, drove them back, and entered with the

---

[1] *Wars*, iii. 8: 8, 9.

[2] The great fast for the destruction of the Temple is celebrated on the ninth day of the month *Ab*, corresponding nearly to August: Jos. *Wars*, vi. 4: 5; Mishna, *Taanith*, iv. 6; cf. Dion Cass. lxvi. 7.

fugitives, pell-mell, into the Temple. A soldier, "without any order being given, and as if driven on by a supernatural force," seized a flaming rafter, and, calling to one of his fellows to "give him a lift," threw in the glowing brand by a window that opened upon the northern porch. The flame and smoke spread rapidly. Titus was just then reposing in his tent. As they ran to warn him (if we may believe Josephus), a sort of struggle ensued between him and the soldiers. Titus, by voice and gesture, gave orders to put out the fire; but in the confusion he was not understood, and those who could not mistake his intention made as if they did not hear him. Instead of checking the flames, the legionaries piled on more brands. Dragged along by the stream of assailants, Titus was borne into the very Temple. The flames had not yet reached the central building, and he saw, unharmed, that sanctuary of which Josephus, Agrippa, and Berenice had so often spoken to him with admiration, finding it (says Josephus) yet more magnificent than he had been told. He redoubled his efforts; commanded the interior to be cleared of men; and even gave orders to Liberalis, a centurion of his guard, to strike those who disobeyed. All at once a jet of flame and smoke shot out from the Temple door. At the moment of their disorderly retreat, a soldier had set fire to the interior. The flames spread on all sides; the position could no longer be held, and Titus came away.

 This account of Josephus is unlikely on more accounts than one. It is not easy to suppose that Roman legions were so slack in obeying a victorious commander. Dion Cassius, on the contrary, asserts that Titus had to use force to compel his men to enter a place so encompassed by dread,[1] where every trespasser was said to have been smitten with death. Only one thing is sure, — that a few years later Titus was very glad to have the matter told in the Jewish world as Josephus has done it, and the burning of the Temple attributed to the loose discipline of his men, or, rather, to the supernatural act of some unconscious agent of a higher Will.[2] "The War of the Jews" was written toward the end of Vespasian's reign, not earlier than 76, when Titus was already ambitious to be known as "the joy of mankind" (*deliciæ humani generis*), and wished to pass as a model of mildness and bounty. In earlier years, and in another world than that of Jews, he would surely have accepted another style of praise. Among the scenes exhibited in the triumph of 71 was a picture of "fire set to temples,"[3] certainly without the least intention, then, of exhibiting this deed as anything else than glorious. About the same time the court poet, Valerius Flaccus, proposes to Domitian, as the finest task for his poetic gift, to sing the war in Judæa, and to show his brother scattering firebrands on every side : —

>   . . . Solymo nigrantem pulvere fratrem,
> Spargentemque faces, et in omni turre furentem.[4]

---

[1] Dion Cass. lxvi. 6; comp. Jos. xi. 2: 3. Josephus is very precise in some details, having been himself an eye-witness; but his story as a whole is warped by all manner of inventions and afterthoughts.

[2] "Under some dæmonic impulse," says Josephus, *Wars*, vi. 4 : 5; "by the will of a divinity" (*dei nutu*), says Sulpicius Severus, ii. 30. Josephus goes so far as to charge his own countrymen with being the first cause of the calamity: "the beginning and the guilt of the flames were from the citizens" (vi. 2: 9).

[3] Jos. *Wars*, vii. 5: 5.

[4] *Argonautica*, i. 43. The burning of the Temple is attributed, in the Talmud, to "Titus the Wicked" (Bab. Talm. *Gittin*, 56 a).

The conflict, meanwhile, was hot in the courts and open spaces. There was fearful slaughter about the Altar. This was a sort of truncated pyramid, surmounted by a platform, which stood in front of the Temple: the bodies of those slain on the platform rolled down the steps, making a heap at the foot. Streams of blood flowed on every side, and everywhere were heard the sharp screams of those who were being slain, and who died while crying aloud to heaven. There was still time to take refuge in the upper city; but many chose rather to expose themselves to death, esteeming it an enviable fate to die for their sanctuary. Others threw themselves into the flames; others, again, upon the swords of the Romans; while yet others stabbed themselves or one another.[1] Some priests, who had succeeded in reaching the ridge-pole of the Temple roof, tore out the metallic points there with the lead fastenings, and hurled them down upon the Romans, and continued to do this till overtaken by the flames. A large number of Jews had gathered about the Holy Place, on the word of a prophet who had assured them that this was the moment when God would display to them the signals of deliverance.[2] A gallery whither six thousand poor wretches had retreated, mostly women and children, was burned. Two doors of the Temple and a part of the Women's Court were left unharmed a little while; the Romans planted their standards where the sanctuary had been, and offered them the worship to which they had been accustomed.

There remained the ancient Zion, the upper town, the strongest part of the city, with its defences still untouched. Hither had retreated John of Gischala,

---

[1] Dion Cassius, lxvi. 6.   [2] Jos. *Wars*, vi. 5: 2.

Simon the son of Gioras, and a large number of the fighting men, who had succeeded in clearing themselves a passage through the conquerors. This stronghold of desperate men required a fresh siege. John and Simon had fixed their centre of resistance in the palace of the Herods, near the site of the present citadel, covered by the three enormous towers, Hippicus, Phasael, and Mariamne. In order to carry this last rallying-place of Jewish obstinacy, the Romans had to construct embankments (*aggeres*) against the western wall of the city, opposite the palace, — that is, the wall which starts from the present citadel, enclosing the gardens of the Armenians.[1] The four legions spent eighteen days — from the 20th of August to the 6th of September — upon this task. Meanwhile, Titus pushed the conflagration into those parts of the city which were in his power. The lower town, especially, and Ophel as far as Siloam, were systematically destroyed. Many Jews of the middling class succeeded in escaping. Those of the lower orders were sold at a very low price. They made the beginning of a large population of Jewish slaves, who, when cast upon the Italian and other Mediterranean shores, brought with them the elements of a new and zealous propaganda. Their number is estimated by Josephus at ninety-seven thousand.[2] Titus granted pardon to the princes of Adiabene. The priestly vestments, jewelry, tables, bowls, candlesticks, and hangings were delivered to him. He ordered them to be carefully kept, to serve in the triumph he was preparing, to which he wished to give a special stamp of foreign splendour, by displaying in it the rich material of Jewish worship.

---

[1] Saulcy, *Last Days*, etc., 409, 410; pl. 222.
[2] Jos. *Wars*, vi. 9: 3.

When the embankments were finished, the Romans began to batter the wall of the upper town. At the first attack, on the 7th of September, they overthrew a part of the wall, with several towers. Shrunken by famine, sapped by fever and rage, the defenders were now mere skeletons. The legions marched in without difficulty. All day long the soldiers burned and killed. Most of the houses which they entered for plunder were full of corpses. The wretches who could escape fled to Acra, which was mostly deserted by the Roman force, and into the vast underground cavities which honeycomb the subsoil of Jerusalem.[1] Just at this point John and Simon weakened.[2] They still held the towers Hippicus, Phasael, and Mariamne, the most astonishing military constructions of all antiquity.[3] The battering-ram was impotent against those enormous blocks of stone, which were put together with matchless skill, and fastened with iron clamps. Dizzied, with wits astray, John and Simon left these impregnable defences, and tried to force the besieging lines on the side of Siloam. Failing in this, they went to join those of their partisans who had hidden in the drains.

On the eighth all resistance was at an end. The soldiers were broken down with fatigue. The weak, who could not walk, were put to death. The remnant, with women and children, were driven, like a herd of cattle, into the Temple enclosure, and shut up in the

---

[1] See Dion Cass. lxvi. 5; Jos. *Antiq.* xv. 11: 7; *Wars*, v. 3: 1; Tac. *Hist.* v. 12; Catherwood, *Plan;* Vogüé, *l. c.*, pl. i. xvii

[2] The charge of cowardice laid against them by Josephus is most likely groundless, and due only to his hatred of them.

[3] Jos. *Wars*, vi. 9: 1. The lower courses of one of these towers still exist, and create astonishment, though the blocks have been detached and misfitted.

inner court which had escaped the burning.[1] In this great crowd, herded together for death or slavery, lines of distinction were drawn. Every one who had borne arms was slaughtered. Seven hundred young men, the tallest and handsomest, were reserved to follow in the triumph of Titus. Among the rest those who had passed the age of seventeen were sent into Egypt, with their feet in fetters, to forced labour, or were distributed among the provinces to perish in the amphitheatres. Those under seventeen were sold. The assorting of the captives lasted several days, during which, it is said, thousands died, some for lack of food, some because they would not eat.

The Romans spent the ensuing days in burning the remainder of the city, undermining its walls, and breaking up the drains and underground-works. Here they found great wealth. Many of the insurgents, who were found alive, were killed on the spot. More than two thousand dead bodies were unearthed, and some few prisoners whom the terrorists had confined there. John of Gischala, compelled by hunger to surrender, begged for quarter, and was sentenced to imprisonment for life. Simon, son of Gioras, who had a supply of food, kept hid till the end of October. Then, in lack of provision, he took a singular course. Clad in a close-fitting white tunic, with a purple mantle, he suddenly emerged from under ground, on the spot where the Temple had stood.[2] He fancied that he should bewilder the Romans by a seeming resurrection, and possibly pass himself off as the Messiah. The soldiers

---

[1] The enclosure, of about 360 feet by 300, was very scanty for the numbers that Josephus crowds into it. But he was an eye-witness (*Life*, 75).

[2] There are many subterranean retreats beneath the site of the *haram*.

were at first, in fact, no little astonished. Simon would give his name to no one but their commander, Terentius Rufus; who put him in chains, sent word to Titus (then at Paneas), and ordered his captive to be taken to Cæsarea.

The Temple, with its huge constructions, was demolished to the foundation; the substructions, however, were preserved,[1] and make what is now called the *Haram esh-sherif*. Titus also wished to preserve the three great towers, Hippicus, Phasael, and Mariamne, to inform posterity against what defences he had fought. The western wall was left standing to shelter the tenth legion (*Fretensis*), which was detailed to garrison the ruins of the captured city. Finally, a few buildings at the end of Mount Zion escaped destruction and remained as isolated ruins, while all the rest disappeared.[2] From the month of September, 70, till about the year 122, when Hadrian rebuilt it under the name *Ælia Capitolina,* Jerusalem was nothing but a field of ruins,[3] in a corner of which was set up the encampment of a legion,[4] always on guard. At any moment,

---

[1] Jerome, *In Zach.* xiv. 2. The extraordinary height of this sub-basement could not be known before the English excavations. The foundations of the Temple itself could be seen till the time of Julian. Comp. Hegesippus in Euseb. ii. 23: 18.

[2] Jos. *Wars*, vii. 1: 1; Luke xix. 44; Epiphan. *De mensuris*, 14; Lact. *Inst. div.* iv. 21; Oros. vii. 9. The contrary statements of Eusebius (*Dem. evang.* vi. 18) and Jerome (*In Zach.* xiv.) came from the wish to find the fulfilment of prophecy. The destruction, evidently, means simply the dismantling and overthrow of the walls of stone.

[3] I shall examine later, in detail, what was the condition of Jerusalem during these fifty-two years, and in what sense it can be said that there was during that time a church at Jerusalem.

[4] On the spot which is now the seat of the Latin patriarchate. See Jos. *Wars*, vii. 1: 1; Clermont-Ganneau, *Comptes rendus de l'Acad. des Inscr.*, 1872, 158 *et seq.*

it was thought, might blaze out the conflagration that smouldered under these calcined rocks. Men trembled lest the spirit of life should return to those corpses which seemed, from below the charnel-heap, to lift their arms in affirmation that there still remained with them the promise of eternity.

CHAPTER XX.

RESULTS OF THE FALL OF JERUSALEM — A. D. 71-73.

TITUS seems to have remained about a month in the neighbourhood of Jerusalem, offering sacrifices, and giving bounties to his men.[1] The spoils and captives were sent to Cæsarea. The season was too far advanced to allow the youthful commander to set out for Rome. He spent the winter in visiting several eastern cities, and in giving feasts. Troops of Jewish prisoners, whom he dragged about with him, were cast to wild beasts, burned alive, or forced to fight one another.[2] At Paneas, on the twenty-fourth of October (his brother Domitian's birthday), more than twenty-five hundred Jews perished in the flames, or else in the horrid sports of the amphitheatre. At Beyrout, on the seventeenth of November, an equal number were sacrificed to celebrate the birthday of Vespasian. Hatred of Jews was the ruling passion of the Syrian towns; and these frightful massacres were hailed with delight. The most shocking thing of all is, perhaps, that Josephus and Agrippa did not quit Titus during this time, and were witnesses of these atrocities.

Titus then made a long journey in Syria and beyond the Euphrates. At Antioch he found the population

---
[1] Inscription in *Mém de l'Acad. des Inscr.* xxvi. 290.
[2] Jos. *Wars*, vii. 2; 3: 1; 5: 1.

enraged against the Jews, who were accused of starting a conflagration that had nearly destroyed the city; but he did no more than to cancel the bronze tablets on which their privileges were inscribed.[1] He further presented to the city the winged *cherubim* which overspread the ark. This curious trophy was set in front of the great western gate, which took the name of the Gate of Cherubim. Near this he dedicated a four-horse chariot to the Moon, in gratitude for the help given him by that luminary during the siege. At Daphne he erected a theatre on the site of the Jewish synagogue, with an inscription signifying that this structure was built from the spoil got in Judæa.[2]

From Antioch he returned to Jerusalem, where he found the legion *Fretensis*, under command of Terentius Rufus, still occupied in searching the hollows beneath the ruined city. The apparition of Simon, son of Gioras, emerging from the drains, when it was supposed that no one was left there, had revived the subterranean hunt. Every day, indeed, some wretched fugitive or some new treasure was discovered. At sight of the solitude he had made, Titus, it is said, could not refrain from an emotion of pity. The Jews who came to him had an increasing influence upon him: the vision of an oriental empire, which had been displayed before the eyes of Nero and Vespasian, began to glow about him, and even stirred some suspicion at Rome.[3] Agrippa, Berenice, Josephus, and Tiberius Alexander were more than ever in favour with him, and there were many who argued that Berenice might play the part of a new Cleopatra. Some anger was felt at seeing people of

---

[1] Jos. *Wars*, vii. 3: 2–4.   [2] Malala (ed. Bonn), 261, 281.
[3] Suet. *Titus*, 5.

that class honoured and all-powerful, when the rebellion had but just been put down.[1] On his own part, Titus listened more and more willingly to the suggestion that he was fulfilling a providential mission; and he took pleasure in hearing prophetic passages which, he was assured, referred to him. Josephus asserts that he ascribed his victory to God, and acknowledged himself to have been the object of special divine favour.[2] We are struck by finding that Philostratus, a hundred and twenty years later, in his "Life of Apollonius" (vi. 29), fully admits the statement, and makes it the occasion of a correspondence between Titus and his own philosophic hero. If we may believe him, Titus refused the crowns that were offered him, saying that not he was the conqueror of Jerusalem; that he had only lent his own service to an angry God. Now, it is hardly to be supposed that Philostratus knew the passage in Josephus: it was part of the trite legend of Titus's moderation.

Titus returned to Rome in May or June of the year 71, bent upon a triumph which should surpass everything in that kind that had ever been seen. The simplicity, gravity, and somewhat commonplace manners of Vespasian were not such as to appeal to the fancy of a population accustomed to demand of its sovereigns, first of all, prodigality and an air of grandeur. Titus thought that a stately entrance would have a fine effect,

---

[1] Juvenal, *Sat.* i. 128-130, a passage referring to Tiberius Alexander.

[2] Jos. *Wars*, vi. 9: 1. No doubt we may suspect in this a deliberate afterthought of the historian (see above, note on pp. 387, 388; also pp. 391-394). But since Titus is said some years after to have approved these statements (Jos. *Life*, 65), we may conclude that at some points they reflect his nature and thought. And, even if we doubt the fact, at any rate Josephus thought to make favour at court by asserting it.

and succeeded in conquering the prejudices of his old-fashioned father about it. The ceremony was set forth with all the skill of the Roman decorative artists of that period. Especially it was marked by the care taken to ensure local colour and historic realism.[1] It was also a favourite device to reproduce the simple and austere Roman rites as if on purpose to set them in relief against the vanquished religion. At the opening of the ceremony, Vespasian officiated as pontiff, with his head more than half covered by the toga, and made the formal prayers, Titus then following him with the same formalities. The procession was amazing. All the curiosities and rarities of the world, the costly products of Oriental art, were displayed in it, beside the finished work of Greek and Roman skill. Having just escaped the greatest danger the Empire had ever run, it would seem the most pompous display must be made of its wealth and splendour. Scaffoldings on wheels, rising three or four stages in height, were the object of universal admiration. Here were seen displayed all the episodes of the war, each series ending with an exhibition, to the life, of the strange figure made by Bar-Gioras as he emerged from his hiding-place, and the method of his capture. The pale features and sunken eyes of the captives were disguised under the superb garments they were dressed in. In the midst was Bar-Gioras himself, conducted in great pomp to his death. Then came the spoils of the Temple,—the golden table, the golden candlestick with seven branches, the purple veil of the Holy of Holies, and, to end the series of trophies, the captive, the vanquished, the specially guilty one—the Book of

---

[1] Jos. *Wars*, vii. 5: 3-7.

the Law (*Torah*). The parade of victorious soldiers closed the march. Vespasian and Titus were borne in two separate chariots.[1] Titus was radiant; while Vespasian, seeing in all this pomp only a day lost for business, was very weary of it, and did not try to hide the dull look of a busy man, expressing his impatience that the procession did not move faster, and grumbling to himself, "A very pretty mess! . . . Well, I have deserved it. What a fool I have made of myself . . . a man of my age, too!"[2] Domitian, sumptuously attired and mounted on a noble charger, pranced here and there about his father and elder brother.

Thus they arrived, by the Sacred Way, at the temple of Jupiter Capitolinus, the usual goal of the triumphal march. At the foot of the Capitol Hill they made a halt, in order to avoid the distressing part of the ceremony, the execution of the chief captives. This hateful custom was observed to the letter. Bar-Gioras was taken out from the troop of prisoners, and dragged, with a cord about his neck, the butt of unseemly insults, to the Tarpeian Rock, where he was put to death. When a cry proclaimed that the enemy of Rome was no more, there went up a mighty shout, and the sacrifices began. After the customary invocations, the princes retired to the Palatine, and the rest of the day was spent by all the city in festival and rejoicing.

The Book of the Law and the hangings of the Temple were carried to the imperial palace. The furnish-

---

[1] Positively so stated by Josephus, who witnessed the ceremony. Zonaras (xi. 17) puts them, though not so precisely, on the same chariot.

[2] Suet. *Vesp.* 12.

ings of gold, especially the table for shew-bread and the candlestick, were laid aside in a great building constructed by Vespasian over against the Palatine, across the Sacred Way, called the Temple of Peace, which made a sort of Museum under the Flavian emperors.[1] A triumphal arch of Pentelican marble, still standing, kept the memory of this extraordinary triumph, with figures of the chief objects which were carried in it.[2] Father and son on this occasion took each the title of *imperator*, but refused that of *Judaicus*,[3] either because there was something of scorn or ridicule in it,[4] or to show that the victory in Judæa was not in a campaign against a foreign nation, but was only the suppression of a revolt of slaves; or, again, from some secret motive, such as Josephus and Philostratus have hinted at in exaggerated terms. A coin, or medal, representing Judæa in chains, weeping under a palm-tree, with the legend IVDAEA CAPTA, IVDAEA DEVICTA, preserved the memory of the one great exploit of the Flavian dynasty. This coin continued to be struck till the days of Domitian.[5]

The victory was complete. A commander of Gallic race and blood — one, I may say, of ourselves,[6] at the head of legions, in whose register, if we could read it,

---

[1] This temple, dedicated in 75, was entirely destroyed by fire under Commodus. Little dependence can be placed on what Procopius says in his Vandal War (ii. 5).

[2] This [the so-called Arch of Titus] was not finished till the reign of Domitian. See inscr. 758, in Orelli.

[3] Dion Cassius, lxvi. 7.

[4] See Cicero's jest (*Hierosolymarius*), *Ad Att.* ii. 9.

[5] Madden, "Jewish Coinage," 183-197.

[6] The Flavian family originated in Cisalpine Gaul. The portraits of Titus and Vespasian show us very common features, like those most familiar to us.

we should find many an ancestor of our own — had demolished the citadel of Semitic faith, and had inflicted on the theocracy, that formidable foe to civilisation, the most crushing defeat it had ever sustained. It was the triumph of the Roman Law — or, rather, the Law of Reason, a wholly philosophic structure, with no groundwork of revelation — over the Jewish Book of the Law (*Torah*), which claims to be revealed. This Law — the *Jus Romanum*, whose roots were partly Greek, but so largely due to the practical genius of the Latins — was the noble gift which Rome bestowed on vanquished nations in recompense of their lost independence. Every victory of Rome was a step in the advance of Reason. Rome introduced into the world a principle better in many respects than that of the Jews, — I mean the Secular State, resting on a purely civil conception of society. Every patriotic struggle is to be honoured. But the Zealots were not merely patriots; they were fanatics, armed tools of an intolerable tyranny. What they wished was to uphold a bloody code, which ordained stoning as the penalty of wrong thinking. What they fought against was the common right, the layman's right, a right free to all, which does not disturb itself about private opinion. Liberty of conscience was destined to result at length from Roman Law, while it could never have been born of Judaism. Out of this could come only the Synagogue or the Church, censorship of manners, compulsory morality, the convent, — a world like that in the fifth century, in which the human race would have lost all its vigour, unless the Barbarians had brought the remedy. Better, in truth, the reign of the Warrior than the temporal rule of the Priest! For the warrior harms not the spirit: one can think freely under him; while the priest requires of his subjects that which is impossible, — namely, belief in certain things, and the pledge to find them always true.

The triumph of Rome was, therefore, in some respects well deserved. Jerusalem had become an impossibility. The Jews, if left to themselves, would have reduced it to ruins. But a great void was to deprive this victory of its fruits. Our Western races, with all their superiority, have always shown lamentable religious impotence. It was utterly impossible to get from the Roman or Gallic religion anything akin to the Christian Church. But any advantage gained over one religion is futile, unless its place is filled by another that gives at least equal satisfaction to the needs of the heart. Jerusalem was destined to avenge herself for her defeat: to conquer Rome through Christianity, and Persia through Islam; to destroy the old political structure, and to become for all finer natures a City of the Soul. The most perilous tendency of its Code (*Torah*) — a Law at once ethical and civil, giving precedence to social questions over matters military and political — was to become dominant in the Church. Throughout the Middle Age, censured and spied upon by the community, the individual would dread the homily, and tremble before the sentence of excommunication. This was just amends for the moral indifference of pagan society, and a protest against the impotence of Roman institutions to benefit the individual. Certainly, there is something hateful in the power of coercion granted to religious bodies over their members. The worst of errors is to think that any one religion has the monopoly of goodness. For every man that religion is good which makes him gentle, upright, humble, and kind. But to govern mankind is a hard task. The ideal is very high, and the earth is very low. Outside the sterile province of philosophy, what we meet at every step is unreason, folly, and passion. The wise men of antiquity succeeded in winning to themselves some little authority only by impostures, which gave them a hold upon the imagination, in their lack of physical force. Where would civilisation have been if men had not believed for centuries that the Brahman could cast a thunderbolt by his glance; or if the barbarians had not been awestruck by the terrible vengeance of Saint Martin of Tours? Man has need of a moral discipline, for which the cares of Family and State are not enough.

In the intoxication of success Rome did not easily keep in mind that the Jewish insurrection was still alive in the valley of the Dead Sea. Three fortresses — Herodium, Machærus, and Masada[1] — remained in the hands of the Jews. What kept any hope in them after the capture of Jerusalem must have been their firm resolution to shut their eyes to all evidence. The rebels defended themselves as fiercely as if the struggle were just beginning. Herodium was little more than a fortified palace, and was taken without much difficulty by Lucilius Bassus. Machærus held out obstinately; and atrocities, massacres, and the sale of whole troops of Jewish captives were renewed. Masada made one of the most heroic defences recorded in the history of

---

[1] Saulcy, Travels in the Holy Land (i. 168) and about the Dead Sea (i. 199, with plates xi., xii., xiii.); Guérin, *Descr. of Palestine*, iii. 122; Parent, *Machærous* (Paris, 1868); Vignes, notes; G. Rey, *Voyage dans le Haouran*, 285; pl. xxv., xxvi.

war. Eleazar, son of Jairus, grandson of Judas the Gaulonite, had seized this fortress early in the revolt, and made it a resort of Zealots and armed partisans. Masada occupies the level summit of an immense cliff, some sixteen hundred feet in height, on the margin of the Dead Sea. To gain possession of such a stronghold, Fulvius Silva was compelled to make enormous efforts. The Jews were cast into immeasurable despair when they found themselves stormed in a retreat they had deemed impregnable. At the instigation of Eleazar, they slew one another, and set fire to the heap they had made of their possessions. So perished nine hundred and sixty persons. This bloody tragedy befell on the 15th of April, 72.

By these events Judæa was left desolated from end to end. Vespasian ordered the sale of all lands that had become ownerless by the death or captivity of their proprietors.[1] It seems to have been proposed to him to rebuild Jerusalem under another name and found a colony there, — a scheme afterwards carried out by Hadrian. He declined to do this, and annexed the entire territory to the emperor's private domain.[2] He only gave to eight hundred veterans the village of Emmaus, near Jerusalem,[3] making of it a little colony, of which a trace is preserved in the name of the pretty village *Kuloniê*. A special tribute was assessed upon the Jews throughout the Empire, who were to pay

---

[1] Jos. *Wars*, vii. 6: 6.

[2] The words of Josephus (*l. c.*) are, ἰδίαν αὐτῷ τὴν χώραν φυλάττων, meaning, probably, that he kept the price of sale (comparing the phrase elsewhere, κελεύων . . . ἀποδόσθαι). On the meaning of ἰδίαν, comp. *Corpus inscr. græc.*, 3751; Mommsen, *Inscr. regni Neap.*, 4636; Henzen, 6926; Strabo, xvii. 1: 12.

[3] See note at the beginning of chap. xiii.

yearly to the Capitol the amount of two drachmas [about forty cents], which they had previously paid to the Temple at Jerusalem.[1] The little band of reconciled Jews — Josephus, Agrippa, Berenice, Tiberius Alexander — chose Rome for their residence. We shall meet them there, playing a considerable part, sometimes winning some moments of court favour for their countrymen, sometimes pursued by the hatred of fanatical believers, more than once indulging hopes, — notably, when Berenice seemed likely to become the wife of Titus, and to hold the sceptre of the world.

Judæa was now reduced to a solitude, and seemed at rest. But the prodigious disturbance she had felt was repeated in lesser shocks in the adjoining regions. This effervescence continued till near the end of 73. The Zealots who had escaped massacre, those who had enlisted in the siege, all the crazy-heads of Jerusalem, spread abroad into Egypt and Cyrenaïca. The communities of these regions, wealthy and conservative, and very far away from the fanaticism of Palestine, felt the danger brought among them by these desperate men; and so undertook the task of arresting and handing them over to the Romans. Many fled as far as to Upper Egypt, whither they were tracked and hunted like wild beasts.[2] At Cyrene a partisan named Jonathas, by trade a weaver, set up for a prophet; and, like all false Messiahs, persuaded two thousand poor men (*ebionim*) to follow him to the desert, where he promised to show them prodigies and astounding appa-

---

[1] Jos. *Wars*, vii. 6: 6; Dion Cass. lxvi. 7; Suet. *Domitian*, 12; Appian, *Syr.* 50; Origen, *Epist. ad Afric.* " de Susanna," i. 28; Martial, vii. 54; Nerva's coinage, Madden, 199.

[2] Jos. *Wars*, vii. 10: 1; Euseb. *Chron. ann.* 73.

ritions.¹ Cool-headed Jews denounced him to Catullus, governor of the district; but he retaliated by laying charges against them, which brought on them endless troubles. Almost the entire Jewish population of Cyrene, one of the most prosperous in the world,² was exterminated; and its property was confiscated in the emperor's name. Catullus, who had shown much cruelty in this affair, and was disavowed by Vespasian, died a victim to frightful hallucinations, which (it has been thought) became the subject of a dramatic work with fantastic scenery, "The Spectre of Catullus."³

But, strange to say, this long and terrible death-agony was not immediately fatal. Under Trajan and Hadrian, as we shall see, the Jewish nationality revived, and proved still capable of a bloody struggle; but clearly the die was cast, the Zealot was crushed beyond recovery. The way pointed out by Jesus, and instinctively followed by the heads of the church in Jerusalem who took refuge in Peræa, became emphatically the true way for Israel. The secular kingdom of the Jews had been hateful, hard, and cruel. The time of the Asmonæan kings, when they enjoyed national independence, was their gloomiest period. Had they to regret the Herodian monarchy, or the rule of Sadducees, that shameful alliance of an ignoble princedom with a dishonoured priesthood? Surely not. That was not the true vocation of the "people of God." One must be blind not to see that the ideal institutions to which "the Israel of God" aspired did not admit of national independence. Since these institutions could

---

[1] Jos. *Wars*, vii. 11: 1.

[2] Strabo, cited by Josephus, *Antiq.* xiv. 7: 2.

[3] Juvenal, *Sat.* viii. 5: 186.

not create an army, they could exist only in a vassal State under a great Empire, which leaves much freedom to its alien subjects (*rayahs*), while it relieves them of the cares of politics by requiring of them no military service. The rule of the Persian monarchy fully satisfied these conditions of Jewish life. At a later day the Caliphate, the Ottoman Empire, were again to satisfy them, and to watch the unfolding, beneath their shield, of free communities like those of the Armenians, Parsees, and Greeks, — nations without a country; brotherhoods, making good the lack of political and military independence by the autonomy of the College and the Church.

The Roman Empire was not flexible enough thus to meet the needs of the communities it embraced in its dominion. Of the Four Empires this was, in the opinion of the Jews, the cruellest and wickedest.[1] Like Antiochus Epiphanes, the Roman Empire forced the Jewish people from its true vocation, thus leading it, by reaction, to the attempt at forming a separate kingdom or State. This attempt was not due to those who represented the true genius of the Hebrew race. In some regards, they would prefer Romans for their rulers. The idea of a Jewish nationality was coming every day to be an idea of the past, — an idea of madmen and fanatics, against which the pious made no scruple of appealing to the protection of their conquerors. The true Jew — clinging to the Law (*Torah*), making the sacred books (as Christians do) his rule of life, absorbed in his hope of the kingdom of God — more and more renounced the thought of earthly na-

---

[1] Apocalypse of Baruch in Ceriani: *Monum. sacra et profana*, i. 82; v. 136.

tionality. The principles of Judas the Gaulonite, which were the soul of the great revolt, were principles of Anarchy. According to them, since God is Master, no man may claim that title. And thus, while these principles could lead forth bands of fanatics like Cromwell's "Independents," they could found nothing that would last. Such tempestuous explosions were an indication how thoroughly the heart of Israel had been wrenched by the awful task laid upon it. Forced to wrestle with bloody sweat for humanity at large, he must perish, as he did, in a death of frightful agony.

A people must, in fact, choose between the long, tranquil, and obscure career of one who lives for himself, and the stormy and vexed career of one who lives for man. A nation whose heart is divided by social and religious problems is almost always weak as a nation. Every country that dreams of a kingdom of God, that lives for universal ideas, and undertakes a task for the general advantage, sacrifices by that course its own particular destiny. It enfeebles and annihilates the part it might sustain as a political entity. So it was with Judæa, with Greece, with Italy; so it may yet be with France. It is not with impunity that one carries fire in his heart. Jerusalem, as a capital of commonplace citizens, might have pursued indefinitely a commonplace career. Because it had the unparalleled glory of being the cradle of Christianity, it became a prey to such chieftains as John of Gischala and Simon Bar-Gioras, — seemingly scourges of their country, really the means of its transfiguration. Those Zealots whom Josephus regards as brigands and assassins were the basest of politicians, and the most incompetent of captains; but they ruined heroically a country which was incapable of being saved. They destroyed the visible city; but they opened the realm of a spiritual Jerusalem, which, seated in her desolation, was far more glorious than she had been in the day of Herod or of Solomon.

What, in truth, was the aim of the conservatives, the Sadducees? It was a small and paltry aim. It was to maintain a city of priests, like Emesa, Tyana, or Comana. Surely they spoke the truth when they said that the uprising of enthusiasts would be the ruin of the nation. Revolution and Messianism were indeed the ruin of the Jewish people considered as a nation; but they were the true vocation of that people, its one contribution to the structure of a world-wide civilisation. In like manner we speak truly when we say to France, "Renounce the Revolution, or thou art lost!" But, if any one of the ideas obscurely working out in the people's heart has the promise of the future, it will be found that France shall be fully recompensed for that which in 1870 and 1871 made her weakness and her misery. Unless by some very violent wrenching of the truth (which is always possible), our sons of the Revolution[1] will never be great citizens; but let each man do his part, and we shall see, perhaps, that such men were more in the secrets of the future than cooler heads.

How, now, shall Judaism take new shape, when deprived of its holy city and its temple? How will the situation which events have brought to pass for Israel give birth to the spirit of the Talmud? This will appear in the succeeding volume. In one sense, Judaism had no longer an excuse for living after Christianity

[1] In the original, *nos Bar-Gioras, nos Jean de Gischala.*

had been brought forth. From that hour the spirit of life was departed from Jerusalem. The mother-church gave all to the child of her sorrows, and spent her force in that sore travail. That was a true voice of the ancient Divinity (*Elohim*) which men thought they heard in the sanctuary, murmuring, "Let us go hence!" The law of every great creation is that its creator, in bestowing existence upon another, virtually gives away his own. After the complete transfusion of life to him who is to bear it on, the giver remains but a sapless stem, an exhausted stock. Still, this sentence of Nature is rarely executed upon the spot. The plant which has borne the flower does not yet consent to die. The world is full of walking skeletons which outlive the decree that has been passed upon them. Modern Judaism is one of these. History has no stranger spectacle than this,—the spectral existence of a people which for more than a thousand years has lost the sense of fact; which has written not a single page that can be read, or given a single precept that can be obeyed. Can we wonder if, after having lived for centuries out of the atmosphere of human life,—in a cavern, if I may say so, in a condition partially demented,—it should come forth pallid, bewildered by the light, and bloodless?

The consequences which resulted to Christianity from the fall of Jerusalem are so evident that, from this time forth, it is easy to point them out. I have already had several occasions to speak of them.[1]

The ruin of Jerusalem and of the Temple was a piece of unexampled good fortune for Christianity. If Tacitus correctly reports the opinion of Titus,[2] the con-

---

[1] See "Saint Paul," chap. xvii. (end). [2] See above, p. 392.

queror believed that Christianity and Judaism would perish alike in the destruction of the Temple. There was never a more complete misjudgment. The Romans supposed that, in tearing away the root, they had torn away the shoot. But the shoot was already a tree, living its own life. If the Temple had remained, Christianity would certainly have been smothered in its growth. The Temple would have continued to be the centre of everything that Judaism had produced. It would never have ceased to be looked on as the holiest spot on earth.[1] Hither would come pilgrimages; here would be offered pious gifts. Clinging about the sacred courts, the church at Jerusalem would have continued, in virtue of its primacy, to receive homage from every land, to persecute the followers of Paul, to require circumcision and the observance of the Mosaic code as the condition of claiming discipleship to Jesus. Every way of fruitful expansion would have been cut off; every missionary must sign a pledge of obedience to the hierarchy at Jerusalem.[2] A centre of inviolable authority would have been established, with a patriarchate consisting (so to speak) of a college of cardinals under the presidency of such men as James, — Jews of unmixed blood, belonging to the family of Jesus.[3] This would have been a monstrous danger for

---

[1] See above, p. 313.

[2] See "Saint Paul," chap. x., and the letters prefixed to the Clementine "Homilies."

[3] Something like this is taking place among the Jews of our day, and seems likely to grow into a serious thing. All the Jews of Jerusalem are regarded as *hakamim*, or "learned," having no other occupation than to meditate upon the Law. As such, they have a right to receive alms, and feel that they ought to be supported by the Jews of all the world. Their begging agents circulate throughout the East, and even rich Israelites of Europe hold themselves in duty bound to contribute to their demands

the growing Church. When we see Saint Paul, after all the ill-treatment he had received, remaining still attached to the church at Jerusalem, we may conceive the difficulty of any break with these holy personages. Such a schism would have been regarded as an enormity, as the same thing as to renounce Christianity outright. Separation from Judaism would have been impossible. But this separation was as essential to the existence of the new religion as the cutting of the umbilical cord is to the life of the new-born child. The mother would else deprive her child of life. On the contrary, the Temple once destroyed, Christians no longer think of it; soon they will even hold it to be an unholy place,—"effete and empty," says Orosius,[1] "and fit for no good use." For them Jesus will be all.

By the same blow the church at Jerusalem was brought down to a second rank. We shall see it rallying anew about the element that gave it strength, —the members of the family of Jesus (δεσπόσυνοι, "the Princes") the sons of Cleopas; but it will reign no more. With the destruction of that centre of hatred and exclusion, the reconciliation of opposite parties in the Church becomes easy. Peter and Paul are officially made at one, and the alarming duality of infant Christianity ceases at length to be a deadly hurt. The little group that clung to the relatives of Jesus—to James or Cleopas—lives forgotten, secluded in Batanæa and

(see "Saint Paul," chap. iii., xv.). Again, the decisions of the Great Rabbi at Jerusalem tend to gain universal authority, while formerly the doctors were of equal rank, their credit depending on their personal reputation. Thus the future may, perhaps, see a doctrinal tribunal of Judaism having its seat at Jerusalem.

[1] *Hist. adv. paganos*, vii. 9 (early in the fifth century).

the Hauran. Here, as the Ebionitish sect, it lingers out a slow death of sterility and insignificance.

In many respects its situation was like that of Catholicism in our day. No religious community has ever had more inward activity, more readiness to put forth its own original productions, than the Catholicism of the last sixty years. All these efforts, however, have been void of result from a single cause, — the autocratic rule of the court of Rome. This it is which has driven from the Church such minds as Lamennais, Hermes, Döllinger, Loyson (*le Père Hyacinthe*), — all the apologists who have defended it with any success. It is the Roman *Curia* that has reduced Lacordaire and Montalembert to despair and impotence. It is this that, by its Syllabus and its Council, has cut away all future from the liberal Catholics. When will this lamentable state of things have an end? It will be when Rome shall be no longer the pontifical city; when the dangerous oligarchy which holds Catholicism in its grasp has ceased to be. The occupation of Rome by the King of Italy will probably be reckoned in Catholic history an event as happy as the destruction of Jerusalem has proved in Christian history. Most Catholics have deplored it, as no doubt the Jewish Christians of 70 deplored the destruction of the Temple as the most gloomy of disasters. But the sequel shows how superficial was that judgment. While weeping the fall of papal Rome, Catholicism will find that loss its greatest gain. Formal unity with real death will give place in its communion to free discussion, movement, variety, and life.

APPENDIX.

OF PETER'S COMING TO ROME, AND OF JOHN'S STAY AT EPHESUS.

AT the end of the second century, as all are agreed, the general belief of the Christian churches was that the apostle Peter suffered martyrdom at Rome, and that the apostle John lived to extreme old age at Ephesus. Protestant theologians of the sixteenth century argued strongly that Peter never came to Rome, — an opinion which Luther opposed when it first appeared, in 1520, but which Flacius Illyricus and Salmasius made a received belief among Protestants. The belief of John's residence at Ephesus has never been seriously controverted until our own day.

It is easy to detect the motive of the emphasis with which Protestants generally have denied that Peter ever came to Rome. Throughout the Middle Age his residence there was the foundation of the exorbitant claims of the papacy. These claims rested on three assertions which were held to be articles of faith: (1) that Jesus himself conferred upon Peter primacy in his Church; (2) that this primacy must have been transmitted to the successors of Peter; (3) that these successors are the bishops of Rome, since Peter, after remaining a time at Jerusalem and then at Antioch, had fixed his residence definitely at Rome. To disprove this last assertion was, accordingly, to overthrow the entire edifice of Roman theology. Much learning was spent upon the question. It was shown that the Roman tradition was not sustained by very substantial direct testimony; but indirect evidence was treated lightly. In particular, there was weary discussion on the passage, ἀσπάζεται ὑμᾶς ἡ ἐν Βαβυλῶνι συνεκλεκτή (1 Pet. v. 13).[1] Now it cannot be maintained that "Babylon" in this passage really means the city on the Euphrates: first, because "Babylon," in the esoteric language of Christians at this time, always means Rome; secondly, because Christianity in the first century hardly went outside the limits of the Roman Empire, and was very little current among the Parthians.

To us the question is far less important than it was to the Reformers;[2] and we find it easier than they did to discuss it without bias. We do not believe in the least that Jesus had any such design as to establish an official Head in his Church; still less, to attach this headship to the episcopal succession in any particular city. Almost certainly no thought of an episcopate was in his mind; and besides, if there was any city in the world known to him by name, which he could have had no thought of associating with such succession, it unquestionably was Rome. It would surely have inspired him with horror, if he had been told that this city of perdition, this merciless foe to the people of God, would one day vaunt its Satanic royalty as the ground of its own right to inherit the new title of power founded by the Son of God. Whether Peter was ever at Rome or not is, accordingly, not of the slightest importance for us, political or moral. It is, simply, a curious question of history. That is all.

At the outset, the Catholic position is open to most serious attack from its unfortunate assumption (taken from Eusebius and Jerome) that Peter came to Rome in the year 42, thus extending his residence there as pontiff to twenty-three or twenty-four years. This is utterly out of the question. To remove any doubt about it, we have only to consider that the persecution at Jerusalem under Herod Agrippa, in which

---

[1] Rendered in the Revised Version, "She that is in Babylon, elect together with [you], saluteth you." — ED.

[2] The final and most learned form given to Protestant doubts upon this subject is found in the two essays of Lipsius: "*Chronologie der römischen Bischöfe bis zur Mitte des vierten Jahrhunderts* (Kiel, 1869); *Die Quellen der römischen Petrussage* (ibid. 1872).

Peter suffered imprisonment and exile (as related in Acts xii. 3-19), occurred in the same year with the death of Herod; that is, in 44.[1] Apollonius, the anti-Montanist, at the end of the second century,[2] and Lactantius, at the beginning of the fourth,[3] surely did not believe that Peter had been at Rome in 42: the former affirming the tradition that Jesus had forbidden his apostles to leave Jerusalem within twelve years after his death; the latter asserting that they devoted the twenty-five years following their Master's death to preaching the gospel in the provinces, and that Peter did not go to Rome till after the accession of Nero. It would be idle to contend at length against an assumption which no reasonable person can defend. I may go farther, and say that Peter had not yet arrived in Rome when Paul was brought thither as a prisoner in 61. We find a further argument in Paul's Epistle to the Romans, written about 58, — at all events not more than two and a half years before his arrival in Rome; for we cannot easily imagine that he should write to a community of which Peter was the head without the slightest mention of him. Still more decisive is the last chapter of Acts. This chapter — especially the verses (17-29) telling of Paul's interview with the Jews at Rome — cannot be explained if Peter was there when Paul arrived. I may assume it, then, as absolutely proved, that Peter did not go to Rome before Paul, — that is, before 61, or thereabout.

But did he not go there after Paul? This the Protestant critics have never succeeded in disproving. Not only is there no impossibility in such a later journey, but strong reasons may be urged in its favour. I think that those who will read consecutively the account which I have given will find that everything shapes itself easily to this view. The evidence of the Fathers of the second and third centuries has some weight in the decision; and there are, besides, three arguments which appear to me worth considering.

---

[1] Jos. *Ant.* xix. 8:2; see "The Apostles," chap. xiv.
[2] Euseb. v. 18:14.
[3] *De mortibus persecutorum*, 2.

First, the fact is not to be disputed that Peter suffered martyrdom. The testimonies of the Fourth Gospel, the Roman Clement, the fragment called "Canon of Muratori," Dionysius of Corinth, Caius, and Tertullian leave no doubt upon it.[1] Granting that the Fourth Gospel is apocryphal, and that the twenty-first chapter is a later addition, still it is clear that the verses (18–19) in which Jesus predicts to Peter a death like his own give expression to an opinion well fixed in the churches before 120 or 130, alluded to here and elsewhere as a fact known to all. Now we cannot easily put it to ourselves that Peter suffered a martyr's death anywhere else than at Rome. Nero's persecution, in fact, was hardly violent excepting there. At Jerusalem or Antioch, the martyrdom of Peter is far less intelligible.

In the second place, the name "Babylon," in the epistle commonly ascribed to Peter (v. 13), evidently points to Rome. If the epistle is genuine, the passage is decisive. If it is apocryphal, the inference to be drawn from the words is equally strong. Whoever the writer may be, he wishes us to believe that the epistle is Peter's own. Hence, to give his fraud the semblance of truth, he must so arrange the local circumstances as to conform to what he knew himself, or to what was generally believed in his time, about the life of Peter. If, with this motive, he dated the epistle at Rome, we may be sure that the common opinion of the time when it was written was that Peter had lived in Rome. On any theory it is a very ancient work, of early and great authority.[2]

Again, the theory which underlies the Ebionite "Acts of Peter" is also well worthy of consideration. In this view Peter is shown to us as everywhere following the steps of Simon Magus (by which name we understand that Paul is meant), to contend against his errors. This curious legend has been analysed by Lipsius[3] with admirable critical acu-

---

[1] See above, pp. 161–163.   [2] See p. 4, above.
[3] In *Römische Petrussage*, p. 13 *et seq.*, esp. 16, 18, 41, 42. Comp. the "Clementine Recognitions," i. 74; iii. 65; also the apocryphal epistle of Clement addressed to James, at the beginning of the "Homilies," chap. i.

men. He shows us that the basis of the various versions of the legends that have come down to us was an original account, written about 130. In this account Peter comes to Rome to defeat Simon-Paul at the centre of his power, and here meets his death, after he has overthrown this father of all heresies. It is hard to see how the Ebionite writer, at so remote a date, could have ascribed so much importance to Peter's journey to Rome if he never really made it. The Ebionite legend has, doubtless, some ground of truth notwithstanding the errors mingled in it. We may admit that Peter came to Rome, as he came to Antioch, in the footsteps of Paul, and in part to neutralise his influence. The Christian community, toward the year 60, was in a state of mind not at all like that calm waiting of the twenty years succeeding the death of Jesus. The missionary journeys of Paul, and the ease with which the Jews went from place to place, had brought about a custom of distant travel. In the same way an old and persistent tradition represents the apostle Philip as coming to make his abode in Hierapolis.

I hold, then, as very probable, the tradition of Peter's stay in Rome; but I regard this stay as very short, and believe that he suffered martyrdom not long after his arrival. The account of Tacitus in his "Annals" (xv. 44) falls in favourably with this view. In this account we find a very natural occasion for connecting with it the death of Peter. As the leader of the Judæo-Christians, he undoubtedly helped make up the list of victims described by Tacitus as *crucibus adfixi*; and among the holy martyrs of the year 64, who rejoice in the ruin of the city where they perished, the Seer of the Apocalypse has done well to include "apostles" along with "saints and prophets" (xviii. 20).

The coming of John to Ephesus was an event of far less doctrinal importance that that of Peter to Rome, and has not given rise to so extended controversy. Until a very recent time the commonly accepted opinion has been that John the apostle, son of Zebedee, died at a very advanced age in the capital of the province of Asia. Even those who declined to believe that during his stay here he composed the Gospel and the Epistles bearing his name, even those who denied that he was the writer of the Apocalypse, continued to believe that his journey thither, attested by tradition, was real. Some rational doubts were raised upon this point by Lützelberger, in 1840; but little heed was given to them. Critics who can surely be charged with no excess of credulity, — Baur, Strauss, Schwegler, Zeller, Hilgenfeld, Volkmar, — while holding a large part of the accounts of John's residence at Ephesus to be legendary, have yet regarded as historical the main fact of his coming into this region. This opinion was seriously challenged, in 1867, by Keim, in the first volume of his "Life of Jesus," [1] his position being that "John the Elder" has been confused with "John the Apostle," and that what ecclesiastical writers have asserted of the latter should be understood as of the former; and in this view he was followed by Wittichen and Holtzmann. Still more recently Professor Scholten, of the University of Leyden, has sought in an extended treatise to overthrow, one by one, all the evidences of the commonly received opinion, and to prove that John the Apostle never set foot in Asia.[2]

Scholten's essay is a real masterpiece of argument and method. He passes in review not only all the testimonies cited for or against the tradition, but all writings, besides, in which the question might be, or (as he thinks) should be, entertained. The learned professor had once been of a different mind. In his extended reasonings against the genuineness of the Fourth Gospel, he had strongly urged the passage in which Polycrates of Ephesus, near the end of the second century, represents John as having been one of the pillars of the Jewish and Quartodeciman party in Asia. But, in a difficult question like this, it is not for a friend of truth to count the cost of changing or correcting a position once taken.

[1] Pages 161–167; compare vol. iii. (1871–72), pp. 44, 45; 477, *notes*.
[2] *De apostel Johannes in Klein-Azië* (Leyden, 1871). The question has been resumed by Holtzmann in his *Kritik der Eph. und Kolosserbriefe* (Leipzig, 1872), pp. 314–324.

To me the arguments of Professor Scholten are not convincing. In them the removal of John into Asia Minor is shown to be an open question. But they do not make it out to be certainly apocryphal; and, as I regard it, the chances still are that the tradition is true. It is less probable, indeed, than the tradition of Peter's residence in Rome, but still it has its probability; and, on various points, Scholten has given evidence of an exaggerated scepticism. As I have said more than once, a theologian is never quite satisfying as a critic. Professor Scholten has a mind too elevated to allow himself ever to be controlled by motives of advocacy or of dogma; but a theologian is by habit so apt to subordinate the fact to the idea, that he rarely regards a point in dispute with the eyes of an unprejudiced historian. In these last five and twenty years especially, we have seen the Liberal Protestant school committing itself to a drift of extreme negation, where impartial science, finding in these topics purely matter of interesting research, may well hesitate to follow. The religious situation has come to such a pass that the defence of supernaturalist dogma is thought to be made easier by handling texts with a free hand and making large sacrifice of them than by urging their authenticity. And I am confident that a critical method clear of all theological bias will one day find that the liberal Protestant theologians of our day have gone too far in their negations; and that in some of its results — certainly not in its spirit — such a method will approach more nearly to the old traditionary schools.

Among the documents passed in review by Professor Scholten, the Apocalypse naturally stands in the foremost rank; and it is just here that this able critic shows himself weakest. We have our choice of three positions: that the Apocalypse is the work of the Apostle John; or that it is by some one writing under a false name who wishes to make it pass as a work of the apostle John; or that it is by some one of the same name — for example, John Mark, or the enigmatical "John the Elder." In the last case the Apocalypse, clearly, has nothing to do with the apostle's residence in Asia; but the hypothesis is little likely in itself, and it is not that adopted by Scholten. He is in favour of the second of the three cases supposed. He holds the Apocalypse to be an apocryphal work like the book of Daniel; and thinks that the composer (following a common Jewish practice of the time) wished to shield himself under an honoured name, choosing that of the apostle John as one of the pillars of the church at Jerusalem, and addressing the churches in Asia in the person of that venerated leader. Since such a forgery can scarcely be imagined in the lifetime of the apostle, Scholten holds that John had died before the year 68.

But this view rests on real impossibilities. However it may be with the genuineness of the Apocalypse, I venture to say that the argument founded on that book for the residence of John in Asia is quite as strong in the second of the cases supposed as in the first. We have not here to do with a book like "Daniel," written hundreds of years after the assumed writer's death. The Apocalypse was circulated among the disciples in Asia during the winter of 68–69, while the conflict among the generals for succession to the Empire, and the appearance of the pretended Nero at Cythnos, held all the world in feverish expectation. If the apostle John was dead, as Scholten supposed, his death was very recent. In any event, on this theory, the disciples at Ephesus, Smyrna, and elsewhere, knew perfectly well at that time that he had never been in Asia. How would they have received the story of a vision claiming to have taken place at Patmos, only a few leagues from Ephesus ? That story is addressed to the seven leading churches of Asia by a man assumed to know the hidden windings of their conscience. To some he allots the sharpest reproach, to others the most exalted praise. He speaks to them in the tone of undisputed authority. He exhibits himself as a sharer in their sufferings. And yet this man has never set foot in Patmos or in Asia; they must think of him as still sitting quietly in Jerusalem! The writer, we must suppose, had very little sense, to heap together with a light heart so many reasons for ill-will against his book.

Why does he put the scene of the vision at Patmos? Up to this time that island had been a place of no note, no significance. It was a mere way-station on the sail from Ephesus to Rome or from Rome to Ephesus. On these trips, Patmos offered a convenient port of relay, at a short day's sail from Ephesus,— the first or the last landing in such petty voyages as those described in Acts, where the main point was to stop over, if possible, every night. It was not of consequence enough to be the object of a voyage; it was likely to be visited only by some one going to or coming from Ephesus. Even granting the Apocalypse to be a forgery, the first three chapters make a strong argument for the residence of John in Asia; just as First Peter, even if apocryphal, gives very good reason to believe that Peter abode in Rome. A forger, however credulous the public he addresses, always seeks to make the circumstances of his invention such that it will be easily received. If the writer of First Peter believes himself bound to date his epistle from Rome,— if the writer of the Apocalypse thinks to provide a good prelude to his vision by making it date from the very threshold of Asia, almost in front of Ephesus, and fitting it out with counsels such as might be given by a spiritual director to the churches in Asia,— the reason is that Peter was in Rome, and John in Asia. Dionysius of Alexandria, at the end of the third century, had a clear sense of the embarrassing nature of the question so stated.[1] Feeling that antipathy against the Apocalypse common to all the Greek Fathers filled with the true Hellenic spirit, he brings together all the objections to ascribing such a work to the apostle John; but he acknowledges that it can have been composed only by some one who has lived in Asia, and so comes down to men of the same name: so clearly does it stand in relief that the real or supposed writer of the Apocalypse was some one in near relation with [the churches in] Asia.

We are indebted to Professor Scholten for a valuable discussion on the text of Papias. This "ancient man" (ἀρχαῖος

---

[1] Comp. Euseb. vii.'25.

ἀνήρ) has had the fortune to be misunderstood, from Irenæus, who wrongly make him a hearer of the apostle John, to Eusebius, who wrongly supposes that he had personal knowledge of "John the Elder." Keim had already shown that the text of Papias, rightly understood, tells rather against than for the residence of the apostle John in Asia. Scholten goes farther, and concludes from the same passage that John the Elder also was a stranger to Asia Minor, holding that he — whom he regards as distinct from the apostle — lived in Palestine and was a contemporary of Papias. I grant that, if the passage of Papias is correct, it bears against the residence of the apostle John in Asia. But is it correct? The words ἢ τί 'Ιωάννης may be an interpolation. If any think the rejection of them to be arbitrary, I would reply that, if those words be retained, then the words οἱ τοῦ Κυρίου μαθηταί, put after Aristion and John the Elder, make the entire clause odd and incoherent. Scholten's doubts, however, are confirmed by a passage of Papias quoted by George Hamartolus,[1] stating that John was put to death by the Jews. This tradition seems to have been invented to fulfil certain words of Jesus, — "Ye shall drink indeed of my cup,"[2] etc.; it is irreconcilable with John's stay at Ephesus; and if Papias really adopted it,[3] he certainly never once thought of him as living in the Province of Asia. It would surely surprise us to find a man like Papias, an eager inquirer into the apostolic tradition, ignorant of so essential a fact in the annals of his own country.

The fact that no mention of John's residence in Asia is

[1] First published by the Abbé Norle in the *Theol. Quartalschrift* (a journal of Catholic theology at Tübingen), 1862, p. 466. Comp. Holtzmann, *Krit. der Eph. und Kol.*, p. 322; Keim, *Gesch. Jesu von Nazara*, iii. 44, 45 n.; and the later observations of Scholten in the *Theologisch Tijdschrift* (Amsterdam and Leyden), 1872, p. 325 *et seq.*

[2] Matt. xx. 23; Mark x. 39.

[3] As to which there is some doubt. George Hamartolus adds that Origen was of the same opinion, which is utterly untrue. See Origen, *In Matt.*, vol. xvi. 6. Heracleon, too, includes John among the apostles who were martyrs: Clem. Alex. *Strom.* iv. 9. Such incidents as that of the boiling oil, and the passage Revel. i. 9, are enough to warrant the expression.

found in the epistles ascribed to Ignatius, or in Hegesippus, suggests a doubt. On the other hand, the tradition of it is constant from the year 180. Apollonius the anti-Montanist, Polycrates, Irenæus, Clement of Alexandria, and Origen make no question of the great honour which came thus to the city of Ephesus. Among the texts that may be cited,[1] two are especially noteworthy: that of Polycrates, bishop of Ephesus about 196, and that of Irenæus in his letter to Florinus of nearly the same date. Professor Scholten treats too lightly the language of Polycrates. It is a weighty point, to find the tradition so firmly established at Ephesus within a century. "The very uncritical mind of Polycrates," he says, "appears in his representing John as decorated with the *petalon* [the golden badge of the high-priest], thus by an anachronism carrying back to the apostolic period a custom of his own time, which assigned the rank of high-priest to a Christian bishop." But Professor Scholten did not always think so. He formerly found in the *petalon*, and in the title of "priest," given to John by Polycrates, a proof that this apostle was chief of the Judæo-Christian party in Asia. He was right. The *petalon*, far from being a bishop's badge in the second century, is ascribed to only two persons, both of the first century,— James and John, both belonging to the Judæo-Christian party, whom this party thought to exalt by assigning to them the insignia of the Jewish high-priest. Both Keim and Scholten make it a charge against Polycrates, that he believes the Philip who came with his prophetess-daughters to live in Hierapolis to have been Philip the apostle. I think that Polycrates is right; and that, if we compare the passage in Acts[2] [which speaks of "Philip the Evangelist"] with the passages of Papias, Proclus, Polycrates, and Clement, which speak of Philip and his daughters resident in Hierapolis,[3] we shall be satisfied that it is the apostle who is meant. The verse in Acts has all the appearance of an interpolation. Holtzmann[4] seems to adopt,

---

[1] See note on pp. 175, 176, above.   [2] Acts xxi. 8.
[3] See pp. 273-275, above; also "The Apostles," chap. ix.
[4] *Judenthum und Christenthum*, p. 719.

as to this, the view which I had offered in "The Apostles," and of which I am more convinced than ever.

The most curious passage of all in the Church Fathers on the question in hand is a fragment of Irenæus's letter to Florinus, preserved to us in Eusebius (v. 20). It is one of the choice passages in the Christian literature of the second century: "Those opinions, Florinus, are not of sound doctrine. . . . They are not such as were handed down by the elders who preceded us, or were known to the Apostles. I remember that when I was a boy in Lower Asia, where you held high office at court, I saw you with Polycarp, seeking to win his good esteem. I remember what happened then better than I do things that have happened since; for what we have learned in childhood grows with the mind, and comes to be a part of it. So that I could tell you the very spot where the blessed Polycarp sat and talked, his gait and habit, his ways of living, his personal appearance and manner of converse with his companions, how he would tell of his familiar acquaintance with John and others who had seen our Lord. He would relate to us, also, what he had heard them say about our Lord, and about his wonderful works and doctrine, as having received these things from eye-witnesses of the Word of Life, all in conformity with the Scriptures. Thanks to God's goodness, I would listen diligently to these things, and write them down, not on paper but in my heart; and, thank God, I always record them truly. And I may assert, in God's presence, that if that blessed and apostolic old man had heard anything like your doctrines, he would have stopped his ears, and cried out, as he would sometimes do, 'O good God! to what a time hast thou preserved me, that I should endure such discourse?' And he would have fled away from the place where he had heard them."

We see that Irenæus does not appeal here, as in most other passages where he speaks of John's residence in Asia, to a vague tradition. He recalls to Florinus the memories of childhood about their common master Polycarp, one of which is that Polycarp would often speak of his relations with the apostle John. Professor Scholten has clearly seen that he must admit these reports as genuine, or else make the epistle to Florinus to be apocryphal. He takes the latter alternative, for reasons which seem to me weak. In the first place, Irenæus expresses himself in the work "Against Heresies" (iii. 3:4) almost exactly as he does in the letter to Florinus. Scholten's chief objection turns on this: that to explain such relations between John and Polycarp, we must suppose all three — John, Polycarp, and Irenæus — to have been unusually long-lived. This does not disturb me much. The death of John, at the earliest, was not before somewhere between A. D. 80 and 90, while Irenæus wrote about 180. That is, Irenæus was about as far from the last years of John as we are from those of Voltaire. Now, without any miracle of longevity, my colleague and friend M. Rémusat knew intimately the abbé Morellet, who would talk to him at length about Voltaire. The supposed difficulty in the circumstance reported by Irenæus comes from assigning the martyrdom of Polycarp to the reign of Marcus Aurelius, somewhere between 166 and 169. At his death Polycarp was eighty-six years old, which would carry back his birth to 80–83, making him very young at the time of John's death. But the date of his martyrdom must be corrected. It took place under the proconsulate of Quadratus in Asia; and this has been shown by Waddington, in a manner which hardly admits of doubt, to have been in 154–155, under Antoninus Pius.[1] This carries back the birth of Polycarp to 68 or 69; and if John was living as late as 90, — in which there is no difficulty, as he may have been ten years younger than Jesus, — it is not unlikely that Polycarp may have listened to him when a child. The reign of Marcus Aurelius is not given as the date of Polycarp's martyrdom in the "Acts" relating that event; but Eusebius, by a false reckoning, as made fully clear by Waddington, supposed that the proconsulate of Quadratus fell within that reign.

A journey to Rome, taken by Polycarp during the pontifi-

---

[1] *Mém. de l'Acad. des Inscr.*, etc., **xxvi.** part 2 (1867), 232 *et seq.* Comp. Waddington, *Fasti of the Asiatic Provinces*, 1872, part 1, 219–221.

cate of Anicetus, offers a difficulty in the chronological reckoning just proposed.[1] Anicetus, as commonly held, became bishop of Rome not earlier than 154, so that we are rather crowded to find room for Polycarp's journey. If, consistently with Waddington's view (which seems to be decisive), it were necessary to set back a little the accession of Anicetus, we need not hesitate to do so, especially since the pontifical lists are confused just here, and some lists put Anicetus before Pius. Lipsius, who has lately put out an excellent treatise on the chronology of the Bishops of Rome down to the fourth century, was, unfortunately, ignorant of Waddington's memoir. He would have found in it material for valuable discussion.

"Is it likely," says Professor Scholten, "that an old man, already nearing his hundredth year, would undertake such a journey, at a time, too, when travelling was far more difficult than now?" But the journey from Ephesus or Smyrna to Rome was the easiest thing in the world. A merchant of Hierapolis tells us, in his epitaph,[2] that he had journeyed from Hierapolis to Italy, round Cape Malea, seventy-two times. He therefore must have continued his passages till he was quite as old as Polycarp when he went to Rome. Such voyages in summer — for hardly any one travelled then in winter — were not in the least fatiguing. We may suppose that Polycarp went to Rome in the summer of 154, and suffered martyrdom at Smyrna on the twenty-third of February, 155.[3] Keim's theory,[4] that the John known to Polycarp was not the Apostle, but the Elder, is full of difficulties. If this Elder was (as I think) a person of inferior consequence, a disciple of the Apostle, who flourished about A. D. 110–120, we cannot imagine that Polycarp or Irenæus should have confused the two. That the Elder was really a man of the great apostolic period, equal in dignity to the apostles, whom any one might confound with them, I have given elsewhere

---

[1] Euseb. *Hist. eccl.* iv. 14; *Chron. ann.* 155.
[2] *Corpus inscr. græc.* 3920.
[3] *Mém. de l'Acad.* xxvi. 240.
[4] *Gesch. Jesu von Nazara*, i. 161 *et seq.*

my reasons for disbelieving.[1] Even in that case (I may add), the error of Polycarp is about equally difficult to explain.

One of the most curious parts of Scholten's work is that in which he returns upon the question of the Fourth Gospel, already discussed by him so fully a few years back. He not only refuses to admit this as the work of John, but denies that it has anything to do with John; he denies that John was the disciple whom it several times mentions with a certain mystery, calling him "the disciple whom Jesus loved." That disciple, according to him, is not a real person. The disciple who knows not death, — who, unlike all the rest, is to live through the power of his spirit till the end of time, — whose testimony, resting on spiritual contemplation, is of absolute authority, — cannot be identified with any one of the Galilæan apostles: he is an ideal person. It is wholly impossible for me to accept such a theory. But let us not complicate one difficult question by another still more difficult. Professor Scholten has shaken some of the props which once sustained the belief that the apostle John lived in Asia. He has shown that this fact does not stand out clear from the half-shadow which envelops almost every fact of the apostolic story. Regarding Papias he has raised an objection hard to meet. Still, he has not refuted all that may be alleged in favour of the tradition. The first chapters of the Apocalypse, the letter of Irenæus to Florinus, and the passage in Polycrates remain, three solid supports, on which we may not, indeed, erect a certainty, but which Professor Scholten, with all the stress of his logic, has not overthrown.

[1] See Introduction to the present volume, pp. 13, 14.

INDEX.

ABADDON, 310.
Abomination of Desolation, 228.
Acte, 124, 253.
Agrippa II., 64, 213, 376, 385.
Amphitheatre, 121, 146.
Angels in Enoch, 287; of nations, 311; of winds, etc., 305.
Annæus, house of, 38.
Apocalypse ("Revelation"): book and writer, 12-24; 28, 54, 139, 174, 260, 279, 282, 286, 292-298, 366, 369; structure and events, 299-352; later theories and comments, 28, 29, 354-357; its theology, 357-364.
Apocryphal writings, 7, 15, 70, 84, 354.
Apostates, 237.
Apostolic missions, 74; in Asia, 272.
Armageddon, 331, 332, 355.
Armenia, supposed retreat of Nero, 256.
Art in Rome, 129.
Asia Minor, 90, 98, 160, 174; sects, 92.
Asmonœan monarchy, 191, 192.
Assyrian mythology, 364.
Atonement, sacrifice of, 160.
Augustus (the title), 321.
Aurelius, 101.

BABYLON, a name of Rome, 54, 115, 328; in Apocalypse, 328, 333; its downfall, 340-342.
Baiæ, 266.
Barabbas, 228.
Barnabas, 9, 177; probable author of Hebrews, 178; apocr. epistle of, 362.
Beast (of Revelation), 156, 277, 281, 283, ($\zeta\tilde{\omega}a$) 299, ($\theta\eta\rho\iota o\nu$) 314, 319, 320, 322, 329, 335; mark of, 281, 322-324; worship of, 324, 328; the second Beast, 325-327.
Berenice, 201; her influence with Titus, 376, 387, 394, 400, 404, 413.

Boëthus, 64, 65.
Bowls (phials) of divine wrath, 330.

CALIGULA, 119, 120, 122.
Campania (volcanic features), 37.
Canon of Muratori, 104, 169.
Cestius Gallus in Judæa, 213-216.
Christ in Apocalypse, 300.
Christians in Jerusalem, 235; in Rome, 36-39, 54-61, 138-143.
Christology, 87-89.
Church of Jerusalem, 66, 68, 419, 420.
Churches in Asia, 275; letters to, in Apocalypse, 288-292.
Coinage of Jews, 224.
Colossæ, destroyed, 98.
Colossians, epistle to, 93-97.
Conflagration of Rome, 116, 132-135.
Cythnos (island of false Nero), 257, 280; events at, 338.

DAMASCUS, massacre of Jews in, 221.
Danaïds and Dirces, 149, 159, 168.
Daniel, Book of, 284, 313.
Disasters, ominous, 262.
Divination, 261.
Dragon, image of, 240; bound for a thousand years, 344.

EARTHQUAKES, as signs, 264, 268.
Ebionites, 51, 57, 73, 421.
Ecclesiastes, Book of, 62, 100.
Edessa, 75.
Eleazar in Jerusalem, 202, 204, 222, 224, 382; at Machærus, 412.
Emmaus, 244.
Emperors of Rome (in Apocalypse), 335, 371.
Empire and its chiefs, 336.
End of the earth, 369.
Enoch, Book of, 223, 266, 284, 287, 365.

Epaphras (Epaphroditus), 43, 90, 92, 96.
Ephesians, Epistle to, 178.
Ephesus, 156, 176; John in, 276, 427–436.
Epictetus, 273.
Epistles of New Testament, 2.
Ezekiel, imagery of, 284, 312, 359.

FALSE Prophet, 59.
Farnese Bull, 150.
Flight to Pella, 240–243.
Florus, governor of Judæa, 200, 210.

GALBA, his revolt, 248, 250, 251; death, 282, 352, 372.
Galilee, slaughter in, 226, 227.
Gauls, revolt of, under Vindex, 247, 249, 259.
German critics, as historians, 3, 25, 424.
Gnostics, 83, 91, 95.
Gog and Magog, 345, 346, 359.
Golden House of Nero, 130, 135.

HANAN (the younger), 76, 78, 224; his death, 231.
Hatred of the pagan world, 365–367.
Hebrews, Epistle to, author and structure, 8–11, 177–183, 186.
Hermas, "Shepherd" of, 15, 19.
Hierapolis, 272, 273.
Horses (in Apocal.), 302, 308.

IMMORTALITY, Jewish view of, 360.
Incarnation, 89.
Incendiary mania, 131.
India, missions in, 74.
Islam, 191.

JAMES the Apostle (*Obliam*), Epistle of, 7, 63–69; death, 77.
Jerusalem, parties in, 66, 78, 382; Christians in, 5, 60, 80; siege and destruction of, 385–400; effect on Christianity, 419–421; New, 347–350.
Jesus of Nazareth, kindred of, 239; son of Hanan, 78.
Jews in Rome, 35, 38; as persecutors, 143; under foreign rule, 190, 207; under Roman rule, 192–195; in the modern world, 193, 198; charities, 272; the Jewish household, 309; paradoxical character, 212, 374.

Joachim, on Apocalypse, 357.
John the Apostle, 15, 23, 168, 276–278, 292; his harsh character, 16, 277; sufferings in Rome, 168, 175; in Ephesus, 175, 276, 281, 427–436; as writer of Apocalypse, 15–18, 21, 23, 292; bitterness toward Paul, 16, 278.
John the Elder, 13, 429, 432.
John of Gischala, 225; in Jerusalem, 228, 373, 400.
Josephus, 225, 377, 391, 393; at Rome, 413.
Jotapata, siege of, 226.
Judæa, churches in, 62; *Judæa Capta*, 408; after the conquest, 412.
Judæo-Christians, 73, 328.
Judas the Gaulonite, 416.
Judgment day (in Apocalypse), 329.

KINDRED of Jesus (*desposynoi*), 80, 239, 243.
Knights of Augustus (under Nero), 119.
Kulonié (Emmaus), 244, 412.

LAMB (symbol in Apocalypse), 18, 112, 301.
Laocoön, as work of art, 121.
Laodicea, 98, 269, 292.
Laureolus, 60, 149.
Law (Jewish), abolished, 86; (Roman), 195, 409.
Logos, 87.

MACHÆRUS (Machero), 204, 379, 411, 412.
Malvenda on Antichrist, 368.
Man of Sorrows, 208.
Mark (friend of Peter and Paul), 107.
Mark of the Beast, 281, 322–324.
Martyrs in Apocalypse, 306; souls of, 172, 258, 303.
Martyrdom (epic of the amphitheatre), 152; of Peter, 161; Paul, 181; James, 77; code of, 106.
Masada, the fortress, 201; stormed by Romans, 204, 412.
Massacres in Palestine, 206, 207, 210–213, 221.
Messiah in Apocalypse, 300; birth, 317.
Messianic ideas, 36, 141; predictions, 199, 227, 360.
Millenarianism, 22, 362.

INDEX.   441

Missions in Asia, 74.
Moderates in Jerusalem, 229.
Montanism, 21, 92.
Monuments ("trophies") of apostles in Rome, 164-167.
Mosaic Law, 189, 409

NERO, 1; his character and rule, 31-34, 116, 119, 126, 140, 254-256; as Antichrist, 156, 325, 343, 354, 356; ambitious schemes, 217; insane vanity, 218; on the stage, 219; in Greece, 220, 245-247; terror under the revolt of Vindex, 250; his popularity, 255, 375; his death, 253; supposed revival, 256, 279, 325; restoration, 283; false Nero at Cythnos, 257, 280, 338; Nero a second founder of the Christian Church, 155, 368.
New Jerusalem, 347, 361, 365.
Number of the Beast (in Apocalypse), 29, 323, 353, 355.

OMENS and signs (apocalyptic), 261.
Otho, succeeds Galba, 255, 282; an admirer of Nero, 353, 372.

PARTHIA, 218, 223, 256, 281, 331, 339; supposed retreat of Nero, 256; cavalry (in Apocal.), 311.
Parties in Jerusalem, 196, 221.
Patmos (as scene of the Apocalypse), 294-296.
Paul in Rome, 34, 42; hostility towards him, 53, 278, 367; his last days, 81, 101-105, 166; his later views, 84, 95, 170; proposed last journey, 103, 104.
Pella (retreat of Christians beyond Jordan), 241-243, 317, 319.
Persecution of Christians, 56, 144-151, 279, 285; impotence of, 173.
Persian Empire, 190.
Peter in Rome, 24, 48, 50, 56, 423, 429; Epistle of, 4, 52, 107, 109-114; crucifixion, 161-163; relations with Paul, 51-53, 176; their reconciliation, 170.
Petronius, 128, 173, 266.
Philip the Apostle, 273-275.
Philippians, Epistle to, 41, 43-47, 99.
Philo, 187.
Pomponia Græcina, 32.
Poppæa, 123, 141, 157.

Prayers of Saints, 139.
Predictions ascribed to Jesus, 270.
Provinces of Empire, 321.
Pseudonymous writings, 15.
Puteoli, 37; the region and its population, 265, 266, 310.

RETRIBUTION in history, 232.
Revelation, see *Apocalypse*.
Revolt against Nero, 247; of Jews in Judæa, 159, 189.
Rod of iron, 317.
Roman and Jewish Law, 409.
Roman rule in Judæa, 192; policy in the Provinces, 207.
Romans, Epistle to, 94.
Rome, old and new, 136; as a holy city for Christians, 155.

SACRIFICE, 64, 180, 186.
Sadducees as a party, 62, 196, 234, 414, 417; they perish, 232.
Satan, 318, 322, 346.
Scarlet woman (in Apocalypse), 333.
Sea (in the Apocalypse), 297.
Sects in Asia Minor, 92.
Seneca, 117, 120.
Seven a sacred number, 364.
Sheol, 346.
Sibylline poems, 269, 354.
Simon Magus, 39, 49, 54, 59, 60, 143, 325.
Simon son of Gioras, 214, 224, 382, 390, 400, 404.
Solfatara as a volcanic region, 265, 267, 310.
Sosiosh (the Zoroastrian Messiah), 364.
Spain as the aim of Paul's travel, 104.
Suffering not punishment but discipline, 183; of the Messiah, 111.
Symbolism, classic and apocalyptic, 365.
Synagogue as opposed to City, 191.
Synoptic Gospels, 71, 72, 88, 185, 368.
Syrian and Jewish Massacres, 209-212.

TALMUD, 65.
Temple in Jerusalem, 187, 233, 313, 353; storming of, 392; its fall, 395, 396.
Terror during siege, 234.
Theatre in Rome, 121.
Theocracy, 191, 193, 409.
Thera (in imagery of Apocalypse), 269, 308.

Thousand-year period, 344, 362.
Thraseas, 42, 123.
Three-and-a-half years' period, 313.
Tiberius Alexander, a recreant Jew, 141, 196, 324, 377, 379, 385, 404.
Tigellinus, 35, 128, 173.
Titus, son of Vespasian, 374, 376, 378; his schemes, 374, 387, 392, 405; character, 394; in Jerusalem, 386, 392–394, 404; at Rome, 405; arch of, 408.
Torah and Roman Law, 409.
Triumph of Rome over Judæa, 410.
Trophies of apostles and martyrs in Rome and elsewhere, 164–167.
Trumpets in Apocalypse, 307–311.

VESPASIAN, 220; in Galilee, 225, 374; campaign of (A. D. 68), 244; messianic attitude, 374; emperor, 375, 379, 380; his triumph, 406–408.

Vindex, his revolt against Nero, 247–250, 259, 282.
Vitellius, 255, 282, 372; an admirer of Nero, 375.
Volcanic phenomena in Italy, etc., 264, 267, 310.

WITNESSES (the two) in Apocalypse, 313.
Women among the Christian martyrs, 148, 153, 157.
Word of God (applied to Christ), 178, 343.
Wormwood (the apocalyptic star), 309.

ZACHARIAS, son of Barachias, 235, 239.
Zealots in Jerusalem, 197–209, 214, 230–236; after the conquest, 413.
Zoroastrianism in Apocalypse, 363.

Messrs. Roberts Brothers' Publications.

LIFE OF JESUS.

BY ERNEST RENAN,
Author of "History of the People of Israel," "The Future of Science."

From the twenty-third French edition. With notes. Revised and enlarged. 8vo. Cloth. $2.50.

The new edition, recently published in this city by the enterprising house of Roberts Brothers, of Ernest Renan's "Life of Jesus," uniform in style with this great scholar and writer's "History of the People of Israel," will for all future time be the standard edition in English of what is now "widely recognized as the one great literary monument of a century of New Testament criticism." The translation has been newly revised from the twenty-third and final edition, which was revised and corrected with the greatest care by Renan. The editor of this edition is Joseph Henry Allen, of Cambridge, a well-known scholar, who is eminently fitted for the important task which he has here undertaken. Mr. Allen has revised the two best known English translations existing, recasting nearly every sentence, and scrupulously weighing the whole, phrase by phrase, with the original. He has also verified every one of Renan's multitude of citations. It seems to us that the entire work could not have been more perfectly rendered into English. A wonderful change has taken place in the general Christian world during the past thirty years in its attitude towards Renan and his "Life of Jesus." He was for years, after the appearance of the earliest editions of his book, denounced as an agnostic, an atheist, and a blasphemer by evangelical Christians who are ready now to acknowledge the wonderful scholarship, the genius, the purity of motive, the devout reverence of his work, while of course totally disagreeing with Renan in his rejection of the supernatural and the divinity of Jesus. It has become the standard work of its kind among theologians; for the honesty of purpose and sincerity of its author, together with the wonderful beauty and devoutness displayed throughout the entire work, is freely recognized. No writer ever treated Jesus in a more tender and appreciative spirit than has Renan. It seems to us that, while the believer in the New Testament record in its entirety will not have his faith shaken in the supernatural portion, he will rise from a reading of this book with a more intense love for Christ, and a fuller realization of the stupendous mission which was involved in his brief active life upon the earth. — *Boston Home Journal.*

Sold by all Booksellers. Mailed, postpaid, on receipt of price, by the Publishers,

ROBERTS BROTHERS, Boston.

Messrs. Roberts Brothers' Publications.

THE BIBLE FOR LEARNERS.

By Dr. H. OORT, Professor of Oriental Languages at Amsterdam, and Dr. L. HOOYKAAS, Pastor at Rotterdam, with the assistance of Dr. A. KUENEN, Professor of Theology at Leiden. Translated from the Dutch, by Rev. P. H. WICKSTEED, of London. With a Comprehensive Index, made specially for this edition, and Maps. 3 vols. 12mo. Cloth.

OLD TESTAMENT. Vol. I. Patriarchs, Moses, Judges. — Vol. II. Kings, and Prophets. $4.00.

NEW TESTAMENT. Vol. III. The New Testament. $2.00.

"This work emanates from the Dutch school of theologians. Nowhere in Europe," said the lamented J. J. Tayler, "has theological science assumed a bolder or more decisive tone than in Holland, though always within the limits of profound reverence, and an unenfeebled attachment to the divine essence of the gospel. . . . We know of no work done here which gives such evidence of solid scholarship joined to a deep and strong religious spirit."

It is the Bible story, told in a connected form, with a history of the book and of the Bible countries and peoples. It properly treats of the Bible as the book of religion, — not of one particular form, but of religion itself, — "because the place of honor, in the religious life of mankind and of each man in particular, belongs to the person of Jesus, and because it is upon Jesus that the whole Bible turns." It is by keeping in sight the fact that the Bible is a religious book, and is meant to furnish answers to the questions "Who and what is God?" and "What are we to do and what leave undone?" — and is not nor was meant to be a book of science or history, that the authors have made so valuable a work. — *Golden Rule.*

As a working manual for the Sunday-school teacher it will be found of great value. Notwithstanding its title, it is a work for all, with or without Bible learning. The scholar will value it for its conciseness and labor-saving references; the general reader for the interest it possesses as a clear and interesting narrative, easily understood, in which the explanations, thoughts, and ideas of every great expounder have a greater or less place. — *Boston Transcript.*

The object of the work has been to reduce the narratives of Scripture to the understanding of youth and the unlearned, with such additional information as will serve to better elucidate the record and lead the reader to value its contents as a guide. Its simplicity of diction and the writer's infusion of a zealous spirit into some of its narratives will commend it to a favorable consideration. — *Chicago Journal.*

Sold everywhere by all Booksellers. Mailed, post-paid, by the Publishers,

ROBERTS BROTHERS, BOSTON.

Messrs. Roberts Brothers' Publications.

HISTORY OF THE PEOPLE OF ISRAEL.

By ERNEST RENAN,

Author of "Life of Jesus."

VOL.
I. Till the Time of King David.
II. From the Reign of David up to the Capture of Samaria.
III. From the time of Hezekiah till the Return from Babylon.
IV. From the Rule of the Persians to that of the Greeks.
V. Period of Jewish Independence and Judea under Roman Rule. (With Index.)

8vo. Cloth. Price, $2.50 per volume.

Renan's "History of Israel" may be said to consist of three parts. The first two volumes contain the analysis of the events that led up to the rise of the prophets; in the third, he unfolds his view of those prophets; while the last two illustrate the course of the prophetical ideas, steadily making their way, despite constantly recurring backsets, till their final triumph in Jesus. Viewing the five volumes as a whole, their interest centres in Renan's interpretation of Hebrew history; and it may safely be said that nothing that he has done reveals the brilliancy of his mind and the greatness of his intellectual grasp as does this monument, which he was fortunately permitted to finish before his life came to an end.

These last pages, written with all the vigor that characterizes his earliest productions, furnish an admirable means of forming a fair estimate of the man Renan himself. To those who are fond of denouncing him as a cynic, the sympathy which hi last words breathe for suffering and struggling humanity constitute the best reply. H. has often been called a sceptic, and yet one may search far and wide through modern literature for stronger expressions of true religious faith than are to be found in Renan's works. Above all, the testimony must be given to him which he most valued, — that his whole life was actuated by a love of truth He made personal sacrifices for what he considered to be the truth. He investigated fearlessly; and when he spoke, the ring of sincerity in his utterances was never wanting, while the boldness of these utterances was always tempered with a proper consideration for those who held opinions differing from his. All this is applicable in a marked degree to the last work that issued from his restless pen.

It may safely be predicted that Renan's latest production will take rank as his most important since the "Life of Jesus" There is the same charming style, the same brilliancy of treatment, the same clear judgment and delicate touches, the deep thoughts and thorough mastery of his subject, which have made Renan one of the most fascinating of modern writers. — *New York Times.*

To all who know anything of M. Renan's "Life of Jesus" it will be no surprise that the same writer has told the "History of the People of Israel till the Time of King David" as it was never told before nor is ever like to be told again. For but once in centuries does a Renan arise, and to any other hand this work were impossible. Throughout it is the perfection of paradox, for, dealing wholly with what we are al' taught to lisp at the mother's knee, it is more original than the wildest romance; more heterodox than heterodoxy, it is yet full of large and tender reverence for that supreme religion that brightens all time as it transcends all creeds. — *The Commercial Advertiser.*

Sold by all Booksellers. Mailed, postpaid, on receipt of price, by the Publishers,

ROBERTS BROTHERS, BOSTON, MASS.

Messrs. Roberts Brothers' Publications.

THE RELIGION OF ISRAEL.

A MANUAL.

Translated from the Dutch of J. Knappert, Pastor of Leiden.
By RICHARD ARMSTRONG, B. A.

16mo.   Price $1.00.

From the Boston Daily Advertiser.

Its purpose is to give a faithful and accurate account of the results of modern research into the early development of the Israelitish religion. Without attempting to set forth the facts and considerations by which the most thorough and accomplished scholars have reached their conclusions respecting the origin and date of the several books of the Old Testament, those conclusions are briefly stated, and the gradual development of the Jewish form of religion traced down to the Christian era. . . .

The translator says that there may be those who will be painfully startled by some of the statements which are made in the work. In his view, however, it is far better that the young especially should learn from those who are friendly to religion what is now known of the actual origin of the Scriptures, rather than to be left in ignorance till they are rudely awakened by the enemies of Christianity from a blind and unreasoning faith in the supernatural inspiration of the Scriptures.

From the Providence Journal.

If this Manual were not an exponent of Dutch theologians in high repute among their own countrymen, and if it were not an expression of the honest conviction of Rev. J. Knappert, the pastor of the Dutch Reformed Church at Leiden, we should feel inclined to pass it by, for it is not pleasant to have doctrines and facts rudely questioned that have been firmly held as sacred truths for a lifetime. And yet one cannot read "The Religion of Israel" without feeling that the writer is an earnest seeker after the truth, and has carefully weighed and diligently examined the premises on which his arguments are based, and the conclusions which he presents as the result of his researches. . . .

The book is one of singular and stirring interest: it speaks with an air of authority that will command attention; and, though it ruthlessly transforms time-honored beliefs into myths and poetic allegories, it makes its bold attacks with a reverent hand, and an evident desire to present the truth and nothing but the truth.

From the Boston Christian Register.

Here we have, for a dollar. just what many liberal Sunday schools are praying for, — a book which gives in a compact form the conclusions of the "advanced scholarship" concerning the Old Testament record. Taking Kuenen's great 'History of Israel" for a guide, Dr. Knappert has outlined what may be called the reverently rational view of that religious literature and development which led up to "the fulness of times," or the beginning of Christianity.

Sold everywhere by all Booksellers. Mailed, postpaid, by the Publishers,

ROBERTS BROTHERS, BOSTON.

POSITIVE RELIGION.
ESSAYS, FRAGMENTS, AND HINTS.

By JOSEPH HENRY ALLEN,

Author of "Christian History in its Three Great Periods,"
"Hebrew Men and Times," etc.

16MO. CLOTH. PRICE, $1.25.

Among the subjects treated may be noted the following, viz.: "How Religions Grow," "A Religion of Trust," "The World-Religions," "The Death of Jesus," "The Question of a Future Life," "The Bright Side," "Religion and Modern Life," etc.

The subjects are discussed, as one will indeed plainly see, by a learned Christian scholar, and from that height in life's experience which one reaches at three score and ten years. They treat of the growth of religion; of religion as an experience; of the terms "Agnostic" and "God"; of the mystery of pain, of immortality and kindred topics. The author is among the best known of the older Unitarians, and the breadth of his views, together with his modesty of statement and ripeness of judgment, give the book a charm not too common in religious works. The literary style is also pleasing. — *Advertiser.*

This little volume of 260 pages contains much that is fresh and interesting and some things which are true only from a Unitarian standpoint. It is always delightful to read an author who knows what he is writing about, and can present his thoughts in a clear and forcible manner. His intention is to exhibit religion not so much "as a thing of opinion, of emotion, or of ceremony, as an element in men's own experience, or a force, mighty and even passionate, in the world's affairs." Such an endeavor is highly laudable, and the work has been well done. — *Christian Mirror.*

A collection of a acute, reverent, and suggestive talks on some of the great themes of religion. Many Christians will dissent from his free handling of certain traditional views, dogmas of Christianity, but they will be at once with him in his love of goodness and truth, and in his contention that religion finds its complete fruition in the lives rather than the speculative opinions of men. — *N. Y. Tribune.*

Mr. Allen strikes straight out from the shoulder, with energy that shows his natural force not only unabated, but increased with added years. "At Sixty: A New Year Letter" is sweet and mellow with the sunshine of the years that bring the philosophic mind. But we are doing what we said that we must not, and must make an arbitrary end. Yet not without a word of admiration for the splendid force and beauty of many passages. These are the product of no artifice, but are uniformly an expression of that humanity which is the writer's constant end and inspiration. In proportion as this finds free and full expression, the style assumes a warmth and color that not only give an intellectual pleasure, but make the heart leap up with sympathetic courage and resolve. — *J. W. C.*

Sold everywhere.

ROBERTS BROTHERS, Publishers.

CHRISTIAN HISTORY

IN ITS THREE GREAT PERIODS. FIRST PERIOD: *Early Christianity.* By JOSEPH HENRY ALLEN, Lecturer on Ecclesiastical History in Harvard University. With Chronological Outline and Index, and an Introduction on the Study of Christian History. 16mo. Cloth. Price, $1.25.

TOPICS: 1. The Messiah and the Christ; 2. Saint Paul; 3. Christian Thought of the Second Century; 4. The Mind of Paganism; 5. The Arian Controversy; 6. Saint Augustine; 7. Leo the Great; 8. Monasticism as a Moral Force; 9. Christianity in the East; 10. Conversion of the Barbarians; 11. The Holy Roman Empire; 12. The Christian Schools.

"In whatever way we regard the origin and early growth of Christianity, whether as special revelation or as historic evolution, the key to it is to be found not in its speculative dogma, not in its ecclesiastical organization, not even in what strictly constitutes its religious life, but in its fundamentally ethical character. In either way of understanding it, it is first of all a gospel for the salvation of human life." — *Preface.*

"I have read your Fragments of Christian History with instruction and delight. You are a miracle of candor and comprehensiveness. . . . You and Dr. Hedge are almost the only men who know thoroughly the whole grand field of Ecclesiastical History. . . . I most cordially send you my thanks for such an illumination as you have given me, on many obscure points of Christian History." — *E. P. Whipple to the Author.*

"We do not desire to state an unqualified agreement with all the conclusions of Professor Allen, and yet we are free to confess that we know of no work of the same scope which could be put into the hands of a thoughtful young man, in which he could find so much sound philosophy, valuable historical review, and devout apprehension of essential Christianity as he will find in 'Fragments of Christian History.'" — *Chicago Alliance.*

Sold everywhere by all booksellers. Mailed, post-paid, by the publishers,

ROBERTS BROTHERS, BOSTON.

www.ingramcontent.com/pod-product-compliance
Lightning Source LLC
Chambersburg PA
CBHW032008300426
44117CB00008B/938